25.00

D1263298

FIREARMS OF THE CONFEDERACY

FIREARMS
OF THE
CONFEDERACY

Claud E. Fuller

and

Richard D. Steuart

QUARTERMAN PUBLICATIONS, INC.

Lawrence, Massachusetts

Copyright 1944 Standard Publications, Inc.

This Quarterman edition contains a facsimile reproduction
of the text of the original.

International Standard Book Number: 0–88000–103–8
Library of Congress Catalog Card Number: 77–74784

Printed in the United States of America

Quarterman Publications, Inc.
5 South Union Street
Lawrence, Massachusetts 01843

INTRODUCTION

It has been said there have been published nearly seven thousand volumes covering virtually every detail of the Civil War and every public library in the country contains hundreds of books devoted to this most critical period of our National History.

To the present day student of the arms used by the Confederates during this great conflict, however, there is lacking any source of information that can be relied upon—most historians have ignored this most important subject.

The Official Records of the Government containing the available information on the subject are combined with such a mass of other data, that even where they are accessible to the student, they afford a very unsatisfactory source of information on the details involved.

Just as the collector and student would like to know more about the contractors who made arms, and the other sources of supply of arms used by the colonial troops in the Revolutionary War, the student of the arms with which the Confederate soldier gave such a good account of himself will want to know what kind of arms were used and just where and how they were secured.

For this reason the attempt has been made to cover all the arms used by the Confederates, with special emphasis upon those manufactured in the South during the war, which are, of course, of prime importance to the collector.

While the Official Records of the War of the Rebellion have been relied upon for a great deal of the data used, other sources have contributed liberally and we acknowledge with deep appreciation permission to use material from Francis Bannermans Sons, New York City; Hobby Magazine, Chicago; The Army Ordnance Association, Washington, D. C.; Dexters Arms Manual, Topeka, Kansas; and we also take this opportunity to express our sincere thanks and appreciation to Mr. Herman P. Dean, of Huntington, W. Va., whose keen interest in the subject and hearty cooperation has made the publication of this volume possible.

We probably never have had a more ardent, conscientious and persistent collector of Confederate arms and Confederate data than the late E. Berkley Bowie, of Baltimore, Maryland, and as much of the material he collected has been made available to, and used freely by the present compilers, this volume is in a sense a memorial to his life's labor of love.

The Steuart Confederate collection, and the Fuller collection devoted entirely to American Military Shoulder arms have provided specimens for photographing with descriptions and measurements so that this first-hand data can be relied upon.

This book is presented in as complete detail as the present limited data permits but THERE IS SO MUCH WE DO NOT KNOW that it will devolve upon some future writer, with more complete information, to give the final story; in the meantime, however, the compilers invite such criticism and suggestions that may present themselves and will be sincerely grateful for any additional data or information on Confederate arms to the end that the material may be included in a supplement to the present volume or in a reprint of it.

Richard D. Steuart,
703 W. University Parkway,
Baltimore, Maryland.

Claud E. Fuller,
Fulleridge, R. R. 6,
Chattanooga, Tenn.

CONTENTS

ILLUSTRATIONS

Page

ILLUSTRATIONS (continued)

ILLUSTRATIONS (continued)

ILLUSTRATIONS (continued)

Photographs of the Shoulder Arms of the Fuller Collection in Part I are by Roy B. Stewart, Nashville, Tenn.

PART I

This type of cartridge in calibers .54, .577, .58 and .69 formed the bulk of the small arms ammunition of the Civil War. The soldier had to bite or tear the end off to charge his muzzle-loader properly. Major General Hindman wrote from Arkansas in 1862:

"As illustrating the pitiable scarcity of material in the country, the fact may be stated that it was found necessary to use public documents of the State library for cartridge paper."

CHAPTER I

REPORTS AND CORRESPONDENCE ON ARMS SUPPLIED TO THE SOUTHERN STATES ON THEIR QUOTA REQUISITION. ARMS PURCHASED IN THE NORTH AND SEIZED FROM THE UNITED STATES ARSENALS WITH DESCRIPTIONS OF THE ARMS INVOLVED.

ARMS SUPPLIED ON QUOTA REQUISITION

THE charge has often been made that John B. Floyd, while Secretary of War, depleted the Northern United States arsenals and sent the arms to the Southern arsenals, and this charge has about as often been denied, and the fact that Floyd was completely exonerated by an investigating committee, whose findings were concurred in by the then President, Buchanan, is cited as conclusive evidence refuting the charge.

The following reports and correspondence are interesting and attention.is invited to some of the outstanding details.

On November 12, 1859, Col. Craig reported to Secretary Floyd the number of arms then on hand at the different U. S. armories and arsenals as:

561,400 Muskets

48,862 Rifles

excluding from the report 23,894 Flintlock muskets and 652 Flintlock Rifles.

In the annual report of Oct. 30, 1860 the Chief of Ordnance reported as on hand only 530,000 muskets, and calling attention to the diminished number being manufactured recommended to the Secretary of War that no more arms be disposed of until the stock had been increased to the estimated requirements of at least 700,000 muskets.

The law of April 23, 1808 provided for the supply of State's arms on a regular quota basis, and the regulation established by President Jackson in 1835 and reconfirmed by President Pierce in 1855 prohibited the issue of these in advance, as set forth in Col. Craig's letter of Nov. 15, 1860 to William Gist.

Despite this regulation the letter from Col. Craig to Secretary Floyd of Nov. 3, 1860 states that the State of Virginia had on that date received its full quota for 1861, and arms equivalent to 203 muskets on the 1862 quota.

On January 8, 1861 Governor Letcher of Virginia requested the issue of his State's quota for 1862, which request, however, was denied by Sec. Holt, and as late as April 12, 1861 orders were given to issue from Harper's Ferry the quota for that year to the State of North Carolina.

In addition to the arms issued to the States on their quotas there appears to have been transferred to the Southern arsenals during the year 1860 arms to the total of 115,000, many of which were of the latest improved patterns, all of which arms were subsequently seized by the various States.

When it is remembered that South Carolina passed an ordinance of secession on December 20, 1860, and that Provisional Government of the Confederate States was established by the States of South Carolina, Georgia, Florida, Alabama, Mississippi, Louisiana and Texas on Feb. 8, 1861 these requisitions for, and issues of arms are hard to explain, especially since it appears that the impending trouble was anticipated by almost everyone familiar with the affairs of the day.

ORDNANCE OFFICE,
Washington, November 12, 1859.

Hon. JOHN B. FLOYD,
    Secretary of War:

    SIR: In compliance with your orders of the 10th instant, I transmit the inclosed tabular statement of the muskets and rifles on hand at each of the armories and arsenals. It does not include the 23,894 flintlock muskets and 652 flintlock rifles still remaining unaltered.

    I am, sir, with much respect, your obedient servant,

        H. K. CRAIG,
        Colonel of Ordnance.

[INCLOSURE]

FIREARMS OF THE CONFEDERACY

[INCLOSURE]

Statement of the number of serviceable muskets and rifles on hand at each armory and arsenal.

Name of the armory or arsenal	Muskets.						Rifles.			
	Altered to percussion, cal. .69.	Altered to Maynard lock, cal. .69.	Made as percussion, cal. .69.	Percussion, since rifled, cal. .69.	Rifled musket, cal. .58.	Total muskets.	Altered to percussion, cal. .54.	Made as percussion, cal. .54.	New model rifle, cal. .58.	Total rifles.
Kennebec Arsenal, Me	24,313					24,313				
Watertown Arsenal, Mass	18,050	1	55			18,106		12,855		12,855
Springfield Armory, Mass	99,446	1	133,973	4,253	5,303	242,976				
Watervliet Arsenal, N. Y	44,888	1	1,825	2	5	46,721		9,686	2	9,688
New York Arsenal, N. Y	884	6	445		764	2,099		8,307		8,307
Detroit Arsenal, Mich			346		100	446				
Frandford Arsenal, Pa	5,169	8,348	206	2,681		16,404		19		19
Allegheny Arsenal, Pa	824	1	10,365		35	11,225		1,603		1,603
Pikesville Arsenal, Md			50		1	51		2		2
Washington Arsenal, D. C	23,325		50,004	176	152	73,657		2,300	19	2,319
Harper's Ferry Armory, Va	149	2	4,569	737	8,599	14,056		696	3,570	4,266
Fort Monroe Arsenal, Va			301	20		321		31	20	51
Fayetteville Arsenal, N. C	4,817		2,861			7,678		1,685		1,685
Charleston Arsenal, S. C			2,413			2,413		814		814
Mount Vernon Arsenal, Ala	2,364					2,364		32		32
Baton Rouge Arsenal, La	8,266	400	1,596	800	610	11,672	1,385	103		1,488
San Antonio Arsenal, Tex	77	396	285		543	1,301		260		260
Little Rock Arsenal, Ark			349			349		54		54
Saint Louis Arsenal, Mo	25,990	1,502	325	4,488	710	33,015		236	483	719
Benicia Arsenal, Cal	14,649	107	2,650	10,812	2,252	30,470		4,574		4,574
Vancouver Arsenal, Wash. Ter.	2,533		537	662	31	3,763		118	8	126
In transitu from armories and Frankford to California.		4,000		9,000	5,000	18,000				
Totals	275,744	14,765	213,155	33,631	24,105	561,400	1,385	43,375	4,102	48,862

H. K. CRAIG,
Colonel of Ordnance.
ORDNANCE OFFICE, Washington, November 12, 1859.

ADJUTANT GENERAL'S OFFICE,
Richmond, Va., November 1, 1860.

Hon. JOHN B. FLOYD,
Secretary of War:

SIR: I am instructed by the Governor of Virginia to inform you that there exists in this State an extended and daily increasing apprehension of insecurity and danger, resulting, among other causes, from manifesta . . . requests that you will authorize an advance to the State immediately of a number of the original army percussioned muskets with accouterments, equivalent to the quota of arms which may be due to the State under the act of Congress of 1808 for the year 1861, estimated by the Colonel of Ordnance at about 682 muskets. This would not be asked except under the pressure of extraordinary circumstances. I am further instructed to say that the money value of the arms shall be promptly paid to the United States if Congress shall so require, or the arms returned in kind and of equal value so soon as they can be fabricated at the armory of the State now going into operation.

If this request be . . . for the advance upon the next year's quota, I hope, therefore, will arise, and especially as you are personally aware of the urgency of our necessities.

I have the honor to be, very respectfully, your obedient servant,
WM. H. RICHARDSON,
Adjutant General.

3

FIREARMS OF THE CONFEDERACY

ORDNANCE OFFICE,
Washington, November 3, 1860.

Hon. JOHN B. FLOYD,
  Secretary of War:
  SIR: In answer to the letter of General Richardson of the 1st
instant, referred to this office for a report, I have the honor to state
that the State of Virginia, as fully communicated to General Richardson
in my letter to him of the 15th of September last, is charged with its
full quota for 1861 and arms equivalent to 203 muskets on account of
the quota for 1862. The . . . The letter of General Richardson is herewith returned.
  Respectfully, your obedient servant,
                                             H. K. CRAIG,
                                             Colonel of Ordnance.

EXECUTIVE OFFICE,
Jackson, Miss., November 6, 1860.

Hon. JOHN B. FLOYD,
  DEAR SIR: The State of Mississippi has 160 flintlock muskets in
perfect order, never having been used. I wish to exchange them for
rifles. If you have the power to make this exchange, please write me
on what terms. Please write me also how and when I can purchase of
the Federal Government a few thousand muskets with percussion locks,
or rifles.
  Very respectfully,
                                             JOHN J. PETTUS

EXECUTIVE DEPARTMENT,
Columbia, S. C., November 12, 1860.

Col. H. K. CRAIG:
  DEAR SIR: I learn that some of the States have received their quota
of arms for next year, and I should be pleased to have the quota for
South Carolina. I wish the whole quota in "rifled muskets and appendages, new patterns, caliber .58." Send them immediately to Charleston, S. C., to Maj. P. F. Stevens, superintendent of the Citadel Academy.
  Very respectfully,
                                             WM. H. GIST.

WAR DEPARTMENT,
Washington, November 14, 1860

His Excellency JOHN J. PETTUS,
  Governor of Mississippi, Jackson:
  SIR: I have the honor to acknowledge the receipt this day from
the Hon. Jacob Thompson of your letter of the 6th instant, and in reply
to inform you that there is no authority in this Department to exchange
rifles for flintlock muskets, as proposed by you. We have percussion
muskets altered from flintlock at the Baton Rouge and Saint Louis
arsenals, which are for sale at $2.50 each. Should you desire to pur-
chase any of them, and will advise me of the number, I will issue the
necessary orders to comply with your request. Two thousand can be
delivered at Baton Rouge, and any larger number at St. Louis.
  Very respectfully, your obedient servant,
                                             JOHN B. FLOYD,
                                             Secretary of War.

FIREARMS OF THE CONFEDERACY

ORDNANCE OFFICE,
Washington, November 15, 1860
His Excellency WILLIAM H. GIST,
Governor of South Carolina, Columbia, S. C.:

SIR: I have the honor to acknowledge the receipt of your letter of the 12th instant, and in answer to state that according to a regulation established by President Jackson on the 29th of June, 1835 and reconfirmed by President Pierce April 30, 1855, issues in advance to the State and Territories under the law of 23d of April, 1808, are not authorized to be made. This rule has, however, in several instances been recently departed from by issuing arms to some of the States for 1861. If you desire it, and will so indicate to me, I will refer your letter to the Secretary of War for his action in the case.

Respectfully, &c.,

H. K. CRAIG,
Colonel of Ordnance.

EXECUTIVE OFFICE,
Jackson, December 31, 1860.
Hon. JOHN B. FLOYD,
Secretary of War:

SIR: I write to request you to send the quota of arms for the State of Mississippi for 1862, and if you have the Map (sic) patent breechloading rifles at your disposal, I would prefer them. If not, please send me the rifle known here as the Mississippi rifle.

Very respectfully,

JOHN J. PETTUS,
Governor of Mississippi.

WAR DEPARTMENT,
Washington, January 3, 1861.
Hon. BENJAMIN STANTON,
Chairman of Committee on Military Affairs, House of Representatives:

SIR: In answer to your letter, asking for information on certain points specified in a resolution adopted by the Committee on Military Affairs of the House of Representatives on the 18th ultimo, I have the honor to state as follows: . . .

The other information asked for in regard to the number and description of arms "distributed since the 1st day of January, 1860, and to whom and at what price," will be found in the accompanying statements (Nos. 2 and 3) from the Ordnance Bureau. It is deemed proper to state, in further explanation of statement No. 2, that where no distribution appears to have been made to the State or Territory, or where the amount of the distribution is small, it is because such State or Territory has not called for all the arms due on its quotas and remains a creditor for dues not distributed, which can be obtained at any time on requisition therefor.

Very respectfully, your obedient servant,

J. HOLT,
Secretary of War ad interim.

Number and description of arms distributed since the 1st of January, 1860, &c.

States and Territories.	Rifle muskets, caliber .58-inch.		Percussion muskets, caliber .69-inch.		Cadet muskets, caliber .58-inch.		Musketoons, caliber .69-inch.	
	No.	Price.	No.	Price.	No.	Price.	No.	Price.
Maine	300	$13.93						
Massachusetts	800							
Vermont	150							
Connecticut	240							
New York	192							
Maryland	400							
Virginia			450	$13.25				
South Carolina	646							
Georgia	390				122	$15.20		
Florida	100							
Alabama	170				150			
Louisiana					185			
Tennessee	701				381			
Ohio	600							
Michigan	160							
Indiana	573							
Illinois	80		120	13.25	80		1	$11.00
Wisconsin	80							
Missouri	252							
Iowa	100							
California	115							
Minnesota	283							
Kansas Territory	52				30			
District of Columbia	458						4	11.00
Pennsylvania	1,011							
Total	7,853		570		948		5	

States and Territories	Long range rifles, caliber .58 inch.		Percussion rifles, caliber .54 inch.		Colt rifles.		Hall carbines.	
	No.	Price.	No.	Price.	No.	Price.	No.	Price.
Massachusetts	100	$17.43						
New York	420				1	$42.50		
New Jersey	100							
Virginia	50							
North Carolina	311							
Louisiana	104							
Mississippi	212							
Tennessee	1							
Kentucky	80							
Indiana	170							
Illinois	1						1	$17.00
Wisconsin			40	$12.88				
Iowa	12							
California	115							
Washington Territory					2	42.50		
Kansas Territory	10							
New Mexico Territory			220	12.88	10	42.50		
Pennsylvania	42	17.43	40	12.88				
Total	1,728		300		13		1	

FIREARMS OF THE CONFEDERACY

Number and description of arms distributed since the 1st of January, 1860, &c.
—Continued.

States and Territories.	Sharps carbines.		Colt artillery carbines.		Colt cavalry carbines.		Percussion pistols.		Colt belt pistols.	
	No.	Price.	No.	Price.	No.	Price.	No.	Price.	No.	Price.
New York........	1	$30.00	1	$35.00	1	$32.50				
Georgia..........									40	$18.00
Louisiana........							60	$7.00	8	
Tennessee........	1	30.00					1		1	
Illinois..........	1	30.00	1	35.00	1	32.50	40	7.00	20	
Wisconsin........									3	
Missouri.........									8	
Washington Territory.								—	4	
Nebraska Territory.									40	
Kansas Territory..	10	30.00					20	7.00	20	
New Mexico Territory.	20								20	
Pennsylvania.....							158	7.00		
Total.......	33		2		2		279		164	

States and Territories.	Colt holster pistols.		Adams belt pistols.		Colt holster pistols, with attachment.		Cavalry sabers, heavy.	
	No.	Price.	No.	Price.	No.	Price per Pair.	No.	Price.
New Hampshire........							132	$7.50
New York.............					1	$50.00		
Virginia.............							100	7.50
Georgia.............							40	7.50
Louisiana............						—	30	7.50
Illinois.............							40	7.50
Washington Territory.					33	50.00		
Nebraska Territory....	30	$22.50			5		10	7.50
Pennsylvania.........			27	$18.00			74	7.50
Total...............	30		27		39		426	

States and Territories.	Cavalry sabers, light.		Horse artillery sabers.		Non-commissioned officers' swords.		Musicians' swords.		Artillery swords.	
	No.	Price.	No.	Price.	No.	Price.	No.	Price.	No.	Price.
New Hampshire...									50	$4.00
New Jersey.......					50	$5.50			50	4.00
Florida..........	132	$8.50								
Louisiana					10		10	$4.40		
Tennessee........	1	8.50	1	$5.50	1		1		1	4.00
Ohio.............			50		50		50			
Michigan.........					50					
Illinois..........			100							
Wisconsin........					12				20	4.00
Missouri.........					8					
Kansas Territory..									10	4.00
Dist. of Columbia..	50	8.50	25		20		6	4.40		
Pennsylvania.....					65	5.50	36	4.40		
Total.......	183		176		266		103		131	

WM. MAYNADIER,
Captain of Ordnance.
ORDNANCE OFFICE, Washington, December 21, 1860.

FIREARMS OF THE CONFEDERACY

WASHINGTON, January 8, 1861.

Hon. JOSEPH HOLT,
Secretary of War:

DEAR SIR: It has long been a custom of the War Department to permit the States to draw their respective quotas of arms one year in advance. Virginia has drawn hers for this year. Two companies in every district want arms from our State and we cannot furnish them. Governor Letcher informs me he will draw on you for them if you will honor his order. Please inform me what you will do in the premises. Before Governor Floyd resigned I had assurances from his chief clerk, Colonel Drinkard, that he would grant the arms. An early answer is desired.
Your friend and obedient servant,
JOHN T. HARRIS.

ORDNANCE OFFICE,
Washington, January 8, 1861.

Hon. JOSEPH HOLT,
Secretary of War:

SIR: In my last annual report, dated 30th of October, 1860, I had the honor, among other matters, to state as follows:

The number of arms manufactured at the national armories during the last year was not as great as the available funds would have justified. This diminution is in a measure attributable to the diversion of armory operations from the manufacture of arms of the established model to the alteration of arms according to plans of patentees and to getting up models of arms for inventors. Our store of muskets of all kinds at this time does not exceed 530,000, dispersed among the arsenals of the country—nowhere more than 130,000 arms being together. As this supply of arms is applicable to the equipment of the Army, the Navy, the Marine Corps, and the militia of the country, it is certainly too small, and every effort should be made to increase the number of our new-model guns, whilst no further reduction by sale of the old-model serviceable arms should be allowed until our arsenals are better supplied. Our store of muskets has in former years reached nearly 700,000, and was not then considered too great for the country, as was evidenced by the liberal appropriations made for the further increase and for the construction of more perfect and productive machinery for the fabrication of small arms.

Since that date 127,635 serviceable muskets altered to percussion have been ordered to be sold, many of which have already been disposed of and passed out of the possession of Government. I have now respectfully to recommend that no more arms on the orders already given be disposed of, and that no further sales be made except in the manner authorized by the act of March 3, 1825.
Very respectfully, your obedient servant,
H. K. CRAIG,
Chief of Ordnance.
[INDORSEMENT]

APPROVED:

J. HOLT,
Acting Secretary of War ad interim.

WASHINGTON, January 11, 1861.

Hon. J. HOLT,
Secretary of War:

SIR: Will you have the goodness to furnish me, for the information of the Committee on Military Affairs, with a statement of the distribu-

tion of arms from the armories of the United States to the U. S. arsenals, and other places of deposit for safe-keeping, from the 1st day of January, A. D. 1860, to the 1st day of January, A. D. 1861, showing the number sent from each armory to each arsenal, or other place of deposit, and the time when each parcel was sent; also whether any portion of the arms so distributed have been taken from the custody and control of the officers or persons charged with their custody or safe-keeping, and, if so, when and by whom they have been so taken. An early reply will very much oblige,
Yours, respectfully,
B. STANTON,
Chairman Committee on Military Affairs

HOUSE OF REPRESENTATIVES,
January 18, 1861.
Hon. JOSEPH HOLT,
Secretary of War:
SIR: Will you please inform me what number of improved arms, now recognized as suitable for the service, are now in possession of the Department, and how large a force the Department can now arm with the latest improved arms.
Very respectfully, yours, &c.,
B. STANTON.

WASHINGTON, January 18, 1861.
Hon. JOSEPH HOLT,
Secretary of War:
SIR: Please send me, for use of the Committee on Military Affairs, a copy of the order of the Secretary of War of December 30 (29), 1859, in relation to the distribution of arms, referred to in the letter of Colonel Craig to you of the 15th instant, and also the orders of January 30, 1860, referred to in the same letter, under which 115,000 stand of arms were distributed to sundry arsenals in the Southern States.
You will also please advise me whether any arms have been distributed to any of the States for the year 1861, and, if so, the number and description distributed to each, and the date of the distribution.
It has seemed to me that there has been unnecessary delay in answering my former inquiries in relation to the distribution of arms.
You will oblige me, therefore, by furnishing me the information now asked for at your earliest convenience,
Very respectfully, yours, &c.,
B. STANTON.

WAR DEPARTMENT,
Washington, January 21, 1861.
Hon. B. STANTON,
Chairman Committee on Military Affairs, House of Representatives:
SIR: In reply to your letter of the 18th instant I have the honor to inclose to you a report of the Chief of Ordnance, showing the number of arms in our arsenals and armories suitable for the service.
Very respectfully, your obedient servant,
J. HOLT,
Secretary of War ad interim.
[INCLOSURES.]

9

FIREARMS OF THE CONFEDERACY

ORDNANCE OFFICE,

Hon. J. HOLT,   Washington, D. C., January 21, 1861.
Secretary of War:

SIR: In answer to the letter of the Hon. B. Stanton of the 18th instant I have to state that it appears by the last returns that there were remaining in the U. S. arsenals and armories as follows: Percussion muskets and muskets altered to percussion (caliber .69), 499,554, and percussion rifles (caliber .54), 42,011; total 541,565. If from this number are deducted the numbers of the same description that were in the arsenals in South Carolina, Alabama, and Louisiana, which arsenals have been officially reported to have been taken possession of by the authorities of those States, 60,878, it leaves this number, 480,687: the whole of which are "recognized as suitable for the service." In addition to these there are, rifle muskets, model of 1855 (caliber .58), 22,827: rifles, model of 1855 (caliber .58), 12,508; total, 35,335; which are "the latest improved arms."

The letter of Mr. Stanton is herewith returned.

I am, sir, very respectfully, &c.,

H. K. CRAIG,
Colonel of Ordnance.

NOTE: Of the above 480,687 muskets and rifles, 22,000 of them are in the arsenal at Augusta, Ga., and 36,362 in the arsenal at Fayetteville, N. C.

Serviceable arms at the U. S. forts and arsenals within the several States and Territories, per the last inventories and returns, excluding flintlock arms, as well as Colt revolvers and all other patent arms.

States and Territories.	Muskets. All descriptions now used and usable.	Rifles, &c. Rifles and all other U. S. arms now used and usable.	Total small-arms.	Sea-coast. 8 and 10 inch columbiads and howitzers, and 42 and 32 pounder guns, and 24-pounder flank howitzers.	Siege and garrison. 8-inch howitzers, and 24, 18, and 12 pounder guns.	Field. Brass field guns and howitzers.	Total artillery.
Maine	24,313		24,313	2	13	4	19
New Hampshire					20	2	22
Massachusetts	155,566	12,177	167,743	138	107	20	265
Rhode Island				100	49	2	151
Connecticut				49	22	2	73
New York	42,005	28,406	70,411	506	209	29	744
Pennsylvania	27,443	5,493	32,936	213	61	21	295
Maryland	50		50	56	24	1	81
District of Columbia	73,778	2,285	76,063	310	179	1	490
Virginia	10,646	6,868	17,514	680	177	7	864
North Carolina	32,678	3,636	36,364		37	4	41
South Carolina	17,413	2,817	20,230	109	20	4	133
Georgia	20,001	2,000	22,001	20		2	22
Florida				339	121	4	464
Alabama	17,359	2,000	19,359	64	15		79
Louisiana	12,364	6,141	18,505	63	124		187
Texas	3,253	2,204	5,457			10	10
Arkansas	1,310	54	1,364			10	10
Missouri	32,468	5,673	38,141		2	9	11
Kansas	1,385	2,193	3,578			4	4
New Mexico	2,333	2,248	4,581			5	5
California	47,501	7,218	54,719	146	29	22	197
Washington Territory	4,082	470	4,552				
Total	525,948	91,933	617,881	2,795	1,209	163	4,167

FIREARMS OF THE CONFEDERACY

ORDNANCE OFFICE,
Hon. JOSEPH HOLT,   Washington, January 21, 1861.
Secretary of War:
SIR: In compliance with the request in the letter from the Hon.
B. Stanton of 18th instant, referred by you to this office, I have the
honor to transmit herewith the following papers:

First. Copy of directions from the Secretary of War, dated December 30 (29), 1859, for the transfer of arms to Southern arsenals.

Second. Copies of three orders for supplies from this office, dated
January 30, 1860, these orders being the necessary action for carrying
into effect the previous directions of the Secretary of War, December
30 (29), 1859.

Third. A statement of arms issued on account of the quotas due
the States for 1861 in advance, the date of the orders directing the issue,
and States to which issued.

Mr. Stanton's letter is herewith returned.

Very respectfully, &c.,

H. K. CRAIG,
Colonel of Ordnance.

[INCLOSURE No. 1.]
WAR DEPARTMENT,
December 29, 1859.

The Colonel of Ordnance will give the requisite orders for supplying the arsenals at Fayetteville, N. C.; Charleston, S. C.; Augusta, Ga.;
Mount Vernon, Ala., and Baton Rouge, La., with the following arms,
in addition to those on hand at those arsenals, viz.: 65,000 percussion
muskets (caliber .69) and 40,000 altered to percussion (caliber .69)
from Springfield Armory; also 6,000 percussion rifles (caliber .54)
from Watertown Arsenal and 4,000 percussion rifles (caliber .54) from
Watervliet Arsenal. These orders will be given from time to time as
may be most suitable for economy and convenience of transportation.
The distribution to the five first named arsenals will be in proportion
to their respective means of proper storage.

JOHN B. FLOYD,
Secretary of War.

Order for supplies, No. 55.
ORDNANCE OFFICE, WAR DEPARTMENT,
Washington, D. C., January 30, 1860.
J. D. WHITNEY, Esq.,
Superintendent U. S. Armory, Springfield:
SIR: You are hereby required to issue to the officers stated below
the following ordnance stores, viz:

To whom to be issued.	Percussion muskets, caliber .69, with appendages.	Muskets, caliber .69, altered to percussion, with appendages.
Capt. J. Gorgas, Charleston Arsenal.	9,280	5,720
Capt. J. A. J. Bradford, North Carolina Arsenal	15,480	9,520
John M. Galt, military store-keeper, Augusta Arsenal, Ga.	12,380	7,620
Capt. J. L. Reno, Mount Vernon Arsenal.	9,280	5,720
Theo. Lewis, esq., military store-keeper, Baton Rouge Arsenal.	18,580	11,420
	65,000	40,000

11

FIREARMS OF THE CONFEDERACY

The within rifles will be held in readiness for issue at such time as you may be called upon by the Quartermaster's Department. Copy of a letter to that department from this office is inclosed herewith for your information and government.

H. K. CRAIG,
Colonel of Ordnance.

Order for supplies, No. 56.
ORDNANCE OFFICE, WAR DEPARTMENT,
Washington, D. C., January 30, 1860.
Maj. A. MORDECAI,
Watervliet Arsenal:

SIR: You are hereby required to issue to Capt. J. Gorgas, Charleston Arsenal, the following ordnance stores, viz: 2,000 percussion rifles, caliber .54, with appendages. To Capt. J. A. J. Bradford, North Carolina Arsenal, 2,000 percussion rifles, caliber .54, with appendages.

The within rifles will be held in readiness for issue at such time as you may be called upon by the Quartermaster's Department. Copy of a letter to that department from this office is inclosed herewith for your information and government.

H. K. CRAIG,
Colonel of Ordnance.

Order for supplies, No. 57.
ORDNANCE OFFICE, WAR DEPARTMENT,
Washington, D. C., January 30, 1860.
Capt. T. J. RODMAN,
Watertown Arsenal:

SIR: You are hereby required to issue to John M. Galt, Esq., military storekeeper, &c., Augusta Arsenal, Ga., the following ordnance stores, viz: 2,000 percussion rifles, caliber .54, with appendages; to Bvt. Capt. J. L. Reno, Mount Vernon Arsenal, 2,000 percussion rifles, caliber .54, with appendages; to Theo. Lewis, Esq., military storekeeper, Baton Rouge Arsenal, 2,000 percussion rifles, caliber .54, and appendages.

The within rifles will be held in readiness for issue at such time as you may be called upon by the Quartermaster's Department. Copy of a letter to that department from this office is inclosed herewith for your information and government.

H. K. CRAIG,
Colonel of Ordnance.

[SUB-INCLOSURE.]
ORDNANCE OFFICE, WAR DEPARTMENT,
Washington, January 28, 1860.
Major General JESUP,
Quartermaster General U. S. Army:

SIR: I have to request that transportation may be provided for the following number of boxes of muskets and rifles to be supplied to the arsenals at Fayetteville, N. C., Charleston, S. C., Augusta, Ga., Mount Vernon, Ala., and Baton Rouge, La., by direction of the Secretary of War:

FIREARMS OF THE CONFEDERACY

	Boxes
From Springfield Armory to Charleston Arsenal	750
From Watervliet Arsenal to Charleston Arsenal	100
From Springfield Armory to North Carolina Arsenal	1,250
From Watervliet Arsenal to North Carolina Arsenal	100
From Springfield Armory to Mount Vernon Arsenal	750
From Springfield Armory to Augusta Arsenal	1,000
From Watertown Arsenal to Augusta Arsenal	100
From Watertown Arsenal to Mount Vernon Arsenal	100
From Springfield Armory to Baton Rouge Arsenal	1,500
From Watertown Arsenal to Baton Rouge Arsenal	100
Total	5,750

Each box contains 20 arms, weight about 300 pounds, and occupies about 10 cubic feet. The transfers of these arms may be made from time to time as may be most suitable for economy and convenience of transportation, and they will be held in readiness for delivery from Springfield Armory and Watervliet and Watertown Arsenals at such times and in such parcels as may best suit the arrangements which your department may make for their transfer.

Respectfully, &c.,

H. K. CRAIG,
Colonel of Ordnance.

STATE OF NORTH CAROLINA, EXECUTIVE OFFICE,
Raleigh, April 2, 1861.

Hon. SIMON CAMERON,
Secretary of War, Washington, D. C.:

SIR: I have the honor, agreeably to instructions from His Excellency Governor Ellis, to address you with regard to the quota of arms due this State from the General Government.

Governor E., having been notified as usual that the quota of arms due North Carolina was subject to his draft, drew the entire quota in long-range rifles (pattern of 1859) with sword-bayonets. No notice having been taken of the latter, he made a second application, and was informed on the 4th of February last, by the Chief of the Ordnance Department, that orders had been issued to the U. S. Armory at Harper's Ferry to forward to his address "334 long-range rifles with sword-bayonets and appendages," being the equivalent of 453 muskets, the quota due North Carolina. Up to this date nothing further has been heard from them, and application is now made directly to you, sir, in the hope that you will cause the matter to receive proper attention without further delay.

With much respect, yours, &c.,

GRAHAM DAVES,
Private Secretary.

WAR DEPARTMENT,
April 12, 1861.

His Excellency JOHN W. ELLIS,
Governor of North Carolina, Raleigh:

SIR: I have the honor to acknowledge the receipt of a letter addressed to this Department on the 2d instant by Graham Daves, Esq., your private secretary, inquiring the cause of the delay in the issue of the arms called for by you on account of North Carolina's quota for the current year.

The rifles were ordered to be sent to you on the 4th of February last from the Harper's Ferry Armory, but their issue has probably been retarded by numerous prior engagements, the rule, unless in special cases, being to execute the orders for issues according to priority of receipt at the armory. The superintendent of the armory has been requested to make the issue to your State at the earliest moment possible.

Very respectfully, your obedient servant,
SIMON CAMERON,
Secretary of War.

ARMS PURCHASED BY THE SOUTHERN STATES FROM U. S. GOVERNMENT AND NORTHERN MANUFACTURERS

Despite the unsettled condition of the national affairs for several years prior to the war, and especially during the latter part of 1859 and 1860 the policy of selling arms destined to the Southern States seemed to go unchecked, and it seems that these sales were made direct, without the usual notice of public auction as provided for in the act of March 3, 1825 for the disposal of arms after condemnation.

During 1860 alone there was sold to or for the Southern States 24,130 arms which arms were flintlocks altered to percussion of .69 caliber, at the price of $2.50 each, and it appears that these sales were discontinued only after the recommendations of the Ordnance officers and the appointment of J. Holt as Secretary of War.

The protest of Gen. Wool of December 27, 1860 in reference to the arms sold at Watervliet and the action of Supt. of N. Y. police, Kennedy, as reported in his letter to Sec. Holt of Jan. 23, 1861 illustrate the attitude of those not in authority on the subject.

On February 9, 1861 Jefferson Davis was elected President of the Confederate States and on the 21st of that month he sent Capt. R. Semmes north to purchase arms and munitions of War, including machinery for the manufacture of arms and percussion caps. As the embargo on shipments of arms to the Southern States was not declared until April 19, 1861 he was able to contract for a vast amount of material.

The Hon. John Forsyth, then in Washington, was also acting in a confidential capacity for the Confederacy, and arranged for the purchase and shipment of many arms and a large stock of powder from Northern manufacturers and dealers.

These gentlemen were also active in reporting to their chiefs all happenings in the Capitol, and securing for the Confederate service such government employees and officers as they could.

FIREARMS OF THE CONFEDERACY

Prior to this time the various States had their agents in the North making all the purchases they could. Adjutant General W. L. Sykes for Mississippi made a contract June 6, 1860 with Eli Whitney for 1500 so-called Mississippi rifles with saber bayonets.

Sixty sample arms supplied under this contract, upon examination were found to be "old arms fitted up" and the contract was cancelled, though the sixty arms were kept as an experiment.

Governor Moore of Alabama reported to Sec. Walker on March 4, 1861 that his State had purchased during the past nine months 9,500 stand of arms consisting of muskets, rifles and carbines, besides a vast amount of other war material.

In addition to the purchases being made in the North the Confederate officials sent their agents through the Southern states purchasing all kinds of arms. Thos. B. Mills of the C. S. Navy reported to Sec. Walker on July 7, 1861 that he had secured nearly 400 rifles, which he had shipped to Fort Smith.

NEW YORK, November 21, 1860.
Hon. JOHN B. FLOYD,
　　Secretary of War:
　　SIR: I understand that you have a large quantity of muskets changed from flint to percussion now at Watervliet for sale.
　　Will you do me the favor to state the lowest price and terms of payment for 10,000 stand, with the privilege of taking 40,000 more on the same terms; and whether they can be delivered here immediately, or whether they must be received at Watervliet? The former would be preferred, if it causes no delay.
　　A prompt reply will be acceptable, by telegraph or otherwise.
　　Very respectfully,
　　　　G. B. LAMAR.
　　P. S. I presume they are all packed, ready for transportation.

WAR DEPARTMENT,
Washington, November 24, 1860.
G. B. LAMAR,
　　New York:
　　SIR: I have the honor to acknowledge the receipt of your letter of the 21st instant, and in reply have to say that I have directed 10,000 altered percussion muskets to be delivered at Watervliet Arsenal to you, on your order, on payment of $2.50 each for the same. This sale covers all the arms that I am at liberty to sell.
　　Very respectfully, your obedient servant,
　　　　JOHN B. FLOYD,
　　　　Secretary of War.

FIREARMS OF THE CONFEDERACY

WAR DEPARTMENT,
Washington, December 15, 1860.

Hon. JOHN SLIDELL, Senate:

SIR: As requested by Governor Moore in his telegraphic dispatch to you, I have directed that 5,000 altered percussion muskets at Baton Rouge Arsenal, be delivered to the order of the Governor on the payment of $2.50 each for the same. Instructions to that effect have been sent by telegraph to the commanding officer of the arsenal. I return Governor Moore's dispatch.

Very respectfully, your obedient servant,

JOHN B. FLOYD,
Secretary of War.

ORDNANCE OFFICE,
Washington, D. C., January 21, 1861.

Hon. JOSEPH HOLT,
Secretary of War:

SIR: In reply to that portion of the resolution of the House of Representatives of the 31st ultimo communicated in the letter of Hon. B. Stanton, of the 8th instant, which relates to the distribution of arms from January 1, 1860, to January 1, 1861, I transmit herewith a statement giving the information desired, so far as it is understood to call for. I have not embraced the arms which were sold under the act of March 3, 1825, after regular condemnation, by public auction, under the supposition that this was not required. It may be proper, also, to state that on November 2, last, a proposition was made to the Secretary of War by A. A. Belknap for the purchase of from "100,000 to 250,000 of the U. S. flintlock and altered percussion muskets, and to have the same delivered to me or my agent in the city of New York. I respectfully ask the privilege of taking the whole or any part thereof within the next sixty-five days upon the payment of $2.15 per gun on delivery as aforesaid," which proposition was accepted by the Secretary of War on November 22, in these words:

The within proposition is accepted to the extent of 100,000 muskets, and as many more, up to the maximum number, as the service will spare.

This accepted proposition was subsequently modified by the Secretary of War on December 26, as follows:

The acceptance of the within proposition of A. A. Belknap was made under the belief that the price offered was $2.50 per gun. That was the price I distinctly understood was to be paid, as it is the least I will consent to sell the muskets for. This decision on the proposition will supersede the indorsement of November 22, 1860, which was signed under an erroneous impression as to the proposition then before me.

All further action in relation to this sale has, however, been arrested by your approval of my proposition of the 8th instant, to the effect that no more arms be disposed of under the orders given and that "no more muskets be sold."

Very respectfully, &c.,

H. K. CRAIG,
Colonel of Ordnance.

[SUB-INCLOSURE]

16

FIREARMS OF THE CONFEDERACY

[SUB-INCLOSURE.]

Statement of arms distributed by sale, by order of the Secretary of War, from January 1, 1860, to January 1, 1861, showing to whom, how, the number, kind, price, and date when sold, and place of delivery.

To whom sold.	How sold.	Number.	Kind of arms.	Price each.	Date.	Place of delivery.
					1860.	
J. W. Zacharie & Co..	Private sale.	4,000	Muskets altered to percussion.	$2.50	Feb. 3	Saint Louis Arsenal, Mo.
J. T. Ames............	....do....	1,000	......do..........	2.50	Mar. 14	New York Arsenal, N. Y.
Capt. G. Barry........	...do....	80	......do..........	2.00	June 11	Saint Louis Arsenal, Mo.
W. C. N. Swift........	....do....	400	......do..........	2.50	Aug. 31	Springfield Armory, Mass.
Do...............	....do....	80	......do..........	2.50	Nov. 13	Do.
State of Alabama.....	....do....	1,000	......do..........	2.50	Sept. 27	Baton Rouge Arsenal, La.
Do...............	....do....	2,500	......do..........	2.50	Nov. 14	Do.
State of Virginia......	....do....	5,000	......do..........	2.50	Nov. 6	Washington Arsenal, D. C.
Phillips County...... (Ark.) Volunteers.	...do....	50	......do..........	2.00	Nov. 16	Saint Louis Arsenal, Mo.
G. B. Lamar..........	...do....	10,000	......do..........	2.50	Nov. 24	Watervliet Arsenal, N. Y.
State of Mississippi...	...do....	5,000	......do..........	2.50	Dec. 4	Baton Rouge Arsenal, La.
State of Louisiana a..	...do....	5,000	......do..........	2.50	Dec. 15	Do.

a Of these the State of Louisiana took and paid for 2,500 only.

H. K. CRAIG,
Colonel of Ordnance.

ORDNANCE OFFICE, January 21, 1861.

WASHINGTON, D. C., April 8, 1861.

Hon. L. P. WALKER:

Do you want arms? Ten thousand Colt pistols, army and navy size, and 2,000 Sharps rifles are offered to be delivered at Richmond. Answer immediately.

JOHN FORSYTH.

WASHINGTON, April 9, 1861.

Hon. L. P. WALKER:

Have ordered 2,000 Colt new army pistols, at $25; Sharps carbine, new (army) improvement, held at $30; Sharps rifle, with sword-bayonet, $42.50. Colt carbine, $30. Two hundred to three hundred tons Hazard's (Government) powder offered at 20 cents. Answer immediately.

JOHN FORSYTH.

MONTGOMERY, April 9, 1861.

Hon. JOHN FORSYTH,
Washington:

The rifles are too high. Would take 2,000 Sharps rifles, with sword-bayonets, at $30. Do not want the other guns. If the powder has been tested and is cannon-powder will take it. You had better ascertain and know certainly all about it. Answer fully.

L. P. WALKER.

WASHINGTON, D. C., April 9, 1861.

Hon. L. P. WALKER:

The price named for rifles and carbines are the lowest market, and in great demand. Probably they could not be had twenty-four hours hence. The powder mentioned at 20 cents is the best Government, and the highest-priced cannon-powder is cheaper. How much powder shall I order? Both arms and powder offered at prices paid by this Government.

JOHN FORSYTH.

MONTGOMERY, April 9, 1861.

Hon. JOHN FORSYTH,
    Washington:

Two thousand Colt pistols; 2,000 Sharps rifles. The former at $25; the latter at $22.50.

L. P. WALKER.

MONTGOMERY, April 9, 1861.

TUCKER, COOPER & CO.,
    No. 70 South Street, New York:

Increase weekly supply of "rope" (gunpowder) to the utmost.

L. P. WALKER.

MONTGOMERY, April 10, 1861.

JOHN FORSYTH,
    Washington, D. C.:

Will take, to be delivered at once, ninety tons cannon and ten tons musket powder. Let there be no mistake as to its quality, and let me know terms, &c. Will not take rifles.

L. P. WALKER.

WASHINGTON, April 10, 1861.

L. P. WALKER,
    Secretary of War:

I have ordered 200 tons best Hazard's cannon-powder at price paid by United States Government, to be delivered in same manner as the pistols.

JNO. FORSYTH.

MONTGOMERY, April 11, 1861.

Hon. JOHN FORSYTH,
    Washington:

Is the powder ready for delivery? If not, we have an order covering the point. The object in replying as I did to you was to get immediate supply. If to be manufactured, nothing is gained. The order to you was for ninety tons cannon and ten tons musket powder. Reply specially, and state time of delivery.

L. P. WALKER.

MONTGOMERY, May 3, 1861.

Governor THOMAS O. MOORE,
    New Orleans:

Your dispatch of the 3d (1st?) to the President received. Buy all the muskets, rifles, powder, and caps that you can. The funds will be provided as you suggest. The Secretary of the Treasury will see to this.

L. P. WALKER.

FIREARMS OF THE CONFEDERACY

CHARLESTON, S. C., July 7, 1861.

Hon. L. P. WALKER:

SIR: I reached this place this morning from Augusta, Ga., where I spent two days with moderate success in purchasing rifles. It being Sunday, I am unable to say with what success I shall meet here, but I am satisfied that I shall be able to procure at least fifty rifles. I have shipped up to this date nearly 400 rifles, in good condition, to the commanding officer at Fort Smith. I now propose to go through the States of South Carolina and North Carolina, and perhaps Tennessee again, relying upon procuring the rest of the rifles in the two former States. I shall proceed from this place to Columbia, S. C., where I respectfully request that you will send me a draft for $250 (payable in gold) for traveling purposes. It is of great advantage to me to have gold, as I find the greatest difficulty in passing the bank notes of one State at par, in an adjoining State even. I will be in Columbia, S. C., by the time the draft reaches there. I find everywhere I go that there are other persons in the market purchasing rifles, even at prices which I do not feel myself justified in giving. It is therefore very necessary for me to have the proper currency and the ready money to move expeditiously from place to place, and take advantage of every opportunity which offers itself to make purchases. I respectfully request that as little delay as possible may attend the forwarding of the funds.

I am, sir, your obedient servant,

THOS. B. MILLS,
C. S. Navy.

ARMS SEIZED BY THE SOUTHERN STATES

As early as November 10, 1860 the movement to seize the U. S. forts and arsenals seems to have been under way and while the different State authorities apparently all acted more or less independently, the movement, once started, soon covered all the seceding States.

In the order of the number of arms secured the arsenals were seized as follows:

Baton Rouge by Louisiana, Jan. 10, 1861...... 47,372 arms
Fayetteville by North Carolina, Apr. 23,
    1861 .... 37,000 arms
Augusta by Georgia, Jan. 24, 1861............ 22,714 arms
Charleston by South Carolina, Dec. 27,
    1860 .... 22,469 arms
Mount Vernon by Alabama, Jan. 4, 1861...... 19,455 arms
Little Rock by Arkansas...................... 10,000 arms

In addition to the above, all of the smaller arsenals and barracks were taken possession of along with the forts located in the Southern States, the principal ones being:

Moultrie—South Carolina...................December 27, 1860
Morgan—Alabama...........................January 5, 1861
Baton Rouge—Louisiana....................January 10, 1861
Jackson—Louisiana.........................January 11, 1861
Saint Phillip—Louisiana...................January 14, 1861
Oglethorpe—Georgia.......................January 26, 1861

FIREARMS OF THE CONFEDERACY

With the exception of Fayetteville all of the seizures above were made prior to January 27, 1861 and, as the property was all located within the bounds of the seceding States, the authorities at Washington were probably in no position to protect them.

At this late date the capture of Harper's Ferry on April 18, 1861 by a body of State troops is indeed hard to explain, as this property was nearer Washington than Richmond, and troops for its protection could have been sent there without passing them through hostile territory.

The call for the first 75,000 volunteers was made April 15, 1861, which indicated that the Government had abandoned the idea of a peaceful settlement of the question, and the movement of troops after that date could not jeopardize any peace plans; but there seems to have been no effort made to reinforce the small body of troops guarding that place, thereby permitting the Confederates to acquire property that was of immense value to them at the time.

CHARLESTON ARSENAL, S. C.,
December 31, 1860.
SIR: I have the honor to submit the correspondence relative to the surrender of this post yesterday to the authorities of this State. Trusting that my course may meet the approval of the Department,
I am, sir, very respectfully,
F. C. HUMPHREYS,
Military Storekeeper Ordnance, U. S. A.
Capt. WM. MAYNADIER,
In charge of Ordnance Bureau, Washington, D. C.

[INCLOSURES.]
CHARLESTON, December 30, 1860 - 10½ o'clock a. m.
SIR: I herewith demand an immediate surrender of the U. S. Arsenal at this place and under your charge, and a delivery to me of the keys and contents of the arsenals, magazines, &c.

I am already proceeding to occupy it with a strong armed detachment of troops.

I make the demand in the name of the State of South Carolina, and by virtue of an order from its governor, a copy of which is inclosed.
Very respectfully,
JOHN CUNNINGHAM,
Colonel Seventeenth Reg. Inf., S. C. M.
Capt. F. C. HUMPHREYS,
Military Storekeeper Ordnance.

HEADQUARTERS, CHARLESTON, S. C.
December 29, 1860.
SIR: In the morning, after reporting yourself to Major General Schneirle, and informing him of this order, you are directed to get from him a detachment of select men, and in the most discreet and

forbearing manner you will proceed to the U. S. Arsenal in Charleston, and there demand, in my name, its entire possession, and state distinctly that you do this with a view to prevent any destruction of public property that may occur in the present excited state of the public mind, and also as due to the public safety. You will then proceed to take, in the most systematic manner, a correct inventory of every thing in said arsenal, and the exact state of all arms, &c.

You will read this order to Captain Humphreys, who is the United States officer at the arsenal.

I do not apprehend any difficulty in giving up the same, but if refused, then you are to take it, using no more force than may be absolutely necessary, and with the greatest discretion and liberality to Captain Humphreys, who is at perfect liberty to remain in his present quarters as long as it may be agreeable for himself, and he is requested to do so. Report as soon as possible to me.

F. W. PICKENS.

Col. JOHN CUNNINGHAM.

Report of Ordnance Sergeant S. Patterson, U. S. Army, of the Seizure of Fort Morgan

MOBILE, JANUARY 5, 1861.

DEAR SIR: I have been superseded by Colonel Todd, of the Militia of Alabama, and he took and receipted for all the property belonging to the Ordnance Department and fort.

I wait for orders from the Adjutant General.

I am, very respectfully,

S. PATTERSON,
Ordnance Sergeant, U. S. Army.

The ADJUTANT GENERAL.

Report of Lieut. John W. Todd, U. S. Ordnance Department, of the Seizure of the Arsenal at Baton Rouge

BATON ROUGE, January 10, 1861.

The arsenal was surrendered this evening to the governor of Louisiana. Please give me instructions where to proceed with the detachment under my command.

J. W. TODD,
Lieutenant, Ordnance Corps.

Col. H. K. CRAIG:
Chief of Ordnance Department, U. S. Army.

U. S. ARSENAL, CHATTAHOOCHEE, FLA.,
January 6, 1861.

SIR: I have the honor herewith to inclose a copy of the order given to Colonel Dunn, the commander of the troops which took possession of this arsenal. I telegraphed this morning to you.

I am, sir, very respectfully, your obedient servant,

E. POWELL,
Ordnance Sergeant, U. S. Army.

Capt. W. MAYNADIER,
Chief of Ordnance, Washington, D. C.

FIREARMS OF THE CONFEDERACY

[INCLOSURE]
STATE OF FLORIDA, EXECUTIVE CHAMBER,
Tallahassee, January 5, 1861.
SIR: Reposing special confidence in your patriotism, discretion, and integrity, I hereby authorize and empower you to raise a company of picked men and proceed to the Apalchicola River and seize and possess the arsenal, arms, ammunition, stores, buildings, and other property now in the possession of the General Government, and retain the same subject to my orders. You are requested to act with secrecy and discretion. You are further authorized to call out the Seventh Regiment Florida Militia for all aid in its power to render that you may deem necessary to retain occupation of said arsenal.

By the governor State Florida:

M. S. PERRY.

T. S. VILLEPIGUE, Secretary of State.

BATON ROUGE BARRACKS, LA.,
January 11, 1861.

COLONEL: It is my painful duty to announce to you the surrender of the arsenal and barracks at this place to the governor of this State.

The governor collected a large force in the city here yesterday and about 5 p. m. sent me, by his aides-de-camp, Colonels Bragg and Taylor, a summons, a copy of which I herewith inclose.

Having no assurance of reinforcements or support, I deemed it proper, after consulting with the officers here, to yield to the demand. I also inclose a copy of the paper signed this morning.

I am, colonel, very respectfully, your obedient servant,

J. A. HASKINS,
Brevet Major, and Captain, First Artillery.

Col. S. COOPER, Adjutant General U. S. Army, Washington, D. C.

P. S. I telegraphed to you yesterday for orders, and shall take the first boat I can for Cairo without I receive contrary orders.

J. H. HASKIN,
Brevet Major, and Captain, First Artillery.

[INCLOSURES.]
EXECUTIVE OFFICE,
BATON ROUGE, LA., January 10, 1861.

SIR: The safety of the State of Louisiana demands that I take possession of all Government property within her limits. You are, therefore, summoned hereby to deliver up the barracks, arsenal, and public property now under your command.

With the large force at my disposal this demand will be enforced. Any attempt at defense on your part will be a rash sacrifice of life.

The highest consideration will be extended to yourself and command.

THOMAS O. MOORE,
Governor and Commander-in-Chief Militia
of Louisiana.

The COMMANDING OFFICER,
Baton Rouge Barracks, Baton Rouge, La.

FIREARMS OF THE CONFEDERACY

ORDNANCE OFFICE,
Washington, D. C., January 15, 1861.

Hon. JOSEPH HOLT,
Secretary of War:

SIR: I have the honor to acknowledge the reference of a letter from the Hon. B. Stanton, chairman of the Committee on Military Affairs of the House of Representatives, asking for the statement of the distribution of arms from the armories to the arsenals and other places of deposit, for safe-keeping, from January 1, 1860, to January 1, 1861, &c., and in compliance with your directions, have to report that on December 30, 1859, an order was received from the War Department directing the transfer of 115,000 arms from the Springfield Armory and the Watertown and Watervliet Arsenals to different arsenals in the South.

Orders were given, in obedience to these instructions, on January 30, 1860, and the arms were removed during the past spring from and to the places as follows, viz:

From Springfield Armory, 65,000 percussion muskets, caliber of .69, and 40,000 muskets, altered from flintlock to percussion, cal. .69. From Watertown Arsenal, 6,000 percussion rifles, caliber of .54. From Watervliet Arsenal, 4,000 percussion rifles, caliber of .54. Of which there were sent to Charleston Arsenal, 9,280 percussion muskets, 5,720 altered muskets, and 2,000 rifles; North Carolina Arsenal, 15,480 percussion muskets, 9,520 altered muskets, and 2,000 rifles; Augusta Arsenal, 12,380 percussion muskets, 7,620 altered muskets, and 2,000 rifles; Mount Vernon Arsenal, 9,280 percussion muskets, 5,720 altered muskets, and 2,000 rifles; Baton Rouge Arsenal, 18,580 percussion muskets, 11,420 altered muskets and 2,000 rifles.

The arms thus transferred, which were at the Charleston Arsenal, the Mount Vernon Arsenal, and the Baton Rouge Arsenal, have been seized by the authorities of the several States of South Carolina, Alabama, and Louisiana, and are no longer in possession of the Ordnance Department. Those stored at Augusta Arsenal and at North Carolina are still in charge of officers of this department.

In addition to the foregoing there have been transfers of arms from the armories to different arsenals, but only in such quantities as the exigencies of the service demand for immediate issues to the Army and to the States, under the act of April 23, 1808, and which I infer are not intended to be embraced in the call of the Hon. Mr. Stanton, whose letter is herewith returned.

Very respectfully, &c.,

H. K. CRAIG,
Colonel of Ordnance.

AUGUSTA ARSENAL, GA., January 24, 1861.

SIR: I have the honor to report that the arsenal was surrendered this morning to the governor of Georgia upon honorable terms, herewith inclosed.

I am, sir, very respectfully, your obedient servant,

ARNOLD ELZEY,
Captain, Second Artillery.

Col. S. COOPER, Adjutant General,
U. S. Army, Washington, D. C.

AUGUSTA ARSENAL, GA., January 24, 1861.

His Excellency the Governor of Georgia having demanded the United States Arsenal at Augusta, commanded by Capt. Arnold Elzey, Second Artillery, U. S. Army, the following terms are agreed upon, to-wit:

1st. The flag to be saluted and lowered by the United States troops.

4th. The public property to be receipted for by the State authorities and accounted for upon adjustment between the State of Georgia and the United States of America.

5th. The troops to have unobstructed passage through and out of the State, by water, to New York, via Savannah.

JOSEPH E. BROWN,
*Governor and Commander-in-Chief
of the Army of the State of Georgia.*
ARNOLD ELZEY,
*Captain, Second Artillery,
Commanding Augusta Arsenal.*

Report of Ordnance Storekeeper John M. Galt, U. S. Army, of the seizure of Augusta Arsenal.

AUGUSTA ARSENAL, GA., January 25, 1861.

SIR: I have the honor to report that this post was surrendered to the authorities of the State of Georgia on a demand made by the governor in person, backed by a very superior force of the military of the State. The company of Second U. S. Artillery stationed here is under orders for New York, and as we are required to evacuate the post as soon as practicable, I would respectfully recommend the immediate discharge of the detachment of Ordnance, and would request that four or six months' leave of absence be granted to me. It may be well in making the application for leave of absence to say that I have had none for fourteen years, with one exception, of which I did avail myself. Full and complete receipts will be taken for all the public property in my charge.

I am, sir, very respectfully, your obedient servant,

JOHN M. GALT,
Military Storekeeper of Ordnance.

Col. H. K. CRAIG:
Ordnance Office, Washington, D. C.

WAR DEPARTMENT,
February 7, 1861.

Hon. B. STANTON,
Chairman Committee on Military Affairs:

SIR: In answer to the inquiries contained in your letter of the 4th instant I have the honor to state that it appears from dispatches received by the Department that the following works have been taken possession of by parties acting in the name and under authority of the States in which they are respectively situated, viz:

First. Fort Moultrie, S. C., December 27, 1860.
Second. Fort Morgan, Ala., January 5, 1861.
Third. Baton Rouge Barracks, La., January 10, 1861.
Fourth. Forts Jackson, and
Fifth. Saint Philip, La., January 11, 1861.
Sixth. Fort Pike, La., January 14, 1861.
Seventh. Oglethorpe Barracks, Ga., January 27 (26), 1861.

FIREARMS OF THE CONFEDERACY

The surrender of the Charleston, Augusta, Mount Vernon, and Baton Rouge arsenals was communicated in my letter of the 22d ultimo. Besides these posts, it is understood that the arsenal at Chattahoochee, Forts McRee and Barrancas, and Barrancas Barracks have been seized by the authorities of Florida, but no official information to that effect has so far reached the Department.

Very respectfully, your obedient servant,

J. HOLT,
Secretary of War.

Report of Capt. R. H. K. Whiteley, U. S. Ordnance Department, of the Seizure of the U. S. Arsenal at San Antonio, Tex.

TEXAS ARSENAL,
San Antonio, February 16, 1861.

COLONEL: I have the honor to inform you that the troops of Texas entered San Antonio early this morning, and have taken possession of the arsenal and all public storehouses in the city. No property has been disturbed to this hour (1 o'clock p. m.), and I think matters will remain in status quo until the 2nd proximo, when an agent will be sent by the convention of the people of Texas to receive and receipt for public property.

I am, sir, very respectfully, your obedient servant,

R. H. K. WHITELEY,
Captain of Ordnance.

Col. H. K. CRAIG:
Chief of Ordnance Department, Washington, City, D. C.

DESTRUCTION OF THE UNITED STATES ARMORY AT HARPER'S FERRY, W. VA., APRIL 18, 1861

REPORTS, ETC.

Reports of First Lieut. R. Jones, Mounted Rifles, U. S. Army

HEADQUARTERS UNITED STATES ARMORY,
Harper's Ferry, Va., April 18, 1861—9 p. m.

SIR: Up to the present time no assault or attempt to seize the Government property here has been made, but there is decided evidence that the subject is in contemplation, and has been all day, by a large number of people living in the direction of Charlestown; and at sundown this evening several companies of troops had assembled at Halltown, about three or four miles from here on the road to Charlestown with the intention of seizing the Government property, and the last report is that the attack will be made tonight. I telegraphed this evening to General Scott that I had received information confirming his dispatch of this morning, and later to the Adjutant General that I expected an attack tonight. I have taken steps which ought to insure my receiving early intelligence of the advance of any forces, and my determination is to destroy what I cannot defend, and if the forces sent against me are clearly overwhelming, my present intention is to retreat into Pennsylvania.

The steps I have taken to destroy the arsenal, which contains nearly 15,000 stand of arms, are so complete that I can conceive of nothing that will prevent their entire destruction.

If the Government purposes maintaining its authority here, no time should be lost in sending large bodies of troops to my assistance and as many of them as possible should be regulars.

A courier has just reported the advance of the troops from Halltown.

Respectfully, I am, sir, your obedient servant,

R. JONES,
First Lieutenant, Mounted Riflemen,
Commanding

To the ASSISTANT ADJUTANT GENERAL,
Headquarters of the Army, Washington, D. C.

CHAMBERSBURG, April 19, 1861.

Finding my position untenable, shortly after 10 o'clock last night I destroyed the arsenal, containing 15,000 stand of arms, and burned up the armory building proper, and under cover of the night withdrew my command almost in the presence of twenty-five hundred or three thousand troops. This was accomplished with but four casualties. I believe the destruction must have been complete. I will await orders at Carlisle.

R. JONES.

General WINFIELD SCOTT.

Report of Lieut. Col. William Maynadier, U. S. Ordnance Department, of the Expenditures and Losses at the Armory

ORDNANCE OFFICE,
Washington, November 16, 1861.

SIR: In answer to the letter (following) of the Hon. John P. Hale, chairman of the committee of the Senate, which you referred to this office, I have the honor to report that U. S. Armory at Harper's Ferry was established in the year 1796.

The amount expended on the same is—

For land purchased at different times..............$	45,477
For improvements thereon for water power, canals, walls, embankments, and water privileges, and for hydraulic machinery and buildings of all kinds..............	1,787,430

Total, exclusive of the amount expended in the manufacture and repair of arms...................$1,832,907

The latest annual inventory of the property belonging to the United States at that armory is dated June 30, 1860, in which the value of all the property on hand at that date is appraised as follows, viz:

1,669½ acres of land..$		37,457
Milldams, canals, water powers & hydraulic machinery		233,279
Forges, rolling mills, machine shops, storehouses, dwellings, and other buildings..........		341,221
Amount of real estate.........................$		611,957
Machines used in workshops...........$270,235		
Tools used in service....................... 109,560	$	379,795
Unwrought materials on hand........ 100,043		
Parts of arms in progress................ 93,573		193,616
20,507 arms of different models in store...........		285,145
Total appraised value June 30, 1860...........$1,470,513		

FIREARMS OF THE CONFEDERACY

By the latest returns received at this office from the armory, it appears that the number of arms in store when the armory was destroyed in April, 1861, was reduced to 4,287, the value of which was about $64,000.

We may assume that the quantity and value of all other property than the arms in store remained without material change from June, 1860, to April, 1861. The diminished number of arms in store at the latter date reduces that item in the inventory from $285,145 to $164,300, and the total appraised value of all the property from $1,470,513 to $1,207,668.

Respectfully, &c.,

WM. MAYNADIER,
Lieutenant Colonel, Ordnance.

Hon. SIMON CAMERON,
Secretary of War:

Report of Bvt. Maj. S. S. Anderson, Second U. S. Artillery, of the seizure of the U. S. Arsenal at Fayetteville, N. C.

HEADQUARTERS TROOPS NORTH CAROLINA ARSENAL,
Fayetteville, N. C., April 23, 1861.

COLONEL: I have to report that this arsenal was surrendered to the State of North Carolina yesterday, on demand of the Governor of the State, which demand was sustained by a force of one thousand and fifty rank and file of State troops, well armed and equipped. The demand for the surrender being made, supported by such an overwhelming force, after consulting with Captain Bradford, the commander of the arsenal, we did not deem it necessary to offer a resistance, which in the end could be of no avail other than the total annihilation of my command (which at the time consisted of only forty-two effective muskets), as there was no probability, or possibility I may say, I could or would be reinforced. I inclose a certified copy of the terms agreed upon between myself and the governor's aide-de-camp with regard to the withdrawal of my command.

I have today ordered Lieutenant DeLagnel to Wilmington, N. C. for the purpose of procuring transportation for the troops to one of the northern posts.

Captain Bradford, the commander of the arsenal, and on whom the demand for surrender was made, has made an official report to the chief of his corps, which embraces all the particulars regarding the surrender.

I am, sir, very respectfully, your obedient servant,

S. S. ANDERSON, Capt.

Col. L. THOMAS, Adj. Gen. U. S. Army.

Statement of small arms on hand at the different arsenals when taken possession of by the several States.

Names of arsenals.	Rifle muskets, U. S. model.	Muskets, rifled, caliber .69.	Muskets, percussion, new and altered.	Muskets, flint.	Harper's Ferry rifles.	Colt rifles.	Hall rifles.	Carbines, various patterns.	Pistols, percussion.	Colt pistols.	Total.
Baton Rouge..........	1,099	972	29,222	8,283	2,158	73	2,287	735	2,075	468	47,372
Mount Vernon........	20	......	a17,370	......	2,032	......	......	......	33	......	19,455
Charleston............	646	......	18,723	......	2,800	......	......	......	300	......	22,469
Augusta...............	......	......	20,000	......	2,000	......	714	......	......	......	22,714
Little Rock (reported)..	......	......	......	......	......	......	......	......	......	......	10,000
Fayetteville (reported)..	......	......	......	......	......	......	......	......	......	......	37,000
Total...........	1,765	972	85,315	8,283	8,990	73	3,001	735	2,408	468	159,010

a A portion of the arms at the arsenal had already been removed at the date of the report rendered. Of cartridges for small-arms, there are on hand at all the arsenals, number, 3,200,000. Of musket and rifle powder, there are now on hand, pounds, 168,000. (This amount of powder will make 1,500,000 cartridges.) Of cannon-powder, the supply is nearly all at the forts, with a small quantity in reserve. Of fixed ammunition for field batteries, there is enough at Baton Rouge alone to supply ten batteries of six guns each. Of percussion caps, there are here (750,000 belonging to this State) over 2,000,000, and there are a good many at the arsenals and bundled with the cartridges. It is understood that the State of Georgia has 150 tons of saltpeter, with a proportionate quantity of sulphur; this will make quite 200 tons of powder.

J. GORGAS,
Major and Chief of Ordnance.

May 7, 1861.
Hon. F. S. BARTOW,
Chairman Committee of Military Affairs.

DESCRIPTION OF THE U. S. REGULATION ARMS USED BY THE CONFEDERATES — THE FLINTLOCK RIFLES AND MUSKETS ALTERED TO PERCUSSION — THE REGULAR PERCUSSION ARMS UP TO THE MODEL 1861.

While the regulation U. S. arms that were used by the Confederates are of little interest to present day collectors, a description of those forming a bulk of their supply at the beginning of hostilities is included here for reference.

It is, of course, impossible to determine for a certainty whether any particular arm of this class was actually in the Confederate service or not, as there was no official marking put upon them, and the traditions handed down, or the markings indicating Confederate use found on some arms, are not to be entirely depended upon.

It is evident from the records available that the several Southern states had in their armories, arms of all description as used by the U. S. Army, and the Government arsenals in the South contained a quantity of all the models then in use.

PLATE I

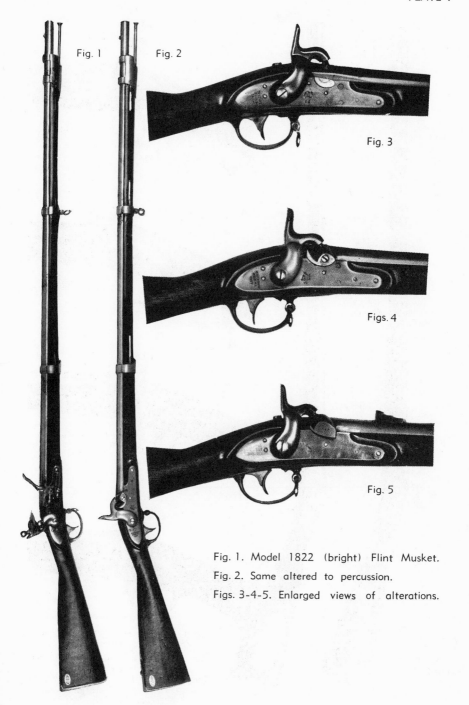

Fig. 1

Fig. 2

Fig. 3

Figs. 4

Fig. 5

Fig. 1. Model 1822 (bright) Flint Musket.
Fig. 2. Same altered to percussion.
Figs. 3-4-5. Enlarged views of alterations.

PLATE II

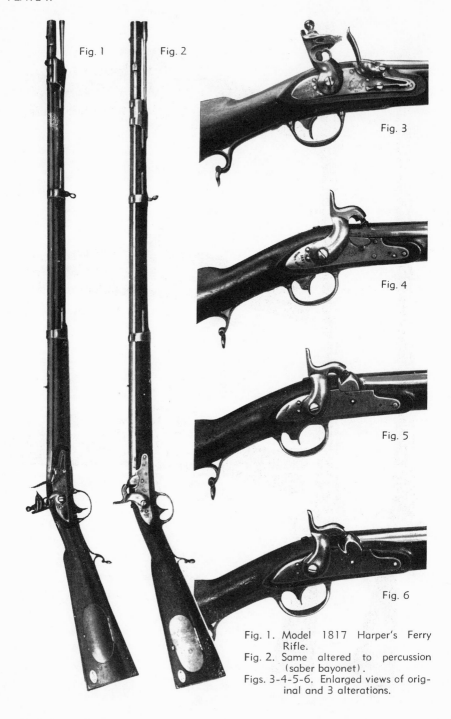

Fig. 1

Fig. 2

Fig. 3

Fig. 4

Fig. 5

Fig. 6

Fig. 1. Model 1817 Harper's Ferry Rifle.
Fig. 2. Same altered to percussion (saber bayonet).
Figs. 3-4-5-6. Enlarged views of original and 3 alterations.

U. S. FLINTLOCK MUSKETS ALTERED TO PERCUSSION CAL. .69

On Oct. 13, 1843, after the adoption of the percussion system for all regulation arms, the Secretary of War ordered a classification of all flintlock arms on hand for the purpose of altering all those suitable to the percussion system.

This work was interrupted by the Mexican War but in 1848 was finally completed and Col. Talcott reported:

Muskets made since 1831.. 164,965
Made between 1821 and 1831.................................... 160,374

Total destined to be altered............ 325,339

The Springfield Armory altered 86,565 of these during 1849-1850-1851 and Harper's Ferry also did considerable of this work, but the records from there are not compiled.

In November, 1859 Col. Craig reported the following quantities of these in the Southern Arsenals:

Harper's Ferry Armory.. 149
Fayetteville, N. C., Arsenal.. 4,817
Mount Vernon, Alabama, Arsenal............................... 2,364
Baton Rouge, Louisiana, Arsenal.............................. 8,266
San Antonio, Texas, Arsenal... 77

Total.................................. 15,673

On orders from Sec. Floyd dated Dec. 29, 1859 the following transfers were made early in 1860.

From Springfield Armory to:
Charleston Arsenal.. 5,720
Fayetteville Arsenal.. 9,520
Augusta Arsenal.. 7,620
Mount Vernon Arsenal... 5,720
Baton Rouge Arsenal... 11,420

Total.................................. 40,000

And on Dec. 21, 1860 Capt. Maynadier reported that during that year 24,110 of these arms had been sold for $2.50 each and as all of these were purchased for Southern States it brings the total number of these arms in possession of the South, after they had seized the several arsenals, to 79,783 not counting those issued to them on their regular yearly quota.

Col. Craig's report of Nov. 12, 1859 indicates that there were on hand at that time 23,894 unaltered flintlock muskets, and these were evidently altered after the war started by independent contractors, as many of them are now found dated 1861 and 1862. Owing to the shortage of arms in the North these and other altered muskets in the arsenals of the North were issued for service in the field. Gen. Grant relates in his Memoirs that upon the fall of Vicksburg his troops exchanged their .69 caliber altered flintlock arms for the Enfields captured from the South.

The above referred to letter of October 13, 1843 is here quoted in full:

ORDNANCE OFFICE, WAR DEPARTMENT,
Washington, October 13, 1843.

SIR: On the inquiry concerning the inspection of United States muskets, contained in Mr. Hallett's letter to the Secretary of the Navy of the 7th instant, which has been referred to this office, I have to report, that the adoption of the percussion musket by most of the European nations, and its advantages over arms with flintlocks, led to the determination to introduce it into our service.

To effect this, it was deemed proper to alter the arms already in store so far as they were of a quality suited to receive percussion locks, and to make such locks for all arms hereafter to be manufactured.

It was well known that many of the arms on hand, made in the infancy of our manufactures, and when proper mechanical skill and suitable materials were not abundant in the country, were unfit for the alteration, and even for service, when compared with the improved arms more recently fabricated. A thorough inspection, therefore, of all the muskets in our arsenals, made prior to 1832, for the purpose of classifying them according to their qualities and disposing of such as should be found unserviceable, was recommended, and sanctioned by the Secretary of War.

This duty was directed to be performed by two inspectors from the national armories, under the supervision of an ordnance officer, to whom the following general instructions, in substance, were given for their guidance in making the classification.

All good and serviceable arms made since 1831 were to constitute the first class.

The second class was to include all good and serviceable arms made from 1821 to 1831 inclusive; such arms to be issued for all ordinary purposes and held as suitable for alteration to percussion.

The third class was to include all serviceable arms made from 1812 to 1820 inclusive, such arms not being considered suitable for ordinary issues, nor for alteration to percussion, but being still such as ought to be retained for use in case of emergency.

The fourth and last class was to include all arms made prior to 1812, as also the unserviceable arms made at later periods, and the damaged arms not worth repairing. These were to be collected at depots for sale under future orders.

The above classification by dates was founded upon the progressive improvements which have been made in the models and manufacture of arms in this country. This inspection has been completed at many of the arsenals, and the persons designated for the service are still engaged in its performances.

The result will show that, of the stock on hand (over 600,000 muskets), at least one-tenth, if not more, will be found defective and fall into the fourth class, or those ordered to be prepared for sale.

Sales have already been made at auction, and at private sale after the arms at auction, under the provisions of the law passed 3d March, 1825, and the Ordnance Regulations, articles 101 and 102, the proceeds of which have been deposited to the credit of the Treasurer of the United States.

Mr. Hallet's letter is herewith returned.
Respectfully, your obedient servant,
G. TALCOTT,
Lieutenant Colonel of Ordnance.
Hon. J. M. PORTER,
Secretary of War:
No. 51. Pages 490-491. (Letters to W. D. Vol. 8, Pg. 159).

From the above it will be seen that this classification was based upon the "progressive improvements" that had been made in the models of arms as manufactured, and those considered suitable for alteration were the Models 1821 - 1831 and Model 1840 the last of the flintlocks.

The model 1821 which is generally referred to as the model 1822 constituted the bulk of the arms to be altered, and is very similar to the model 1831 except that the latter was finished "bright" in place of "brown" and generally the brass pan was provided with a fence.

Included in the first class was also the model 1840 muskets but as the production of these was limited, and as they were the latest improved flintlocks their alteration was probably not commenced until the other classes had been completed.

Figure 1, Plate I

This shows the Model 1822 in the original flintlock and the general description of it applies to the altered arm shown in Figure 2.

The BARREL is caliber .69, smooth-bore, 42 inches long, with bayonet lug on top. The STOCK is black walnut 54 inches long and made without a comb. The MOUNTINGS are all of iron, the top band being double and carrying the knife blade front sight.

Total length from butt to muzzle 57.64 inches. With bayonet fixed 73.64 in. Weight without bayonet, 10 lbs. 1/4 ounce.

This arm was made in large quantities by both Springfield and Harper's Ferry armories and contracts were let for many thousand, the records show that on Dec. 31, 1821 there were due on contracts the following:

Adam Carruth, Greenville, S. C. 7,750
Eli Whitney, New Haven, Conn. 2,000
Alexander McRae, Richmond, Va. 10,000
Asa Waters, Millbury, Mass. 6,000
Lemuel Pomeroy, Pittsfield, Mass. 3,340
Marine T. Wickham, Philadelphia, Pa. 5,000

In addition to these the following contractors are known to have made this model:

P. & E. W. Blake   W. L. Evans
Henry Derringer   N. Starr
John Rogers   B. Evans
          P. & J. D. Johnson

Derringer and Johnson changed their contracts from Hall rifles to muskets and so far as known but very few guns of this model were made by McRae or Rogers.

The first regularly adopted method of altering these arms is shown in Figure 3, and is described in the ordnance manual of 1850 as follows:

ALTERATION OF FLINT MUSKETS TO PERCUSSION

THE BARREL is altered: 1st by closing the vent in the side, and boring a new vent on the upper part of the barrel; 2nd, by upsetting a cone seat in the metal of the barrel, and putting in a percussion cone. The screw thread of the cone for altered muskets is a little shorter than for the new muskets, so that it may not project into the bore.

THE LOCK is altered: 1st, by removing the cock, the battery, battery screw, battery spring, and battery spring screw; 2nd, by cutting off the pan, near the face of the lock plate, filling up the hollow of the remaining part with brass, soldered in, and dressing off the upper surface even with the top of the lock plate; 3rd, replacing the cock by a percussion hammer; 4th, filling up the holes of the battery screw and the battery spring screw with pieces of those screws, rounded on the outer end, and filling the pivot hole of the battery spring with wire.

Later the method of cutting off the end of the barrel and supplying a forging with a bolster for the nipple seat was used. Fig. 4 shows the first of this kind provided with a side screw for cleaning the passage, and later that shown in Fig. 5 was used, especially by the contractors on this work during the war. In most cases the last two alterations included rifling the barrel.

U.S. FLINTLOCK RIFLE MODEL 1817—CAL. .54 WITH ALTERATIONS

Plate II

The manufacture of this, the second regulation rifle to be adopted by the Government commenced in 1817 and continued to 1847, a period of thirty years without any material changes.

Harper's Ferry produced 7,817 of these arms and during the years 1820 to 1843 many thousand more were manufactured for the Government by contractors S. North, N. Starr, R. & D. Johnson all of Middletown, Conn., and H. Derringer of Philadelphia.

The workmanship on this arm was of the very highest quality and compared favorably with that of the best sporting arms. The barrel which is 36 inches long, .54 caliber, was finished a dark brown, while the full length stock was treated with several coats of linseed oil rubbed to a high finish. The mountings, all of iron, were heat blued, and the ramrod finished bright with a brass tip. The extension from the trigger guard to carry the rear swivel and forming a hand grip, and the oval patch box in the stock are characteristic of this arm, though a few of them made by Derringer did not have the extended guard. The total length of the arm is 51½ in. and the weight with bayonet, 10¼ pounds.

The original specimen shown on Plate II, Fig. 1, is marked on the lock plate, Harper's Ferry, 1817, with the large spread eagle. It differs from most of the contractor arms, in being provided with a bayonet lug on the barrel and the front sight on the top band in place of the front sight on the barrel with no provision for attaching the bayonet.

Fig. 2 shows a specimen probably altered after 1856, for besides the change to percussion, the alteration includes the shortening of the stock to permit the attachment of a lug for a saber bayonet.

Figs. 3, 4, 5 and 6 show the original lock and three of the principal methods of altering to percussion.

Col. Craig's report of Nov. 12, 1859 shows 1,385 of these altered rifles in store at Baton Rouge, and while it is impossible to arrive at the exact number in the different State arsenals there is frequent mention of them in all of the correspondence, and it will be noted that many of the State militia were armed with the original flintlocks at the commencement of the war.

Some of these Model 1817 rifles belonging to the State of North Carolina were altered to percussion at Fayetteville in 1861. A knob for sword bayonet was also added. Figure 1, Plate XXIV shows one of these guns, dated 1825, and marked on the barrel: "N. Carolina" and on the lock plate: "M. A. Baker, Fayetteville, N. C."

U. S. REGULATION PERCUSSION ARMS — MODEL 1842
U. S. MODEL 1842 MUSKET
Figure 1, Plate III

The musket of this model, shown in Fig. 1, Plate III, marks an important step in the development of our firearms, it being the last smooth-bore and first percussion arm regularly issued.

It also has the distinction of being the first arm (except the Hall breech-loading arm manufactured at Harper's Ferry) to be produced on the complete interchangeable plan as indicated by the report of Col. Craig to Jeff'n Davis, Secretary of War, dated March 17, 1854 which reads in part as follows:

"As applicable to the question concerning the quality of the arms made under the superintendence by military officers, I submit the following extract from an official report by the United States Inspector of Armories of his inspection of Harper's Ferry Armory in July, 1852:

'The completeness of the present system (of superintendence by military officers) so far as uniformity in construction is concerned, is made manifest by the late submersion of some 20,000 arms during the highest flood ever known at the place. In cleaning these arms 9,000 percussion muskets have been stripped and completely dismantled, their parts being thrown into great masses, and after being repaired the arms are reassembled from these lots of 9,000 components having no distinguished mark, every limb filling its appropriate place with perfectness. Had not this perfect uniformity existed, the parts of each arm must have been separately distributed, boxes must have been provided for these several and numerous parcels, great care would have been requisite to avoid a mixture. Every limb of every musket must have been numbered and the expense of the operation would have been greatly increased.

'All these inconveniences have been obviated by that system of uniform dimensions, even in the simplest and minutest components of the arm, which obtains in such perfection at this armory.

'To determine whether this general uniformity extended to the fabrication of both national armories, I caused a musket of the manufacture of 1851 of each armory to be taken to pieces, and then applied all the components of one to the other, mixing them in almost every possible manner, and applying the parts likewise to the receiving gauge. The result was, the components, as well as the whole, were identical for every practical purpose. Only one almost inappreciable variation in the length of the front end of the lock plates being detected, and this did not prevent a perfect assembling of the arms.

'With the use of the percussion caps came trouble from the damage to the cone from the hammer striking the cone when no cap was on as indicated by the Ordnance Office correspondence on the subject.' "

The specimen shown is marked on lock plate Harper's Ferry, with the usual spread eagle and dated 1844. Length of barrel, 3 feet 6 inches. Total length, 4 feet 9½ inches. Weight, 10 lbs. The bayonet lug is on the bottom side of the barrel and the bayonet is supplied with a clamping band, the first of this type issued since the experimental ones of 1801. As issued these arms were .69 cal. smooth-bore, but later many of them were rifled and provided with a long range rear sight as shown by the specimen illustrated.

Except for a few made by contractor B. Flagg & Co., Millbury, in 1849 and those made by the Palmetto Armory, this musket was produced only at the Springfield and Harper's Ferry armories during the years from 1843 to 1855 inclusive.

Col. Craig's report of Nov. 12, 1859 shows the following number of these arms in the U. S. armories and arsenals of the Southern States:

Harper's Ferry	5,306
Fort Monroe	321
Fayetteville	2,861
Charleston	2,413
Baton Rouge	2,396
San Antonio	285
Little Rock	349
Total	13,931

Of the above, 1557 were rifled and sighted.

On orders from Secretary of War Floyd dated Dec. 29, 1859, the following transfers were made:

From Springfield Armory to:

Charleston arsenal	9,280
Fayetteville arsenal	15,480
Augusta arsenal	12,380
Baton Rouge arsenal	18,580
Mount Vernon arsenal	9,280
Total	65,000

To this total of 78,931 should be added those in possession of the various States of which there is no compiled record available, but from the numerous reference to them in the correspondence they formed a considerable portion of the arms used by their militia, and even allowing for those destroyed at Harper's Ferry it appears that this arm comprised an important factor in arming the Southern Army.

U. S. CADET MUSKET MODEL 1842

Figure 2, Plate III

There is no record of this arm, known as the Cadet model 1842, being in any of the U. S. arsenals of the South at the commencement of hostilities, but frequent mention is made of them in the correspondence of the State officials, so it can be assumed that at least a small number of them were used.

It is caliber .54, and otherwise conforms in all details to the regular musket model except that all proportions are reduced in accordance with the reduction of the caliber from .69 to .54.

The specimen shown is marked on lock plate Springfield 1852 and the usual eagle. Length of barrel 3 feet, 4 inches. Total length, 4 feet, 6½ inches. Weight 8½ pounds. Bayonet 14 inches long with regular clasp of this model.

U. S. MODEL 1842 RIFLE

Figure 3, Plate III

The rifle of this model, due to the fact that it was made at Harper's Ferry in 1841, is generally referred to as model of that date, but it was not adopted until the following year. They are also often referred to as Mississippi rifles; Kentucky rifles; Harper's Ferry Yager and Windsor rifles.

During the Mexican War a regiment from Mississippi, commanded by Jeff'n Davis was armed with this rifle and later, a Kentucky regiment was so armed, and as the rifles were great favorites among the troops they acquired the above names.

The terms "Yager" and "Windsor" come from the fact that at about this time some German sharpshooters used a similar rifle called a "Yager," and many of the arms made by contract came from Windsor, Conn., and were so marked.

Harper's Ferry produced the first 700 of these in 1846 and several thousand more the following nine years; Springfield made 3200 in 1849 and many more were made by contractors Whitney, Tryon, Remington, Robbins and Lawrence, and Robbins, Kendal & Lawrence.

The total length is 4 feet and ½ inch; the barrel length 33 inches. The bore without grooves is .52; the grooves at the muzzle are five-thousandths of an inch deep and they increase regularly in depth to thirteen-thousandths at the breech; there are seven of them, almost semi-circular at the breech, segmental at the muzzle, about two-thirds the width of the lands, and having a pitch of one turn in six feet. The weight of the rifle is 9¾ lbs. When new it was not provided with a bayonet.

The charge was a half ounce spherical bullet, patched, and 75 grains of rifle powder. The muzzle velocity was about 1,850 feet per second. At that period in making up fixed ammunition in the Government shops for the Model 1841 and its flintlock predecessors still in use, the bullet was enveloped in a square piece of cloth, or soft thin wash leather, or bladder, and all the puckers were gathered and tied and trimmed; then the entire surface of the patch was saturated with tallow.

The finish of the Model 1841 rifle illustrated seems to be the original finish and acid-browned barrel; heat-blued trigger, screw heads and band springs; exterior lock parts case-hardened gray with faint, mottled colors; bright polished ramrod and sling swivels; polished brass furniture; dull, oil-finished wood.

The changing of the caliber of the Model 1841 from .54 resulted from an order of the Ordnance Board, approved July 5, 1855 by Jefferson Davis, then Secretary of War as follows:

"Percussion Model of 1841—The bore of this arm to be reamed up to caliber .58 and rerifled and a stud and guide attached for sword bayonet."

The object of the change in the bore and grooving was to use in these rifles the .58 caliber Minie bullet, such as the other service arms were to use. And as this bullet had different ballistical properties from the old spherical one, new sights, not mentioned in the order, also were supplied. And, after 1859, triangular bayonets with sockets instead of sword bayonets were fitted to the bulk of the altered arms.

In the fitting of the lug for the sword bayonet there were a number of different methods followed; in some cases the stocks and top bands were shortened, in others the lug was a part of a split band that clamped in place on the barrel, in other cases the lugs were fastened by screws, both of these methods permitting the removal of the bands for the purpose of dismantling the gun.

Col. Craig's report of Nov. 12, 1859 shows the following number of these arms on hand in the Southern arsenals:

Harper's Ferry	696
Fort Monroe	31
Fayetteville	1,685
Charleston	814
Mount Vernon	32
Baton Rouge	103
San Antonio	260
Little Rock	54
Total	3,675

On the order of Dec. 29, 1859 from Secretary of War Floyd, the following transfers were made early in 1860:

From Watervliet to:	
Charleston	2,000
Fayetteville	2,000
And from Watertown to:	
Mount Vernon	2,000
Augusta	2,000
Baton Rouge	2,000
Total	10,000

There is no available record of the number of these arms in the various state arsenals but from the large number of independent rifle companies organized prior to the war, there must have been a fair supply of them.

The high esteem at which the rifle was held by the Southern troops is well illustrated by the letter of January 18, 1861, from Adjt. Sykes to Gov. Pettus which reads in part as follows:

"Relative to the Mississippi rifle, it is but justice to state that every effort has been made to procure them within the power of this department. This arm being renowned for the brilliant victories achieved upon the battlefields of Mexico in the hands of the First Regiment of Mississippi Riflemen, has derived the appellation of Mississippi rifle, and is the principal arm called for by the volunteer corps."

U. S. MODEL 1842 MUSKETOONS
Figure 4, Plate III

The so-called Model 1842 Musketoons were adopted upon the recommendation of the Ordnance Board of 1847, who proposed that the foot artillery be armed with the musketoon without a bayonet, as they carried swords, and they also recommended that two companies of them be armed with the miners and sappers musketoon with the sword bayonet, to ascertain by experience in the field if this arm could not be advantageously substituted for the regular artillery musketoon and sword.

These arms were all .69 caliber, smooth-bore and they otherwise followed the general design of the musket of that model, except all parts are reduced in size to conform to the lesser length of the musketoon.

The general dimensions are as follows:

Caliber	.69	inches
Diameter at muzzle	.85	"
Length of barrel	26.	"
Length of complete arm	41.	"
Length with Artillery bayonet attached	59.	"
Length with Sappers & Miners bayonet	62.1	"
Weight—Cavalry, without bayonet	7.22	pounds
Weight—Artillery, with bayonet	7.70	"
Weight—Sappers & Miners with bayonet	9.35	"

The Sappers & Miners arm was of the same design as the artillery, except for the lugs on barrel and top band for attaching the 22-inch Roman type, double-edge bayonet weighing 2.33 pounds in place of the regular bayonet lug on the bottom side of the barrel.

The cavalry musketoon Figure 5, Plate III, while of the same general design, was mounted with brass in place of iron; a ring and bar substituted for the regular swivels; the top band of entirely different shape, and the ramrod of special shape to work with a swivel attachment.

This ramrod swivel gave considerable trouble from breakage, and was finally replaced with a chain attachment, but as the model was soon after discontinued, the arms with chain attachments are now rather scarce.

Many of these arms were also rifled experimentally, and rear sights applied, and as the regular charge of powder for them was 75 grains many complaints were made of the fearful kick. An attempt to correct this fault was made, by ordering a number of them to Frankfort arsenal where a slug of lead was placed in the butt; these arms can now be easily detected, for in almost every case the shrinkage of the wood has caused the stock to split at this point.

These arms are believed to have been made only at Springfield and the records show that from 1848 to 1856 there was produced:

Artillery 3,359
Sappers & Miners 830
Cavalry 6,703

The Ordnance office reports do not show any of the arms in the Government arsenals of the South at the beginning of hostilities, but the correspondence indicates that there were a number of them belonging to the different states, that had been furnished on their regular quota, and which no doubt were pressed into service at an early date.

U. S. MODEL 1854 CARBINE

Figure 6, Plate III

While this arm is usually referred to as the Model 1854 Carbine it probably represents the efforts of the Ordnance Department to overcome the difficulties encountered with the Model 1842 Musketoons, all of which were caliber .69 and originally smooth-bored but later many of them were rifled. The carbine shown is marked on lock plate with the usual eagle, U. S. Springfield and 1848; the tang of the barrel being also dated 1848 and the barrel having the regular VP and eagle head proof marks. The tang of the butt-plate is marked U. S.

The barrel is rifled caliber .54 and is 21¾ inches long with a large knife blade front sight and two leaf rear sight peculiar to this arm. The ramrod is attached to the barrel with a long loop swivel fitting into a large lug into the barrel, this design evidently being an effort to overcome the difficulties experienced

PLATE III

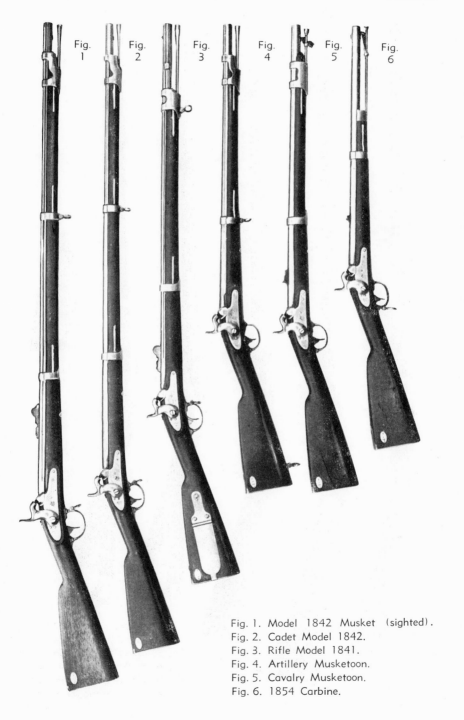

Fig. 1

Fig. 2

Fig. 3

Fig. 4

Fig. 5

Fig. 6

Fig. 1. Model 1842 Musket (sighted).
Fig. 2. Cadet Model 1842.
Fig. 3. Rifle Model 1841.
Fig. 4. Artillery Musketoon.
Fig. 5. Cavalry Musketoon.
Fig. 6. 1854 Carbine.

PLATE IV

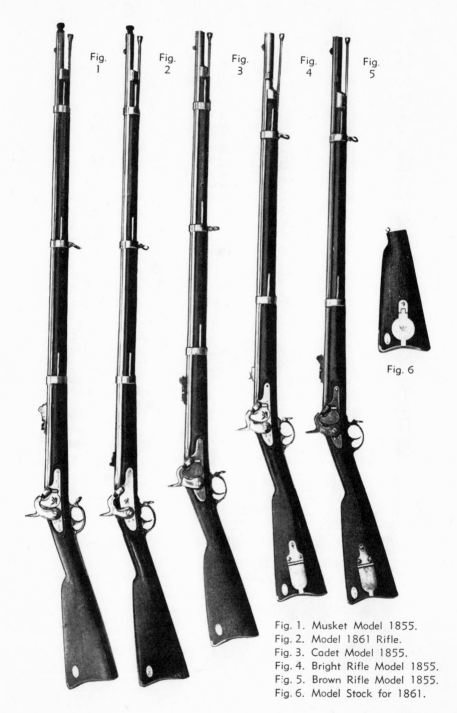

Fig.
1

Fig.
2

Fig.
3

Fig.
4

Fig.
5

Fig. 6

Fig. 1. Musket Model 1855.
Fig. 2. Model 1861 Rifle.
Fig. 3. Cadet Model 1855.
Fig. 4. Bright Rifle Model 1855.
Fig. 5. Brown Rifle Model 1855.
Fig. 6. Model Stock for 1861.

with the short swivels and chain attachments of the musketoon. The circular sling swivel or ring is attached to the rear of the trigger guard which feature also is peculiar to this arm alone.

The lock plate, cone seat and hammer conform to the general outline of the regular model 1842 arm. The records indicate that 300 of these were made in 1855 besides the two made in 1848 probably as experimental pieces.

There is no record of the number of these arms in the possession of the Confederates in the beginning of the war but there is frequent mention of carbines in the hands of State troops.

U. S. REGULATION PERCUSSION ARMS MODEL 1855
Plate IV

The recommendations of the Ordnance Board approved by Jeff'n Davis as Secretary of War, July 5, 1855 mark an important step in the development of military arms. The adoption of the caliber .58 for all arms of the service, the superceding of the smooth-bore by the rifled musket, and the Maynard priming device for all arms being the principal innovations.

Figure 1, Plate IV

The musket of this model, which is 55.85 inches long, weighs 9.18 pounds and has a 40-inch barrel. It was first issued without the patch box in the stock, but in 1859 this was added and used on all arms made thereafter.

This was the latest improved arm in the service at the outbreak of the war, using a 500 grain conical bullet, 60 grains of powder and having a muzzle velocity of 950 feet per second, and a great improvement over the earlier .69 caliber arm.

They were produced in large numbers at both Springfield and Harper's Ferry, and the records indicate that contracts were let for their manufacture to:

E. Whitney	J. D. Mowry	J. Mulholland
A. M. Burt	J. F. Hodge	A. Jenks & Son

but the only contractor arm of this model known to the writer, is the one made by E. Whitney.

The records indicated that the southern arsenals of the Government contain only 9,209 of these arms, but as they had been manufactured since 1856 it is fair to assume that all of the southern States had received a number of them as their regular quota, and that they were in the hands of the different permanent State organizations.

41

Figure 3, Plate IV

The cadet arm of this model is identical with the musket, except the barrel, the stock, the bayonet and the rammer. The caliber is the same as the musket, that is, .58 inches, but the barrel is only 38 inches long; the total length of the arm, 53 inches, and the weight 8.50 pounds. The records indicate that from 1856 to 1860 Springfield produced 2,813 of these arms, and it is now hard to explain their present scarcity, except that they must have been destroyed in service, or as captured property, or included in one of the many sales to individuals abroad after the war.

Figure 4, Plate IV

The rifle of this model with its 33-inch heavy barrel, and using the regulation .58 caliber hollow conical bullet weighing 500 grains, with 60 grains of powder, was probably the best military arm of its period, and was referred to in all the Confederate correspondence as the long-range rifle.

So far as known they were made only at Harper's Ferry, and comprised its principal output from 1856 to April of 1861, but the record of the exact number made has not been compiled.

They were issued in two different finishes: that of Figure 4 being bright, with all iron mountings and small rear sight, while that shown in Figure 5 was finished "brown" with brass mountings and a large rear sight; the stock tip of this type is somewhat different than the iron-mounted types. All were provided with lugs for saber bayonets, which were part of the standard equipment of the arm, and they were all provided with the patch box in the stock. The total length of the arm, 49.3 inches. Weight without bayonet, 9.93 lbs.

The records show 3,590 of these arms in the U. S. arsenals of the South on Nov. 12, 1859 and the correspondence indicates issue to the several States on their quotas after that date of a large number of them, so with those of previous issues it is fair to assume that this was the arm of the best equipped rifle companies of the South at the beginning of the war.

FIREARMS OF THE CONFEDERACY

U. S. MODEL 1861 RIFLED MUSKET

Figure 2, Plate IV

This was the principal infantry arm of the Federal forces for the war. During that period there were some slight changes made that were known as the Special Model 1861—the Model 1863 and the Model 1864 but these changes did not affect the principal dimensions of the arm which remain the same as the Model 1855.

The length of the barrel is 40 inches. Total length 58½ inches. Weight with 18-inch socket bayonet 9¾ lbs. The caliber is .58, using a hollow bullet of 500 grains and 60 grains of powder. The muzzle velocity was 950 F. S. The pitch of the rifling is one turn in 6 feet, uniform twist. There are 3 grooves each .3 of an inch wide, .005 of an inch deep at the muzzle, increasing regularly in depth to .015 at the breech.

Adverse reports on the Maynard primers used on all arms of the 1855 lead to the adoption of this new Model 1861 omitting the priming devices and making one or two minor changes on the barrel to provide for attaching the new rear sight. The rectangular patch box added to the model 1855 arms in 1859 were to have been replaced by a round patch box and many of the ordnance manuals show guns with this round patch box in the packing cases.

The model of a round patch box shown on Plate IV came from Springfield armory and is marked A—117/60, and considering the fact that cuts were made up for the ordnance manuals with this type of patch box, it is the assumption that the 1861 model was to be so equipped, but owing to the extreme need of arms and the necessity of contracting for many thousands of them for the Civil War, they were omitted.

The records show that Springfield armory manufactured 793,434 of these arms during the war period, and from 1861 to to 1865 the government contracted for and received an additional 882,561 of them, making a total of 1,675,995.

Our present interest in this arm lies in the fact that it also constituted one of the principal arms of the Confederates as a large percentage of their captures were probably of this model. It has been estimated on good authority that the Battle of the Wilderness netted 35,000 small arms, Second Manassas 20,000, Harper's Ferry 11,000, Fredericksburg 9,000, Antietam and

Shiloh 15,000 and the Tennessee campaign of late 1862 netted them around 27,500 small arms, totalling around 117,000 arms.

Chancellorsville and Chickamauga added another 35,000 to this so that by the middle of 1863 there were quite likely more arms of this model in the Confederate service than any other of one kind.

CHAPTER II

HISTORICAL SKETCH OF VIRGINIA MANUFACTORY ARMORY AND HARPER'S FERRY — DESCRIPTIONS OF SOME OF THEIR ARMS — PALMETTO ARMS — REPUBLIC OF TEXAS RIFLE — HISTORICAL SKETCH OF HALL AND HIS ARMS MADE AT HARPER'S FERRY — THE WHITNEY CONFEDERATE ARMS — MORSE AND HIS BREECHLOADERS.

WHILE the Palmetto armory machinery seems to have played a minor role in supplying arms to the Confederacy, the great importance of the Virginia Manufactory armory and Harper's Ferry to the Southern cause cannot be overestimated.

The vast amount of machinery, component parts of arms, tools and other necessary equipment secured at Harper's Ferry was of vital importance to the Confederacy as it greatly expedited the early production of arms. Of great importance in this connection was the securing of a large number (variously estimated at from 17 to 30,000) of seasoned gunstocks. The kiln drying of lumber for use in gunmaking had not been practiced to any extent at that time and the extremely slow process of air seasoning requiring two or three years was considered necessary.

Of still greater importance, however, was the fact that these two armories probably furnished more mechanics trained in the art of large scale production of arms with modern machinery than were included in all the rest of the Confederacy. It is interesting to note that Mr. Solomon Adams who was master armorer of the Virginia State Armory in 1860 was occupying that same position in the Richmond armory in 1864 and had undoubtedly played an important role in its operations.

THE VIRGINIA MANUFACTORY ARMORY
Richmond, Va.

In 1797 it was enacted that the executive of the State of Virginia be empowered to establish a manufactory of arms within the vicinity of Richmond. The armory was located at the western limit of the city on the James river, the river and the Kennawha canal bounded it on the north and later the Tredegar Iron Works adjoined it on the west.

John Clarke was commissioned to build the armory. He visited Boston and other New England arms centers and was much impressed by Eli Whitney's system of uniformity of parts. Erection of the armory began in 1801, and George Williamson was appointed master armorer. Manufacture began in March 1802, and by October 1803, 2,151 muskets had been finished. In 1807, Clarke wrote the governor that he had in storage 3,272 muskets, 14 rifles, 470 pistols, 405 cavalry swords, 50 artillery swords and 12 powderhorns. See Bruce's "History of the Iron Industry in Virginia."

All military arms including muskets, rifles and pistols required by the State were manufactured here and in the early days it was an important source of supply; on July 28, 1817, Alexander McRae, then operating the armory, contracted with the U. S. Government for 10,000 muskets. He, however, failed to deliver the arms according to terms of the contract and a suit was instituted against him July 20, 1820. Pending the suit he proposed to transfer his interest to John Rogers & Brooks Evans of Valley Forge, Pa., without loss to the Government which transfer was agreed to.

From this time until the activities in preparation for the rebellion there appears to have been no arms manufactured, the armory being used merely as a storage.

The letter of November 3, 1860 by George W. Randolph to Secretary of War Floyd, indicates this renewed activity as the master armorer, Mr. Solomon Adams, was sent to Springfield to prepare a model arm and John R. Anderson of the Tredegar Iron Works was given a contract for the necessary machinery for producing a modern arm, permission being granted them by Secretary Floyd to make the required drawings for the tools and fixtures at Springfield, the armory at this time being under the direction of J. H. Burton, late master armorer at Enfield, England.

The machinery for manufacturing the rifled musket, which was captured at Harper's Ferry, was transferred to this armory and put into operation by the Virginia State authorities under the direction of C. Dimmock, Col. of Ordnance for that State. The letter of George W. Munford to Jefferson Davis of July 12,

1861 and the letter of C. Dimmock to Secretary of War Walker outlined some of the details of the transfer of this property to the Confederate authorities who developed the facilities into the principal arms manufactory of the Confederacy. The arms made after this date being marked C. S., Richmond, Va.

Richmond, November 3, 1860.

Hon. JOHN B. FLOYD,
Secretary of War:

SIR: I am instructed by the armory board of commissioners of Virginia to make the following requests of the War Department:

First. That we shall be allowed to purchase from the Government 5,000 muskets altered from flintlock to percussion, and said to be for sale at $2.50 apiece. Our necessity for these is immediate, in consequence of the small number of arms in the State and the rumors of insurrection which, whether well- or ill-founded, disturb the public mind and render it necessary for our repose that our military should be armed. Capt. Charles Dimmock will visit Washington immediately to receive these muskets, and we respectfully request that every facility may be afforded to him in forwarding the arms to this place without delay. We shall be prepared to pay for them at such time as the department may indicate.

Second. We are informed that the Government has 130,000 seasoned musket-stocks at Harper's Ferry, and that the consumption does not exceed 12,000 per annum. We suppose, therefore, that 20,000 of these seasoned stocks might be replaced by green ones without injury to the public service, and we ask leave to make such substitution. The green stocks can be purchased by the superintendent at Harper's Ferry and we will pay for them. The seasoned stocks are intended for use a year or two hence, or possibly a little earlier, as the operations of our armory may require, and unless we can get them from the Government we shall have barrels without stocks until the green stocks shall season. We are informed that a stock does not season properly in less than three years.

Third. We are engaged in making a model arm at Springfield, under an order which the War Department was so obliging to give, and we should be greatly aided by permission to use the Government patterns and take drawings of them. We request that our master armorer, Mr. Solomon Adams, may be allowed to do this at our expense, and so far as it may be done without detriment to the public service.

I have the honor to remain, your most obedient servant,

GEO. W. RANDOLPH.

[INDORSEMENT.]
WAR DEPARTMENT,
November 6, 1860.

The proposition for the purchase of 5,000 altered muskets, at $2.50 each, made within, is accepted. The Colonel of Ordnance will take the necessary measures to have them delivered as requested. The arms to be selected by Captain Dimmock.

J. B. FLOYD,
Secretary of War.

FIREARMS OF THE CONFEDERACY

Springfield, Mass., November 24, 1860.

Hon. J. B. FLOYD,
Secretary of War:

MY DEAR SIR: Please allow me to address a line on a matter that deeply interests your State.

Having been engaged in the Springfield Armory for fifteen years last past, and knowing that assistance has been rendered and privileges granted to foreign Governments and to some of our own States, as well as to private individuals, I desire the same favors granted to the State of Virginia.

I have no hopes of any favors from Colonel Craig, for in a conversation with him a few months since I found him deadly opposed to the Virginia Armory.

We wish to use some of the armory patterns for the Richmond machinery, and the privilege of taking drawings of fixtures, tools, &c.

I desire that the honorable Secretary issue an order to the superintendents of the Springfield and Harper's Ferry armories to give the master armorer of the Virginia State Armory and Joseph R. Anderson or his agents every facility they may need in said armories, at the same time not interfering with the legitimate business of the armory.

I desire to get all the assistance we can from the national armories before our much honored and esteemed Secretary of War vacates his office, for I have no hopes of any assistance after a Black Republican takes possession of the War Department. Should the honorable Secretary see fit to grant the request of the petitioner, I wish a copy of the order be sent to me at Springfield, Mass., as I shall be engaged here for a couple of months getting up a model gun for the State of Virginia.

Your humble servant,

S. ADAMS,
Master Armorer, State Armory, Virginia.

Richmond, December 1, 1860.

Hon. JOHN B. FLOYD,
Secretary of War, Washington:

SIR: I take the liberty of introducing to you Mr. J. H. Burton, late master armorer at Enfield, England, and now engaged with Joseph R. Anderson & Co., of this place, in executing a contract for the machinery of the Virginia Armory. It will facilitate their operations to be allowed free access to the drawings, machines, tools, &c., and the use of the patterns for castings at the Springfield and Harper's Ferry armories, and as this privilege was accorded to the British Government, I respectfully ask that it may be granted to the agents of the State of Virginia.

I have the honor to remain, very respectfully, your obedient servant,

GEO. W. RANDOLPH.

[INDORSEMENT.]
WAR DEPARTMENT,
December 4, 1860.

The Secretary directs that the privilege within asked for to be granted. By order:

W. R. DRINKARD.

FIREARMS OF THE CONFEDERACY

RICHMOND, VA., July 12, 1861.

His Excellency JEFFERSON DAVIS,
President of the Confederate States of America:

SIR: Your letter of the 9th instant to Governor Letcher was forwarded to him, as he was absent from the city upon its receipt. He has addressed a brief note to me, in which he says that as he desires no delay in all arrangements necessary to forward the public interests of Virginia and all the Confederate States, he requests that I will attend to this matter, and take such action as I and Mr. Tucker (the attorney general) may deem right in the premises. He further says that as the injunction of secrecy was not removed from the resolutions to which you refer, he had not heard and did not know of these proceedings until he was informed of the action of the War Department in respect to them. He says that he will approve what I may do and will carry it out upon his return to the city. Acting under this authority, in the name of the Governor of Virginia, and for him, I have the honor to turn over and transfer to the Government of the Confederate States, for use during the war, all the machinery and stores captured by the Virginia forces at Harper's Ferry, now in possession of the State, reserving the right of property therein. The Governor is directed by one of the resolutions to preserve an inventory of all property thus turned over, &c. In order to do this it will be my pleasure on his behalf to direct the Colonel of Ordnance of Virginia, in conjunction with any officer to be detailed by your orders, to take the necessary steps for a correct and fair inventory, as required. The Governor of Virginia believes it was the desire and purpose of the convention to have the machinery put up in the armory at Richmond; hence in the third resolution it provided "that the Governor of Virginia be authorized to allow the Confederate Government, on such terms as he may deem just and reasonable, the use of the Armory buildings at Richmond for the operation of said machinery." In accordance with this authority vested in the Governor, I beg leave in his name to tender the use of the Armory buildings for operating said machinery, and to express the desire that the tender be accepted. The armory has been in operation in this city to a certain extent since the memorable year of 1800, and was then established with a view to the great crisis of that period. Virginia is anxious to continue it with the enlarged facility afforded by the machinery in question, and while she cheerfully yields its use to the Confederate Government for the common cause of all the States, I may add the expression of the opinion and feeling of the Governor that it was the intention of the convention that the machinery should be used in the buildings now tendered to your service, unless its safety would thereby be imperiled or its value to the Confederacy be seriously impaired.

I am, sir, with high respect, yours,

GEORGE W. MUNFORD,
Secretary of the Commonwealth.

CONFEDERATE STATES OF AMERICA, WAR DEPARTMENT,
Richmond, July 29, 1861.

His Excellency JOHN LETCHER,
Governor of Virginia:

SIR: The letter of the Secretary of the Commonwealth of Virginia detailing the operations in the Virginia armory at Richmond, now in charge of the authorities of the State of Virginia, has been received. This Department is gratified to know that its late letter on the subject of the proposed transfer was satisfactory to Your Excellency, and cordially reciprocates the kindly feelings expressed by Your Excellency toward the Confederate Government. The operations referred to are only such as this Department fully approves, and will doubtless be faithfully and satisfactorily executed by the officers now charged with them. It is finally stated that—

As soon as a suitable person is assigned to the duty by the proper department of the Confederate States, and suitable arrangements can be made to meet the circumstances detailed in the previous part of this (your) letter, the Governor will designate a proper person to whom the duty of the transfer will be designed, and a written agreement can be signed by the parties.

Major Gorgas is authorized to represent this Government in the transfer proposed, and will, therefore, as soon as the arrangements referred to are completed, enter on the part of the Government with the written agreement proposed.

Very respectfully,

L. P. WALKER,
Secretary of War.

ORDNANCE DEPARTMENT OF VIRGINIA,
November 2, 1861.

His Excellency GOVERNOR LETCHER:

SIR: I understand that a number of Virginia manufactured muskets made at the armory here many years ago, and that have been issued from this department, are being gathered into the Confederate Ordnance Department to be altered into percussion, and, as I may suppose, to be reissued to troops generally as an issue from the Confederate States. Now, there is no objection to these arms going into the field to any troops if Virginia has the credit of such issue. As there is to be a final settlement between all the States of the South, when the value of all issues will be an element of credit to the State issuing, if Virginia's arms are to be issued by the Confederate authorities the State is not only deprived of the credit due her, but the issue thus made will become in part a charge upon her in the final settlement. Virginia has issued 10,000 percussion muskets, United States, and 50,000 Virginia flintlock muskets, these last plainly known by the stamp "Virginia" upon the lock. I think it but fair to this State that the Ordnance Department of the Confederate Army be instructed by the Honorable Secretary of War to turn over to this department all thus marked, that I may put them in good order for reissue. In addition to the Virginia flintlocks this State has issued 10,000 U. S. flintlocks, which she received from the Federal Government years ago. These have no distinctive mark, and therefore cannot be recognized as belonging to this State; yet, as they are also coming in to be altered for reissue, ought not a due proportion of these be turned over to this department, when they fall into the hands of the Confederate Department, for like reasons? My impression is that but very few of flintlock muskets have gone into the field except from Virginia. If this be so, then all flintlock muskets gathered into the Ordnance Department of the Confederate States should be turned over to this armory, that they be put in order and held subject to proper order. This is a matter of large consideration, and I think that if the Honorable Secretary of War is made to understand it he will correct the wrong.

I am, very respectfully,

C. DIMMICK,
Chief of Ordnance of Virginia.

PLATE V

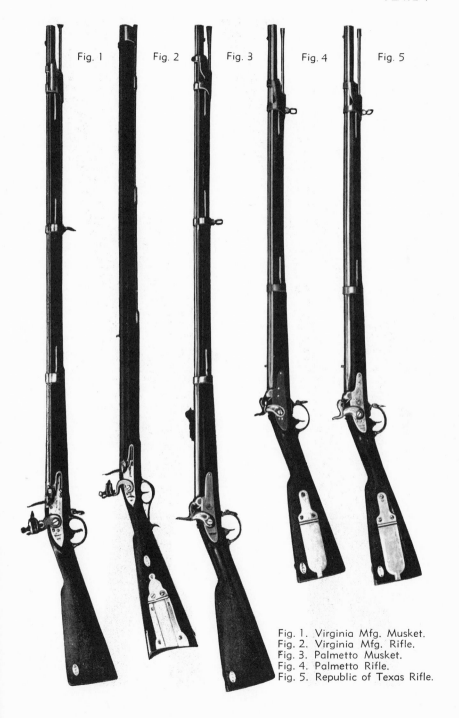

Fig. 1   Fig. 2   Fig. 3   Fig. 4   Fig. 5

Fig. 1. Virginia Mfg. Musket.
Fig. 2. Virginia Mfg. Rifle.
Fig. 3. Palmetto Musket.
Fig. 4. Palmetto Rifle.
Fig. 5. Republic of Texas Rifle.

PLATE V (a)

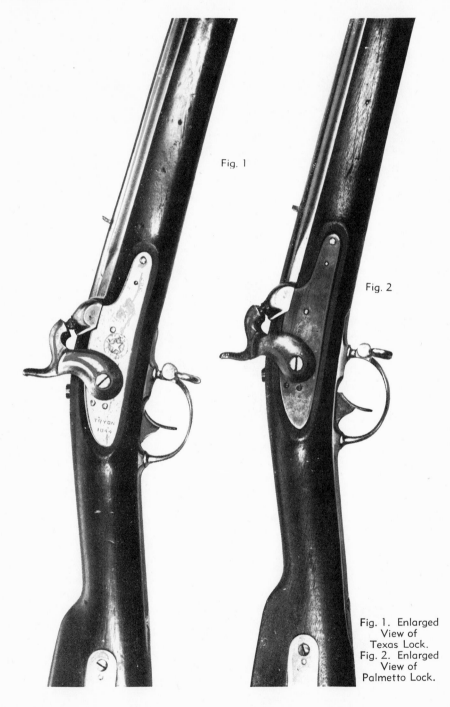

Fig. 1

Fig. 2

Fig. 1. Enlarged
View of
Texas Lock.
Fig. 2. Enlarged
View of
Palmetto Lock.

Colonel Gorgas in his account of the Ordnance Department of the Confederacy wrote concerning the armory as follows:

"The State of Virginia claimed all the machinery captured at Harper's Ferry, and was bringing it all to Richmond. It was agreed, however, with the State of North Carolina that that part of the machinery which was specially adapted to make the Mississippi rifle (caliber 54) should go to Fayetteville, where there was an arsenal with good steam power, the machinery to be returned at the close of the war to the State of Virginia. Colonel Burton, an admirably-educated machinist, superintended the re-erection of the works at Richmond. He was subsequently made Superintendent of Armories, and given full charge of the entire subject of manufacture of arms in the Confederacy. The machinery of the rifle-musket (caliber 58), retained at Richmond, got to work as early as September, 1861. If we had possessed the necessary number of workmen this "plant" could have been so filled in as to have easily produced 5,000 stands per month, working night and day. As it was, I don't think it ever turned out more than 1,500 in any one month."

The armory buildings were all destroyed by fire upon the evacuation of Richmond, April 3, 1865.

THE VIRGINIA MANUFACTORY FLINTLOCK MUSKET
Figure 1, Plate V

This arm marked on lock plate Virginia Manufactory (Manufactory in script) between cock and pan and rear of cock, Richmond in a curve and dated 1818. Length of barrel, 41½ inches. Total length of arm, 56½ inches. Caliber .69. Weight, 9 lbs., 8 ounces. This is an exceptionally well made arm and seems to be somewhat in advance of the type of that date, it being provided with a brass pan and having the band springs of the lower and middle bands located forward of the bands. The lower sling swivel is carried on the customary stud used to retain the trigger guard in place, this guard and trigger plate being of the usual design.

THE VIRGINIA MANUFACTORY FLINTLOCK RIFLE
Figure 2, Plate V

This arm is patterned somewhat after the Kentucky rifle of that period, it having a full octagon barrel 39 inches long, caliber .54. Full length of arm 54½ inches. Weight, 9 lbs., 14 ounces. The walnut stock extends to the extreme end of the barrel and has the heavy brass tip. The ramrod is of wood carried by three brass ramrod pipes, and the trigger guard, butt plate and patch box cover are also of brass; the spring catch to the patch box cover being located at the bottom of the stock in place of the top as in the U. S. arm of this date.

The lock plate is marked VIRGINIA between cock and pan and to the rear of the cock is the word RICHMOND in a curve with the date 1817. The word Richmond in this case being reversed to that of the same name on the musket. The cock is of the gooseneck type but as this arm has been converted to percussion and then changed back to the original flintlock this cock may not be of the proper type.

For purposes of comparison, Plate XXV shows: Figure 1—the Virginia Manufactory flintlock rifle, with 44-inch octagonal barrel, all iron mountings, dated 1809, issued to Virginia troops in 1861. Figure 2—Virginia Manufactory rifle, altered to percussion, dated 1806, with ornamental patch box with the legend: "Don't Tread on Me," issued to Virginia troops in 1861. Figure 3—Virginia Manufactory flintlock musket, all iron mountings, dated 1808, issued to Virginia troops in 1861, marked on barrel: "74 Va. Regt." Figure 4—Virginia Manufactory musket, dated 1812, altered to percussion in 1861 and barrel cut down to 30 inches, used in the Confederate Army.

* * * * *

PALMETTO ARMORY, COLUMBIA, S. C.

There is very little known by the compiler on the establishment and activities of the armory but it appears that it dates from the adjournment "sine die" of the first Secession Convention held at Columbia in 1852 at which time it became apparent that there were no arms on hand to make good their position as an independent state.

Before adjournment of this meeting a contract for 24,000 arms to consist of muskets, rifles and pistols was awarded to the firm of Boatwright and Glaze.

This firm immediately purchased the necessary machinery from A. E. Waters of Millbury, Mass., and erected it and went into production that same year 1852. As the only arms of this manufacture known are dated 1852 and 1853 it is probable that operations ceased after that time and were not again taken up until the Civil War.

PALMETTO RIFLED MUSKET
Figure 3, Plate V

This arm follows in all details the U. S. model 1842 musket described under Fig. 1, Plate III and besides being rifled is provided with a long range rear sight. Marked on lock plate PALMETTO ARMORY, S. C., in a circle around a palmetto tree and behind hammer COLUMBIA, S. C., 1852. The tang of the butt plate is also marked S. C.

PALMETTO RIFLE
Figure 4, Plate V

This arm conforms in general with the regular U. S. model 1841 rifle as described under Figure 3, Plate III—the lock plate being stamped PALMETTO ARMORY, S. C., in a circle around the palmetto tree and behind hammer, COLUMBIA, S. C., indicating that the arm was made for South Carolina and not for the U. S. Government as claimed by some authorities.

In Lieut. Col. T. G. Baylor's report of April 7, 1865 (see page 317) 500 Palmetto rifles were included in the arms destroyed at Columbia, S. C.

There seems to be no direct evidence that any arms were made at this armory during the war and it is not definitely established where this machinery was used but it appears evident that the plant during the war was devoted to the building of machinery for the Confederate powder mills and other ordnance requirements. Mr. G. A. Shields was connected with the enterprise and active in its operation throughout the war.

After the war T. W. Radcliffe was associated with Mr. Wm. Glaze in the sporting goods business evidently on a very large scale for there are a number of double-barreled shotguns of post-war vintage bearing the name of Radcliffe & Glaze but these guns were undoubtedly made elsewhere and merely stamped with the merchant's name.

* * * * *

THE REPUBLIC OF TEXAS RIFLE
Figure 5, Plate V

This is a regulation 1841 (see Fig. 3, Plate III for details) rifle and while there is no direct evidence that they were used by or for the Confederates, the fact that these guns were held in such high esteem by all military men of the time, they were always well taken care of and many of them must have survived the Mexican War to be turned over to the State in 1845 when it became a part of the Union.

On April 3, 1840 the firm of Tryon Son & Co., of Philadelphia, secured a contract for 1,500 of the Model 1841 rifles for the Republic of Texas and the U. S. Government accepted a suspended delivery after Texas was annexed to the U. S. as evidenced by the following:[1]

ORDNANCE OFFICE,
Washington, 1846.

TRYON SON & CO.

GENTLEMEN: The object of this note is to inquire whether you have manufactured the (640) muskets that remain to be delivered on your contract with the late Republic of Texas, and if so, where are they now deposited?

I am, respectfully yours,

G. TALCOTT,
Ordnance Office.

The specimen shown is a regular Model 1841 with caliber .54 barrel, which carries the inspection initials J.C.B., but does not have the U. S. proof marks. The tang is dated 1844.

The lock plate is marked forward of the hammer REPUBLIC of TEXAS in a circle surrounding a five pointed star with the number 387 at the extreme end of plate. Rear of hammer is TRYON 1844.

In describing the arm covered by the above contract the catalogue goes on to state:

"This '1841' musket was built by contract at a number of individual gun factories, but the government also manufactured a great number at the Harper's Ferry shops; hence, this model has been frequently called the 'Harper's Ferry rifle,' but more frequently it has been termed the Mississippi rifle, because early issued to a Mississippi regiment.

"The Tryon Company built these muskets continuously for the government from 1841 to 1848. While those in collections today are apparently .58 caliber, yet the original model of the '41' was .54 caliber with the rifling making one turn in six feet and using a round ball; 33-inch barrel, without bayonet."

* * * * *

HARPER'S FERRY ARMORY

While the Confederates did not secure a large number of arms by the capture of Harper's Ferry, the machinery and supplies saved from the fire was of the utmost importance to them,

---

[1] Edwin K. Tryon Co., 1911 Anniversary Catalogue.

forming, as it did the nucleus of the equipment required for the factories, and enabling them to start work on the production and repair of arms much sooner than they otherwise could.

The story of its devolment, capture and final disposition is here included as an important part of the history of arming the Confederates, and while it entails considerable repetition of the foregoing data, is used as originally compiled from what are thought to be reliable sources.

Harper's Ferry was named after Robert Harper, an English millwright, who obtained a grant of it in 1748 from the owner, Lord Fairfax, a friend of George Washington, who first surveyed it.

In 1792 Congress authorized the President to establish two National arsenals, that is, places for the storage of arms, and two years later in 1794 he was instructed to establish two places for the manufacture of arms, that is, armories. President Washington chose for both purposes Springfield in the north and Harper's Ferry in the south.

No records or guns are to be found which show any manufacturing of arms at the Ferry before 1801. Little of interest, outside of Hall's going there in 1819, is attached to the Ferry until the John Brown raid, followed by the destruction of the arsenal in 1861. The first superintendent at the armory was a Mr. Perkins, an English Moravian.

The capacity of the Harper's Ferry armory was from 1,500 to 2,000 guns a month, and the rifles made there were considered the best in the world. The Harper's Ferry Yager enjoyed, in its day, a reputation second to no weapon of the small arms kind in the world. It was known as the Mississippi rifle, Jefferson Davis' regiment coming from that State and being armed with the Yager in the Mexican War.

The armory was surrendered to a body of State troops, April 18, 1861, after having been fired and partially destroyed. All the records of the armory were lost in this fire.

The arsenal, between 4,000 and 5,000 finished rifles and muskets, and the carpenter shop were totally destroyed. A large portion of the gunmaking machinery, material and unfinished arms were saved, and when boxed were sent by rail to Winchester (the terminus of the road), thence by wagons to Strasburg, at which place the confiscated property was turned over to the Manassas Gap Railroad, and forwarded to Richmond,

Va. By the 18th of June all of this material was removed. The machinery thus secured was divided between the arsenals established by the Confederates at Richmond, Va., and Fayetteville, N. C., and when installed, supplied to a great extent the want which existed in the South, of means for the alteration and repair of old or injured arms, and finally contributed to increase the scanty supply of arms which existed in the Confederacy at the outbreak of the Civil War.

The superintendent, Mr. A. M. Barbour joined the Confederate cause and Master Armorer Ball went to Fayetteville, N. C., with the machinery sent there.

The Confederates held and operated it until the following June when they were forced to evacuate at which time they destroyed the arsenal and armory and the bridge across the Potomac. The village was afterwards held by a Union garrison of 12,000 men, who, however, on the 15th of September, 1862, after a strong resistance of several days, surrendered to a Confederate force under Jackson and A. P. Hill. After the battle of Antietam, on the 17th of the same month, it was occupied by the army of the Potomac under General M'Clellan, who left a strong garrison in the place. In June 1863 it was again abandoned to the Confederates on their march to Pennsylvania. After their defeat at Gettysburg, the town again fell into the hands of the Federal troops, who held it until the demonstration against Washington in July 1864. After the battle of Monocacy on July 9th it was occupied by the United States forces, and held by them until the end of the war.

That the Confederates did operate the armory for the production of rifles is indicated by the following:

> DIVISION HEADQUARTERS,
> Harper's Ferry, Va., May 7, 1861.
> Major General LEE, Commanding Virginia Forces:
> GENERAL: I forward herewith a statement of the strength . . .
> Mr. Burkhart, who is in charge of the rifle-factory, reports that he can finish fifteen hundred rifle-muskets in thirty days. I have, in obedience to the orders of Governor Letcher, directed the rifle-factory machinery to be removed immediately after that of the musket factory. My object is to keep the former factory working as long as practicable without interfering with its rapid removal . . .
> I am, general, very respectfully, your obedient servant,
> T. J. JACKSON,
> *Colonel, Virginia Volunteers,*
> *Commanding.*

Gen. Harper reports April 22, 1861:

"My object has been to secure all the efficient arms here, and to remove the machinery in such a manner as to readily set up again as well as the unfinished arms. My information is there are components to fit up from 7-10,000 stand, exclusive of those rescued uninjured. I have employed artificers to put these together and am turning out daily several hundred Minie muskets."

There is no evidence that any distinguishing marks were put upon any of the arms turned out after April 18, 1861, so that any of the Harper's Ferry arms dated 1861 can be either of United States or Confederate fabrication.

From the Calendar of Virginia State Papers:—

Martin E. Price, in charge of removal of Harper's Ferry machinery to Richmond, to General Harper, April 24, 1861 — "I have examined some of the 14,000 arms that were burned in the Armory and find I can make serviceable guns of them. The stocks are here and can be made up."

Machinery from Harper's Ferry for making the rifled musket installed in the Virginia State Armory at the southern end of Fifth Street, between the James River and the Kanawha Canal. Substantial brick buildings, two stories high, forming a quadrangle enclosing a large area, the right and left sides dropping down on terraces to the river. General Gorgas and family lived in brick dwelling on upper terrace. Water power of James River used to drive machinery of the armory, and the Tredegar Iron Works, which adjoined the armory.

The following letters show the material captured and the final disposition of the property as given by the Government records:

FIREARMS OF THE CONFEDERACY

HARPER'S FERRY PROPERTY.
(13 W. D., page 216.)

ORDNANCE OFFICE, WAR DEPARTMENT,
Washington, November 16, 1861.

Hon. SIMON CAMERON,
Secretary of War:

SIR: In answer to the letter of the Hon. John P. Hale, chairman of
the committee of the Senate, which you referred to this office, I have
the honor to report that the United States Armory at Harper's Ferry
was established in the year 1796.

The amount expended on the same is for land purchased at
different times ....$ 45,477

For improvements thereon, for water power, canals, embank-
ments, walls, and water privileges, and for hydraulic
machinery, and buildings of all kinds 1,787,430

       Total, exclusive of the amount expended in the manu-
       facture and repair of arms $1,832,907

The latest annual inventory of the property belonging to the United
States at that armory is dated June 30, 1860, in which the value of all
the property on hand at that date is appraised as follows, vis:

1,669½ acres of land ....$ 37,457

Milldams, canals, water powers, and hydraulic machinery........   233,279

Forges, rolling mills, machine shops, storehouses, dwellings,
and other buildings   341,221

       Amount of real estate ....$ 611,957

Machines used in workshops ....$ 270,235

Tools used in service   109,560

       Total..............................$ 379,795

Unwrought materials on hand ....$ 100,043

Parts of arms in progress   93,573

       Total..............................$ 193,616

20,507 arms of different models in store   285,145

       Total appraised value June 30, 1860...........$1,470,513

By the latest returns received at this office from the armory it
appears that the number of arms in store when the armory was destroyed in April, 1861, was reduced to 4,287; the value of which was
about $64,000.

We may assume that the quantity and value of all other property
than the arms in store remained without material change from June,
1860 to April, 1861. The diminished number of arms in store at the
latter date reduces that item in the inventory from $285,145 to $164,300;
and the total appraised value of all the property from $1,470,513 to
$1,207,668.

Respectfully, etc.,

       WM. MAYNADIER,
       Lieutenant-Colonel of Ordnance.

Ordnance Reports, Vol. IV, pp. 1043-1044.

FIREARMS OF THE CONFEDERACY

(17 W. D., page 246.)

Letter of Hon. H. G. Davis asking for information relative to the Harper's Ferry sale.

[INDORSEMENT.]

ORDNANCE OFFICE, WAR DEPARTMENT,
December 20, 1872.

Respectfully returned to the Secretary of War, with the following memorandum of sale of Harper's Ferry property, viz:

Water power on Potomac, sold for	$ 176,000.00
Water power on Shenandoah, sold for	30,000.00
Shenandoah ferry, sold for	1,790.00
Wood tract, sold for	3,600.00
Ore bed, sold for	13,100.00
Dwellings, lots, etc., sold for	73,303.50
	$ 297,793.50

The sum of $4,048.50 has been received in payment for dwellings and lots sold.

By order of the Chief of Ordnance:

S. V. BENET,
Major of Ordnance.

(19 W. D., page 89.)

War Department refers House of Representatives resolution inquiring as to the purchase by the Government of the water power and land formerly used as a national armory at Harper's Ferry, W. Va., and the uses to which it will be put. (Referred by Hon. A. A. Hardenberg, sub-committee on Military Affairs.)

ORDNANCE OFFICE, WAR DEPARTMENT,
Washington, December 13, 1876.

Respectfully returned to the Secretary of War with the recommendation that reference be made to the Department of Justice for the information desired. As to the expediency of reestablishing the national armory at Harper's Ferry, I have the honor to remark that it is the policy of the War Department to concentrate ordnance manufactures at three arsenals and the Springfield Armory, as recommended in recent annual reports from this office, the reports of the Secretary of War, and the President's message, and that neither the necessities of the public service nor a judicious economy would render such reestablishment expedient.

S. V. BENET,
Brigadier General, Chief of Ordnance.

Ordnance Reports, Vol. IV, pp. 1053-1054.

D.—Statement of the expenditures at the United States armory at Harper's Ferry, Va., &c.—Continued.

Years	Made																	Repaired				Total value of arms made and repaired, estimated in new muskets.
	Muskets	Rifles	Pistols	Pattern muskets	Pattern rifles	Pattern pistols	Wall pieces	Harpoon guns	Torpedo-locks	Torpedo lock-boxes	Cannon-locks	Ball-screws	Screw-drivers	Bullet-molds	Wipers	Rifle-charges	Spring-vices	Muskets	Rifles and carbines	Pistols and swords	Value of repaired arms in new muskets	
1796																						
1797																						
1798																						
1799																						
1800	293																					
1801	1,472																					
1802	1,048																					
1803	156																					
1804																						
1805	136	772					1					772		772	772	772						
1806	50	1,716		4	4		6					1,716		1,716	1,716	1,716						
1807	3,051	1,381	2,880			8						1,381		1,381	1,381	1,381						
1808	7,348	146	1,208									146		146	146	146						
1809	9,400																					
1810	10,000																					
1811	10,200																	5,500				
1812	9,000										6											
1813	10,400									25								590				
1814	5,340			5	4	4		4	40									691				
1815	6,416	1,600										1,600		1,600	1,600	1,600		1,392				
1816	8,513	1,508		5								1,508		1,508	1,508	1,508		2,113		581		
1817	9,892	2,052		6								2,052		2,052	2,052	2,052		612	531			
1818	7,020	2,726		8								2,726	6,750	2,726	2,726	2,726		548	231			
1819	9,856	2,700		2	9	6						2,700	12,500	2,700	2,700	2,700		23	16			
1820	10,320	3,324			2							3,324	10,000	3,324	3,324	3,324	3,768		2			
1821		1,793										1,793	8,500	1,793	1,793	1,793	2,266					
Total.	119,911	19,718	4,088	30	19	18	7	4	40	25	6	19,718	37,750	19,718	19,718	19,718	6,034	11,469	780	581	$3,208	$151,550

NOTE.—In some of the years the expenditures and products of the armory appear to be disproportionate. This has arisen partly by the purchase of a greater or less quantity of stock and materials in a year than was consumed within it, and partly by the payments of debts in one year which had been contracted in the year preceding.

ORDNANCE OFFICE, WAR DEPARTMENT, November 30, 1822.

G. BOMFORD,

Lieutenant Colonel, on Ordnance Duty.

B.—Statement of expenditures at the United States Armory at Harper's Ferry, &c.—Continued.

Years	Articles manufactured.													
	Flintlock muskets.	Percussion muskets.	Rifles.	Pistols.	Hall's patent rifles.	Carbines, Hall's.	Ball screws.	Wipers.	Screw-drivers.	Bullet molds.	Spring vices.	Flint caps.	Rifle charges and flasks.	Arm-chests.
From its establishment, in 1798, to—	119,911		19,718	4,088			19,718	19,718	37,750	19,718	6,034		19,718	
31st December, 1821	10,000							8,173	5,594					500
31st December, 1822	12,200							11,000	10,343					921
31st December, 1823	10,559							31,827	6,922					212
31st December, 1824	14,000				1,000		5,000	34,998	26,926	1,000			1,000	848
31st December, 1825	8,720						5,327	25,000	53,112		10,100			888
31st December, 1826	12,020								8,475					772
31st December, 1827	10,000				1,000				35,679	1,000			1,000	1,164
31st December, 1828	8,895								3,653					837
31st December, 1829	10,130													564
31st December, 1830	11,160				4,360			4,360	4,360					274
31st December, 1831	12,000				3,670			19,100	3,682					137
31st December, 1832	12,000				970		6,896	22,360	25,941					102
31st December, 1833	12,000				1,714			1,714	1,714	436	436		20	74
31st December, 1834	10,000				1,809			1,770	1,770	367	367		20	226
31st December, 1835	9,150				1,200			17,435	22,809	47		51,575	4,734	447
31st December, 1836	8,200						614	22,914	25,424	171	171	7,454		626
31st December, 1837	12,000						1,136	10,940	29,000	177	177	6,632		1,563
31st December, 1838	5,850				2,934	1,017		4,428	5,202	301	200	17,084	3,000	669
30th September, 1839	8,304				1,023			14,867	4,199	395	1,334	2,000	881	2
30th September, 1840	8,650				190			1,999	10,685		4,941	10,000		132
30th September, 1841	6,575					1,003	1,663	15,815	1,950	55	3,418	70,000		298
30th September, 1842	3,105							7,472	3,123	25	49	3,000		112
30th June, 1843	608				300	1,001	73	6,547			567			307
30th June, 1844					2,700		524	3,749		131	501			311
30th June, 1845		2,225					478	7,857	8,631	3,191	304	10,080		1,084
30th June, 1846		12,203	*700				2,747		19,562	2	1,241	14,817		606
30th June, 1847		12,000	*3,054				834		9,908	435	3,100	3,234		523
31st March, 1848		8,200	*2,202							336	1,019			
Total	336,037	34,628	25,674	4,088	22,870	3,021	45,010	334,562	366,314	27,787	34,006	201,876	30,373	14,199

*Percussion.

ORDNANCE OFFICE, Washington, 10th June, 1848.

61

DESCRIPTION OF ARMS MADE AT HARPER'S FERRY BEFORE THE CIVIL WAR

While the arms made at Harper's Ferry are not directly connected with the Confederacy they are of considerable interest to collectors of this class of weapons, and the fact that this armory was seized by the Southern authorities, and all of the machinery removed South and used for supplying arms lends added interest for the student of Confederate history.

Included here is the table showing the arms made there from the beginning of 1801 up to and including March 31, 1848 which is the last Government tabulation that is available.

Besides the regular muskets made at the armory in the early days it will be noted from the tabulation that they produced a variety of other arms including the 1804 rifles, the 1817 rifles, together with pistols, wall pieces, harpoons and many pattern muskets besides the Hall's arms which were produced there exclusively except for those made by North at Middletown, Conn. In addition to the arms mentioned in the former chapter the following is a description of some of the other arms produced at this armory.

U. S. MODEL 1804 RIFLE
Figure 2, Plate VI

This arm is sometimes referred to as the Model 1800 and while the pattern arms may have been made at this early date it will be noted from the tabulation that the first regular output was in 1804.

This is the first regulation rifle adopted by the Government and plainly indicates the influence of the Kentucky rifle as it resembles a Kentucky more than any other of our military arms. They were made with a number of slight variations and with barrels from thirty-two to thirty-six inches long and though the caliber remained constant, various styles of boring and rifling were employed.

They are marked on the lock plate with the date of manufacture, Harper's Ferry, and a spread eagle bearing U. S. on a shield. The specimen illustrated is dated 1816. Its total length is four feet and one and one-half inches; the length of the barrel thirty-three and three-eighths inches. The caliber is .54 with grooves four one-hundredths of an inch deep using a half ounce

PLATE VI

Fig.
1

Fig.
2

Fig.
3

Fig.
4

Fig.
5

Fig. 1. Musket Magazine Primer.
Fig. 2. Harper's Ferry Flint Rifle.
Fig. 3. Special Model 1819 Short Musket.
Fig. 4. Blunderbuss.
Fig. 5. Musketcon.

PLATE VII

Fig. 1

Fig. 2

Fig. 3

Fig. 1. Hall's Flint Rifle.
Fig. 2. Hall's Flint Musketoon.
Fig. 3. Hall's Percussion Carbine.

ball, the diameter of which was .525. There are seven grooves with pitch of one-half turn in the length of the barrel. The regular charge for the rifles was 90 to 100 grains of fine rifle powder and a one-half ounce lead ball loaded with a greased patch. The muzzle velocity was about 2,000 feet seconds. The rifle does not take a bayonet and weighs nine and one-fourth pounds with its steel ramrod.

The stock is of walnut, well finished, and is what is known as half stock; the barrel being attached with a single, flat key. The furniture is polished brass while the lock, trigger and ramrod are of steel. The barrel has a rib underneath to which is attached a thimble for carrying the rod. The patch box opens by pressing upon a spring stud set in the top of the butt plate. Both the front and rear sight are rigidly fixed and set for a range of about fifty yards.

EXPERIMENTAL MODEL 1812 FLINTLOCK MUSKET
Figure 1, Plate VI

This arm is one of the interesting experimental pieces made by the Government at Harper's Ferry. It is the third pattern of the Model 1812 having the band retainers for the bottom and middle bands placed forward while it retains the other features of the older patterns consisting of the lug for the bottom swivel to hold the trigger guard in place; the flat faced lock plate and flat cock. It has the regulation heavy stock with the high comb of that model. Marked on the barrel U. S. with the eagle head and M. On lock plate between cock and pan with the large spread eagle looking rearward below which is U. S. and behind cock Harper's Ferry, 1818 in three lines across the plate.

The arm is equipped with a magazine primer which acts also as the battery for the flint. One-half turn of the projecting lever permits enough powder for a priming to be fed into the pan while a screw cap allows the soldier to fill the magazine with sufficient powder for a number of charges. There is no record available as to the number of these arms made but they probably proved unsatisfactory owing to the danger of the magazine exploding.

SPECIAL MODEL FLINTLOCK MUSKET

Figure 3, Plate VI

Marked on lock plate, Harper's Ferry, 1819, U. S. and spread eagle. On top of barrel, V. P., an eagle head, also I, a 48 and dated 1819. While this arm is commonly referred to as a Cadet the records do not show this, and it may be for some other special service. It follows the regular musket in all details except the length of barrel and placement of the bands. The trigger guard and trigger plate are separate pieces and the rear swivel is held by a stud forward of guard. The band springs are forward of the bands. Length of barrel 36 inches. Breech to first band 10⅜ inches, to second band 20⅜ inches and to top band 30⅝ inches. This band placement indicates that the arm was specially made up and not a standard musket cut down. The available Harper's Ferry records do not classify the output, but Springfield records show that from 1818 to 1821 they made 1,640 36-inch barrel muskets. While this arm has the band arrangement and swivel stud attachment of the third pattern of the model 1812 it has a stock shaped like the model 1821 and is also equipped with a brass pan similar to the pans of this latter model.

HARPER'S FERRY BLUNDERBUSS

Figure 4, Plate VI

Length of barrel, 27¾ inches. Total length, 43 inches. Weight, 9½ pounds. The barrel half octagon—1¾ inches across the square at the breech—at muzzle 3 by 2 inches. Two brass ramrod thimbles and brass plate for lock screws, otherwise iron mounted. Trigger guard being a typical 1795 model. Butt plate of iron, marked U. S. Forward sling swivels attached to stock and rear swivel screws into stock near butt plate. Lock marked U. S. in script, spread eagle and Harper's Ferry, and dated 1808. This type of arm was used in Colonial times and during the Revolutionary War. The Ordnance returns of 1793 shows 2,262 of them on hand and the Ordnance Report for 1805 shows 4 blunderbusses. These guns were used aboard ships and were also used as wall pieces in the frontier forts, and are later referred to as wall pieces. The Harper's Ferry armory reports show that one wall piece was made in 1807 and 6 in 1808.

A number of these arms were made by contract probably for service in the War of 1812 by T. French at Canton, Mass., in 1811 differing from the one shown in that the barrels were shorter and the muzzle round instead of elliptical; specimens of this arm being in the Government museum at West Point.

MODEL 1840 FLINTLOCK MUSKETOON

Figure 5, Plate VI

The barrel is 26 inches long with a bayonet stud 2 inches from the end of the barrel and located on the bottom of the barrel. The breech tang is 2 inches long. The barrel is .84 inch in diameter at the muzzle, thus taking the standard 1840 bayonet. Marked at breech V. P. and eagle head.

The stock is of black walnut, 38 inches long with a ¾ inch comb 8 inches from the butt. The grip is 1¾ inches by 1½ inches in diameter.

The Furniture. All mountings are iron. The bottom band is ⅝ inches wide on top and 1 inch wide on the bottom, and is retained by a 2⅜-inch band spring forward of the band. The forward swivel is carried on a lug on this band and has a sling opening of 1⅜ inches. The top band has two rings; the forward ring being ½ inch wide carries the brass knife blade sight; the rear ring is ½ inch wide. The total length of the band is 2⁹⁄₁₆ inches with the body cut out square between the bands and with a bottom projection ½ inch to the rear. The band retainer is 2¾ inches long and is to the rear of the band with a lug to engage a hole in the band. The butt plate is 4¼ inches long and marked on tang U. S. The trigger guard plate is 9½ inches long attached by two screws, and the trigger guard is separate and the threaded shanks pass through the plate and are provided with round nuts. The trigger is carried on a stud that is a part of the plate. The trigger guard is plain and not provided with a sling swivel. The rear sling swivel is the same size as the forward swivel and is carried on a 2½-inch plate at butt of the stock. The ramrod is 25.7 inches long and has the trumpet shaped end. It is held in place by a "spring" or "spoon" and the rod channel has a metal stop.

The lock is 6¼ inches long by 1³⁄₁₆ inches wide with the rear portion rounded and more pointed than previous models. The cock is rounded and is ⁷⁄₁₆ inch thick, and is provided with

a round hole ½ inch in diameter, thus being entirely different than any previous model. The brass pan lies horizontal
with the barrel and has a very high fence. The total weight of
lock with side screws, 1 pound, 3¾ ounces. It is marked between
cock and pan with the spread eagle looking rearward below
which is the U. S. and to the rear of cock Harper's Ferry, 1839
in three lines. All parts of this arm are also marked U. S. M.,
indicating it is a model piece. The total length of the arm from
butt to muzzle is 41 inches, with bayonet attached 59 inches.
Weight complete without bayonet, 7 pounds, 3 ounces.

The records indicate that the regular production of this
arm was at Springfield armory and it is probable that only the
Model pieces were made at Harper's Ferry and it is to be noted
that the Springfield production differs from the model piece
in the shape of the top band which in the model follows the band
shape of the 1821 musket while the regular issue of this arm had
a top band shaped like the top band of the 1840 musket.

* * * * *

HALL'S BREECH-LOADING ARMS

The numerous references to Hall's arms in the official reports indicates that there were a good many of these used by
the Confederate troops and the fact that they were developed
and manufactured almost entirely at Harper's Ferry which is
so closely associated with the Confederate arms history entitles
them to more than passing notice.

The Hall arms represent the achievements of John H. Hall,
who was granted a patent covering it on May 21, 1811 and who
succeeded in getting an order from the Government for one
hundred of them in 1816—the result of the trial order being the
contract with the War Department dated March 19, 1819 whereby Hall entered the Government employ at Harper's Ferry for
the specific purpose of building the necessary machinery and
manufacturing these guns for the Government thereby making
the Hall arm the first breechloader to be adopted into the regular
military service of any country.

Hall, in his development of the breech-loading system, did
not have the benefit of present day literature, as is evidenced
by his letter addressed to Col. Bomford of the Bureau of Ordnance dated Jan. 24, 1815, in which he writes as follows:

"I invented the improvement in 1811, being at that time but little acquainted with rifles, and being perfectly ignorant of any method whatever of loading guns at the breech." The outstanding achievement of Hall, however, was not the introduction of the breechloader into the military service but the fact that he early conceived the idea of making the arms on a completely interchangeable system which had long been considered insurmountable even by the experts of European nations, therefore Hall's accomplishments in persuading the officials of his day to undertake the development of such a plan marks him as a salesman of the highest order. That he conceived the idea of thus producing his arms very early in his work there can be little doubt for in his correspondence with the War Department after the first successful trial by troops in 1816 he writes:

"Only one point now remains to bring the rifles to the utmost perfection, which I shall attempt, if the Government contracts with me for the guns to any considerable amount, vis: to make every similar part of every gun so much alike that it will suit every gun, so that if a thousand guns were taken apart and the limbs thrown promiscuously together in one heap, they may be taken promiscuously from the heap and will all come right. This important point I conceive practicable, and although in the first instance it will probably prove expensive, yet ultimately it will prove most economical, and be attended with great advantages."

"A favorite and important part of the American small-arms would then be at the height of perfection, and would vastly excel those of any other nation. They would be strong, durable and simple, easily kept in order, easily repaired when out of order, perfectly accurate and capable of being fired with the greatest quickness which a gun can admit of, and we have more marksmen capable of using them to advantage than can be found in the army of any other nation."

Claims are made for both North and Whitney, giving them credit for having introduced the interchangeable system in mass production but to anyone who has worked with the early output of either of their armories the best that can be conceded is that they attained "similarity" of parts, which is considerably different than exact interchangeability.

That Hall did achieve his object early in his operations is attested to by the report of Jan. 6, 1827 of the Commissioners appointed to investigate Hall's work, from which is quoted:

"It is well known, we believe, that arms have never yet been made so exactly similar to each other by any other process as to require no marking of the several parts and so that those parts, on being changed, would suit equally well when applied to every other arm. But the machines we have examined effect this with a certainty and precision we should not have believed till we witnessed the operations. To determine this point and test their uniformity beyond all controversy, we requested Colonel Lee, superintendent of the United States armory at this place, to send to Hall's armory five boxes containing 100 rifles manufactured by him in 1824, and which had been in the arsenal since that period. We then directed two of his workmen to strip off the work from the stocks of the whole 100, and also to take to pieces the several parts of the receivers, so called, and to scatter them promiscuously over a large joiner's work bench. One hundred stocks were then brought from Hall's armory which had been just finished, and on which no work or mounting had ever been put. The workmen then commenced putting the work taken from off the stocks brought from the United States arsenal on to the one hundred new stocks, the work having been repeatedly mixed and changed by us and the workmen also, all this was done in our presence, and the arms, as fast as they were put together, were handed to us and minutely examined. We were unable to discover any inaccuracy in any of their parts fitting each other, and are fully persuaded that the parts fitted, after all the changes they must have undergone by the workmen, as well as those made designedly by us in the course of two or three days, with as much accuracy and correctness as they did when on the stocks to which they originally belonged. If uniformity, therefore, in the component parts of small arms is an important desideratum (which we presume will not be doubted by anyone the least conversant with the subject) it is in our opinion completely accomplished by the plan which Hall has carried into effect. By no other process known to us (and we have seen most, if not all, that are in use in the United States) could arms be made so exactly alike as to interchange and require no marks on the different parts. And we very much doubt whether the best workmen that may be selected from any armory, with the aid of the best machines in use elsewhere, could, in a whole life, make a hundred rifles or muskets that would, after being promiscuously mixed together, fit each other with that exact nicety that is to be found in those manufactured by Hall."

This rather definitely fixes the Hall as being the first arm to be manufactured on a production basis that was completely interchangeable and a careful search of early works on mechanical arts gives it the further distinction of being the first commodity of any kind made up of numerous parts to be so produced any place in the world. It will be recalled that the regular output of the United States armories were not considered interchangeable until the Model of 1842 went into production.

The cost of developing and building the machinery and manufacturing the rifles is set forth in the following:

Statement of the amount expended at Harper's Ferry, from May 1819, to December 31, 1826, in constructing implements and machinery for the fabrication of Hall's patent rifles, so as to insure a perfect uniformity in all their component parts; and also of the amount expended in fabricating the rifles and their accouterments. Amount expended on the implements and machinery, viz:

For materials	$ 18,320.75
For labor, including superintendence	38,756.07

Total amount expended for implements and machinery	$ 57,076.82

Amount expended in fabricating the first parcel of 1,000 rifles and their accouterments, viz:

For materials	$ 4,030.53
For labor, including superintendence	15,561.97
For privilege of patent right	1,000.00

Total cost of 1,000 rifles and 1,000 sets of accouterments	$ 20,592.50
Amount expended on the second parcel of 1,000 rifles which are not yet completed, per statement D	$ 9,821.79

Total amount expended on the implements, machinery, and rifles from the commencement to the close of the year 1826	$ 87,491.11

The total cost of the 1,000 rifles and sets of accouterments which have been completed has been expended upon the several articles made, in the following proportion, viz:

1,000 rifles and bayonets at $17.82½	$ 17,825.00
1,000 ammunition flasks at $1.04 each	1,040.00
1,000 bullet-moulds at 31 cents each	310.00
1,000 wipers, at 19 cents each	190.00
100 spring vises at 20 cents each	20.00
1,000 screw-drivers at 7 cents each	70.00
50 packing boxes (for rifles at $2 each)	100.00
50 packing boxes (for accouterments) at 75c each	37.50

	$ 19,592.50
Privileges of patent rights, $1 each	1,000.00

Total cost, as above	$ 20,592.50

G. BOMFORD,
Brevet Colonel.

ORDNANCE OFFICE, WAR DEPARTMENT,
Washington, January 31, 1827.

Hall, who continued in the Government service until his death, February 26, 1841, received for his services and patent rights, according to Talcott's report, May 2, 1842, the following:

"Mr. Hall had been paid, from March, 1827 to October, 1834, being 7 years and 7 months, an average compensation of $2,636.81 per annum. Or in the whole for that period for his personal services and the use of his inventions.................$ 19,995.82

From that time to the time of his decease, 26th of February, 1841, being 6 years and 5 months, he was allowed at the rate of $2,600 per annum, $1,000 of which was for his personal services and $1,600 for the use of his machinery and improvements, amounting to.................... 16,687.50

And for the use of the machinery and improvements from thence to the 1st of July, 1841, his son was allowed at the same rate of $1,600...................... 870.00

Making the whole sum paid.................................$ 37,553.32

In this same report Talcott writes:

"I have to reply that the principle of the invention as regards the rifle is still considered a valuable one, and although but about 23,500 of the rifles have been manufactured for the Government at the national and private armories, and no more are now in the process of manufacture, as there is no rifle corps in service, yet the same principle is applied to the manufacture of carbines, of which 13,684 have been made, and the manufacture of them is still in progress."

The private armory referred to in the above paragraph was that of North's who was the only contractor to manufacture guns of the Hall pattern for the Government. He was the first official pistol maker and had furnished a great many model 1817 rifles to the Government and so developed his armory facilities that complete interchangeability of parts was attained and on December 15, 1828 he undertook a contract for making 5,000 Hall rifles at $17.50 each, which was successfully filled, and a contract for 1,000 Hall carbines at $20.00 each was taken by him in 1833.

So successful was North in these undertakings that he continued to receive orders for Hall carbines until 1850 as indicated by the following letter:

Middletown, Connecticut, February the 7th, 1850.
General GEORGE TALCOTT,
    Washington, D. C.

HON. SIR: Yours of the 5th came to hand this day, by which I have pleasure to receive notice of an addition of Three Thousand Carbines to my contract. Dr. Sir, permit me to tender to you my grateful acknowledgments for the favor.

Your proposition to make two Carbines for the purpose . . .

I am Sir very truly, your obt. Servant,
                SIMEON NORTH.

HALL'S BREECH-LOADING RIFLE
Figure 1, Plate VII

The specimen of Hall's rifle shown is marked on the receiver, J. H. Hall, U. S., 1837 and is of the following weights and dimensions:

DIMENSIONS

		Inches
Barrel	Diameter of bore	0.52
	Variation allowed, more	0.008
	Depth of groove	0.01
	Diameter of the muzzle	0.785
	Diameter at the breech	1.07
	Length	32.7
Receiver	Exterior diameter	1.
	Diameter of bore	0.545
	Diameter of chamber	0.1
	Depth of bore	1.1
	Depth of chamber	1.3
Bayonet	Length of blade	16.5
Arm Complete	Length from butt to muzzle	52.5
	Length with bayonet fixed	68.5
Ramrod	Length	32.0

WEIGHTS

		Lbs.	*Oz.*
Barrel, with supporters		4	13
Arm complete	without bayonet	10	4
	with bayonet	10	15

The stock is of American black walnut and the pores were not filled, but the finished surface received the usual protective coatings of linseed oil. The breech block and the external lock parts show dull colors of case hardening. The ramrod and bayonet are of polished steel. All screw heads are blued. The barrel and all other steel or iron is coated with brown lacquer. As lacquer does not appear on U. S. Government arms after the destruction of the Harper's Ferry works in 1861 presumably the formula was lost with the other burned records, because this lacquer is an admirable preservative and of excellent wearing qualities; it is not affected by water, oil, or acid; it is tough, hard, and so adhesive that it can only be removed by scraping.

The rifling of this arm is, so far as known, different than any other ever used by the Government, being as follows: Caliber of bore without grooves .51. Depth of grooves one-hundredth of an inch. Number of grooves, 16. Pitch, 1 turn in 8 feet. At the muzzle the lands are reamed out for a distance of an inch and a half, which is as far back as the rear edge of the front sight; looking into the muzzle, the rifle could easily be mistaken for a smooth-bore. Presumably the object was to facilitate loading at the muzzle in case the arm became defective as a breechloader. Possibly it was intended to increase accuracy; in either case the depth of reaming seems excessive.

The breech consists of a receiver, which contains the charge, and to which the lock is attached, it (the receiver) has two shoulders near its muzzle or fore-end, by which it is kept to the barrel and is prevented from recoiling when it is discharged. The receiver is prevented from recoiling wholly by these shoulders, which bear against the case-hardened chocks placed behind the shoulders. But no direct support is given by the butt piece behind the receiver, nor by the axis pin on which the receiver turns; on the contrary, the receiver does not even touch the butt piece; a vacancy is left between that and the end of the receiver to freely permit all the expansion which takes place in the receiver as it grows warm with repeated discharges, viz: all the expansion from the back part of the shoulders to the back end of the receiver. That expansion which takes place forward of the shoulders is provided for in the joint where the receiver meets the barrel. The holes in the receiver through which the axis pin passes are made long for the same purpose, viz: to freely admit of expansion in the after part of the receiver. The bore of the barrel increases gradually in size toward the breech, beginning about one foot from the muzzle and enlarging very rapidly in the last half inch next to the receiver somewhat in the form of a trumpet, so as to be rather larger at the butt than the bore of the receiver, to permit the ready passage of the bullet, even if its bore were not exactly to correspond with the bore of the barrel.

The charge was 100 grains of rifle powder, and ten grains were used for priming. The bullet was spherical and weighed one-half ounce; its normal diameter was .525; it was shot bare.

Owing to the escape of gas at the breech the muzzle velocity was several hundred foot seconds less than that of the regulation muzzle-loading rifles.

The sights are fixed, and in order to allow for the obstruction of pan and hammer they are offset from the vertical axis of the barrel. The bayonet lug is offset and the front sight carried on the lug is also offset to one side of it. In altering these arms to percussion at a later date the sights were not changed, although with the percussion type the sights can be carried on the vertical axis of the barrel. As the receivers of practically all models of this arm are interchangeable and as the markings are almost always on the receivers, a great deal of confusion has been caused by putting flint receivers into arms that were never made flintlock, but that were of the percussion period only. The offset was necessary on the flintlock and was not used on the percussion but it is not uncommon to find Hall carbines with flintlocks, and with sights on the vertical axis of the barrels which are totally obscured by the pan and hammer.

The socket bayonet used on this gun can be distinguished from other bayonets of the period by the slot for the stud; the slot having an offset recess to accommodate the sight.

A unique feature of the action generally overlooked by the student of this arm is the adjustable hair trigger. This consists of an adjusting screw passing through the sear by means of which any desired trigger pull can be secured and is a refinement in a military arm many years in advance of its day.

The three bands of this arm are retained in their position by pins or rivets passing through the stock but as this method was extremely unhandy when dismounting the piece it was later changed to the regular band spring method.

The records indicate the number of these rifles made at Harper's Ferry to be as follows, and it is believed that they were all made flintlocks:

1824	1,000	1836	1,809
1827	1,000	1837	1,200
1832	4,360	1838	2,934
1833	3,670	1840	1,023
1834	970	1841	190
1835	1,714	1843	300
		1844	2,700
	12,714		10,156

Total............................22,870

HALL'S FLINTLOCK CARBINE, SMOOTH-BORE
Figure 2, Plate VII

The records show that Harper's Ferry armory made 1,017 of these in 1837 and 1,003 in 1840 and while they also show 1,001 made in 1843 it is believed that this applies to the percussion model that was adopted in 1842.

The stock of this flintlock carbine is the same as that of the rifle except for the changes necessary in making the shorter arm and on part of them the patch box, and using the ramrod type of bayonet in place of the regular ramrod. This ramrod type of bayonet was first introduced into the service on this arm and was later used on one of the .45 caliber breech-loading Springfields and again on the first model 1903 Springfield.

Part of these carbines were made with a patch box which opened from the bottom of the stock and was covered by a hinged lid that formed a prolongation of the trigger guard plate.

In place of the sling-strap swivels of the rifle, the carbine had an Eye Bolt passing through the grip of the stock, in which to attach the sling strap. It will be noted that the same trigger guard is used as on the rifle but that it has not been drilled for attaching the sling swivel.

The carbine shown is marked on the receiver J. H. Hall, H. Ferry, U. S. 1837 and is of the following dimensions and weights:

DIMENSIONS

		Inches.
Barrel	Diameter of bore	0.64
	Diameter at the muzzle	0.84
	Diameter of the breech	1.12
	Length	23.00
Receiver	Exterior diameter	1.12
	Diameter of bore	0.69
	Depth of chamber	2.48
Bayonet	Length of blade	21.50
Arm Complete	Length from butt to muzzle	43.00
	Length with bayonet fixed	61.25

WEIGHTS

	Lbs.
Barrel, with supporters	3.60
Barrel, with bayonet	8.40
Arms complete without bayonet	8.15

HALL'S PERCUSSION CARBINE SMOOTH-BORE
Figure 3, Plate VII

This carbine, known as the U. S. Model 1840 embodies a number of changes in design besides the change of flintlock to percussion, and the most pronounced of these being the reduction of the caliber, use of the so-called Fish Tail lever for moving the receiver, and the omission of the bayonet.

The specimen shown is marked on receiver, H. Ferry, U. S., 1842, and is of the following dimensions and weights:

DIMENSIONS

		Inches
Barrel	Diameter of bore	0.52
	Diameter at the muzzle	0.84
	Diameter of the breech	1.1
	Length	21.00
Receiver	Exterior of diameter	1.00
	Diameter of bore	0.56
	Diameter of chamber	0.46
	Depth of bore	1.4
	Depth of chamber	0.98
Ramrod	Length	19.50
Arm Complete	Length from butt to muzzle	40.00

WEIGHTS

	Lbs.
Barrel, with supporters	3
Arm complete, without bayonet	7

This is the model of a Hall carbine as made by North, of Middletown, Connecticut, that figured so prominently in the Civil War scandal, which scandal, by the way, has been a sweet morsel for all those who indulged in the great American peace-time pastime of condemning everyone connected with the manufacture or sale of firearms.

The story of how the foundation of the Morgan fortune was laid by swindling the Government out of vast sums of money in connection with the sale of some five thousand Hall's carbines has been told and retold with almost endless variation.

In 1910, Myers in his HISTORY OF THE GREAT AMERI-
CAN FORTUNES devoted considerable space to this episode at
the beginning of Morgan's career.

Since Myers was more or less a recognized authority, subsequent writers seemed to have merely taken his version of the
transaction and rehashed it to suit their particular theme. Good
examples of these being THE HOUSE OF MORGAN, by Lewis
Corey, published in 1930; THE ROBBER BARONS, by Matthew
Josephson; and THE MERCHANTS OF DEATH, by Engel-
brecht & Hanighen, published in 1934.

Mr. R. Gordon Wasson, in his THE HALL CARBINE
AFFAIR, printed in 1941, cites the above and many other
writers in showing how history is developed into legend, and in
addition to this he compiles a record of the case based entirely
upon official government records—Reports of Congressional
Committees, Court trials and testimony, and such other source
material required to present the details of the transaction as it
really happened, and sums up the evidence with the following:

"The facts in the Hall carbine affair are clear. Before pur-
suing their metamorphosis into legend, it will be well to recapitu-
late them.

"Late in the spring of 1861, when the War of Secession was
just getting under way, the Chief of Ordnance of the United
States Army, James W. Ripley, agreed to sell a lot of more than
5,000 smooth-bore guns to one Arthur M. Eastman at $3.50 each,
being all of the Hall model that the Government owned.

"Though no one questions Ripley's good faith, his sale
of the Hall arms proved a blunder. It should have been evident
to him that in the emergency no serviceable arms could be spared.
Of those that he was selling, 5,000 were carbines in new condition, in their original packing boxes. They had been made on
Government order between 1848 and 1852 by Simeon North at
Middletown, Conn. The Government had inspected, accepted,
and paid for them. The Hall model had enjoyed considerable
vogue in the '30's, but the ensuing decades saw rapid progress in
the designing of small arms, and it passed out of favor. General
Ripley later alleged that all Hall arms had been recommended
for sale in 1857; but the fact is that those in good condition had
not been sold, and documentary support for his allegation has
not been found. Furthermore, in 1857, when sensible persons
were still not expecting war, the Secretary of War had favored
the sale of even serviceable arms of all older models to make

room in the arsenals for the new guns that were superseding all others. There is no convincing evidence that any responsible army authority had ever condemned the Hall carbines as unserviceable. At most the authorities may have thought in 1857 that there would never be a call for the Hall carbines, and that therefore they should be sold. These guns were a well built, serviceable weapon, and when war threatened, it was madness to sell them at any price.

"Eastman had no money to carry out his contract. He tried to resell the guns to others, but with no success until after the rout of the Union forces at Bull Run, late in July, when a stampede began for arms of every description. He then encountered a man named Simon Stevens, who agreed to pay him $12.50 for 5,000 rifled Hall carbines in new condition. Later the price was cut to $11.50, the rifling to be left to Stevens. Payment was to be in two installments—$20,000 within a few days, and the balance of $37,500 a few weeks later. Eastman hid from Stevens the fact that the arms were still held by the Government.

"Stevens at once re-offered the arms by telegraph to his friend, General John C. Fremont at $22.00 apiece. Fremont was in command of the Western Department with headquarters at St. Louis, and he accepted instantly, for his troops wanted guns badly. At that time Stevens did not tell Eastman of the sale to Fremont.

"Stevens now needed $20,000 for the initial payment to Eastman, and he sought a loan of that amount from a young man in New York, J. Pierpont Morgan, who had only recently started in business for himself.

"Morgan lent $20,000 to Stevens on August 7. He took the arms as collateral: by the most conservative valuation, they were worth two or three times the amount of his advance. He stipulated that when Stevens sold them, the bills should be made out in his favor, so that he would be reimbursed out of the first proceeds. He advanced certain additional sums to pay for the rifling of the carbines and incidental expenses. On September 14, 1861, thirty-eight days after he made his loan, payment for the first half of the arms reached him. He deducted $26,343.54 in liquidation of his loans, including interest and commission, and he never had any further interest in the Hall carbine affair. In due course all the carbines reached Fremont's troops; they appear to have given good service and caused no serious complaints.

"Early in the fall of 1861 the shocking circumstances of the Hall carbine transaction became known—how one branch of the Government had sold for $3.50 smooth-bores that another branch had bought, after rifling, for $22.00. The Government at once held up payment for the second half of the arms, and there was a general hue and cry. A Congressional committee held hearings and submitted tentative findings. The War Department took testimony, assembled documents, and made recommendations. General Ripley submitted certain information to Congress in a special report. General Fremont was questioned by the famous Joint Committee on the Conduct of the War. There was a debate on the Hall carbine affair in the House of Representatives, and scattered comment appeared in the press.

"Stevens persisted in his claim for his final payment, supported by a financial backer named Morries Ketchum. Ultimately Stevens brought suit in the Court of Claims, Ketchum, however, having the chief interest in the claim. In defending the case, the Government invoked a legal technicality, the United States Solicitor contending that under an old law Fremont had no authority to buy arms except through regular ordnance channels. He also contended that $22.00 was an unreasonable price for the carbines in August 1861. The Court of Claims made short work of the defense. Brushing aside the technicality, it held that a general commanding an army in the field would expose himself to something worse than censure, if he failed to equip his troops as best he could to meet the enemy. On the strength of substantial evidence, it held that the price, in view of the conditions in the arms market at the time, had been reasonable. The Government had a weak case to start with, and it did not carry the case to the higher court.

"It must be rare in history that an episode so unimportant as the Hall carbine affair is so thoroughly documented. The various hearings and reports and depositions make possible an accurate cross-check of almost every phase of the transaction. In the person of Ripley the Government displayed that lack of business sense which often afflicts democracies, and Eastman, the speculator, stood at his elbow to profit thereby. Stevens, another speculator, exploited his friendship with Fremont and the latter's needs to make another large profit. At the same time, in fairness to Stevens, it should be borne in mind that no fraud tainted his transaction. Fremont knew exactly what he was buying, and he received exactly what he ordered.

78

"As for Morgan, he had no part in initiating the purchase from the Government or the sale to the Government. In thirty-eight days his loan was paid off. He was never called to testify, much less did he ever push a claim—he had none to push—and no one ever disputed his right to reimbursement. In the contemporary discussion of the case, the press ignored his minor role; neither the House Investigating Committee nor the War Department in their reports singled him out for criticism; in the Congressional debate his name was mentioned only once, and then only to emphasize his circumscribed interest.

"When young Morgan made his $20,000 loan to Stevens on August 7, 1861, he knew that the proceeds were going for the purchase of arms from the Federal Government. He was in a position to satisfy himself that the sale of the arms by the Government had been approved by the Chief of Ordnance and the Secretary of War. On the other hand, though the documentation concerning the whole affair is extraordinarily complete, there is an absence of evidence to show that Morgan knew, when he made his loan, of Steven's re-sale of the arms to Fremont. There is circumstantial evidence to support the supposition that he was not privy to the Fremont contract. Before the month of August was out, and weeks before the public scandal broke, Stevens was in acute need of more money to pay off the balance that he owed to Eastman, but Morgan, far from accommodating him further, was himself demanding immediate repayment of the loan he had already made. Stevens got relief finally from Ketchum, a friend of Morgan's; however, Stevens met Ketchum, not through Morgan's good offices, but through another man's. Clearly Morgan's relations with Stevens became strained, for some reason, soon after he made his loan.

"At the time of the Hall carbine transaction, Morgan, then 24 years old, had had no previous dealings with Stevens; if they had known each other at all, the acquaintanceship was slight."

An interesting sidelight is contained in a communication from Mr. Wasson, dated June 16, 1942, which reads in part as follows:

"Since the book was printed, I have learned an interesting fact about the Hall arm that I will include in the text if it is ever reprinted. Has anyone ever called your attention to the fact that when Commodore Perry went on his famous embassy to Japan, among the impressive gifts that he took to the Mikado were several Hall guns? Undoubtedly they were included because of the high regard in which they were held. They appear in the list of gifts presented to the Japanese that was published in the official account of the embassy printed afterwards by our Government."

* * * * *

THE WHITNEY CONTRACT

One of the most interesting incidents to present day collectors in connection with the purchase of arms in the North for use by the Confederates is the Whitney contract with the State of Mississippi.

In the report of Jan. 18, 1861 by Adjutant General W. L. Sykes to Governor John J. Pettus of that State, relating to the efforts to supply the demand for the Mississippi rifle he writes:

"Relative to the Mississippi rifle, it is but justice to state that every effort has been made to procure them within the power of this department. This arm being renowned for the brilliant victories achieved upon the battlefields of Mexico in the hands of the First Regiment of Mississippi Riflemen, has derived the appellation of Mississippi rifle, and is the principal arm called for by the volunteer corps. In consequence of the numerous applications for this rifle the adjutant general, in compliance with verbal instructions, proceeded North in May last for the purpose of making contracts for this rifle to supply the demand existing up to the time of departure. This was effected after much difficulty in finding a suitable armory for its manufacture. On the 6th of June a contract was closed with Eli Whitney, of Connecticut, for 1,500 of these rifles with bayonets, 1,000 of which were to be delivered by the 1st of December, 1860. At the time of the first delivery of arms, October 15, said Whitney raised a point relative to the inspection, fearing an inspection by an officer of the Army, and refused to have them examined, and therefore shipped but sixty of said arms as samples, he said, of what he could furnish. The arms were received and examined and proved to be old guns fixed up. Such an act being a violation of the letter and spirit of the contract, none of the arms were taken as a part of the contract, though the sixty were taken as an experiment. The affair is now being adjusted between a U. S. Senator and said Whitney, but owing to the bad faith of Whitney the arms will probably never be received and the companies will have to resort to whatever can be furnished."

PLATE VIII

Fig.
1

Fig. 2

Fig.
4

Fig. 3

Fig. 1. Whitney Con-
federate Musket.
Fig. 2. Whitney En-
field Rifle.
Fig. 3.-4. Enlarged
Views of 1 - 2.

PLATE IX

Fig. 1

Fig. 2

Fig. 3

Fig. 1. Morse Altera-
tion Flint Musket.
Fig. 2. Enlarged
View.
Fig. 3. Morse
Carbine.

WHITNEY-ENFIELD RIFLE
Figure 2, Plate VIII

The arm shown seems to be made up from several types. The stock is a typical Enfield model 1858 except that band springs have been used instead of the regular clamping bands of that model. The butt plate is of iron instead of the regular brass type but has the Enfield shape. The trigger guard is of brass set in plate of iron made up similar to the U. S. method instead of the one-piece all brass Enfield type. The barrel, cone seat and tang follow closely the U. S. Model 1861 but the barrel is provided with a heavy lug for attaching saber bayonet. The ramrod differs from either the U. S. or Enfield models of the period, as does also the lock plate, while the hammer resembles somewhat the U. S. 1861 model. Sling-strap swivels attach to trigger guard and front band. Front sight is a heavy knife blade type and rear sight is a single leaf elevating one, both differing from either the regular Enfield or U. S. models.

Total length, 49 inches. Length of barrel, 33 inches. Weight, 7¼ pounds. Caliber at muzzle, .61 inch. The rifling consists of 7 grooves, differing from the regular Enfield which had 3 grooves, or the "Short" Enfield, which had 6 grooves, or the U. S. model of 1861 which had 3 grooves. Total length of the stock is 44 inches, leaving 5 inches of barrel protruding, which is considerably more than the regular Enfields. Marked on lock plate, E. WHITNEY. There being no other marks or dates.

As Whitney had furnished a great deal of machinery to the British Government for the Royal Small Arms Factory at Enfield, and is believed to have also furnished them a large number of arms to meet the pressing need arising from the war with Russia, 1854-1856, it may be that these arms furnished to Mississippi were made up of remnants of the British contract.

WHITNEY RIFLED MUSKET
Figure 1, Plate VIII

There are no definite records available concerning this arm but it is supposed to have been made by Whitney for the Confederates early in the war before such shipments were completely stopped—or possibly the lock only was furnished for use in making up complete guns at Richmond before they were fully organized.

81

FIREARMS OF THE CONFEDERACY

It is a regulation U. S. model 1855 including rear sight of that model (see Fig. 1, Plate IV, for complete details) but the barrel is minus any markings and the butt plate is of brass.

The lock is exactly like those made at Richmond by the Confederates during the first two years of the war but is marked E. WHITNEY, New Haven, and while the lock shows very little wear and was never rusty, the name can only be detected under favorable light conditions.

* * * * *

THE MORSE BREECHLOADER

The arms made by George W. Morse, besides being the earliest breech-loading arms to use a metallic self-primed cartridge, are of particular interest to students of Confederate arms from the fact that at the beginning of the war Mr. Morse became actively engaged in the cause of the Confederacy, and before the war was over succeeded in producing quite a number of carbines embodying his patents.

On March 6, 1861 he wrote to Jefferson Davis from Washington regarding his mission North to purchase machinery for the manufactory of arms, reading as follows:

WASHINGTON, D. C., March 6, 1861.
His Excellency, JEFFERSON DAVIS,
President of the Confederate States of America:

SIR: In pursuance of my understanding with you respecting the machinery for arms, I immediately, on my arrival here, went to work to find out the facts relative to the business, and had prepared a letter to you as the result of my investigations, which I took on Sunday evening to Captain Semmes for delivery, as I learned he was going direct to Montgomery. Much to my surprise, he informed me that he had been sent here fully authorized to transact the same business, and instead of going to Alabama he was on his way to the East to see Mr. Ames. Finding myself thus completely ignored in the transaction, I, of course, withhold as useless the communication, as no doubt Capt. Semmes has kept you well informed upon the subject. I regret that I had no knowledge of his appointment, as that would have prevented my placing myself in an unpleasant position with all of the parties with whom I had been for some time in intercourse in reference to the propositions which I had the honor to submit to the military committee of the Congress. I hope that Captain Semmes may succeed in the enterprise, for then I shall have the satisfaction of knowing that my exertions and honest endeavors to benefit the Confederacy will have been crowned with success. I still believe, however, that as I had taken the initiative in this business I could have been of some service in its execution.

I am, sir, very respectfully, your obedient servant,
GEO. W. MORSE.

FIREARMS OF THE CONFEDERACY

Following this we find him addressing a letter to Secretary Walker, July 18, 1861, in which he signs himself superintendent of Tennessee Armory, requesting the loan of certain machinery by the Confederate Government to the State of Tennessee, which machinery was to be used in the manufacture of the Morse carbine. The letter reads as follows:

RICHMOND, July 18, 1861.

Hon. L. P. WALKER,
Secretary of War, Confederate States:

SIR: In accordance with your suggestion I submit the following as the list of machines which I hope to obtain for the purpose set forth in a letter from the Governor of the State of Tennessee to His Excellency, President Davis: One trip-hammer, with such special tools for welding gun barrels as are at hand; 2 small planers; 1 screw machine; 1 cone machine; 2 small lathes; 1 propelling machine; 2 drilling machines, with 3 or 4 spindles each; 6 milling machines; 1 rifling machine; 1 nut-boring machine; 1 smooth-boring machine; 1 barrel-turning lathe; 1 punching press; 1 horizontal milling machine for ramrod, &c.; 1 old breech screw-cutting machine; 1 old index machine. It is the loan of these tools only which is asked for, the value of which may be fairly estimated at from $8,000 to $10,000. There are several good reasons why the request should be granted, and one of them is, that under the representations of General Polk that it would be done the State of Tennessee has purchased buildings and grounds for an armory. Another is that at Nashville workmen from Louisville and Saint Louis are easily obtained to duplicate them and make more of the same kind. Still another reason is that the State has purchased large supplies of war material, and the Confederate Government has not only already availed itself of a part of this in the form of percussion-caps, but will want large supplies of powder from her mills.

All of which is respectfully submitted for your consideration.

I am, sir, your obedient servant,

GEO. W. MORSE.
Superintendent Tennessee Armory.

From the foregoing it appears that Morse very early in the war assumed his duties as superintendent of the Tennessee armory at Nashville where old arms were repaired, sporting arms altered to military pieces and preparations actively undertaken to produce his breech-loading arm.

From the *Nashville Patriot,* Sept. 5 and 7, 1861.

Wanted at the State Armory, Blacksmiths, Gunsmiths, Iron Finishers and gun stockers, to whom fair wages will be paid. Contract for the delivery of a large number of Gun Barrels and gun stocks, finished or in the rough, and for gun locks, or other parts of small arms, will be entered into on application to

GEORGE W. MORSE,
Supt.

Aug. 11, 1 m.

The approach of the Federal armies forced the removal of the machinery and equipment of this armory to Atlanta, Georgia, sometime between February 17th and 20th of 1862 indicating that this armory was in operation about eighteen months.

From the Journal of the Secession Convention Report of the General Superintendent of the State Works, page 722, we read:

OFFICE GEN. SUPT. OF STATE WORKS,
Greenville, August 15, 1862.

Hon. W. H. GIST,
Chief of Construction and Manufacture:

SIR: In accordance with your directions, I herewith beg leave to report that under instructions for Col. J. Chesnut, Jr. . . .

When Nashville, Tenn., was evacuated by the Confederate authorities in April (Feb.) last, a part of the machinery and stock was saved from the Armory which that State had commenced to establish, and carried to Atlanta, Ga. I opened a correspondence with Governor Harris and found that the State of Tennessee would place at the disposal of this State all the machinery and stock saved. By direction of the Governor and Council I proceeded to Atlanta, and succeeded in obtaining it all. Governor Harris directed his agents to turn it all over to the State of South Carolina, subject to future settlement. As agent of the State I received it and secured the services of such workmen as had been engaged in the Nashville Armory and workshops, removing the machinery and stock to this place, the workmen to the shops in Columbia to be employed in altering and repairing small arms, while, at the same time, I commenced erecting a shop at these works to receive and put in operation the machinery. Paper No. 2 is an inventory of all articles received from the State of Tennessee and I refer you to my report of May 1st, 1862 for the full particulars relating to the subject.

The workshop for this department is completed, the machinery set up and in operation; much of it was injured and some parts lost in its removal from Nashville, and some had never been completed; which have been repaired, replaced, and completed, and I am now making and obtaining what new machines are necessary to commence the manufacturing of arms . . .

DAVID LOPEZ,
Gen. Supt. State Works.

This machinery and equipment at the time of the transfer from the State of Tennessee to the State of South Carolina was valued at $23,000, and the detailed inventory made at the time indicates that most of the work at Nashville had been devoted to the repairing and remodeling of arms and not the fabricating of new ones. The outstanding exception is an item in the inventory of one stamp TENNESSEE ARMORY which could have been intended for use on new arms though many small armories such as Sutherland, at Richmond, and Memphis Armory did stamp their converted arms.

From the same source, on page 703, is found:

DISBURSEMENTS FOR DEPARTMENT OF CONSTRUCTION AND MANUFACTURE

Feb. 25, 1862. To paid David Lopez for manufacture of arms $	200.00
March 22, 1862. To paid David Lopez for the State Works for Manufacture of Arms	5,000.00
April 2, 1862. To David Lopez for machinery, tools, Hardware for State Works	7,110.00
April 23, 1862. To Hon. W. H. Gist, Chief Dept. Construction and Manufacture and pay mechanics	4,054.00
May 12, 1862. To Hon. W. H. Gist, Chief, etc., for estimate of David Lopez for Armory	29,379.39
May 31, 1862. To David Lopez on estimate State Armory	10,165.00
May 31, 1862. To C. J. Bollin freight on machinery and materials for State Armory	1,241.31
July 10, 1862. To David Lopez for one gun	30.00
July 10, 1862. To David Lopez, on estimate for State Works	16,180.00

The Greenville Armory evidently got into operation late in the spring of 1863 and continued until the fall of 1864. They probably experienced the same shortage of manpower that curtailed work in all the other armories as indicated by the following:

From the *Tri-Weekly Carolinians,* Oct. 17, 1863.

STATE WORKS, GREENVILLE, S. C.

Wanted: at these works good machinists and gunsmiths to whom liberal wages will be paid. Good references required.

J. RALPH SMITH,
Gen. Supt.

That the armory did cease operation in the fall of 1864 is indicated by the advertisement in *The Daily South Carolinian,* Columbia, S. C., November 2, 1864:

"Sale of the State Military Works at Greenville, S. C. To be sold at public auction on the 15th day of November, 1864 at 12 M all the lands, buildings, machinery, tools, materials and other property of the State. By order of the Governor."

This sale did not take place then, as indicated by the following from the *Augusta Constitutionalist,* Tuesday, Nov. 15, 1864:

"Postponement of Sale—The sale of the Military works at Greenville, advertised to take place at Columbia on the 15th inst., has been postponed by order of the Governor."

The exact number of carbines made at this armory has never been definitely determined. As indicated elsewhere, when the

Federal troops took possession of Columbia, S. C., they found 400 Morse carbines stored there and the records are not clear as to whether they were removed or destroyed along with the other property. A rather complete list of the serial numbers would indicate that they were not destroyed at that time for they range up to 736 and of course this does not include all of the arms extant.

Not only were these arms made too late in the war to have seen much active service, but they required special ammunition, the principal patent claims of which read:

"October 28th, 1856, Soft Metal shell, with hard disc attached to base of Projections on the soft metal, by copper eyelet or by pressing into soft metal. May have priming between shell and disc, and internal disc.

"May 11th, 1858. Metal tube has pronged anvil soldered inside. Base closed by cup, which is driven against cap on anvil by hammer in firing.

"June 29th, 1858. Cap on anvil in base of metal tube, surrounded by perforated Disc."

The termination of the active and somewhat hectic career was announced by the *New York Tribune,* March 9, 1888:

"Washington, March 8—Col. G. W. Morse, the inventor of the Morse Cartridge and breech-loading gun, and a nephew of Professor Morse, who invented the telegraph, died at his home in this city today. His funeral will take place Saturday."

MORSE ALTERATION OF FLINTLOCK MUSKET
Figure 1, Plate IX

This is a regular U. S. Model 1831 flintlock musket, caliber .69, altered to a breechloader in which the top of the barrel is cut away and a breech-action hinged in the rear is applied. The firing pin is in the bolt connected to the hinge cover of the action. The original hammer is cut down and used as a cocking piece, the firing pin being attached to the tumbler inside the lock.

Marked on lock plate, U. S., the spread eagle, Springfield and 1839. Weight, with 16-inch bayonet, 10¾ pounds. The Springfield Armory records show that 54 of these were made there in 1860, and there are several varieties of these Morse arms in the National museum at Washington, D. C., and in private collections.

Figure 2, Plate IX

Shows an enlarged view of this breech-action. It will be noted that the forward lock-plate screw has a nut on the outside, made necessary by the reinforcement of the bottom of the barrel which prevents the screw turning. The first arms patent granted to Morse was No. 15995 dated October 28, 1856, the claims of which read:

"First. Inserting the rim N, or its equivalent, without contact, into the chamber O, substantially in the manner and for the purpose described, contact being attained through the medium of a cartridge case.

"Second. The nippers S, and the mode of operating them by the pins r, and the shoulder 7, on the hammer or equivalents therefor, substantially in the manner and for the purpose described.

"Third. The combination of movable parts, or their equivalents, whereby I retract or deliver the gun of a cartridge whether the previous charge was fired or failed to fire, and cock the hammer automatically at one motion, substantially in the manner described."

The second arms patent granted to him was No. 20503, dated June 5, 1858, the claims of which read:

"First. The percussion-rod in a movable breech-piece, in combination with the sliding-bolt E, when so arranged that the lock, in the act of firing, shall both make fast the breech-piece and fire the charge.

"Second. I claim the construction and use of the globular surface on the front end of the movable breech-piece, in combination with the end of the cylindrical cartridge case, for the purpose of more effectually preventing the escape of gas at the joint.

"Third. I claim the construction and use of the lever H, O, l, when arranged substantially as described, for the purpose of retracting the cartridge case."

THE MORSE BREECH-LOADING CARBINE

Figure 3, Plate IX

Caliber .50. A long brass frame with gripping piece in the rear of the trigger guard. Breech-action similar to that described above except that the hammer, which acts as a cocking piece, is swung in the middle. Butternut stock and full length fore piece. Brass ramrod pipes and a lug on the bottom of the barrel for holding ramrod in place.

There are no marks on this arm except the serial number 514. Length of barrel, 20 inches. Total length of arm, 40 inches. Weight, 6½ pounds.

The following letter of March 6, 1875 addressed to the Secretary of War, by S. V. Benet, Chief of Ordnance, gives the official record of Morse's activities in developing the arm and introducing it into the service:

(W. D. 18, Page 248.)

ORDNANCE OFFICE, WAR DEPARTMENT,
Washington, March 6, 1875.

THE SECRETARY OF WAR:—

SIR: I have the honor to return herewith the letter of the Attorney General, of 24th ultimo, asking for a full statement of all facts, circumstances, and evidence in the possession or knowledge of this Department touching the claim of the Morse Arms Manufacturing Company (in the Court of Claims, No. 10,270), and in compliance with the request have to submit the following report:

By the "act making appropriations for the support of the Army for the year ending 30th June, 1855," approved August 5, 1854, the sum of $90,000 was appropriated . . . for the purchase of the best breech-loading rifles in the opinion of the Secretary of War, for the use of the U. S. Army: Provided, that the Secretary of War, after a fair practical test thereof shall deem the purchase advisable and proper. (10 Stat., p. 579.)

The effect of this measure was to stimulate the ingenuity of inventors in devising and perfecting methods of operating arms at the breech; and the records of the Patent Office show, in the number of patents issued for breech-loading arms about this time, that it is here properly that the era of breechloaders in this country begins. The number of patents for such arms previous to this time were comparatively few, and but few had received anything like governmental patronage. And although a board of officers was convened at Washington Arsenal in December, 1854, under Special Orders, No. 199, Adjutant General's Office, 1854, for the purpose of examining such breech-loading rifles as might be presented, with a view of purchasing a sufficient number of the best for practical test in the field under the appropriation of August 5, 1854, the arms ultimately selected for the purchase were required to be carbine pattern for the use of cavalry—the arming of infantry troops with any of the systems of breech-loading rifles then extant not being favored by the War Department throughout Mr. Jefferson Davis' administration of the War Office, and consequently very little of the appropriation for "the purchase of breech-loading rifles" was spent during his term. A balance of $82,143.50 remained unexpended when Mr. Davis retired from the War Office on March 4, 1857. The Morse arm, not being patented until October, 1856, did not compete under the board of December, 1854, but became a strong competitor for participation in the above balance during Mr. John B. Floyd's administration of the War Office, beginning March 4, 1857.

On the day following Mr. Floyd's entrance upon the duties of his office Mr. Morse presented his arm at the Ordnance Office, and was referred by the colonel of ordnance to the commanding officer of the Washington Arsenal, who was directed to test the arm and make report. A very favorable report was made under date of March 6, 1857, and on the 17th of March, 1857, another favorable report was made to the Bureau of Ordnance and Hydrography of the Navy Department by the officer in charge of the Ordnance Department at Washington navy-yard.

These two reports seem to have strongly impressed the Secretary of War in favor of the Morse inventions, and during the summer of 1857, with a view to applying the large balance of the appropriation of 1854, for the purchase of the best breech-loading arms, due public notice was given of a contemplated trial by the Government of breech-loading arms at West Point, N. Y. A board of officers was duly assembled at that place on August 17, 1857, in pursuance of Special Orders, No. 118, Adjutant General's Office, 1857, "for the purpose of making trials of breech-loading rifles, with a view to ascertain which arm of this description is best suited to the military service." Mr. Morse appeared before this board with his gun and cartridge, and submitted several communications descriptive of his inventions, including copies of the two reports of March 6, and 17, 1857, above referred to. The board tried a number of varieties of arms, and finally chose "the breech-loading rifle submitted by A. E. Burnside, of Rhode Island, as the best suited for the military service." The Burnside arm used metallic cartridges, and this therefore was the first official recognition of the merits of this kind of ammunition by the military authorities. The expression of the choice of the board was not, however, unaccompanied by a qualification implying distrust in what they had done. They said:

"In submitting this opinion the board feel it their duty to state that they have seen nothing in these trials to lead them to think that a breech-loading arm has yet been invented which is suited to replace the muzzle-loading gun for foot troops. On the contrary, they have seen much to impress them with an opinion unfavorable to the use of a breech-loading arm for general military purposes."

Owing to this qualified opinion the Secretary of War ordered "carbines" from Burnside on November 9, 1857, but this order was subsequently canceled by consent, and the appropriation of 1854 for the purchase of the best breech-loading rifles was expended in purchase of Colt's, Maynard's, and Sharp's rifles and Joslyn carbines.

During the period of the session of the above board the Secretary of War had had full reports made to him by the colonel of ordnance of "the number of muskets and other small arms on hand which have been made into percussion arms by alteration of the old flintlock," and also the views of that officer regarding "the expediency of selling such arms, or a portion of them." He had, at or about the time of the cancellation of the Burnside order, directed various experiments to be made at the Washington Arsenal in altering old arms to the Morse system of breech-loading. "This application," says the commanding officer of that post in an official report "was to be made with the least possible change or expense in the arms, the object of the Secretary in the experiment being both efficiency and economy—efficiency in producing a more perfect arm than had yet been made, and economy in avoiding the contemplated sales of the old arms, necessarily at a great sacrifice."

On the 5th March, 1858, the Secretary of War directed that 100 of Morse's guns be purchased at $40 apiece, to be paid for in lots of 25 each as soon as inspected and delivered. The order was duly given to and accepted by Mr. Morse, but no arms were ever furnished under the order.

Efforts in behalf of the Morse inventions were made in Congress during the spring and summer of 1858, wherein the Secretary of War took decided action looking to the alteration of the stock of old muzzle-loaders on hand to breechloaders on Morse's plan. The published debates in the House of Representatives during that period on the "act making appropriations for the support of the Army for the year ending

June 30th, 1859," show the extent of the efforts in that behalf; and the debates in the Senate for the same period show the objections urged by Mr. Jefferson Davis, the late Secretary of War, and then a Senator from Mississippi, against the scheme. The clauses in the appropriation bill which were the subject of contention were finally enacted in the following form:

"For the purchase of breech-loading carbines of the best model, to be selected and approved by a board of ordnance officers, $25,000.

"For the alteration of old arms so as to make them breech-loading arms, upon a model to be selected and approved by a board of Ordnance officers, $25,000: Provided, that any portion of said sum not exceeding $5,000 may be expended under direction of the Secretary of War, at his discretion, in applying to the old or new arms any recent improvements in the mode of priming." (11 Stat., p. 335.)

These two clauses are here inserted because each gave rise to a board of ordnance officers before which the Morse inventions were brought.

The act was approved on June 12, 1858, and on the 14th of June, the Secretary of War issued orders for the assembling of a board at West Point, N. Y., on July 12, 1858, to select "the breech-loading carbines of the best model" contemplated in the first item of above appropriation. The board met on July 13, and after testing a number of different arms, including Morse's, submitted their report July 31, 1858, recommending the Burnside carbine as "the least objectionable for use in the hands of the mounted troops." An order was therefore given, on September, 1858, for the Burnside carbines to the full extent of the $25,000 appropriated.

On the 8th of July, 1858, the Secretary of War appointed a board to proceed to West Point to examine all methods of altering old arms that might be submitted, and to report upon the adaptability of the principle of each in the alteration of muzzle-loading arms. This was in pursuance of the second item of the above appropriation. On the same date the Secretary of War directed the arms that had been altered on Morse's plan at Washington Arsenal to be sent to West Point to be submitted to "the boards" to convene at that place.

The board on "alteration of old arms" met at West Point on the 22d July and adjourned to the 26th July, "to allow time to inventors to submit their arms." Six plans of alteration were submitted to the board, including the Morse, accompanied by written description in each case. The board selected Morse's system, and in their report say:

"The board selects Morse's model, inasmuch as it differs from the others by including the new and untried principle of a primed metallic cartridge, which may on actual trial be found of advantage; and they recommend that the appropriation, or so much as the Secretary of War may deem necessary for the purposes of trial by troops in service, be applied to the alteration of old United States arms to breech-loading arms upon Morse's model, with certain modifications suggested by him."

Morse made the following proposal to the Secretary of War on September 9, 1858:

"You may alter 2,500 old arms in any of the Government armories on my plans for the sum of $5 each, or for the sum of $12,500. This will leave of the appropriation $7,500, or $3 each, to pay for the labor and material on each gun. If you fear the cost of alteration will exceed $3 on each arm, retain in your hands a portion of the $12,500 until you are satisfied on that point and have funds to go on with."

This proposal was accepted by the Secretary of War to the extent of 2,000 arms, and the sum of $10,000 was paid Mr. Morse, upon the execution of a license to the United States to alter that number of arms, the agreement to include all his patent privileges for the 2,000 arms.

Immediately upon the execution of the license and payment of the $10,000, Morse repaired to Worcester, Mass., where he had forwarded to him, care of Muzzy & Co., the altered arms which were before the boards at West Point. By the 4th November, 1858, he had prepared a model musket, which, though differing slightly from the arms submitted at West Point, was pronounced by two members of the board that had tried the arms at that place to be according to the general plan or principle of alteration as originally proposed. Mr. Morse named Springfield Armory as the place at which he desired the alteration of the 2,000 arms to be undertaken, and on November 6 and 9, 1858, orders were given the superintendent of that armory to begin the work.

On the 28th June, 1859, some further modifications being suggested by Mr. Morse in his alteration, the same were permitted upon express condition that all work on his alteration should cease as soon as the sum of $4,200, that had been assigned out of the appropriation "for the alteration of old arms to breechloaders" for this particular work should be expended, no matter how many or how few arms should then be altered. On the 12th November, 1859, the superintendent reported that the $4,200 had been expended, that 60 arms had been completed, and that components were in progress for 540 arms. The estimated cost of finishing the 540 arms was $4 each.

The appropriation of June 12, 1858, for the alteration "of old arms so as to make them breech-loading" had by this time become entirely exhausted. The sum of $5,800 had been spent out of it on account of another plan of alteration selected by the Secretary of War, and $5,000 had been paid on account of method of priming. The remainder had been spent as follows:

September 13, 1858, to G. W. Morse, for license to
    alter 2,000 arms $10,000
August 6, 1859, to paymaster, Springfield Armory,
    for Morse alteration   4,200
                                  Total..$14,200

In addition to this amount, there had also been the following expenditures at Washington Arsenal prior to the transfer of the work to the Springfield Armory, viz:

February 22, 1859, for altering 4 service arms to
    Morse's pattern, and work done on his model gun $1,253.92

The faith of the Secretary of War in the ultimate success of the experiments he had inaugurated had not in the least abated, as will appear from his annual report of December 1, 1859, under the heading "Breech-loading arms" (Senate Document, first session, Thirty-sixth Congress, vol. 2.).

On the 6th of February, 1860, George W. Morse and A. Anderson submitted the following proposition to the Secretary of War:

"The undersigned propose to change the order heretofore given by you to G. W. Morse for the manufacture of 100 carbines, at $40 each, and instead of it to sell to the Government the right to manufacture 1,000 carbines, according to Morse's invention for breech-loading arms, and according to the particular plan thereof which has been applied in the alteration of the United States rifle; and they propose to make the conveyance for $3,000, being at the rate of $3 on each gun."

The Secretary of War indorsed on this proposal February 9, 1860:

"The within proposition is accepted, and the colonel of ordnance will make proper arrangement for securing the right to make 1,000 guns, according to Morse's patented invention, on the terms within stated. Payment of $3,000 therefor will be made to Messrs. G. W. Morse and A. Anderson, and the order heretofore given for four thousand dollars' worth of Morse's carbines will be rescinded."

A license was accordingly obtained from G. W. Morse and A. Anderson February 11, 1860, and they obtained $3,000 from the Treasury on February 13, 1860, out of the appropriation for "arming and equipping the militia."

These purchases of patent rights by the Secretary of War became known in Congress during the spring and summer of 1860, and were very objectionable to Mr. Davis, on whose motion a clause was inserted in the "act making appropriations" for the "legislative, executive, and judicial expenses of the Government for the year ending 30th June, 1861," follows:

"No arms nor military supplies whatever, which are of a patented invention, shall be purchased, nor the right of using or applying any patented invention, unless the same shall be authorized by law and the appropriation therefor explicitly set forth that it is for such patented invention."

The 54 Morse arms that had been completed at Springfield Armory were sent to the Washington Arsenal, and on a complaint of Mr. Morse, of April 5, 1860, of "persistant refusal" of the colonel of ordnance to have them made "ready for service," the Secretary of War, on April 9, 1860, ordered as follows:

"The Chief of Ordnance will give directions to have the arms which have been altered to Morse's invention, together with ammunition for them, prepared for service, under Mr. Morse's supervision, at the Washington Arsenal."

On the 28th February, 1860, in pursuance of the license granted to the 11th of that month, the Secretary of War issued the following order, upon which instructions were duly issued by the colonel of ordnance:

"Preparatory to the manufacture of the 1,000 Morse arms, for which the right has been obtained, the colonel of ordnance will give orders to have 4 of these arms for models made at the Springfield Armory under the supervision of the inventor, Mr. George W. Morse. Two of these arms will be made of the caliber of the Harper's Ferry .54-inch rifle and 2 of the caliber of the Colt's army pistol. The other details will be arranged at the Springfield Armory. Directions will also be given for altering 4 Harper's Ferry rifles of .54 caliber to Morse's plan, and to furnish a sufficient number of cartridges, say 200 per arm, for trying the 4 models and the 4 altered rifles. Mr. Morse will be informed of the above instructions."

On the 5th of July, 1860, the following order was given to the colonel of ordnance by the Secretary of War:

"With a view to altering rifles to Morse's plan at Harper's Ferry Armory, you are requested to have sent to that armory from Springfield one of the last models of altered rifles, with its appendages, together with all of the tools which have been made at Springfield, for the purpose of making such alterations; and also the drawings, or copies of them, by which the work has been done, as well as copies of the drawings of the new carbines, now in course of manufacture at Springfield Armory."

And on the 13th following:

"The colonel of ordnance will please instruct the superintendent of Harper's Ferry Armory to proceed as soon as possible after the receipt from Springfield Armory of the altered rifle, with tools, etc., if any, as may be necessary to alter Harper's Ferry rifles of the .54-inch caliber to Morse's plan, and to go on with the alteration according to the Springfield model to the extent for which the right has been obtained. To insure correctness in doing this work Mr. Morse will be permitted to see it as it progresses, and to make any suggestions he may deem proper to aid the master armorer in carrying out the alterations in the best and most effective manner."

FIREARMS OF THE CONFEDERACY

The model, tools, gauges, and mills suited to the Morse alteration were duly received at the Harper's Ferry Armory on July 19, 1860.

Touching these diversions of armory operations from the manufacture of arms of the established model to the alteration of arms according to plans of patentees, and to getting up models of arms for inventors, attention is invited to the annual report of the colonel of ordnance for the year ending June 30, 1860 (Senate Document, second session, Thirty-sixth Congress, vol. 2, page 965). Attention is also invited to the annual report of the Secretary of War for the same year, urging an appropriation of about "$50,000 for experiments for the improvement of arms and military supplies," and complaining of the law which prohibited the purchase of patented arms and military supplies. See also his remarks under the head of "Breech-loading arms" (Senate Document, second session, Thirty-sixth Congress, vol. 2, pages 7-9).

On the 10th November, 1860, Morse suggested the immediate advertisement for proposals to furnish 600,000 rifle cartridge cases of his model for use in the rifles and carbines then making. The colonel of ordnance recommended that if this number were to be made the work should be undertaken at the Frankford Arsenal, where the manufacture of metallic cartridges was then in progress adapted to the Burnside and Maynard carbines. This recommendation being approved by the Secretary of War, instructions in accordance therewith were issued on December 7, 1860.

On the 27th December, 1860, only a few days before the resignation of Mr. Floyd as Secretary of War, the following order was issued by him, and directions were given for the Ordnance Office accordingly:

"The Ordnance Bureau will direct that the alteration of the rifles at Harper's Ferry Armory to Morse's plan, ordered last July, be carried on with all possible dispatch, and 1,000 of them be finished as soon as possible, and 100 cartridges for each of the altered rifles be procured from the manufactury of Waterbury, Conn., and sent to Harper's Ferry, to be put up and forwarded with the rifles to the United States arsenal at San Antonio, Tex."

The above is the last paper from the War Office, previous to the war, on the subject of the Morse arms. In April, 1861, Harper's Ferry Armory fell into the hands of the rebels, the storehouses being previously burned, and in June, 1861, the place was evacuated by them, the machinery, etc., being carried off with them.

In the "Decisions of the Commissioner of Patents" for 1872, in the matter of the application of George W. Morse for extension of a patent for improvement in cartridge cases, the Commissioner finds as follows, on page 106:

"It is proven that just before the Government troops took possession of Alexandria, in the spring of 1861, the applicant left his family in Washington and went to Richmond; remained in Richmond until after the battle of Manassas Gap; then went to Nashville, Tenn., in charge of machinery for making his cartridges, which machinery had been stolen by the rebels from the Government works at Harper's Ferry . . . He was forced back with the machinery first to Chattanooga and later to Atlanta and then to Greenville, S. C. At the latter place he entered into contract with the governor of South Carolina to manufacture arms, and actually made arms for a company of rebel soldiers, as he declares, for State use to keep the peace, which probably meant to enforce the Confederate conscript laws."

It is not known at this Bureau that there was any machinery at Harper's Ferry for the manufacture of Morse's cartridges, and the probabilities are that the machinery above referred to as having "been stolen by the rebels from the Government works at Harper's Ferry" was the same that had been sent to that post from Springfield Armory, and was what was used by Morse at Greenville, S. C., in the manufacture of arms for the company of rebel soldiers. Wherever this machinery may be at the present time it is legally the property of the United States.

The foregoing is a succinct history of the Morse inventions down to the period of the beginning of the war, so far as the same is known to this Bureau. The Morse experiments were abandoned by the Government at that period, and the machinery for the making or altering of arms on his plan had passed out of its possession. In the face of open hostilities, and the stupendous preparations consequent thereon, there was left no time for continuing experiments with unperfected systems of breech-loading arms, nor to contrive and construct new and untried machinery for the production of arms of that character. As the war progressed the productive energies of the Ordnance Department were taxed to their utmost extent to supply the standard muzzle-loading rifle muskets to meet the continual wastes of service; and, in time, private contractors had to be called in to duplicate the machinery, and aid in the enormous production imperatively demanded by the infantry branch of service. Meanwhile the Morse inventions were stored away at the Springfield Armory and Frankford and Washington Arsenals.

An inspection of the licenses granted by Morse on September 13, 1858, and by Morse and Anderson on February 11, 1860, also of the proposals on which such licenses were based, and the instructions subsequently given in each case, fails to show that the Government at any time undertook the production of arms and ammunition under and according to the Morse patents to a greater extent than named in the licenses themselves. And certain it is that there is no record in this office that Morse ever "entered in a contract of license with the Government of the United States, through the Secretary of War, whereby the Government was licensed to make and use arms and ammunition under and according to the specifications in said letters for and during the life of the same," as described in the claimant's petition; nor will any of the Morse transactions and writing, so far as known to this Bureau, raise such a contract by implication even. The rights granted by Morse to the United States were in each case limited to a specific number of arms. The United States has never made the number of arms of the Morse pattern named in the licenses, but the United States has made nearly or about 130,000 breech-loading arms, and ammunition therefor, and as the petitioners claim "the sum of $5 each on the full number of 130,000 muskets," the claim is reduced to a mere demand for damages for the alleged infringement of a patent right. These arms have all been made since 1865, and after prolonged litigation in the United States circuit court for Massachusetts have been decreed to be an infringement of a patent obtained upon a device which originated in the following manner:

The work of altering old arms at Springfield Armory on Morse's plan had just begun in November, 1858, when one of the clerks at the armory, Mr. J. W. Preston, began experimenting with a view to improving the method of alteration. In his testimony in the above suit Preston says:

Ordnance Reports, Vol. IV, P. 924.

"This work (Morse alteration) was going on in the shops when I conceived the idea that I could invent a simpler and better method. I immediately began drawing and experimenting. I procured a cylindrical piece of wood, bored through the center, and with my knife cut out the model as near as I could. . . . I prepared a caveat for the Patent Office in November, 1858, etc."

This caveat as filed in the Patent Office is dated Nov. 19, 1858; application for a patent was made October 8, 1861, and rejected October 16, 1861, but finally a patent issued in 1867.

Suit was instituted as above stated in the United States circuit court for Massachusetts in October, 1868, on this Preston patent, resulting in the following decree in respect thereto, in September, 1871.

Here is inserted a copy of the decree as printed on page 10, Report of the Chief of Ordnance for 1872.)

In respect to this Morse claim now presented, the real question to be first decided, therefore, is "Do the arms which have been decreed to infringe the Preston patent also infringe the Morse patents?" It is apprehended that the jurisdiction of the Court of Claims, "limited and defined as it is by statutes," does not embrace the solution of this question.

A formal claim was presented to the War Department by Mr. Skilton, as attorney, in June last, founded upon alleged infringement of the Morse patents, but owing to the complex questions of fact and of patent law that were raised thereby between the Morse and other devices in the same line of invention, the Department declined to entertain the claim; principally, however, upon the ground that the Department was not authorized to adjust what was in the nature of unliquidated damages, the claim being for the past unauthorized manufacture and use of what was alleged to be covered by the Morse patents.

The documentary evidence in this case being quite voluminous, I inclose herewith for the perusal of the Attorney General, in accordance with his suggestion, the original papers from the files of this office relating to the Morse case, consisting exclusively of the incoming correspondence.

It is respectfully suggested that the outgoing correspondence, and the reports of the various boards be consulted at this office.

Respectfully, your obedient servant,

S. V. BENET,
Brigadier General, Chief of Ordnance.

For reply to the call of the Court of Claims in this case, see printed report of Morse vs. The United States.

(W. D. 18, page 248.)

CHAPTER III

CORRESPONDENCE AND REPORTS ON THE MANUFAC-
TURE OF ARMS BY THE STATES AND BY THE
CONFEDERATE GOVERNMENT. GEN. GORGAS AND
HIS ACCOUNT OF THE ORDNANCE DEPARTMENT.
THE RICHMOND ARMORY AND ITS OUTPUT—FAY-
ETTEVILLE—TYLER, TEXAS—COOK AND BROTHER,
TALLASSEE ARMORY.

THE achievements of the Southern States, in the production of arms and munitions of war is one of the outstanding
accomplishments of those stirring times, and today the student
of the subject finds a source of wonder and keen admiration in
the story of how a section of the country, devoted almost
entirely to agricultural pursuits, and with few mechanics or
facilities for the difficult task of manufacturing firearms, were
able in a short time to build up the industry.

It is to be much regretted that the details of a great deal
of this work are not available, but the correspondence, reports
and records included here give some idea of the extent of their
operations, and the Confederate-made arms here described and
shown testify to the accomplishments of the Ordnance Department, under the able direction of J. Gorgas, formerly a captain
in the U. S. Army.

It will be noted by the letter of Nov. 3, 1860 that the State
of Virginia was taking active steps to meet the impending
crisis, both by the purchase of arms, and also the purchase of
materials and machinery for the production of arms at the
State Armory at Richmond; Mr. Solomon Adams, Master
Armorer for the State, having been granted permission by the
U. S. Government to make a model arm at Springfield, and to
make drawings of the machinery and tools required for its
production for the use of the Tredegar Iron Works, operated
by J. R. Anderson & Co., who had a contract from the State to
build the machinery.

On February 21, 1861, Capt. R. Semmes, acting as an agent
for the Confederate Government, was sent North by Jefferson
Davis, with instructions to purchase machinery for the manufacture of arms and munitions, and particularly to make ar-

rangements with an employee of the Washington arsenal named Wright for his services and the use of his machines for the production of copper caps. Mr. Barbour, Superintendent of Harper's Ferry Armory, was to be interviewed regarding the set of machinery for making rifles, that had been made for that place, and Mr. Ball, master armorer of Harper's Ferry would accept service with the new Government and probably bring some mechanics with him.

After the capture of Harper's Ferry, the machinery there was promptly moved away, and after a great deal of correspondence on the subject, that part of it necessary for production of the rifled musket was sent to Richmond, and that part of it required for the Harper's Ferry rifle was loaned by the State of Virginia to the State of North Carolina for erection at Fayetteville. Both of these armories were subsequently taken over by the general government.

The firm of Jones, McElwaine & Co., of Holly Springs, Miss., appear to have been the first to receive a contract for arms, an order of 30,000 stand with delivery to commence in November 1861, and they also did a great deal of repairing and remodeling of arms, especially the reboring of the squirrel rifles and fitting them for military use.

Mr. Geo. W. Morse, formerly an employee of the U. S. Government, and signing himself Superintendent of the Tennessee Armory, requested on July 18, 1861, the loan of certain machinery for manufacturing arms from Secretary Walker. This machinery was probably used in the making of the Morse carbine.

In the report to Congress of July 27, 1861, mention is made of the contract to Mr. LeMat, of Louisiana, for five thousand of his revolvers. These revolvers were to be made abroad, however, and owing to the difficulty encountered in their manufacture, very few were delivered.

Mr. Ed. Want, of New Berne, N. C., is also mentioned as having a contract for 5,000 pistols but the details of this are lacking. It was undoubtedly a single shot military pistol as the distinction is made in this report; the LeMat being referred to as revolvers.

The eight or ten arms made per day at Wytheville, from barrels saved from Harper's Ferry, are believed to be the so-called Confederate Hall rifle, a muzzle-loader made up from parts of the Hall breech-loading arm and from the wide variation found in the specimens known at this time, they were evidently fabricated entirely by hand, even to the forming of the stocks, which were plainly not machine made.

The report by Col. Gorgas of January 7, 1863, shows the small arms fabricated in the Government armories as two thousand and fifty per month, including rifles, muskets, carbines and pistols, and the private armories were producing 1550 of these arms per month.

In his indorsement on Col. Boteler's letter of August 10, 1863, Col. Gorgas reports a good breech-loading carbine being made in small numbers at Richmond, that no reliable carbines except muzzle-loaders could be attained abroad, and that a model of a muzzle-loading carbine was then being made, to be submitted to Gen. Stuart for his criticism.

The report of Gov. Pettus, of Mississippi, dated November 3, 1863, indicates some of the handicaps experienced in the production of arms, the State armory having been forced to move twice, first from Panola to Brandon, and later from Brandon to Meridian.

On November 15, 1863, Col. Gorgas, reporting to Secretary of War Seddon, advises that the armories at Richmond, Fayetteville and Asheville had produced an aggregate of 28,000 small arms within the year, and that the private armories had supplied 7,000 during that period. Of this total about thirty thousand were infantry arms, and 5,000 cavalry arms, three thousand of which were Sharps breechloaders, the remainder being muzzle-loaders. He also reports revolver pistols to the extent of about 500 per month being made by contract at Macon, Columbus, and Atlanta, Ga. This report also indicates a total of 127,862 small arms repaired during the period covered.

The letter of Governor Watts of Alabama to Secretary Seddon complaining of the enrollment into the ranks of the army, workmen of the Shakanoosa Arms Mfg. Co., of Dawson, Ga., indicates that this company was under contract to furnish arms to the State of Alabama.

The capacity of the armories under the control of the Ordnance Bureau as given in Col. Gorgas's report of Dec. 31, 1864, was as follows:

Richmond, Va.	25,000
Fayetteville, N. C.	10,000
Columbia, S. C.	4,000
Athens, Ga.	10,000
Tallassee, Ala.	6,000

FIREARMS OF THE CONFEDERACY

Those made at the last mentioned place were to be carbines, and it is indeed to be regretted that the number actually made is not given. This same report shows the arm manufactured and made up from captured parts as follows:

Rifles, .58 caliber	12,778
Carbines	5,354
Pistols	2,353
Total	20,485

At this period of the war workmen to operate the machinery seemed to be the big problem, all the correspondence indicating a shortage of the skilled labor so much required, and this coupled with the depreciated currency finally compelled the general government to take over practically all the private manufactories.

The Confederate States Ordnance Manual was printed in 1863, and was in most details a copy of the U. S. Manual of 1861, only the necessary changes being incorporated to provide for the omission of the Maynard priming lock on the regulation U. S. model 1855 arms. The drawings, pertaining to the small arms taken from this manual, are included here.

AN ACT to provide for munitions of war, and for other purposes.

SEC. 1. Be it enacted by the Confederate States of America in Congress assembled, That the President, or the Secretary of War under his direction, is hereby authorized and empowered to make contracts for the purchase and manufacture of heavy ordnance and small arms; and of machinery for the manufacture or alteration of small arms and munitions of war, and to employ the necessary agents and artisans for these purposes; and to make contracts for the establishment of powder mills and the manufacture of powder; and the President is authorized to make contracts provided for in this act, in such manner and on such terms as in his judgment the public exigencies may require.
Approved February 20, 1861.

Montgomery, Ala., February 21, 1861.
Capt. R. SEMMES:

DEAR SIR: As agent of the Confederate States you are authorized to proceed, as hereinafter set forth, to make purchases and contracts for machinery and munitions, or for the manufacture of arms and munitions of war. Of the proprietor of the Hazard Powder Company, in Connecticut, you will probably be able to obtain cannon and musket powder, the former to be of the coarsest grain, and also to engage with him for the establishment of a powder mill at some point in the limits of our territory. The quantity of powder to be supplied immediately will exceed his stock on hand, and the arrangement for further supply should, if possible, be by manufacture in our own territory. If this is not practicable, means must be sought for further shipments from any and all sources which are reliable. At the arsenal at Washington you will find an artificer named Wright, who has brought the cap-making machine to its present state of efficiency, and who might furnish a cap machine and accompany it to direct its operations. If not in this, I hope you may in some way be able to obtain a cap machine with little delay, and have it sent to the Mount Vernon Arsenal, Ala. We shall require a manufactory of friction-primers, and will, if possible, induce some capable person to establish one in our country. The demand of the Confederate States will be the inducement in this as in the case of the powder mill proposed. A short time since the most improved machinery for the manufacture of rifles, intended for Harper's Ferry Arsenal, was, it was said, for sale by the manufacturer. If it be so at this time, you will procure it for the Government and use the needful precaution in relation to its transportation. Mr. Barbour, the superintendent of the Harper's Ferry Armory, can give you all the information in that connection which you may require. Mr. Ball, the master armorer at Harper's Ferry, is willing to accept service under our Government, and could probably bring with him some skilled workmen. If we get the machinery this will be important. Machinery for grooving muskets and heavy guns, with persons skilled in their use, is, I hope, to be purchased ready-made. If not, you will contract for their manufacture and delivery. You will endeavor to obtain the most improved shot for rifled cannon, and persons skilled in the preparation of shot and other fixed ammunition. Capt. G. W. Smith and Captain Lovell, late of the U. S. Army, and now of New York City, may aid you in your task; and you will please say to them that we would be happy to have their services in our army. You will make such inquiries as your varied knowledge will suggest in relation to the supply of guns of different calibers, especially the largest. I suggest the advantage, if to be obtained, of having a few of the 15-inch guns like the one cast at Pittsburgh. I have not sought to prescribe so as to limit your inquiries, either as to object or place, but only to suggest for your reflection and consideration the points which have chanced to come under my observation. You will use your discretion in visiting places where information of persons or things is to be obtained for the furtherance of the object in view. Any contracts made will be sent to the Hon. L. P. Walker, Secretary of War, for his approval, and the contractor need not fear that delay will be encountered in the action of this Government.

Very respectfully, yours, &c.,

JEFFERSON DAVIS.

CONFEDERATE STATES OF AMERICA, WAR DEPARTMENT,
Montgomery, Ala., May 7, 1861.

Hon. HOWELL COBB,
President of the Congress;

SIR: In answer to the inquiry contained in the resolution adopted by the Congress May 4, asking whether "any measures have been taken to promote and induce manufactures of arms and of powder within the States of this Confederacy or elsewhere," I have to state that until recently reliance was naturally placed on extensive orders to Northern factories of powder for a supply of that material. As soon, however, as it became evident that this resource could no longer be relied on, the attention of the Department was turned toward obtaining supplies of saltpeter, the only mineral constituent of powder which could be obtained from the soil of this country. Information having reached me that deposits of nitrous earth existed in . . .

FIREARMS OF THE CONFEDERACY

In reference to the manufacture of small-arms the prospect is not so satisfactory, and it is probable that the Government will be obliged to initiate steps toward the immediate establishment of a manufactory of this kind of arms. In a matter of this sort, in which prompt action is vital, I recommend, in answer to the latter part of the resolution of Congress asking my opinion as to the action deemed necessary to promote the manufacture of arms and powder that a competent agent be selected and sent without delay to England. At London a complete set of machinery exists, which was made in this country, after the pattern of the machines at Springfield, in the United States. It would, I think, be no difficult matter to get these machines copied and executed on the spot with rapidity. Triplicate machines should be ordered to insure the chances of delivery of at least one set. For this purpose an additional appropriation of $300,000 may be needed, under the appropriation of ordnance and ordnance stores and supplies, for the three sets of machinery. Should they all arrive they will, even if not required by the Government, be easily disposed of. The amount already asked for under the head of armories and arsenals would also require to be increased by an item of $75,000 for a suitable building in which to place this machinery at one of our arsenals, or the machinery, when so procured, might be placed, if thought desirable, in the hands of parties having manufacturing facilities, who could give ample security for its application to the sole uses of this Government. No further action is deemed necessary to stimulate the production of powder than, perhaps, to make advances to parties who offer to engage in its production, to enable them to prosecute researches after saltpeter in remote districts difficult of access. It might be advisable to offer a bonus of, say, $5 per barrel of 100 pounds on every barrel produced and received by the Government within the current year.

Respectfully, your obedient servant,

L. P. WALKER,
Secretary of War.

CONFEDERATE STATES OF AMERICA, WAR DEPARTMENT,
Richmond, July 24, 1861.

To the PRESIDENT:

SIR: I herewith transmit . . . Every possible effort, as you are aware, has been made to procure them. It may not be improper in this connection to state briefly, for the information of Congress, what this Department has done to accomplish this object. It has outstanding contracts with citizens of this Government for the manufacture of 61,200 stand of small-arms, and orders have been sent abroad for 200,000 more, with skillful ordnance officers to see them properly executed. Agents have also been sent to Cuba and Mexico to purchase arms. Thus the contracts and outstanding orders for the purchase and manufacture of arms (not embracing the orders sent to Cuba and Mexico) are for 261,000 stand of the best quality, with corresponding accouterments and equipments.

Besides these contracts and orders, agents have been sent into all the States of the Confederacy, not only to purchase arms, but to encourage by liberal orders their manufacture by all persons who could make them, whether in small or large quantities; and to induce our people to bring into the service of the Government whatever arms they might have, the Department has proposed to pay for them upon assessments of value to be made by officers of the Government. The armories at Richmond and Fayetteville will soon be in a condition to manufacture muskets and rifles on a large scale, which will complete the arrangements of the Department for the supply of small-arms . . . to provide clothing for the Army, feeling satisfied as I do that no army should be left to the hazards of chance or the possibilities of individual supply for either raiment or food.

Very respectfully,

L. P. WALKER,
Secretary of War.

AN ACT to authorize advances to be made in certain cases.

The congress of the Confederate States of America do enact, That the Secretary of War, with the approbation of the President, be authorized during the existence of the present war to make advances upon any contract, not to exceed 33 1-3 per cent, for arms or munition of war: Provided, That security be first taken, to be approved by the Secretary of War, for the performance of the contract, or for a proper accounting for the said money.

Approved August 5, 1861.

CONFEDERATE STATES OF AMERICA,
ORDNANCE OFFICE, WAR DEPARTMENT,
Richmond, Va., August 12, 1861.

Answer to interrogatories under resolution of Congress of July 27.

First interrogatory. What quantity of muskets and rifles has the Government on hand besides those which have already been distributed to the Army?

Answer. All our serviceable muskets and rifles are in the hands of troops in the field, at posts, or in camp. The Government has on hand 3,500 muskets, chiefly flintlocks, and all of which should be passed through the workshop.

Second interrogatory . . .

Sixth interrogatory. Have any small-arms yet been manufactured by and for the Government at any public or private establishment within the Confederate States? If yea, state what arms have been so manufactured, in what quantities, and what establishments. If not, what has prevented or delayed such manufacture?

Answer. Very few arms have yet been manufactured for the Government either at private or public establishments for a very obvious reason—there has not yet been time to get up establishments for this purpose. A few—eight or ten per day for four or five weeks past—it is reported, have been made out of the gun-barrels saved from Harper's Ferry, at Wytheville, for the command of General Floyd. An order for 30,000 stand of arms has been given to Messrs. McElwain & Co., Holly Springs, Miss., the first delivery on which is to be made November 1, and thereafter at the rate of 2,000 per month. Mr. LeMat, of Louisiana, has an order to deliver 5,000 of his revolvers. Mr. Ed. Want, of New Berne, N. C., has an order for the delivery of 5,000 pistols, to begin in three months. Orders are out also for the manufacture of 4,000 swords and 1,000 saber-bayonets. Unlimited orders have also been given to parties to purchase arms in Mexico and Cuba. None have yet been received by this Department. The armory at this place will probably be in working order in six or eight weeks. That at Fayetteville, where some new buildings must be erected, will not be ready under four months. The Department has received from its agents in Europe for the purchase of arms positive information as to the purchase by them of arms, embracing muskets and rifles chiefly, to the amount of $300,000, and also assurances that they will be shipped through in safety. We therefore look forward with confidence to their early arrival.

FIREARMS OF THE CONFEDERACY

CONFEDERATE STATES OF AMERICA, WAR DEPARTMENT,
Richmond, Va., March 12, 1862.
The PRESIDENT:

SIR: I have the honor herewith to submit, in accordance with the resolution of Congress of the 26th ultimo, a "statement of the establishments now engaged in manufacturing small-arms under contract . . . ample supply of arms, powder, and percussion-caps for the use of our Army," I have the honor to report that the establishments for the manufacture of powder and percussion-caps are sufficient for the wants of the Army, but the chief material for the manufacture of powder, to wit, saltpeter, is not sufficiently abundant. The establishments for the manufacture of arms are woefully deficient, and cannot furnish more than one-tenth part of the necessary supply of small-arms. I know of no legislation which could aid the Department in procuring a supply of small-arms. Nearly every mechanic in the Confederacy competent to manufacture small-arms is believed to be engaged in the work. The manufacture of small-arms is a slow and tedious process, of years. When it is considered that the Government of the United States—with all its accumulation of arms for half a century, and all its workshops and arsenals, public and private, and its untrammeled intercourse with foreign nations—has recently been compelled to disband a number of cavalry regiments on account of the difficulty of arming them, and has been driven to the necessity of making purchases of arms in Europe in very large quantities, and of saltpeter by thousands of tons, some faint idea may be formed of the difficulties against which this Department has been and is now struggling in the effort to furnish arms and munitions for our troops.

The difficulty is not in the want of legislation. Laws cannot suddenly convert farmers into gunsmiths. Our people are not artisans, except to a very limited degree. In the very armory here at Richmond the production could be greatly increased if skilled labor could be procured. In the absence of home manufactures no recourse remains but importation, and with our commerce substantially at an end with foreign nations the means of importation are limited. I am unable to perceive in what way we can procure arms by the passage of laws . . . enemy into others, where their labor could be applied to the digging of ore and the furnishing of the fuel necessary for the production of iron.

I am, your obedient servant,

J. P. BENJAMIN,
Secretary of War.

FIREARMS OF THE CONFEDERACY

ORDNANCE BUREAU,
Richmond, January 7, 1863.

Hon. JAMES A. SEDDON,
Secretary of War:

SIR: In reply to the accompanying resolution of the House of Representatives of the Confederate States, transmitted to me by you, I have the honor to state that I have fixed the 1st day of September as the period to which my report is made. From some of the more remote arsenals and depots statements of fabrications and issues have not yet come in. The report is not therefore, as full as could be desired.

Small arms (rifles, muskets, carbines, and pistols):
Fabricated	14,349
Issued	294,753
Remaining on hand	9,876

Infantry accouterments (sets):
Fabricated	248,006
Issued	408,756
Remaining on hand	25,457

Infantry equipments:
Fabricated	137,913
Issue	252,415
Remaining on hand	18,579

Public armories:
Rifles, muskets, and carbines manufactured per month	2,050

Private armories:
Rifles, muskets, carbines, and pistols manufactured per month	1,550
Sabers manufactured per month	3,500

Average cost of—
Rifle or musket	$ 21.50
Carbine	42.50
Saber	18.00

Other private armories are under contract, and it is expected that the supply will be increased from them 500 firearms per month during the present year.

The capacity of the public armories will also be increased and the new and large armory at Macon, Ga., it is hoped, will be in operation before the close of the year.

Very respectfully, your obedient servant,

J. GORGAS,
Colonel and Chief of Ordnance.

August 24, 1863.

Respectfully returned.

Contents noted. A good breech-loading carbine is now making here in small numbers. No reliable carbines except muzzle-loaders are to be obtained abroad. Cavalry officers are not all agreed as to the value of the breech-loading carbine, and officers of great experience pronounce in favor of the muzzle-loading carbine. As the latter can be produced when the former cannot, I have ordered a model to be prepared, and have had it submitted to General Stuart for the criticism of his officers. As soon as its main features are settled it will be adopted . . .

J. GORGAS,
Colonel.

FIREARMS OF THE CONFEDERACY

CONFEDERATE STATES OF AMERICA, WAR DEPARTMENT,
ORDNANCE BUREAU,
Richmond, November 15, 1863.

Hon. JAMES A. SEDDON,
Secretary of War:

SIR: Since the last report rendered from this office the department . . .

SMALL-ARMS

Notwithstanding the heavy losses of arms at Vicksburg, Port Hudson, and at Gettysburg, computed at not less than 75,000 stand, the supply on hand has been steadily increasing. The armories at Richmond, Fayetteville, and Asheville have produced an aggregate of about 28,000 small-arms within the year. Those produced at private establishments will swell this number to full 35,000 (it may be fairly assumed that this number will be increased to 50,000 during the year ending September 30, 1864). Of these about 30,000 are infantry and 5,000 cavalry arms, including among the latter 3,000 Sharps carbines; the remainder are muzzle-loading of the uniform caliber of .5775, adopted for all muzzle-loading arms, whether for infantry, cavalry, or artillery.

Revolver pistols are fabricated under contract at Macon, Columbus, and Atlanta, Ga.; the number produced is about 500 per month now; this will be increased to 1,000 per month in the course of three or four months.

The supply of sabers produced under contract is abundant, though the style of workmanship admits of great improvement. Steps were early taken to establish another armory on an adequate scale; the site chosen was at Macon, where a plot of ground was given to the Confederate States for the purpose. Good progress has been made with the buildings, and Superintendent James H. Burton has just returned from Europe, where contracts have been made for the necessary machinery. A portion will be delivered in December. Meantime, with the tools and machinery saved from places abandoned to the enemy, work is progressing on such part of the gun-making machinery as can be made in this country. This armory will, when completed, be able to turn out from 1,500 to 2,000 stand per week. A portion of the machinery will be in position by the 1st of July next, if it should fortunately escape capture, and the whole establishment will, I hope, be completed as far as now intended in nine to twelve months thereafter. Only the most necessary buildings are now put up permanently, the construction of store-houses, outhouses, &c., being deferred to better days.

ARSENALS, ARMORIES, ETC.

The following are the principal establishments of the Ordnance Department. These employ 5,090 persons, of whom two-thirds are non-conscripts, disabled soldiers, boys, females, and slaves.

Richmond Arsenal, Richmond, Va., Lieut. Col. W. L. Brown; Richmond Armory, Richmond, Va., Superintendent W. S. Downer; harness shops, Clarksville, Va., Superintendent W. S. Downer; Danville Depot, Danville, Va., Captain E. S. Hutter; Lynchburg Depot, Lynchburg, Va., Capt. G. T. Getty; arsenal and armory, Fayetteville, N. C., Major F. L. Childs; foundry, Salisbury, N. C., Capt. A. G. Brenizer; Charleston Arsenal, Charleston, S. C., Maj. J. T. Trezevant; arsenal, foundry, and powder mills, Augusta, Ga., Col. G. W. Rains; Atlanta Arsenal, Atlanta, Ga., Col. M. H. Wright; Macon Arsenal, Macon, Ga., Lieut. Col. R. M. Cuyler; Macon Laboratory, Macon, Ga., Maj. J. W. Mallet; Macon Armory, Macon, Ga., Superintendent J. H. Burton; Montgomery Arsenal, Montgomery, Ala., Maj. C. G. Wagner; Columbus Arsenal, Columbus, Ga., Maj. F. C. Humphreys; Selma Arsenal, Selma, Ala., Lieut. Col. J. L. White.

Firearms of the Confederacy

At the arsenals, armories, workshops, and depots the following are a few of the principal items produced and issued during the year:

	Repaired .	Purchased.	Fabricated.	Issued to the Army.
Heavy artillery....................................	....	46	31	77
Siege artillery and artillery of reserve.....................	....	20	3	86
Field artillery....................................	12	173	79	514
Siege and sea-coast carriages......................	....	159	91	239
Field carriages, caissons, battery wagons, forges, &c........	567	404	302	934
Cavalry saddles....................................	1,763	30,381	6,866	49,357
Saddle blankets....................................	....	45,073	2,315	16,625
Artillery harness (2-horse)............................	373	2,729	2,453	4,221
Horseshoes (pounds)....................................	....	108,721	120,798	266,951
Horseshoe nails (pounds)............................	....	16,700	6,818	18,343
Bridles..	600	31,379	4,478	1,180
Halters..	162	39,172	16,472	396
Small-arms..	127,862	16,246	27,752	145,292
Sabers and swords.................................	3,397	43,559	....	35,144
Saber-belts..	....	22,155	14,054	30,770
Cartridge-boxes....................................	2,123	126,733	34,666	171,251
Cartridge-box belts................................	4,046	109,352	61,766	104,443
Waist-belts..	2,875	132,671	72,750	178,592
Cap-pouches.......................................	1,442	157,402	41,189	185,661
Bayonet-scabbards.................................	1,675	114,858	15,379	167,018
Knapsacks...	....	108,489	27,928	134,100
Haversacks..	....	46,383	226,450	227,020
Canteens..	1,278	73,422	85,291	212,270
Siege and sea-coast ammunition.....................	246	174,329	35,335	76,451
Field ammunition..................................	5,638	178,111	262,970	318,297
Small-arms cartridges..............................	940,440	81,750	36,531,466	44,933,907
Friction-primers...................................	....	16,099	288,526	812,557
McEvoy igniters...................................	....	78,806	....	79,846
Percussion-caps (musket)...........................	....	472,500	46,500,099	55,478,092
Percussion-caps (sporting)..........................	....	979,750	3,358,300	4,844,850
Powder (loose).....................................	....	40,175	1,417,882	1,638,298

Respectfully submitted,

J. Gorgas,
Colonel, Chief of Ordnance.

Adjt. and Insp. General's Office,
Richmond, January 14, 1864.

General Orders, No. 6.

I. Whenever ordnance stores are lost or damaged in any brigade it . . .

VI. The use of the sword-bayonet having been generally disapproved by boards of officers in the field, to whom the question of its usefulness was referred, its manufacture has been ordered to be discontinued. The triangular bayonet will be substituted.

S. Cooper,
Adjutant and Inspector General.

Adjutant and Inspector General's Office,
Richmond, March 19, 1864.

General Orders No. 35.

I. Officers on inspection duty, while traveling under the immediate . . .

IX. The following is published as supplementary to the schedule of average cost of arms, parts of arms, and accouterments, as set forth in General Orders, No. 158, Adjutant and Inspector General's Office, December 3, 1863:

FIREARMS OF THE CONFEDERACY

Carbine (breech-loading)	....$75.00	Horse brush	$ 2.00
Carbine (muzzle-loading)	.... 60.00	Bridle	14.00
Parts of same. (See prices of parts of rifle, model 1855.)		Bit	2.00
		Girth	5.00
		Stirrups	2.00
Skeleton saddles	75.00	Bridle reins	7.00
Halter	12.00	Spurs	1.50
Crupper	3.00	Curry comb	1.25
Stirrup leathers	6.00	Nose bag	2.50
Mess blanket	4.00	Cartridges of all kinds,	
Halter reins	5.00	each	.25
Headstall	7.00	Caps of all kinds, each ..	.02½

The price of bayonets is increased to $11 each.

By order:

S. COOPER,
Adjutant and Inspector General.

C. S. ARMORY,
Richmond, September 22, 1864.

Col. J. GORGAS,
Chief of Ordnance:

COLONEL: I beg to present for your information a list of rifle muskets manufactured North, and their places of manufacture:

Springfield U. S. rifle, manufactured at Springfield, Mass.

Philadelphia U. S. Rifle, manufactured at Philadelphia, Pa.

Bridesburg U. S. rifle, manufactured at Bridesburg, Pa.

Park, Snow & Co. U. S. rifle, manufactured at Meriden, Conn.

Colt U. S. rifle, manufactured at Hartford, Conn.

Whitney U. S. rifle, manufactured at Whitneyville, Conn.

Wm. Muir & Co. U. S. rifle, manufactured at Windsor Locks, Conn.

Norwich U. S. rifle, manufactured at Norwich, Conn.

L. G. & Y. U. S. rifle, manufactured at Windsor, Vt.

Providence Tool Company U. S. rifle, manufactured at Providence, R. I.

E. Robinson U. S. rifle, manufactured at New York.

U. A. Co. U. S. rifle, manufactured at New York.

Remington U. S. rifle, manufactured at Ilion, N. Y.

Watertown U. S. rifle, manufactured at Watertown, Mass.

Wm. Mason U. S. rifle, manufactured at Taunton, Mass.

Eagleville Company U. S. rifle, manufactured at place not known.

Norfolk U. S. rifle, manufactured at Norfolk, Va.

Among the old arms received in this armory for repairs during the current month I have noticed the above arms from a variety of manufacturing establishments, all of them made after the U. S. '55 model and all interchanging with the Richmond rifle musket except in lock plate and mainspring, which have been altered in the Northern arms.

I suppose there are in the north (including breech-loading) not less than thirty-eight armories, all on a large scale, and their total product probably will not fall short of 5,000 arms per day.

I am, colonel, your very obedient servant,

S. ADAMS,
Master Armorer.

FIREARMS OF THE CONFEDERACY

[FIRST INDORSEMENT]

October 16, 1864.

Respectfully forwarded to the President for notice.

This paper exhibits a most marked contrast to our own condition in this respect. We are not making an average of 100 arms per day in the Confederacy, though we have machinery enough to make 300 (including pistols), and would soon have the workmen if they could remain undisturbed.

I cannot help thinking that the policy of the War Department ought to be modified so far as to appropriate to this duty 500 or 600 men liable to military duty. This, with the exempts, would form a sufficient force. It would be necessary to relieve them from all military duty and attach them permanently to this duty.

J. GORGAS,
Chief of Ordnance.

CONFEDERATE STATES OF AMERICA, WAR DEPARTMENT,
ORDNANCE BUREAU,
Richmond, December 31, 1864.

Hon. JAMES A. SEDDEN,
Secretary of War:

SIR: In reply to your inquiry for information as to the means of supplying munitions of war, "confining the answer to the munitions" furnished by this Bureau to the cis-Mississippi, I have the honor to state, first, as to arms: There are enough arms on hand of a mixed character—that is, arms most of which are not as good as those now in the hands of troops in the field—to arm and equip some additional force. The returns of November, 1864, showed on hand at the various arsenals and depots:

Rifles of caliber .58	3,882
Rifles of caliber .54	2,759
Smooth-bore muskets .69	3,564
Smooth-bore muskets .75	636
All other infantry arms	10,504
Carbines	2,596

This amount can be probably increased by 10,000 or 12,000 by a vigorous system of collecting the arms scattered about through the country.

IMPORTATIONS

We have hitherto had no difficulty in importing arms through the blockaded seaports. The total importations for the year have been:

Rifles	39,798
Pistols	1,716
Carbines	4,740

The want of funds necessary to purchase has greatly limited the importations of the expiring year. There are probably not more than 10,000 or 12,000 on the islands awaiting shipment.

MANUFACTURED

The number of arms manufactured and made up of parts derived from capture and other sources for the year ending November 30, 1864, were:

Rifles, caliber .58	12,778
Carbines	5,354
Pistols	2,353

FIREARMS OF THE CONFEDERACY

There is machinery enough under the control of this Bureau to manufacture 55,000 rifles and carbines per annum, provided a sufficient mechanical force be employed as follows:

Armory.	Number of rifles.	Number of workmen.
Richmond	25,000	450
Fayetteville	10,000	250
Columbia, S. C.	4,000	125
Athens, Ga.	10,000	250
Tallassee, Ala.	a6,000	150
Total	55,000	1,225

a Carbines.

The proviso is the workmen, and these must be permanently attached to those establishments and excused from the performance of all military duties, except perhaps local guard duty. The number actually employed is about 425, about 300 less than were employed, say twelve months since. Defection from service in the local forces and losses on the battlefield have thus greatly reduced our force of workmen.

By General Orders, No. 82, over 700 men were placed in the ranks; of these perhaps one-half were competent mechanics, many of them valuable for the service of the armories. The product could not at once be raised to the maximum figures above indicated, but could, with the 800 additional workmen, be so raised, allowing for the time it would take to teach and organize them.

For our cavalry arms we have chiefly to rely on importations, although pistols are being made at several points with success. Want of workmen alone prevents additional results. Sabers can be produced in sufficient numbers, and of pretty good quality, by the detail of a very few workmen from the field . . .

The chief detriment the operations of the Bureau have had has arisen from interference with its workmen for military purposes.

J. GORGAS,
Brigadier-General and Chief of Ordnance.

ADJT. AND INSP. GENERAL'S OFFICE,
Richmond, November 26, 1863

General Orders, No. 154.

I. No ordnance or ordnance stores other than those prescribed in the Ordnance Manual, edition of 1863, or specially approved by the Ordnance Bureau, are allowed to be purchased or fabricated. The permission given to officers by paragraph 1232, Army Regulations (paragraph 9, Ordnance Regulations), to provide ordnance and ordnance stores, "in case of urgent necessity," is to be exercised, subject to the above restrictions.

II. Accounts paid by disbursing officers for the purchase, fabrication, or repair of ordnance and ordnance stores contrary to the foregoing order will not be admitted in the settlement of their accounts.

By order:

S. COOPER,
Adjutant and Inspector General.

BRIGADIER GENERAL JOSIAH GORGAS

Josiah Gorgas, distinguished as chief of ordnance of the Confederate States, was born in Dauphin county, Pennsylvania, July 1, 1818. He was graduated at West Point as No. 6 in the class of 1841, and was assigned to the ordnance department of the United States army. In 1845-46 he was in Europe on leave of absence for the study of his profession in foreign lands, and in the year following his return he went into active service in the Mexican war. March 3, 1847, he was promoted to first lieutenant. He served with distinction in the siege of Vera Cruz and was subsequently in charge of the ordnance depot at that point. On the return of peace he served as assistant ordnance officer at various arsenals until placed in command of Mt. Vernon arsenal, Alabama, in 1853. In December of that year he was married to the daughter of ex-Governor Gayle, of Mobile. He was promoted to captain in 1855, transferred to Kennebec (Maine) arsenal in 1856, commanded the Charleston (S. C.) arsenal until 1860, and was then transferred to Pennsylvania. In the latter year he served as a member of the ordnance board. Resigning in April, 1861, he removed with his family to Alabama, and received from President Davis the appointment of chief of ordnance of the Confederate States, then "the most important scientific and administrative office in the government." Fully appreciating the great poverty of the South in this department, he promptly sent an efficient officer to Europe to procure arms, located arsenals, and made immediate preparation for the manufacture of powder and saltpeter, and the development of lead and copper mines, also preparing elaborate papers showing the proper distribution of heavy armament for effective defense against invasion. At an early date he insisted upon the use of cotton and tobacco to procure military supplies, and arranged for an effective service by blockade runners. Out of his suggestion and practical action grew the bureau of foreign supplies and the mining and niter bureau. He displayed remarkable ability in the selection of officials for the work under his control, and impressed all those brought into intercourse with him as an executive officer of remarkable energy and ability, though his modesty rendered him little known to the general public. "He created the ordnance department out of nothing," was the brief and comprehensive verdict of General J. E. Johnston. After the practical dissolution of the Confederate government at Charlotte, N. C., in the spring of 1865, he returned to Alabama, and promptly turned his activity into industrial channels as superintendent of the Briarfield iron works. Soon afterward he was appointed headmaster and later vice-chancellor of the University of the South at Sewanee, Tennessee. In 1877 he became president of the University of Alabama, but after a brief tenure was compelled by failing health to resign. The trustees desiring his continued presence, he accepted the office of librarian, and was thus connected with the university until his death, May 15, 1883.

From the
CONFEDERATE MILITARY HISTORY
*   *   *   *   *
Atlanta, Ga.
Confederate Publishing Company
1899

*   *   *   *   *

COL. JAMES H. BURTON

Col. James Henry Burton, whose war time papers provide such a valuable source of Confederate small arms information, and who is so often quoted in connection with the activities of the Confederate ordnance department, was born of English parents August 17, 1823, at Shennondale Springs, Jefferson county, Virginia. After receiving an education at Westchester Academy, Pennsylvania, he entered, at the age of 16, a machine shop in Baltimore to learn the business of practical machinist. He was there four years.

In 1844 he took employment at the rifle works of the U. S. Armory at Harper's Ferry and was appointed foreman in 1845. While there he invented the self-expanding bullet.[1] Later he was appointed master armorer, which position he held until 1854. In 1855 he accepted the appointment of chief engineer of the Royal Arms factory at Enfield, near London, England. Five years later, because of failing health, he returned to Virginia.

In June, 1861, Burton was commissioned Lieutenant-Colonel of Ordnance by Governor John Letcher and placed in charge of the Virginia State Armory with instructions to arrange for the removal to that place with the utmost dispatch of the ma-

---

[1] See "Reports of Experiments with Small Arms, 1856," published by the War Department for an account of Burton's experiments.

111

chinery captured at Harper's Ferry. Within 90 days after the date of his commission, he had the machinery in Richmond producing rifles of the U. S. Army pattern.

The following December he was commissioned by President Davis, Superintendent of Armories, with the rank of Lieutenant Colonel. During the summer of 1863 Colonel Burton was sent to Europe on business for the State Department. At the close of the war and after recovering from a severe illness, Colonel Burton and his family spent three years in England. Upon his return he settled in Loudoun county, Va., where he lived until 1871.

In that year he returned to England for a private firm in Leeds, Greenwood and Batley—to direct a contract with the Russian Government for the supply of machinery for a small arms factory at Tula, in Central Russia. The factory was to manufacture the Berdan rifle. In 1873 he resigned and came back to Virginia. From then until his death October 18, 1894, he followed the peaceful pursuit of a farmer near Winchester.

THE FOLLOWING ARTICLE ON
CONFEDERATE ORDNANCE
by
GENERAL GORGAS
was taken from
THE CONFEDERATE SOLDIER IN THE CIVIL WAR
Edited by
Ben La Bree
Published by
The Courier-Journal Job Printing Company
Louisville, Ky.
1895.

It was printed in ARMY ORDNANCE, January-February 1936 with the following notation.

This is an historic document. In it the Chief of Ordnance of the Confederacy narrates many important facts not heretofore generally available.

General Gorgas' manuscript is entitled "Extracts from my notes written chiefly after the close of the war." It was forwarded by his son, the late Maj. Gen. W. C. Gorgas, then head of the Department of Sanitation, Panama Canal Zone, on April 8, 1911 to Major General William Crozier, then Chief of Ordnance of the United States Army. In his letter of transmittal Gen. W. C. Gorgas wrote: "Please find enclosed copy of some notes of my father concerning the Ordnance Department of the Confederacy. Extracts from these notes have been used by President Jefferson Davis in his book concerning the Confederacy, and they will possibly be used elsewhere. I thought they might interest you."

It is doubtful whether there is a more valuable ordnance paper in existence. In the belief that the object lesson it teaches contains great current significance and the record it recounts great tribute to the improvization and ability of a great man and his organization. ARMY ORDNANCE herewith presents the original manuscript. No attempt has been made to supply incomplete references in the original text.— *Editor*.

ORDNANCE DEPARTMENT
of the
CONFEDERATE GOVERNMENT
by
BRIGADIER-GENERAL JOSIAH GORGAS
Chief of Ordnance of the Confederate States.

At the formation of the Government, or, at the beginning of the war, the arms at command were distributed as follows, as nearly as I can recollect:

SMALL ARMS

	Rifles	*Muskets*
At Richmond, Va. (about)	4,000	
Fayetteville Arsenal, North Carolina (about)	2,000	25,000
Charleston Arsenal, South Carolina (about)	2,000	20,000
Augusta Arsenal, Georgia (about)	3,000	28,000
Mount Vernon Arsenal, Alabama	2,000	20,000
Baton Rouge Arsenal, Louisiana	2,000	27,000
	15,000	120,000

There were at Richmond about sixty thousand old, worthless flint muskets, and at Baton Rouge about ten thousand old Hall's rifles and carbines.

Besides the foregoing, there were at Little Rock, Ark., a few thousand stands, and some few at the Texas Arsenals, increasing the aggregate of serviceable arms to, say, one hundred and forty-three thousand. To these must be added the arms owned by the several states and by military organizations throughout the country, giving, say, one hundred and fifty thousand in all for the use of the armies of the Confederacy. The rifles were of the caliber fifty-four, known as Mississippi rifles, except those at Richmond, taken from Harper's Ferry, which were caliber fifty-eight; the muskets were the old flintlock, caliber sixty-nine, altered to percussion. Of sabers there were a few boxes at each arsenal, and some short artillery swords. A few hundred holster pistols were scattered here and there. There were no revolvers.

AMMUNITION, POWDER AND LEAD

There was little ammunition of any kind, or powder, at the arsenals in the South, and that little relics of the Mexican war, stored principally at Baton Rouge and Mount Vernon arsenals. I doubt whether there were a million rounds of small arm cartridges in the Confederacy. Lead there was none in store. Of powder the chief supply was that captured at Norfolk, though there was a small quantity at each of the Southern arsenals, say sixty thousand pounds in all, chiefly old cannon powder. The stock of percussion caps could not have exceeded one-quarter of a million.

ARTILLERY

There were no batteries of serviceable field artillery at any of the Southern arsenals. A few old iron guns, mounted on Gribeaural carriages, fabricated about the time of the War of 1812, composed nearly the entire park, which the Confederate States fell heir to. There were some serviceable batteries belonging to the States, and some which belonged to volunteer companies. There were neither harness, saddles, bridles, blankets, nor other artillery or cavalry equipments.

Thus to furnish one hundred and fifty thousand men on both sides of the Mississippi, on, say, the 1st of May, 1861 there were on hand no infantry accouterments, no cavalry arms or equipments, no artillery, and, above all, no ammunition; nothing save small arms, and these almost wholly smooth-bore, altered from flint to percussion. Let us see what means we had for producing these supplies.

ARSENALS, WORKSHOPS, FOUNDRIES, ETC.

Within the limits of the Confederate States there were no arsenals at which any of the material of war was constructed. No arsenal, except that at Fayetteville, N. C., had a single machine above a foot-lathe. Such arsenals as there were had been used only as depots. All the work of preparation of material had been carried on at the North; not an arm, not a gun, not a gun-carriage, and, except during the Mexican War, scarcely a round of ammunition had for fifty years been prepared in the Confederate States. There were, consequently, no workmen, or very few of them, skilled in these arts. No powder, save perhaps, for blasting, had been made at the South; and there was no salt-peter in store at any point; it was stored wholly at the North. There was no lead, nor any mines of it, except on the northern limit of the Confederacy, in Virginia, and the situation of that made its product precarious. Only one cannon foundry existed—at Richmond. Copper, so necessary for field artillery and for percussion caps, was just being produced in East Tennessee. There was no rolling mill for bar iron south of Richmond, and but few blast furnaces, and these small and, with trifling exceptions, in the border States of Virginia and Tennessee. Such were the supplies and such the situation when I took charge of the Ordnance Department on the 8th of April, 1861.

The first thing to be attended to was the supply of powder. Large orders had been sent to the North, both by the Confederate Government and some of the States, and these were being rapidly filled at the date of the attack on Fort Sumter. The entire product of one large Northern mill was being received at a Southern port. Of course, all the ports were soon sealed to such importations from the North. Attention was at once turned to the production of niter in North Alabama and in Tennessee—in the latter State under the energetic supervision of its Ordnance Department. An adequate supply of sulphur was found in New Orleans, where large quantities were in store to be used in sugar-refining. The entire stock was secured, amounting to some four or five hundred tons.

The erection of a large powdermill was early pressed by President Davis, and about the middle of June, 1861, he directed me to detail an officer to select a site and begin the work. The day after this order was given Colonel G. W. Rains, a graduate of West Point, in every way qualified for this service arrived in Richmond, through the blockade, and at once set out, under written instructions from me, to carry out the President's wishes. He, however, went first to East Tennessee to supervise and systematize the operations of two small private mills, which were then at work for the State of Tennessee.

Thus, in respect to powder and our means of making it, we had, perhaps, at this time (June 1, 1861), two hundred and fifty thousand pounds, chiefly cannon, at Norfolk and in Georgia, and as much more niter (mainly imported by the State of Georgia). We had no powdermills except the two rude ones just referred to, and no experience in making powder or in getting niter. All had to be learned.

As to a further supply of arms, steps had been taken by the president to import these and other ordnance stores from Europe; and Major Caleb Huse, a graduate of West Point, and at that moment professor in the University at Alabama, was selected to go abroad and secure them. He left Montgomery, under instructions, early in April, with credit of ten thousand pounds (!) from Mr. Memminger. The

114

appointment proved a happy one, for he succeeded with a very little money, in buying a good supply, and in running the Ordnance Department into debt for nearly a half million sterling—the very best proof of his fitness for his place, and of a financial ability which supplemented the narrowness of Mr. Memminger's purse.

Before this, and immediately upon the formation of the Confederate Government, Admiral Semmes had been sent to the North by President Davis as purchasing agent of arms and other ordnance stores, and succeeded in making contracts for, and purchases of powder, percussion caps, cap machinery (never delivered), revolvers, etc. He also procured drawings for a bullet-pressing machine and other valuable information.

The sets of machinery for making the rifle with sword bayonet, and the rifle-musket model of 1855, had been seized at Harper's Ferry by the State of Virginia. That for the rifle-musket was being transferred by the State to her ancient armory at Richmond under the direction of Lieutenant Colonel Burton, an officer in the service of Virginia, whose experience in the armories of the United States and in the erection of the works at Enfield, near London, qualified him above all for the work. The other set of machines was sent to Fayetteville, N. C., by consent of the State of Virginia, to be there re-erected, as there was at that point an arsenal with steam power and some good buildings, which had heretofore never been put to any use. These two sets of machinery—capable, if worked with but one set of hands to each, of producing two thousand to two thousand five hundred stands per month in all—were the only prospective resources at home. With additional workmen and some extension of the machinery, much larger results could be obtained. But the workmen were not to be had. As it was, it would take many months to put it in working order. Parts were missing and some injury done in the hasty transfer (partly under fire) from Harper's Ferry. There were no private armories at the South; nor was there any inducement, prior to the war, to turn capital in that direction. Thus, the class of skilled operatives needed were unknown to this region. In New Orleans the Brothers Cook were embarking in the business of making small arms, assisted by the purses and encouraged by the sympathy of patriotic citizens.

In field artillery the production was confined almost entirely to the Tredegar Works in Richmond. Some castings were made in New Orleans, and foundries were rapidly acquiring the necessary experience to produce good bronze castings. The Ordnance Department of Tennessee was also turning its attention to the manufacture of field and siege artillery at Nashville. At Rome, Ga., a foundry—Noble & Son—was induced to undertake the casting of three inch rifles after drawings furnished at Montgomery, but the progress made was necessarily slow. The State of Virginia possessed a number of old four-pounder iron guns, which were reamed out to get a good bore, and were rifled with three grooves, after the manner of Parrott. The army in observation at Harper's Ferry and that at Manassas were supplied with old batteries of six-pounder guns and twelve-pounder howitzers. A few Parrott guns, purchased by the State of Virginia, were with Magruder at Big Bethel.

For the ammunition and equipments required for the infantry and artillery a good laboratory and shops had been established at Richmond by the State, but none of the Southern arsenals were yet in a condition to do much work. The arsenal at Augusta, Ga., was directed to organize for the preparation of ammunition and the making of knapsacks, of which there were none wherewith to equip the troops now daily taking the field. The arsenal at Charleston and the depot at Savannah were occupied chiefly with local work. The arsenal at Baton Rouge was rapidly getting under way, and that at Mt. Vernon, Ala., was also being prepared for work. None of them had had facilities for the work usually done at an arsenal. Fayetteville, N. C., was in the hands of that State, and was occupied chiefly in repairing some arms and in making up a small amount of small arm ammunition. Little artillery ammunition was being made up, except for local purposes, save at Richmond.

Such was the general condition of supplies when the Government, quitting Montgomery, established itself at Richmond.

PROGRESS OF MANUFACTURE

Colonel Rains, in the course of the summer of 1861, established a refinery of saltpeter at or near Nashville, and to this point chiefly were sent the niter obtained from the State of Georgia, and that derived from caves in East and Middle Tennessee. He supplied the two powder-mills in that State with niter properly refined, and good powder was thus produced. A small portion of the Georgia niter was sent to two small mills in South Carolina—at Pendleton and Walhalla—and a powder produced, inferior at first but afterward improved. The State of North Carolina established a mill near Raleigh, under contract with certain parties to whom the State was to furnish the niter, of which a great part was derived from caves in Georgia. A stamping mill was also put up near New Orleans, and powder produced before the fall of the city. Small quantities of powder were also received through the blockade from Wilmington to Galveston, some of it of very inferior quality. The great quantity of artillery placed in position from the Potomac to the Rio Grande required a vast supply of powder (there was no immediate want of projectiles) to furnish even the scant allowance of fifty rounds to each gun. I think we may safely estimate that on the 1st of January, 1862, there were fifteen hundred sea coast guns of various calibers in position from Evansport on the Potomac to Fort Brown on the Rio Grande. If we average their caliber at thirty-two pounders, and the charge at five pounds, it will, at forty rounds per gun, give us six hundred thousand pounds of powder for these. The field artillery, say three hundred guns, with two hundred rounds to the piece, would require, say one hundred and twenty-five thousand pounds and the small-arm cartridges, ten million, would consume one hundred and twenty-five thousand pounds more—making in all eight hundred and fifty thousand pounds. If we deduct two hundred and fifty thousand pounds, supposed to be on hand in various shapes at the beginning of the war, we have an increment of six hundred thousand pounds. Of this perhaps two hundred thousand pounds had been made at the Tennessee and other mills, leaving four hundred thousand to have been supplied through the blockade and before the commencement of actual hostilities.

The site of the Government Powdermills was fixed at Augusta, Ga., on the report of Colonel Rains and progress was made on the work in this year. There were two large buildings, in the Norman (castellated) style of architecture; one contained the refinery and storeroom—the other being the mills, twelve in number. They were arranged in the best way on the canal which supplied water power to Augusta. This canal served as the means of transport for the material from point to point of its manufacture, though the mills were driven by steam. All the machinery, including the very heavy rollers, was made in the Confederate States. The various qualities of powder purchased, captured and produced were sources of irregularity in the ranges of our artillery and small arms—unavoidably so, of course. We were only too glad to take any sort of powder; and we bought some brought into Florida, the best range of which scarcely exceeded one hundred and sixty yards with the eprouvette.

Contracts were made abroad for the delivery of niter through the blockade, and for producing it at home from caves. The amount of the latter delivered by contracts was considerable—chiefly in Tennessee.

FIREARMS OF THE CONFEDERACY

The consumption of lead was in part met by the Virginia Lead Mines (Wytheville), the yield from which was from one hundred thousand to one hundred and fifty thousand pounds per month. A laboratory for the smelting of other ores from the Silver Hill Mines, North Carolina, and Jonesboro, East Tennessee was put up at Petersburg, under the direction of Dr. Piggott, of Baltimore. It was very well constructed; was capable of smelting a good many thousand pounds per day, and was in operation before midsummer of 1862. Mines were opened on account of Government in East Tennessee, near the State Line of Virginia. They were never valuable, and were soon abandoned. Lead was collected in considerable quantities throughout the country by the laborious exertions of agents employed for this purpose. The battlefield of Bull Run was fully gleaned and much lead collected.

By the close of 1861 the following arsenals and depots were at work, having been supplied with some machinery and facilities, and were producing the various munitions and equipments required: Augusta, Ga.; Charleston, S. C.; Fayetteville, N. C.; Richmond, Va.; Savannah, Ga.; Nashville, Tenn.; Memphis, Tenn.; Mount Vernon, Ala.; Baton Rouge, La.; Montgomery, Ala.; Little Rock, Ark.; and San Antonio, Texas—altogether eight arsenals and four depots. It would, of course, have been better, had it been practicable, to have condensed our work and to have had fewer places of manufacture; but the country was deficient in the transportation which would have been required to place the raw material at a few arsenals. In this way only could we avail ourselves of local resources, both labor and material. Thus, by the close of 1861, a good deal had been done in the way of organization to produce the material of war needed by an army, as far as our means permitted. But our troops were still very poorly armed and equipped. The old smooth-bore musket was still the principal weapon of the infantry; the artillery had the 6-pounder gun and 12-pounder howitzer chiefly; and the cavalry were armed with anything they could get—sabers, horse pistols, revolvers, Hall's carbines (a wretched apology), muskets cut off, Sharp's carbines, musketoons, short Enfield rifles, etc. Equipments were, in many cases, made of stout domestic, stitched in triple folds and covered with paint or rubber, varnished.

But poor as were our arms, we had not enough of these to equip the troops which were pressing to the front in July and August, 1861. In the winter of 1861-'62, while McClellan was preparing his great army near Alexandria, we resorted to the making of pikes for the infantry and lances for the cavalry; many thousands of the former were made at the various arsenals, but were little used. No access of enthusiasm could induce our people to rush to the field armed with pikes. I remember a formidable weapon, which was invented at this time, in the shape of a stout wooden sheath containing a two-edged straight sword some two feet long. The sheath or truncheon could be leveled, and the sword, liberated from the compression of a strong spring by touching a trigger, leaped out with sufficient force to transfix an opponent.

About December, 1861, arms began to come in through the purchases of Major Huse, and we had a good many Enfield rifles in the hands of our troops at Shiloh, which were received in time for use there through the blockade. Major Huse had found the market pretty well cleaned of arms by the late war in Europe, but he had succeeded in making contracts with private manufacturers, of which these arms were the result.

I will not attempt to trace the development of our work in its order, as I at first intended, but will note simply what I can recollect, paying some attention to the succession of events.

The winter of 1861-'2 was the darkest period of my department. Powder was called for on every hand—Bragg at Pensacola, for his big 10-inch columbiads; Lovell, at New Orleans, for his extended defenses, and especially for his inadequate artillery at Forts Jackson and

St. Phillips; Polk, at Columbus, Ky.; Johnston, for his numerous batteries on the Potomac; Magruder, at Yorktown. All these were deemed most important points. Then came Wilmington, Georgetown, Port Royal and Fernandina. Not a few of these places sent representatives to press their claims—Mr. Yulee, from Fernandina, and Colonel Gonzales, from Charleston. Heavy guns, too, were called for in all directions—the largest guns for the smallest places.

The abandonment of the line of the Potomac and of the upper Mississippi, from Columbus to Memphis; the evacuation of the works below Pensacola and of Yorktown somewhat relieved us from the pressure for heavy artillery; and after the powder mills at Augusta went into operation in the fall of 1862, we had little trouble in supplying ammunition.

To obtain the iron needed for cannon and projectiles, it became necessary to stimulate its production in Virginia, North Carolina, Tennessee, Georgia and Alabama. To this end, contracts were made with ironmasters in these States on liberal terms and advances of money made to them, to be refunded in products. These contracts were difficult to arrange, as so much had to be done for the contractor. He must have details from the army and the privilege of transport of provisions and other supplies over the railroads. And then the question of the currency was a continually recurring problem. Mr. Benjamin, who succeeded Mr. Walker in the War Department, gave me great assistance in the matter of making contracts, and seemed quite at home in arranging these details. His power of work was amazing to me, and he appeared as fresh at 12 o'clock at night, after a hard day's work, as he had been at 9 o'clock in the morning.

About May, 1862, finding that the production of niter and of iron must be systematically pursued, and to this end thoroughly organized, I sought for the right person to place in charge of this vital duty. My choice fell on Colonel I. M. St. John (afterward Commissary General of Subsistence), and was eminently fortunate. He had the gift of organization, and I placed him in charge of the whole subject of producing niter from caves and from other sources, and of the formation of niter beds, which had already been begun in Richmond. Under his supervision beds were instituted at Columbia, S. C., Charleston, Savannah, Augusta, Mobile, Selma and various other points. We never extracted niter from these beds except for trial; but they were carefully attended to, enriched and extended, and were becoming quite valuable. At the close of 1864 we had, according to General St. John, 2,800,000 cubic feet of earth collected and in various stages of nitrification, of which a large proportion was prepared to yield one and a half pounds of niter per foot of earth, including all the niter beds from Richmond to Florida.

Through Colonel St. John, the whole niter-bearing area of the country was laid off into districts; each district in charge of an officer, who made his monthly reports to the office at Richmond. These officers procured details of workmen, generally from those subject to military duty in the mountain regions where disaffection existed, and carried on extended works in their several districts. In this way we brought up the niter production, in the course of a year, to something like half our total consumption of niter. It was a rude, wild sort of service; and the officers in charge of these districts, especially in East Tennessee, North Carolina and North Alabama, had to show much firmness in their dealings with the turbulent people among whom and by whose aid they worked. It is a curious fact that the district on which we could rely for the most constant yield of niter, having its headquarters at Greensboro, N. C., had no niter caves in it. The niter was produced by the lixiviation of nitrous earth dug from under old houses, barns, etc.

The niter production thus organized, there was added to the Niter Bureau the duty of supervising the production of iron, lead, copper, and, in fine, all the minerals which needed development, including the making of sulphuric and nitric acids; which latter we had to manufacture to insure a supply of fulminate of mercury for our percussion caps. To give an idea of the extent of the duty thus performed: Colonel Morton, Chief of the Niter and Mining Bureau, after the transfer of General St. John, writes: "We were aiding and managing some twenty to thirty furnaces, with an annual yield of fifty thousand tons or more of pig metal. We had erected lead and copper smelting furnaces (at Petersburg, before referred to) with a capacity sufficient for all our wants, and had succeeded in smelting zinc of good quality at the same place." The chemical works were placed at Charlotte, N. C., where a pretty large leaden chamber for sulphuric acid was put up. Our chief supply of chemicals continued to come however from abroad, through the blockade, and these works, as well as our nitraries, were as much preparation against the day when the blockade might seal all foreign supply, as for present use . . . These constituted our reserves for final conflict.

We had not omitted to have a pretty thorough though general exploration of the mountain regions from Virginia to Alabama, with the hope of finding new deposits of lead. One of the earliest of these searches was made by Dr. Maupin, of the University of Virginia. No favourable results came from it. I remember an anecdote he told touching one of his researches. An old settler showed the doctor a small lump of lead which he had extracted from ore like some he had in his possession. There was the lead and here was the ore, but it was not an ore of lead. The doctor cross-examined: "Did he smelt it himself?" "Yes." "What in?" "An iron ladle," (such as is used for running lead balls.) "Was there nothing in the ladle but this sort of ore?" "No, nothing." "Nothing at all? No addition—no flux?" "No, nothing but a little handful of common shot, thrown in to make it melt more easily."

Much of the niter region was close to the lines of the enemy, and here and there along its great extent became debatable ground. Not seldom the whole working force had to be suddenly withdrawn on the approach of the enemy, the "plant" hurried off, to be again returned and work resumed when the enemy had retired. Much of the work, too, lay in "Union" districts where our cause was unpopular and where obstacles of all kinds had to be encountered and overcome. It was no holiday duty, this niter digging, although the service was a good deal decried by such as knew nothing of its nature.

MANUFACTURE OF INFANTRY, ARTILLERY AND CAVALRY EQUIPMENTS

In equipping the armies first sent into the field the supply of these accessories was amazingly scant; and these deficiencies were felt more keenly, perhaps, than the more important want of arms. We had arms, such as they were, for over one hundred thousand men; but we had no accouterments nor equipments; and these had to be extemporized in a great measure. In time, knapsacks were little thought of by the troops, and we at last contented ourselves with supplying haversacks, which the women (Heaven reward their labors) could make, and for which we could get cotton cloth. But cartridge boxes we must have; and as leather was also needed for artillery harness and cavalry saddles, we had to divide the stock of leather the country could produce among these much-neeeded articles. But soldiers' shoes were even more needed than some of these; so that as all could not be fully provided, a scale of preference was established. Shoes and cartridge boxes were most needed, and then saddles and bridles. The President, whose practical sagacity was rarely at fault, early reduced these interests to logical sequence. He said, "For the infantry, men must first be fed, next armed, and even clothing must follow these; for if they are fed and have arms and ammunition they can fight." Thus the Subsistence Department had, in a general way, a preference for its requisitions on the

Treasury; my department came next, and the Quartermaster's followed. Of course the Medical Department had in some things the lead of all, for its duties referred to the men themselves, and it was necessary first of all to keep the hospitals empty and the ranks full.

To economize leather, the cartridge boxes and waist belts were made of prepared cotton cloth, stitched in three or four thicknesses. Bridle-reins were also made, and even cartridge boxes covered with it, except the flap. Saddle skirts, too, were sometimes made in this way, heavily stitched. An ardent admirer of the South came over from Washington to offer his patent for making soldiers' shoes with no leather except the soles. The shoes were approved by all except those who wore them. The soldiers exchanged them with the first prostrate enemy who no longer needed his leathern articles. To get leather each department bargained for its own hides—made contracts with the tanner—procured hands for him by exemption from the army—got transportation over the railroads for the hides and for supplies and, finally, assisted the tanner to procure food for his hands and other supplies for his tannery. One can readily see from this instance how the labors of the heads of the departments became extended. Nothing but thorough organization could accomplish these multiplied and varied duties. We even established a fishery on the Cape Fear River to get oil for mechanical purposes, getting from the sturgeon beef at the same time for our workmen.

In cavalry equipments the main thing was to get a good saddle—one that did not ruin the back of the horse; for that, and not the rider's seat, is the point to be achieved. The rider soon accommodates himself to the seat provided for him. Not so the animal's back, which suffers from a bad saddle. We adopted Jenifer's tree, which did very well while the horses were in good condition, and was praised by that prince of cavalrymen, General J. E. B. Stuart; but it came down on the horse's backbone and withers as soon as the cushion of fat and muscle dwindled. The McClellan tree did better on the whole, and we finally succeeded in making a pretty good saddle of that kind—comfortable enough, but not as durable as the Federal article. In this branch of the service, one of the most difficult wants to supply was the horseshoe for cavalry and artillery. The want of iron and labor both were felt. Of course such a thing as a horseshoe machine, to turn out thousands an hour, was not to be dreamed of; besides we would have had little store of iron wherewith to feed it. Nor could we set up such machinery without much provision; for to concentrate all work on one machine required the transportation of the iron to one point, and the distribution of the shoes from it to all the armies. But the railroads were greatly overtasked, and we were compelled to consider this point. Thus we were led to employ every wayside blacksmith shop accessible, especially those in and near the theater of operations. These, again, had to be looked after, supplied with material, and exempted from service.

BUREAU OF FOREIGN SUPPLIES

It soon became obvious that in the Ordnance Department we must rely greatly on the introduction of articles of prime necessity through the blockade ports. As before stated, President Davis early saw this, and had an officer detailed to go abroad as the agent of the department. To systematize the introduction of the purchases, it was soon found advisable to own and run our own steamers. Major Huse made the suggestion also from that side of the water. Accordingly, he purchased and sent in the Robert E. Lee at a cost of £30,000, a vessel capable of stowing six hundred and fifty bales of cotton. This vessel was kept running between Bermuda and Wilmington, and made some fifteen to eighteen successive trips before she was finally captured—the first twelve with the regularity of a packet. She was commanded first by Captain Wilkinson, of the navy. Soon the Cornubia, named the Lady

FIREARMS OF THE CONFEDERACY

Davis, was added, and ran as successfully as the R. E. Lee. She had a capacity of about four hundred and fifty bales, and was, during the latter part of her career, commanded also by a former naval officer, Captain R. H. Gayle. These vessels were long, low and rather narrow, built for swiftness and with their lights out and with fuel that made little smoke they contrived to slip in and out of Wilmington at pleasure, in spite of a cordon of Federal cruisers eager for the spoils of a blockade runner. Other vessels—the Eugenia, a beautiful ship, the Stag and several others—were added, all devoted to carrying ordnance supplies, and finally general supplies. To supervise shipments at Bermuda, to which point they were brought by neutrals, either by steam or sail, Major Norman Walker was sent there by Mr. Secretary Randolph, about midsummer, 1862. Later, an army officer, Lieutenant Colonel Smith Stansbury, was detached to take charge of the stores accumulated there. Depots were likewise made at Nassau and Havana. Thus much of the foreign organization.

But the organization of the business outside of our own soil was much the simplest part of the service. The home administration. involved a variety of work so foreign to my other duties that I soon looked about for the proper person to discharge them in the most effective manner by exclusive devotion to them; and I had Lieutenant Colonel Bayne detailed to my office for this duty. He had been wounded at Shiloh, and on his recovery joined me about September, 1862.

It was soon found necessary, in order that the vessels coming in through the blockade might have their lading promptly on their arrival, that the bureau should undertake the procuring and shipment of cotton to Wilmington, Charleston and other points, for we had vessels arriving at half a dozen ports from Wilmington to Galveston. This necessitated the establishment of a steam compress at Wilmington, and, affiliated with it, agents to procure the cotton in the interior and see it to its destination; for the railroads were now so overtasked that it was only by placing positive orders from the Secretary of War in the hands of a selected agent that the cotton could be certainly forwarded over the various roads. The steam press was kept fully at work, in charge of Captain James M. Seixas (Washington Artillery). The necessity for transportation over the railroads brought us in contact with them, and gave them claim on us for assistance in the matter of supplies, such as steel, iron, copper, etc. and especially for work at the various foundries and machine shops in which precedence was, of course, claimed for army work, and which were, therefore, in great part controlled by the Ordnance Department. The foreign supplies were not all conveyed through steamers. Contracts were out for supplies through Texas from Mexico.

Finding that the other departments of the Government would naturally claim a share in this avenue for supplies, which had been opened chiefly through my bureau, it was detached at my own instance, but remained in charge of Colonel Bayne, with a good staff of officers and agents, as a separate bureau.

Thus the Ordnance Department consisted of a Bureau proper of Ordnance, having its officers in the field and at the arsenals and depots; of the Niter and Mining Bureau, and of the Bureau of Foreign Supplies.

DEVELOPMENT OF THE ARSENALS, ARMORIES AND OTHER PLACES OF
MANUFACTURE OF ORDNANCE STORES

The arsenal at Richmond soon grew into very large dimensions, and produced all the ordnance stores that an army may require, except cannon and small arms in quantities sufficient to supply the forces in that part of the field. I have, by accident, preserved a copy of the last number of the *Richmond Enquirer*, published under Confederate rule.

It is dated April 1, 1865, and contains the following "Statement of the principal issues from the Richmond arsenal from July 1, 1861, to January 1, 1865":

"Three hundred and forty-one columbiads and siege guns (these were made at the Tredegar works, but issued from the arsenal); 1,306 field pieces made chiefly at Tredegar works or captured; 1,375 gun carriages; 875 Caissons; 152 forges; 6,852 sets of artillery harness; 921,441 rounds field, siege and seacoast ammunition; 1,456,190 friction primers; 1,110,966 fuses; 17,423 port fires; 3,985 rockets; 323,231 infantry arms (most of these were turned in from the army, from battlefields and from the Richmond armory); 34,067 cavalry arms (same remark); 44,877 swords and sabers (from army, battlefield and contractors); 375,510 sets of infantry and cavalry accouterments; 180,-181 knapsacks; 328,977 canteens and straps; 72,413,854 small-arm cartridges; 115,087 gun and carbine slings; 146,901,250 percussion caps; 69,418 cavalry saddles; 85,139 cavalry bridles; 75,611 cavalry halters; 35,464 saddle blankets; 59,624 pairs spurs; 42,285 horse brushes; 56,903 curry combs."

This "statement" appears as an editorial, but the items were furnished from the office of the arsenal, and may be relied on. Its commandant at this time was Lieutenant Colonel Leroy Broun, of Virginia. In the items of cavalry saddles, bridles, harness, infantry accouterments, canteens and other articles of this character much assistance was received from contractors. A small part of the percussion caps also came from other arsenals. When we reflect that the arsenal grew to these great dimensions in a little over two years, it must be confessed that good use was made of the time. The laboratory attached to the arsenal was well conducted and did much work. It covered the island known as Green Island, which was connected with the shore by a bridge built by the Engineer Department especially for the service of this laboratory.

Besides the cap machinery, which was a very large and improved plant, machinery for pressing balls, for driving time fuses, for drawing friction primers and metallic cartridges and other labor-saving machines were invented, made and used with effect. In all respects the establishment, though extemporized and lodged in a cluster of tobacco warehouses, was equal to the first class arsenals of the United States in extent and facilities.

The arsenal of Augusta, Ga., was in great part organized in the city, where suitable buildings were obtained, and did much the same class of work done at Richmond, though on a smaller scale. It was very serviceable to the armies serving in the South and West, and turned out a good deal of field artillery complete, the castings being excellent. Colonel George W. Rains, in charge of arsenal and powder works, found that the fusion of a small per cent of iron with the copper and tin improved the strength of the bronze castings very much.

The powdermills at Augusta, Ga., which I have already mentioned as the direct result of the order of President Davis were wonderfully successful and never met with serious accident—a safe indication of the goodness of its arrangements. It showed, too, that, under able directions, the resources of Southern workshops and the skill of its artisans had already become equal to the execution of great enterprises involving high mechanical skill.

The arsenal and workshops at Charleston were also enlarged, steam introduced, and good work done in various departments.

The arsenal at Mount Vernon, now furnished with steam power and having a good deal of machinery, was considered out of position after the fall of New Orleans, and was moved to Selma, Ala., where it grew into a large well-ordered arsenal of the best class, under the charge of Lieutenant Colonel White. It was relied on to a great extent for the equipment of the troops and fortifications in the southern part of the Confederacy.

THE

ORDNANCE MANUAL

FOR

THE USE OF THE OFFICERS

OF THE

CONFEDERATE STATES ARMY.

———————◆———————

PREPARED UNDER THE DIRECTION OF COL. J. GORGAS, CHIEF OF ORDNANCE, AND
APPROVED BY THE SECRETARY OF WAR.

FIRST EDITION.

RICHMOND:
WEST AND JOHNSTON, 145 MAIN STREET.
1863.

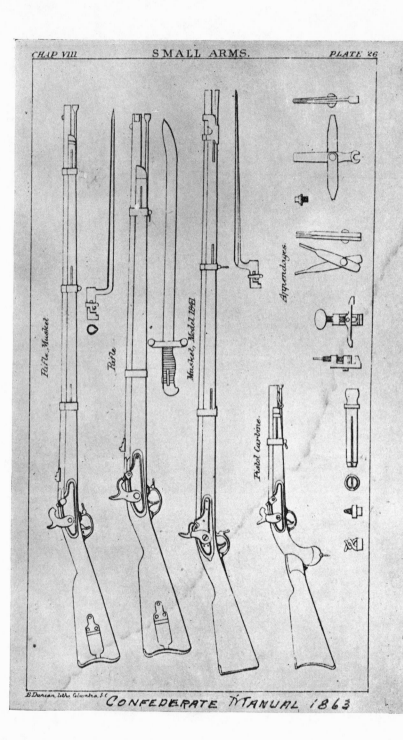

CONFEDERATE MANUAL 1863

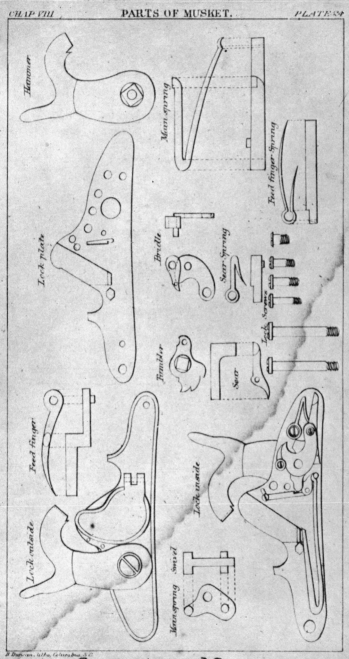

CONFEDERATE MANUAL 1863.

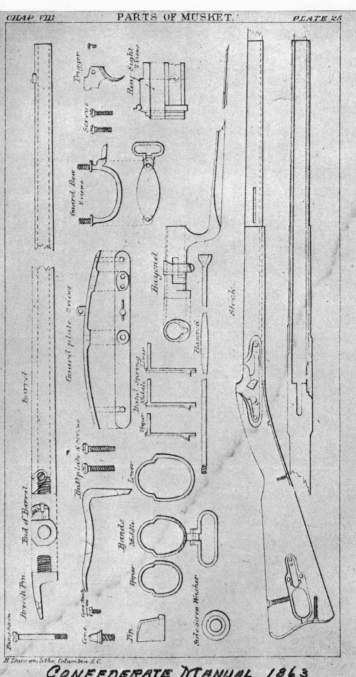

CONFEDERATE MANUAL 1863.

B. Duncan, Litho, Columbia S.C.

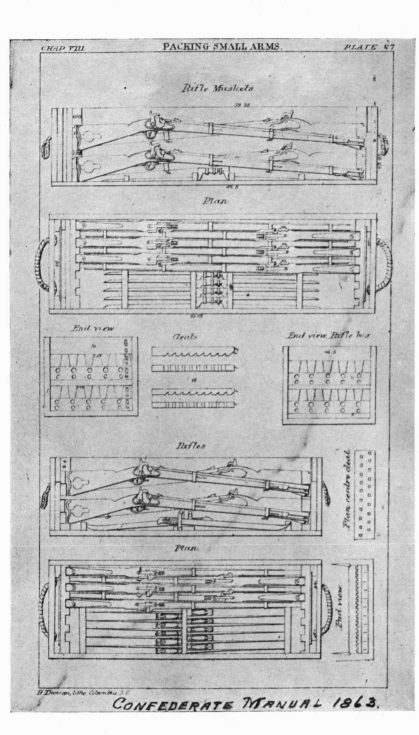

Rifle Muskets.

Plan.

End view. Cleats. End view. Rifle box.

Rifles.

Plan.

Plan centre cleat.

End view.

B. Duncan, litho Columbia S.C.

CONFEDERATE MANUAL 1863.

BRIGADIER–GENERAL JOSIAH GORGAS

FIREARMS OF THE CONFEDERACY

Attracted by the deposits of fine ore immediately north of Selma, made accessible by the Selma, Rome & Dalton Railroad, the War Department accepted the proposition of Mr. Colin McRae to undertake the erection at Selma of a large foundry for the casting of cannon of the heaviest caliber. A large contract was made with him and advances of money made from time to time as the work progressed. After a time Mr. McRae was called on by President Davis to go abroad in connection with Confederate finances. He made it a condition that he should be relieved of his works and contract at Selma without pecuniary loss to himself. The works were thereupon assumed by the War and Navy Departments jointly, and placed at first under the charge of Colonel Rains as general superintendent, while an officer of less rank took immediate charge. Subsequently it was agreed by the War Department that the Navy should take sole charge, and use the works for its own purposes. It was here that Commander Brooke made many of his formidable banded and rifled guns.

The foundry and rolling-mills grew into large proportions, supplied by the iron and coal of that region. Had the Confederacy survived, Selma bid fair to become the Pittsburgh of the South. The iron obtained from the brown haematite at the furnaces in Bibb County (Brierfield), and from the Shelby Works, was admirable, the former being of unusual strength.

Mount Vernon Arsenal was still continued, after being in a great measure dismantled, and was utilized to get lumber and timber for use elsewhere, and to gather and prepare moss for making saddle blankets.

At Montgomery shops were kept up for the repair of small arms, and for the manufacture of articles of leather, of which some supplies were obtained in that region.

There were many other small establishments and depots, some of them connected immediately with the army, as at Dublin, Southwest Va.; Knoxville, Tenn.; and Jackson, Miss. Some shops at Lynchburg, Va., were moved to Danville, near the south line of Virginia, and it grew into place of some value for repairs, etc.

The Ordnance shops at Nashville had been hurriedly transferred to Atlanta, Ga., on the fall of Fort Donelson; and when Atlanta was seriously threatened by the operations of Sherman, the arsenal there, which had become very important, was moved to Columbus, Ga., where there was the nucleus of an Ordnance establishment. Colonel M. H. Wright soon made this nearly as valuable as his arsenal at Atlanta had been.

ARMORIES AND SMALL ARMS

Besides the arsenals, a brief account of which has just been given, we had the armories at Richmond and Fayetteville, N. C.; and arms were also made at other points.

The State of Virginia claimed all the machinery captured at Harper's Ferry, and was bringing it all to Richmond. It was agreed, however, with the State of North Carolina that that part of the machinery which was specially adapted to make the Mississippi rifle (caliber 54) should go to Fayetteville, where there was an arsenal with good steam power, the machinery to be returned at the close of the war to the State of Virginia. Colonel Burton, an admirably-educated machinist, superintended the re-erection of the works at Richmond. He was subsequently made Superintendent of Armories, and given full charge of the entire subject of manufacture of arms in the Confederacy. The machinery of the rifle-musket (caliber 58), retained at Richmond, got to work as early as September, 1861. If we had possessed the necessary number of workmen this "plant" could have been so filled in as to have easily produced 5,000 stands per month, working night and day. As it was, I don't think it ever turned out more than 1,500 in any one month. Fayetteville did not get to work until the spring of 1862, and did not average 400 per month, for want of hands.

To supplement this scarcity of operatives, Colonel Huse was authorized to engage for us a number of skilled workmen, used to work on small arms, and to pay their passage over. They came in through the blockade at Wilmington without difficulty, but we could do nothing with them. They had been engaged to be paid in gold, which meantime had risen to such a price as to make their pay enormous, and would have produced utter disintegration among our own operatives. I offered to pay one-half of the wages promised them in gold, to their families in England, if they would take the remainder in Confederate money, which would support them here. I brought the British Consul to confer with them here. But they stood upon their bond; and foreseeing that their presence would do more harm than good, I simply, with their consent, reshipped them by the next steamer, and paid their passage back. The experiment cost us something like £2,000 in gold, and made us shy of foreign workmen, especially English. I think the Treasury Department did succeed in getting engravers and printers for their purposes at Columbia, S. C., to some extent by importation; but my impression is they were not English. Of all obstinate animals I have ever come in contact with, these English workmen were the most unreasonable.

The Cook Brothers had, as heretofore stated, undertaken the making of rifle-muskets in New Orleans at the very commencement of the war. On the fall of New Orleans their machinery was hurriedly taken off by boats up the Mississippi. They finally selected Athens, Georgia, as their point of manufacture, and under a contract with me, and assisted with funds under that contract, proceeded to reorganize and extend their "plant." They were reasonably successful.

The want of cavalry arms caused me to make a contract with parties in Richmond to make the Sharp's carbine—at that time the best cavalry arm we had. A set of machinery capable of turning out one hundred arms a day was driven to completion in less than a year, nearly all the machinery being built up "from the stumps." The arms were never perfect, chiefly for want of nice workmanship about the "cut-off." It was not gas-tight. We soon bought out the establishment, and converted it into a manufactory of rifle-carbines, caliber fifty-eight, as the best arm our skill would enable us to supply to the cavalry.

Recognizing the necessity of some great central establishment for the production of small arms, plans of buildings and estimates of machinery were made for such a one, to be built at Macon, Ga.,—a point of easy access and near to a fertile corn region out of the way of the enemy. Colonel Burton went to England and easily negotiated for the machinery, which was to have been of sufficient capacity to turn out about ten thousand arms per month. Buildings were immediately obtained for some machinery for pistols, which was transferred there; and Colonel Burton had made good progress in erecting ample buildings for the new machinery, part of which had arrived at Bermuda and Nassau when the Confederacy fell. But about six months before the close of the war, finding that the blockade had become so stringent that the introduction of machinery would be very difficult, and reflecting, too, that as long as the war continued this extended machinery would be of but little use to us, for want of workmen, I got the authority of the Secretary of War to set it up at some point abroad and bring in the arms, which would be less difficult than to bring in the machinery and train the workmen. Colonel Burton was abroad on this duty when the war closed. Had the war been prolonged, we should in twelve months have been making our own arms in a foreign land, under the sanction of a private name. After the war it was proposed to transfer the entire "plant" to the buildings which were in course of construction for it at Macon. Peace would have then found us in possession of a great armory, which I much desired.

FIREARMS OF THE CONFEDERACY

One of the earliest difficulties forced upon us in the manufacture of arms was to find an iron fit for the barrels. The "skelps" found at Harper's Ferry served for awhile, and when these were exhausted Colonel Burton selected an iron produced at a forge in Patrick County, Va., and by placing a skilled workman over the rolling process at the Tredegar Works he soon produced "skelps" with which he was satisfied. We found that almost any of the good brown haematite ores produced an iron of ample strength for the purpose, and the even grain and toughness could be attained by careful rerolling.

Besides the larger armories at Richmond and Fayetteville, smaller establishments grew up at Asheville, N. C., and at Tallassee, Ala. The former was the development of a private enterprise undertaken to repair and fit up old arms, by a citizen (Mr. Pullem) resident there, and afterward as a matter of necessity assumed by the Confederate Government. Most of the machinery was moved before the close of the war to Columbia, S. C., whither, as a place of safety, other arms manufacturing machinery was moved from other points. Tallassee was selected as a good manufacturing point, a large building having been offered to us by the proprietors of the cotton mills there, and some machinery for making pistols moved thither from Columbus, Ga.

A great part of the work of our armories consisted in repairing arms brought in from the battlefield or sent in from the armies in too damaged a condition to be effectually repaired at the arsenals. In this way only could we utilize all the gleanings of the battlefields. My recollection is that we saved nearly ten thousand stands of arms from the field of Bull Run, and that the battlefields about Richmond in 1862 gave us about twenty-five thousand excellent arms through the labors of the armory at Richmond.

The original stock of arms, it will be remembered, consisted almost wholly of smooth-bore muskets, altered from flint to percussion, using ounce balls (caliber .69). There were some 15,000 to 20,000 Mississippi rifles; and then some irregular arms, like Hall's rifles and carbines— some short carbines smooth-bore; and there were even some of the old flintlock muskets. All this original stock disappeared almost wholly from our armies in the first two years of the war, and were replaced by a better class of arms, rifled and percussioned. It is pretty safe to assume that we had altogether, east and west of the Mississippi, 300,000 infantry, pretty well armed, by the middle of 1863. We must therefore have procured at least that number for our troops. But we must also have supplied the inevitable waste of two years of active warfare. Placing the good arms thus lost at the moderate estimate of 100,000, we must have received from various sources 400,000 stands of infantry arms in the two years of fighting ending July 1, 1863. I can only estimate from memory the several sources from which this supply was derived as follows:

Good rifled arms on hand at the beginning of the war (this includes the arms in the hands of volunteer companies)	25,000
New arms manufactured in the Confederacy and in private establishments	40,000
Arms received from the battlefields and put in good order (this includes the great number of arms picked up by the soldiers	150,000
Imported from January 1, 1862 to July 1, 1863	185,000
Total	400,000

This estimate does not include pistols and sabers, of which a small supply was imported.

To account for the very large number obtained from the enemy (rather an under than an over estimate), it must be remembered that in some fights, where our troops were not finally successful, they were so at first, and swept over the camps and positions of the enemy. Whenever a Confederate soldier saw a weapon better than his own he took it and left his inferior arm; and although he may have been finally driven back, he kept his improved musket. So, too, on every field there were partial successes, which in the early part of the war resulted in improved weapons; and although on another part of the field there may have been a reverse, the enemy had not the same advantage; the Confederate arms being generally inferior to those of the adversaries. The difference of arms was not so marked at a later day, except in cavalry arms, in which we were always at a disadvantage, the celebrated Spencer carbine being generally in the hands of the enemy's cavalry during the last two years of the war.

A CENTRAL LABORATORY

The unavoidable variation in the ammunition made at the different arsenals, pointed out, early in the war, that there should be a general superintendent of all the laboratories, invested with authority to inspect and supervise their manipulations and materials. To this end Lieutenant Colonel Mallet, a chemist and scientist of distinction, who had for some years been professor in the University of Alabama, was selected and placed in charge of this delicate and important duty. I attribute much of the improvement in our ammunition to this happy selection. A more earnest and capable officer I cannot imagine. What a set of men we would have had after the war out of which to form an ordnance department had we been successful, Rains, St. John, Mallet, Burton, Wright, White, Baldwin, Rhett, Ellicott, Andrews, Childs, DeLagnel, Hutter and others who would have remained in the service. Then there were some no less admirable, like LeRoy Broun, Allan, Wiley Browne, Morton, Colston, Bayne, Cuyler, E. B. Smith, etc., who would doubtless have returned to their civil avocations.

Among the obvious necessities of a well-regulated service was one large central laboratory, where all ammunition should be made—thus securing absolute uniformity where uniformity was vital. The policy of dissemination so necessary to husband our transportation and to utilize the labor of non-combatants must here yield to the greater necessity of obtaining our ammunition uniform in quality and in dimensions. Authority was, therefore, obtained from the War Department to concentrate this species of work at some central laboratory. Macon, Ga., was selected, and Colonel Mallet placed in charge of the central laboratory, as Burton was later placed in charge of a national armory. Plans of the buildings and of the machinery required were submitted to the Secretary of War, approved, and the work begun with energy. This pile of buildings had a facade of 600 feet, was designed with taste, and comprehended every possible appliance for good and well-organized work. The buildings were nearly ready for occupation at the close of the war, and some of the machinery had arrived at Bermuda. In point of time, this project preceded that of the national armory, and was much nearer completion. These, with our admirable powdermills at Augusta, would have completed a set of works for the Ordnance Department; and in them we would have been in condition to supply arms and munitions to three hundred thousand men. To these would have been added a foundry for heavy guns at Selma or Brierfield, Ala., at which latter place the strongest cast iron in the country was produced, and where we had already purchased and were carrying on a furnace for the production of cold-blast charcoal pig for this special purpose. All these establishments were in the heart of the country not readily reached by the enemy, and were, in fact, never reached by them until just at the close of the war. Being in or near an excellent agricultural region, they would have had the advantage of cheap living for operatives; and they had all sufficient facilities for transportation, being situated on main lines of railroad.

FIREARMS OF THE CONFEDERACY

SUMMARY

I have thus, from memory, faintly traced the development of the means and resources by which our large armies were supplied with arms and ammunition. This involved manufacturing, mining and importation. The last two were confided in time to sub-bureaus created ex necessitate, which were subsequently detached. The first was carried on by the armories, arsenals, laboratories and depots above mentioned. We began in April, 1861, without an arsenal, laboratory or powdermill of any capacity, and with no foundry or rolling mill, except at Richmond, and before the close of 1863, in little over two years, we had built up, during all the harassments of war, holding our own in the field defiantly and successfully against a powerful and determined enemy. Crippled as we were by a depreciated currency; throttled with a blockade that deprived us of nearly all means of getting material or workmen; obliged to send almost every able-bodied man to the field; unable to use the slave labor with which we were abundantly supplied, except in the most unskilled departments of production; hampered by want of transportation even of the commonest supplies of food; with no stock on hand even of the articles, such as steel, copper, lead, iron, leather, which we must have to build up our establishments; and in spite of these deficiencies we persevered at home as determinedly as did our troops in the field against a more tangible opposition, and in a little over two years created, almost literally out of the ground, foundries and rolling mills (at Selma, Richmond, Atlanta and Macon); smelting works (at Petersburg), chemical works (at Charlotte, N. C.), a powdermill far superior to any in the United States and unsurpassed by any across the ocean, and a chain of arsenals, armories and laboratories equal in their capacity and their improved appointments to the best of those in the United States, stretching link by link from Virginia to Alabama. Our people are justly proud of the valor and constancy of the troops which bore their banners bravely in the front of the enemy; but they will also reflect that these creations of skill and labor were the monuments which represented the patience, industry and perseverance of the devoted and patriotic citizens; for of the success which attended the operations of any department of the Confederate Government the larger moiety was due to the cooperation of the body of the people—a cooperation founded in their hearty sympathy with and their entire faith in the cause which that government represented.

ORGANIZATION

The Ordnance Bureau, as finally organized, consisted of one brigadier general, one colonel, and of such additional number of field officers, captains and first lieutenants as the service required. They were artillery officers on ordnance duty.

Appointments to these positions were at first made by selection, on nomination by the Ordnance Bureau, but about October, 1862, Congress created fifty officers of artillery especially for ordnance duty, to which two hundred more were subsequently added. As selection for these offices involved much political contrivance, I obtained the order of the Secretary of War to hold examinations for appointment to the grade of captain and first lieutenant. This plan succeeded entirely and relieved us from a thousand personal solicitations. The first examination was held at Richmond. Of some five hundred applications found on file for ordnance officers, less than one hundred came to the examination, and of these only some forty or fifty passed. The examination for captain involved a fair knowledge of a college course of mathematics, and none, I believe, passed this except the M. A.'s of the University of Virginia. That for first lieutenant embraced only an ordinary English education, with a full examination on the Ordnance Manual. This gave us an excellent set of officers—educated men; and although a few of them were, as was said, "Virginia school-masters," and cannot be said to have distinguished themselves professionally, yet they were all respectable on account of their education, and I am sure there never were in any army a better class of such officers.

These examinations were extended, and were held at the head-quarters of each army in the field by a commission, of which Lieutenant Colonel Leroy Broun and Lieutenant Colonel S. Stansbury, Colonel T. A. Rhett and Major J. Wilcox Browne were the chief members. These, or one of them, went to an army and associated with themselves one or more officers detailed by the general at headquarters. In order to provide for that class of valuable officers, distinguished for excellent qualities developed by service on the field but not prepared for a somewhat technical examination, each general of an army designated one or two of this class, who were appointed on his recommendation alone.

Officers in the field were distributed as follows: To each army a "chief ordnance officer," with the rank of lieutenant colonel; to each army corps, an ordnance officer with the rank of major; to each division, a captain, and to each brigade a first lieutenant; all these attached to the staff of their respective generals, but reporting also directly, if necessary, to the ordnance officer, through his superior in the field, and receiving instructions as to special duties through the same channel. Every regiment had an ordnance sergeant in charge of ordnance wagon, containing the spare arms and the ammunition of each regiment.

The officers in command of the greater ordnance establishments—such as Richmond and Augusta, etc.—had the grade of lieutenant colonel, like the "chief ordnance officers" of armies in the field, while in the lesser establishments the officers had rank according to the gravity of the duties devolving on them.

The Superintendent of Armories, Lieutenant Colonel Burton, and the Superintendent of Laboratories, Lieutenant Colonel Mallet, had also the grade of the higher officers on duty in the field.

The labors and responsibilities of my department closed practically at Charlotte, N. C., on the 26th of April, when the President left that place with an escort for the Trans-Mississippi. My last stated official duty, that I can recall, was to examine a cadet in the Confederate service for promotion to commissioned officer.

On the afternoon of the 25th of April I received due formal notice from the Adjutant General's office that General Lawton, Quartermaster General, General Gilmer, Chief Engineer, and I were constituted a Board of Examiners on Cadet ————. We met a little before sundown, in the ample upper story of a warehouse in Charlotte, N. C., and by the waning light of the last day of the Confederate Government, we went through all the stages of an examination of an expectant lieutenant of the Confederate armies. Lawton, I think, took him on geography and history, Gilmer on the mathematics, while I probably tested his English grammar. He passed the ordeal in triumph and got his commission, which I dare say he prizes very highly, as he ought to do, considering the august body that signed the certificate which pronounced him qualified for it.

DETACHED OBSERVATION
Consumption of Small-Arm Cartridges

It appears that the Richmond laboratory made 72,000,000 cartridges in three and a half years, say one thousand working days. As this laboratory made nearly as much as all the others combined, we may safely place the entire production at 150,000,000, or 150,000 per day. As our reserves remained nearly the same, being but slightly increased toward the latter part of the war, there must have been only a little less than this consumption in the field, say half a cartridge per man per day for the average force of 300,000 men, to cover all the accidents and expenditures of service in the field. An average, then, of half a cartridge per day per man would be a safe assumption for protracted warfare.

In examining the returns of ordnance officers after heavy actions, I found that the reduction of ammunition amounted to from about nineteen to twenty-six rounds per man. At Gettysburg the reports of a few days before the battle and a short time after showed a difference of twenty-five or twenty-six rounds on the average. This was the heaviest consumption to which my attention was called. When our troops first took the field commanders were very nervous because they had only fifty to seventy rounds per man instead of the two hundred rounds prescribed by the Ordnance Manual. Later we raised it to about eighty or ninety rounds. The results of battles show that with proper dispositions for transfer from one corps to another there need be no scarcity with sixty rounds on hand, or even fifty.

Our soldiers were, however, in the habit of supplying themselves with ammunition by throwing away their empty cartridge boxes and taking any well-supplied one that they might espy with the proper cartridges. What splendid fellows they were, taking even better care of their powder and lead than of themselves or of their rations. They were in downright earnest.

CONSUMPTION AND SUPPLY OF LEAD

Allowing for waste, 150,000,000 of cartridges would require 10,-000,000 pounds of lead for these alone, to say nothing of other needs. Where did all this lead come from? I make the following rough calculation:

	Pounds
From Trans-Mississippi mines (early in the war)	400,000
From the mines in Virginia (60,000 lbs. per month)	2,160,000
On hand at arsenals, etc.	140,000
Imported (not over)	2,000,000
Picked up through the country and on battlefields	5,300,000
Total	10,000,000

This leads to the surprising conclusion that we must have picked up throughout the country over 5,300,000 pounds of lead during the four years of the war. I remember that the window-weights and loose lead about houses yielded 200,000 pounds in Charleston alone; while the disused lead water pipes in Mobile supplied, if I am not mistaken, as much more, so that these two items alone supplied one-thirteenth of this vast gleaning of the country.

TRANSFER OF ARMS TO THE SOUTH

It was a charge often repeated against Governor Floyd that, as Secretary of War, he had, with traitorous intent, abused his office by sending arms to the South just before the secession of the States. The transactions which gave rise to this accusation were in the ordinary course of an economical administration of the War Department. After it had been determined to change the old flintlock musket, which the United States possessed, to percussion, it was deemed cheaper to bring all the flintlock arms in store, at Southern arsenals to the Northern arsenals and armories for alteration, rather than to send the necessary machinery and workmen to the South. Consequently, the Southern arsenals were stripped of their deposits, which were sent to Springfield, Watervliet, Pittsburgh, St. Louis, Frankford, Pa., and other points. After the conversion had been completed the denuded Southern arsenals were again supplied with about the same numbers, perhaps slightly augmented, that had formerly been stored there. The quota deposited at the Charleston arsenal, where I was stationed in 1860, arrived there full a year before the opening of the war.

Firearms of the Confederacy

The Napoleon Field-Guns

I think I will be sustained by the artillery in saying that, on the whole, this gun became the favorite for field service, perhaps because our rifle shells with percussion fuses were, as stated by General Alexander, less successful than those of the enemy. When copper became scarce we fabricated an iron Napoleon with a wrought-iron jacket, weighing in all twelve hundred and fifty pounds, which was entirely satisfactory, and was cheerfully accorded by the artillery companionship with their bronze favorites. The simplicity and certainty of the ammunition of this smooth-bore, its capacity for grape and canister, its good range, and its moderate draught, as it was not too heavy for four horses, were certainly strong reasons in its favor. At the distance at which the serious work of the artillery was done, it was an overmatch for rifled artillery.

Heavy Guns

It was, of course, a matter of keen regret to me that we could not rapidly produce guns of heavy caliber for points, the defense of which, against men-of-war, was of vital importance. But the 10-inch columbiad could only be cast at the Tredegar Works, and although this establishment was in able hands and responded nobly to the calls made upon it, yet tasked, as it was, to produce artillery of all calibers—especially field artillery—we could but slowly answer the appeals made with equal vehemence from Pensacola, Yorktown, Charleston and New Orleans.

About the close of 1863, Maj. Huse sent two Blakely rifles of about 13-inch caliber, splendid looking, superbly mounted, and of fearful cost!—£10,000 for two in England, with Fifty rounds each. Charleston claimed them on their arrival at Wilmington, and I was glad to strengthen General Beauregard's hands. Unfortunately one of them cracked in some trial firing, with comparatively weak charges. The full charge, which was never reached, was fifty pounds of powder, and a solid rifle shell of say four hundred and fifty pounds. These guns were built up of a wrought-iron cylinder, closed at the breech with a brass-screw plug, some thirty inches long, and chambered to seven inches. This cylinder had three successive jackets, each shorter than its predecessor, so that from muzzle to breech the thickness of the gun increased by steps of about three and a half inches. The object of the seven-inch chamber in the brass plug was to afford an air or gas space which would diminish the strain on the gun. Such was the theory. General Ripley, however, cut down the big cartridge bags of ten or eleven inches in diameter, so as to introduce the charge into the brass chamber. This not being over three inches thick, cracked, and the crack, I believe, extended into the cylinder. On a report of the facts direct from Charleston to Captain Blakely, he attributed the bursting to the high elevation given, though the highest, I think, had been only about one hundred and fifty; an impotent conclusion for a scientific artillerist to reach. The fact of the introduction of the charge into the air space may have been omitted in the narrative to him, and thus he may have been drawn into this helpless conclusion. I never saw the drawings of the gun until after the report of the accident. Captain Brooke, Chief of Ordnance of the Navy, with me then looked over the drawings and evolved the design of the air-chamber. After this the gun was fired, and with moderate elevations attained fair, but not remarkable ranges, as I was advised. The cracked gun was skillfully repaired at Charleston, and restored to a reliable condition.

Just before the war closed, the Tredegar Works had cast its first 12-inch gun, after the method of Rodman—cast on a hollow core, with water kept flowing in and out of it to cool the castings from the inside. This method of cooling has been found to give a marked increase of strength, and greater hardness and consequent smoothness to the finished bore.

JOSIAH GORGAS,
*Late Brigadier General and
Chief of Ordnance.*

*   *   *   *   *

THE RICHMOND ARMORY

As previously indicated, the Richmond armory which served the Confederates so well during the war probably produced more arms than the combined products of other plants throughout the Confederacy.

Preparations for the production of arms similar to the U. S. models were commenced here by the State of Virginia in the fall of 1860. A contract for the necessary machinery was let to the Tredegar Iron Works, who had in their employ J. H. Burton, late master armorer at Enfield, England. At the same time Mr. Solomon Adams, the master armorer, was in Springfield preparing a model arm and making drawings of the tools and fixtures required for its production.

With the capture of Harper's Ferry armory by the Virginia forces on April 18, 1861, and the removal of all that part of the machinery suitable for manufacturing the rifle-musket to Richmond, the contract with Tredegar Iron Works was cancelled.

Under the direction of Col. Dimmick, Chief of Virginia Ordnance department and with J. H. Burton acting as superintendent, the work of re-erecting the Harper's Ferry machinery was pushed forward rapidly and the production of arms commenced early in the summer of 1861.

The armory was operated by the Virginia State authorities until late in the fall, when it was turned over to the Confederate government who developed it into a capacity of 5,000 stands per month but, as Col. Gorgas reported, because of shortage of labor the output never exceeded 1,500 in any one month.

In September, 1864, the civilian employees were all called out to man the trenches and about February 1, 1865, work on dismantling the machinery and shipping it to Danville, Va., commenced while the armory buildings and such machinery and equipment that had not been moved were destroyed by fire upon the vacuation of Richmond, April 3, 1865.

THE RICHMOND RIFLED MUSKET
Figure 1, Plate X

This is almost an exact copy of the U. S. model 1855 rifled musket. The barrel is 40 inches long, caliber .58. The total length is 55.85 inches and it weighs without bayonet, 9.18 pounds. The regular charge for this arm was 500 grain conical bullet and 60 grains of powder, giving a muzzle velocity of 950 feet per second.

The arm is equipped with the regular 1861 rear sight and has a brass butt plate in place of the regular iron one of the regular issue. The lock is stamped C. S. Richmond, Va., at the forward end of the plate and 1864 at the rear end. The hammer is of the regular 1861 type and does not have the knife edge for cutting the Maynard primers such as were used on the model 1855. There are no proof marks on the barrel but it is stamped near the breech 1864.

RICHMOND NAVY MUSKETOON
Figure 4, Plate X

Like the preceding arm this follows closely the regulation model 1855 and was evidently made up from parts of that arm except for the lock plate and lock mechanism.

The barrel has been cut down to a length of 30 inches, and bored smooth to a caliber of .62 evidently to permit easier handling and more rapid loading on ship service where long range and accuracy was not so important. Total length of arm, 46 inches. Weight, 7 pounds and 8 ounces. Marked on lock plate, C. S. Richmond Va., and dated 1863.

RICHMOND CARBINE
Figure 5, Plate X

This arm was probably made up for cavalry use from parts of the regulation musket. The barrel is 25 inches long, caliber .58. Total length of arm, 40¾ inches. Weight, 7 pounds, 6 ounces. The barrel has been provided with a high front sight. The stock tip and butt plate are bronze, evidently Confederate manufacture. The lock plate is the usual tape-lock blank while a new hammer, not provided with a cutting edge, is used. Only two bands are used and in addition to the sling swivels on the top band and trigger guard, another one has been provided in the butt stock. The lock plate is marked C. S. Richmond, Va., and dated 1863. The barrel is stamped C. S. and dated 1863 and the tang of the butt plate is also stamped C. S.

PLATE X

Fig. 1

Fig. 2

Fig. 3

Fig. 4

Fig. 5

Fig. 1. Richmond Musket.
Fig. 2. Fayetteville Rifle.
Fig. 3. Hall Muzzle-Loading Rifle.
Fig. 4. Richmond Navy Musketoon.
Fig. 5. Richmond Carbine.

PLATE XI

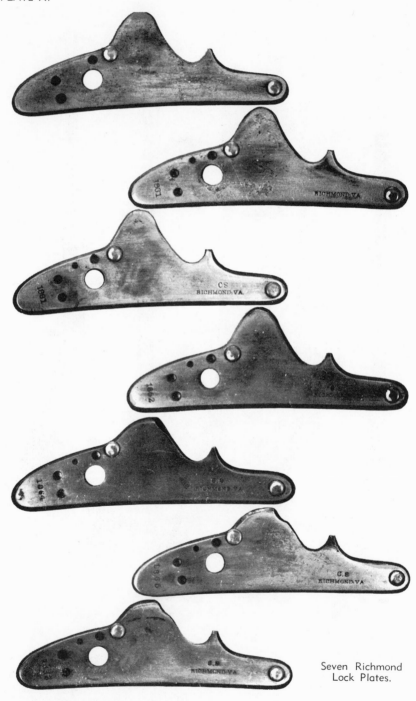

Seven Richmond
Lock Plates.

FIREARMS OF THE CONFEDERACY

LOCK PLATES
FROM CONFEDERATE RIFLED MUSKETS
MADE AT RICHMOND ARMORY

The correspondence included here outlines many of the activities in connection with the operation of the Richmond armory at Richmond, Va., during the war. Many of the details, however, are lacking and it is regrettable that so much is left to conjecture.

In referring to the rifled muskets produced at this armory a statement is generally made that the locks were made from forgings captured at Harper's Ferry or with dies taken from there, and it is probably true that this happened to some extent, but the records are not entirely clear on the question.

As early as November, 1860, the State of Virginia was actively engaged in rebuilding the armory at Richmond and Mr. Solomon Adams, master armorer for the State, was at Springfield making a model arm and also making drawings of the machinery and tools required for its manufacture and the Tredegar Iron Works, operated by J. R. Anderson & Co., had a contract for building the machinery, and it is quite possible that this model arm embodied the lock plate 1855 minus the Maynard primer and that they were providing the necessary tools to manufacture it prior to the capture of Harper's Ferry.

The lock plates shown on the accompanying cut would seem to indicate this and would also suggest that they started the manufacture of them rather hurriedly.

LOCK PLATE NO. I

This plate is without any markings whatever and while it is of the regular Maynard type blank it has a small groove cut in the upper part to permit the use of a hammer of rounded outline in place of the knife edge used in connection with the Maynard tape lock.

LOCK PLATE NO. II

This plate is of the regular Maynard type and does not include the groove referred to in No. I. It is marked Richmond, Va., and dated 1861, and could very probably be a blank secured from Harper's Ferry. This plate likely was used at Richmond by the State of Virginia prior to September, 1861, at which time the Confederate Government took charge, as it does not carry the usual C. S. put upon the plates by them.

LOCK PLATE NO. III

This is a duplicate of Plate No. II but stamped C. S. Richmond, Va., and dated 1861, indicating that it was made after September of that year when the armory was turned over to the Confederate Government by the Virginia officials.

LOCK PLATE NO. IV

This is a duplicate of Plate No. III but is dated 1862 and while Colonel Gorgas' report of January 7, 1863, does not itemize the number of arms of the different armories it states that up to September, 1862, there had been fabricated a total of 14,349 small arms of all kinds and that the public armories could produce 2,030 rifles, muskets and carbines per month. As Richmond was by far the most important armory it is likely that a big part of these were produced there.

LOCK PLATE NO. VII

This is marked C. S. Richmond, Va., and dated 1863, and while it will interchange with the former plates there is a marked difference in the outline of the upper portion as the total height has been reduced by about three-eighths of an inch and chamfered off on a bevel, indicating that a new die differing in this respect from the one suitable for the Maynard blank was in use.

Colonel Gorgas, in his report of November 15, 1863, states that the armories at Richmond, Fayetteville and Asheville produced an aggregate of about 28,000 of small arms within the year, indicating a considerable increase in production over the previous years.

LOCK PLATE NO. V

This is a duplicate of the former plate. Marked C. S. Richmond, Va., and dated 1864, which year probably marks the greatest production at this armory, as the report of September 31, 1864, to James A. Seddon, Secretary of War, by Colonel Gorgas, states that 25,000 arms per year could be produced at Richmond, providing they had 450 workmen, though there was only a total of 12,778 rifles and rifle muskets produced at all the armories during the year on account of the shortage of labor.

LOCK PLATE NO. VI

A duplicate of the 1864 plate. Marked C. S. Richmond, Va., and dated 1865 and interesting in that it shows despite the ad-

CONFEDERATE ARSENAL AND ARMORY AT FAYETTEVILLE, N. C.
(From A Sketch In Harper's Weekly)

CONFEDERATE ARMORY AT HOLLY SPRINGS, MISS.

(From sketch in Harper's Weekly.)

vancing Union troops the armory was kept in production as long as possible, the Union troops taking the city on April 4, 1865.

* * * * *

THE FAYETTEVILLE ARMORY

The U. S. Government had maintained for a long time one of its largest Southern arsenals at Fayetteville, N. C., and this was equipped with steam power and some machinery for the repair of arms. There were stored there at the breaking out of hostilities some 20,000 muskets and 2,000 rifles which were all taken over by the State authorities.

After the capture of Harper's Ferry by the Virginia troops, they operated the rifle machinery there until June of 1861, when it was removed and loaned to the State of North Carolina to be erected at Fayetteville, as indicated by the following letters:

Richmond, May 27, 1861.

President DAVIS:

In reply to your letter of the 23d instant, received this morning, I send the advice of the council. It has been communicated to Governor Ellis by me:

"The council advise that so much of the Harper's Ferry machinery adapted to the manufacture of rifles as can, in the opinion of the ordnance department, be spared without inconvenience to the service of the State, and as can be promptly and advantageously employed at Fayetteville, be loaned to the State of North Carolina for the purpose of immediately commencing the manufacture of small arms at that point, and that the Governor of that State be invited to send suitable machinists to Virginia to take charge of so much of said machinery as it may be desirable and expedient to transfer to Fayetteville for the above-named purpose.

Approved May 22, 1861.

JOHN LETCHER.

ORDNANCE DEPARTMENT,
Richmond, Va., June 15, 1861.

Lieutenant Colonel BURTON:

COLONEL: The authorities of this State having loaned the rifle machinery taken from Harper's Ferry to the authorities of North Carolina, you will please turn over the same to any authorized agent, that he may have it transported to Raleigh, taking care to retain all and any machines or parts thereof that may be necessary for the making up of muskets. The barrels and stocks suitable for the rifle and not fit for the muskets you will also turn over to said agent.

Very respectfully,

C. DIMMOCK,
Colonel of Ordnance.

The master armorer of Harper's Ferry, Armistead M. Ball, and his assistant, Benjamin Mills, joined up with the Southern cause and accompanied the machinery to Fayetteville. Ball died early in the war but Mills after the war returned to his home near Harrodsburg, Kentucky, where he operated a gun shop specializing in fine target rifles and some pistols.

As additional buildings had to be provided and some machinery built, work at Fayetteville was slow in getting under way. Some of the problems in connection with dividing the machinery taken from Harper's Ferry into two separate units are set forth in the following letter:

CONFEDERATE STATES ARMORY
Richmond, July 20, 1861.

Maj. J. GORGAS,
  Chief of Ordnance:

SIR: With reference to the subject of the propriety or expediency of allowing selections to be made from among the machines for the manufacture of rifle muskets—removed to this armory from Harper's Ferry—with a view to the use of the machines so selected at other places, I beg to submit for your information, and in compliance with your request, the following remarks:

It is, I find, a prevailing impression among the several persons interested in the proposed separation of a portion of this machinery for use elsewhere that the plant of machinery now here is composed for the most part of different classes of machines, of which one machine is a type of many; and from this it is argued that the detachment of one or two machines of each class will only have the effect of reducing the product of the armory to the extent of the productive capacities of the machines so detached. This impression is very erroneous, with but little exception.

The most numerous class of machines now in the armory is that known as "milling machines," and, so far as the machines themselves are concerned, one may be regarded as the type of the whole class. But each machine is fitted with a special apparatus for holding the part to be operated upon in one particular position; and it is also fitted with a set of "cutters" of special shape for milling the part so held. In this way the set of milling machines is made up of a number of machines fitted apparently to the unpracticed observer for doing the same work, whilst, in fact, each one is set apart for the performance of some one particular operation, which none of the others can be spared to do without seriously deranging the whole system. In the set of milling machines for milling barrels, for instance, the detachment of any one of the set, of which there is no duplicate employed, would have the effect of rendering it necessary to supply its place with another machine of the same kind, and which could not be spared from any other operation. The result is obvious. And so with reference to the set of machines for milling bayonets or any other important component part of the arm. In some cases there may be duplicate milling machines employed, but it is quite obvious that the detachment of one such duplicate machine, although apparently an insignificant draft upon the entire machinery of the armory, would have the effect of reducing the product of the armory just one-half.

The set of machines for making stocks comprises fifteen distinct machines, each of which differs essentially from the rest. The detachment of any one of them would entirely stop the manufacture of this component by the system now pursued.

The machinery now in this armory comprises a complete set, equal to the production of about 15,000 arms per annum, and there being no surplus or spare machines, the separation of any one or more of them would so seriously affect the productive capacity of the whole that I am constrained to recommend in the strongest terms the preservation of the whole system in its present entirety, as being the course most likely to produce a result satisfactory to the Government, inasmuch as it is expected that in a comparatively short time the whole will be successfully at work producing the minie musket.

I have the honor to be, sir, your most obedient servant,

JAS. H. BURTON,
Lieutenant Colonel, Virginia Ordnance, in Charge.

Under these handicaps they did not commence to manufacture arms until 1862 and shortly thereafter it was taken over and operated by the Confederate authorities.

In his report of Dec. 31, 1864, Gorgas states that Fayetteville had a capacity of 10,000 stands of arms annually, but subsequent reports indicate that their maximum output was something less than 600 for any one month.

Most of the rifles made there were provided with lugs for saber bayonets but the manufacture of this type bayonet was discontinued by General Orders No. 6, of January 14, 1864, after which the regular triangular bayonet was substituted.

This armory was operated until March, 1865, when, upon approach of Sherman's army, most of the machinery was taken to Egypt and hidden in an old mine, where it was recovered by the Federals in May, 1865, and taken to Raleigh.

The buildings and the remaining machinery were completely destroyed early in May, as indicated by the following.

HDQRS. MILITARY DIVISION OF THE MISSISSIPPI,
Goldsborough, N. C., April 4, 1865.

GENERAL: I must now endeavor to group the events of the past three months connected with the armies under my command, in order that . . .

The 12th, 13th, and 14th were passed at Fayetteville, destroying absolutely the U. S. Arsenal and the vast amount of machinery which had formerly belonged to the old Harper's Ferry U. S. Arsenal. Every building was knocked down and burned, and every piece of machinery utterly broken up and ruined by the First Regiment Michigan Engineers, under the immediate supervision of Col. O. M. Poe, chief engineer. Much valuable property of great use to an enemy was here destroyed or cast into the river.

I have the honor to be, your obedient servant,

W. T. SHERMAN,
Major General, Commanding.

Maj. Gen. H. W. HALLECK,
Chief of Staff, Washington City, D. C.

THE FAYETTEVILLE RIFLE
Figure 2, Plate X

The rifle illustrated is marked on lock plate Fayetteville, the spread eagle below which is C. S. A. The "S" inverted and the date 1864. The barrel is 33 inches long. Caliber .58 and is marked with V. P., eagle head, 1864. The total length of the arm is 49 inches. Weight, 8 pounds, 14 ounces. The two bands, stock tip, trigger guard and butt plate are brass, the tang of the latter being marked C. S. A. The barrel is provided with a regular 1861 rear and front sight and the diameter of the barrel permits the use of the regulation bayonet.

The die of the eagle used in stamping the locks on these arms probably came from Harper's Ferry as it is identical with the eagle used on the model 1842 rifles made there, and the fact that the "S" is inverted would substantiate the theory that U. S. of the die had been cut out and replaced with C. S. A. The eagle stamped on the model 1855 rifles being manufactured at Harper's Ferry at the time of its capture was exceptionally large and placed on the cover of the tape box.

* * * * *

THE CONFEDERATE—HALL MUZZLE-LOADING RIFLE
Figure 3, Plate X

This arm is made up, with the exception of the stock and lock, of parts of the Hall breech-loading rifle that was for years made at Harper's Ferry and is one of the curiosities of the war, and the only instance on record of the deliberate conversion of a breechloader to a muzzle-loader for military purposes. The original breech-block frame is removed from the barrel and a most ingenious arrangement consisting of a one-piece brass casting carries the entire action with its center hung hammer.

In the ordnance office report to Congress dated Aug. 12, 1861, it is stated that eight or ten rifles per day were being made at Wytheville for the command of General Floyd, which arms were being made from barrels saved from Harper's Ferry. From a number of these Confederate-Hall rifles now known, all of which plainly indicate that they were fabricated with the use of little or no machinery, it is believed that they are the arms referred to as being made at Wytheville.

There is quite a wide variation in the band arrangement and the stocks were evidently made by hand without particular reference to any pattern as they all differ considerably. The original flintlock sights which were offset from the center line of the barrel, are retained as is also the sixteen groove rifling of that arm which is caliber .54 and probably adapted for use of the .54 caliber ammunition for the Mississippi rifle, many of which have not been bored out to the .58 caliber later adopted as standard.

*   *   *   *   *

THE TYLER, TEXAS, ARMORY

In May, 1862, a partnership was formed at Tyler consisting of George Yarbrough, J. C. Short and W. S. N. Biscoe—the latter two of them gunsmiths—for the purpose of the establishment of an armory that operated under the name of Messrs. Short, Biscoe & Co. They purchased one hundred acres of land one mile south of Tyler, Smith County, Texas and built a large brick factory and purchased all the necessary machinery and materials for making 5,000 guns under a contract with the Military Board at Austin.

From the report of the Military Board, September 30, 1863, is quoted: "On the 5th of November, 1862, Messrs. Short, Biscoe & Co., entered into contract with the Board to manufacture five thousand guns of the style of the Mississippi rifle, with the improved bayonet invented by Mr. Short, which the Board view as a very effective weapon." The price was to be $35.00 per gun.

These parties, immediately after making the contract, proceeded to the erection of buildings, procured a steam engine, manufactured a large number of tools necessary, and laid in a stock of material. They expended in this manner a very considerable sum of money, somewhat as the Board have been informed, over $30,000.00.

In June these parties obtained an advance from the Board of twenty-five thousand dollars to aid them in their operations, for which they gave approved security.

Under date of 17th September (1863), these contractors report as follows to the Board:

"We can deliver one hundred guns in two weeks from this date. We have been much troubled about stock timber, and a large number of our hands have been sick. We have been delayed on account of inexperienced hands, having to take such as we could get, as we have invariably been refused Gunsmiths from the regular army, and we are much annoyed by hands wanting advanced wages, as everything has so much advanced above the usual price of living. We are already losing money at the price of the gun.

"We have five hundred barrels bored and turned ready for the stocks, and two hundred and fifty bored, and fifty welded, making in all 800 barrels. We have made about 500 bayonets, and have nearly ready all the pieces for the locks for the 800. We have a lot of timber seasoning which we will push as we are steaming it, and will put them together as rapidly as possible."

An order has also been issued to turn these guns over to the military authorities for the arming of the State Troops. The high standing of these contractors is a guarantee that they will comply with their agreement.

From the journal of November 14, 1864, Papers of Military Board is quoted: "On October 12, 1863, Capt. W. Spalding Good was informed that there were probably 100 finished guns at Tyler, Texas. The armory was turned over to the Confederate States about this time, and the State of Texas paid for and received only one rifle from Tyler, Texas.

These guns, according to the contract, were to be patterned "after the model of the Misssissippi rifle—length of barrel 33 inches, bore of the size to carry ball of ½ ounce weight, walnut stocks, iron mountings, iron ramrod, two bands with loops, double sighted and single trigger with the improved bayonet invented by Mr. Short."

The bore of this arm was definitely fixed at .577 in compliance with the wishes of the Confederate War Department.

The Tyler armory was located at or near the southeast corner of Mocking Bird Lane and Robertson Avenue, the latter being the old Palestine Road, and while it was pretty well demolished at the close of the war, the records are not exactly clear as to the final disposition of the machinery and buildings.

There are no details available concerning the improved bayonet, invented by Mr. Short, which was to be supplied on the contract but it is assumed that it was some kind of a saber bayonet since at least one specimen of the Texas rifle is known that has a lug for this type of bayonet.

Early in 1862 the State of Texas also made a contract with N. B. Tanner, of Bastrop, for 500 Mississippi rifles with bayonets at the rate of $32.50 each. Tanner, it appears from the correspondence, contracted the making of the barrels and bayonets unfinished at $9.00 each to J. R. Nichols, also of Bastrop.

According to the report of the Military Board, September 30, 1863, there had been delivered on the contract 264 guns which indicates that Mr. Tanner was much more successful than Short, Briscoe & Co.

On August 23, 1863, an Ordnance report of Cooper's Brigade shows 450 Texas rifles in service.

Since there is nothing definite in regard to the marking of these arms, reference to the Texas rifle in the correspondence is a bit confusing, but it is fair to assume that complaints made against Texas rifles early in 1864 applied to the Tanner product in place of the Tyler. A typical complaint is here included:

OFFICE CHIEF ORDNANCE OFFICER,
Dist. Ind. Ter.
Doaksville, Choctaw Nation, February 25, 1864.
Brigadier General MAXEY,
Commanding District of Indian Territory:

GENERAL: I have the honor to report the condition of guns in the First Brigade, Indian Forces . . .

A few Enfield rifles were seen, with a few, very few, Mississippi rifles in the line; the remainder were composed of double-barrel guns, Texas rifles, sporting rifles, &c. . . .

The First Choctaw Regiment of the Second Brigade were armed with an assortment of guns, more of the Texas rifles than any other class of arms. And I would call your attention especially to this arm. A regiment armed complete with these guns are armed but badly. These guns are nothing more than a cheat, badly put together, and very unreliable, being liable, a great number, to burst. The remainder in the regiment were sporting rifles, which with few exceptions were badly wanting repair; double-barrel shot-guns, and a very few muskets. Lieutenant Colonel Wells' battallion were armed with Texas rifles, double-barrel guns, and a very few muskets with very few exceptions. I did not see a gun that was entirely serviceable.

I have the honor, General, to remain, very respectfully, your obedient servant.

J. J. DU BOSE,
Captain and Chief Ordnance Officer,
Dist. Ind. Ter.

With the steady advance of the Federal forces towards Little Rock in the fall of 1863 the Confederates evacuated first that place and soon Arkadelphia—the transfer of the machinery, &c., of the armories being outlined in the accompanying letter:

FIREARMS OF THE CONFEDERACY

OFFICE OF CHIEF OF ORDNANCE AND ARTILLERY,
TRANS-MISSISSIPPI DEPARTMENT,
Shreveport, La., October 22, 1863.

Maj. J. P. JOHNSON,
Assistant Adjutant and Inspector General:

MAJOR: I respectfully report for your information as follows: Establishments for ordnance work were in full operation at Little Rock, Arkadelphia, and Camden, and a shop for repair of arms at Fort Smith; but by reason of movements recently ordered, and the approach of the Federal forces, all these workshops and establishments have been removed to places of safety: the machinery, tools, stores, and men from Little Rock Arsenal to Tyler, Tex.; the machinery, tools, stores, and men from Arkadelphia to Marshall, Texas; and the machinery, tools, stores, and men from Camden to Shreveport, La.

I am establishing at Tyler a laboratory for fabricating battery and small-arms ammunition, carpenters' and blacksmiths' shops, and shop for repairs of arms. I am also in treaty for the purchase of a manufactory of small arms located at that point, and which is now carrying out a contract with the State of Texas for making guns.

At Marshall, Texas, I am having buildings erected for manufacture of small arms, smiths' and carpenters' shop, powdermill and magazine . . .

I am, Major, very respectfully, your obedient servant,
THOS. G. RHETT,
*Major and Chief of Ordnance and
Artillery, Trans-Miss. Dept.*

It is not known definitely whether the work at Arkadelphia included the making of new guns but the evidence is all against this and it is generally concluded that their efforts were confined to repairing damaged guns from the field and rebuilding and reboring country rifles for the military service.

The poor opinion held by the officers on the output of this armory is indicated by a report of Brigadier General W. L. Cabell, C. S. Army:

HEADQUARTERS NORTHWESTERN ARKANSAS,
Ozark, April 25, 1863.

COLONEL: I have the honor to inform you that . . . The Arkadelphia rifles, with the cartridges sent for them are no better than shotguns. I must therefore . . .

I am, sir, very respectfully, your obedient servant,
W. L. CABELL,
*Brigadier General, Commanding,
Northwestern, Ark.*

Col. S. S. ANDERSON,
Adjutant General, District of Arkansas.

With the Confederate Government finally taking over the Tyler armory and combining with it much of the machinery, tools and personnel of the Arkansas armories it seems that real

142

progress was finally made in the production of arms. The *Galveston Weekly News* of July 6, 1864, had this account:

Tyler, June 24, 1864.

Editor *News*: By the way, perhaps, there is no harm telling your numerous readers how well our young Confederacy is getting along in this section in the fabrication of firearms and ordnance stores generally —articles so much needed by our gallant soldiers in this great struggle for liberty. Well, then, I recently had the pleasure to accompany Lieut. Col. G. H. Hill through the extensive works he has caused to be erected near this formerly flourishing town, and I was most agreeably surprised to witness the progress which has been effected. One fine blacksmith shop runs sixteen forges. In another extensive brick structure, the machinery for the manufacture of firearms rolls daily (Sundays excepted), putting up splendid guns, from the first to the last screw, and all going on with perfect order and system. Though this is a Government establishment, I did not see one idle man about the premises; all was quiet, save the roll of the machinery and the clink of the hammer.

Capt. Geo. S. Polleys is superintendent of the work here, and deserves much credit for the orderly manner in which all is carried on.

I do not mention, for particular reasons, the precise number of firearms added to our supply every week from this establishment, but it is by no means inconsiderable.

Col. Hill is engaged in fabricating nearly everything belonging to the ordnance department, excepting cannon, round shot and shell; and certainly no more faithful or skillful officer graces this branch of the service.

THE TYLER, TEXAS, ENFIELD RIFLE
Figure 2, Plate XII

This arm is patterned somewhat after the Enfield rifle and has a barrel 33 inches long, caliber .57, with a five groove rifling. It is provided with a lug for a saber bayonet and a two-leafed rear sight. The mountings are all of brass. The trigger guard is shaped like that of the Enfield while the bands are flat and retained in place by regular band springs.

The butt has a shape like our regulation rifle. The lock plate, which is of the regular Enfield type is 5¼ inches long, and is marked Texas Rifle, Tyler, Cal. .57 in three lines forward of the hammer and to the rear of the hammer C. S. The serial number 11 appears on all of the lock parts and this lock is peculiar in that it is attached to the stock by only one screw just forward of the hammer and is believed to be the only military arm of the period so arranged. The barrel and butt plate tang are both marked C. S. and they likewise carry the serial number 11. Total length of arm 48½ inches. Weight 8½ pounds.

The output of this armory presents quite a number of riddles. Their contract with the Military Board of the State of Texas, dated December 20, 1862, provided that they were to make 5,000 arms after the model of the Mississippi rifle, length of barrel 33 inches, bore .577, walnut stocks and iron mountings and provided with the improved bayonet invented by Mr. Short.

The specimen shown is not the Mississippi type but is of the Enfield type and the mountings are all of brass in place of iron. There is no record of the type of bayonet invented by Mr. Short the contract specifies, but it is most probably a saber bayonet of some kind that the lug on the specimen shown would accommodate.

L. D. Satterlee, writing in Dexter's Quarterly shows a cut of an arm having an Enfield type lock marked Hill Rifle, Tyler, Texas, caliber .54 C. S. 1864, and gives the following description:

"Enfield type, with Mississippi type of rear band. Length 43½ inches over all (6 inches shorter than the Mississippi or Short Enfield), barrel 27 inches, caliber .54. Front and rear sights are of brass, cut in. Numbered 337 in ten different places, every part of the lock is so numbered, including the screw through the tang and frame to trigger guard. Also numbered at front of barrel about 1 inch from muzzle, next to front sight. Lands are about ¼ inch wide and very shallow. Front band gone and woodwork at this point about two-thirds intact, indicates no bayonet was used. First band in place (very light iron) and has spring to hold. Front spring gone, but similar to the English type."

Here again the Enfield type predominates over the Mississippi type—the barrel is 6 inches shorter than the contract specified and the caliber .54 in place of .577. The mountings are iron in place of brass as on specimen shown and there are no provisions for a bayonet. Since the Satterlee specimen has a front sight with the serial number stamped on the barrel one inch from the muzzle it would indicate that this is the length as originally made and that it has not been cut down for a rabbit gun since the war.

THE TYLER, TEXAS, AUSTRIAN RIFLE
Figure 1, Plate XII

The specimen shown is a crudely made arm of the typical Austrian pattern of that period. The total length is 53 inches

PLATE XII

Fig.
1

Fig. 2

Figs. 3-4

Fig. 1. Tyler Texas
Austrian Rifle.
Fig. 2. Tyler Texas
Enfield Rifle.
Fig. 3.-4. Enlarged
View of Locks
on Guns.

PLATE XIII

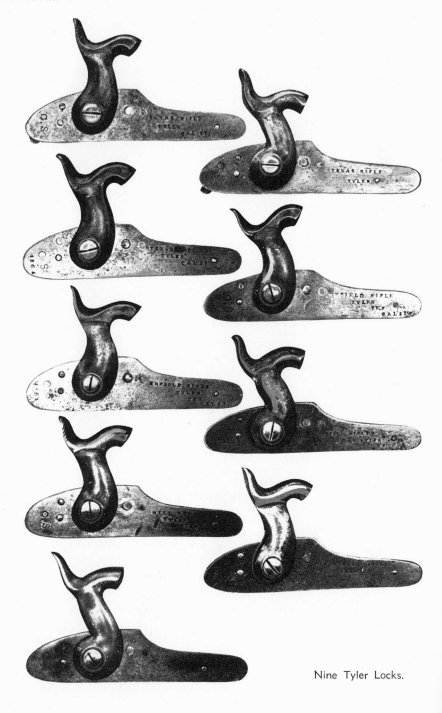

Nine Tyler Locks.

and the barrel is caliber .54 and is 37¼ inches long, provided with a regular U. S. type 1861 rear sight. The mountings are all of iron, two bands, with sling swivels attached to top band and trigger guard. The lock is marked forward of the hammer "AUSTRIAN RIFLE, TYLER, TEX. Cal. .54" To rear of hammer C. S. 1865 and as in all Tyler arms the lock is attached to the stock with but one screw.

Like the preceding specimen shown, this arm is also serial number 11, which number appears on all lock parts, the barrel, butt plate and guard. Except for having an Enfield type lock there are no other resemblances to the above specimen, leaving a very large question mark as to why arms differing so radically were made at the same armory.

TYLER, TEXAS, RIFLE LOCKS

Plate XIII

The different markings on the following locks, which were obviously all intended for the same style of gun, discloses the possibility that the Confederate authorities had put into operation a system of manufacture wherein the various parts of the arms were made at different armories, with the intention of assembly into a complete arm, at some central armory, and it seems likely that these locks were all made at one place for use on arms produced at other points, and the variation was made to accommodate the different equipment of the various armories producing the barrels.

Twenty-nine of these locks came to light in 1931 and all give indications of having been in use, as many of the screws holding the lock to the stock were broken off, and the hammers show evidence of contact with the nipples of the gun.

These locks are all of the same type, having the single screwhole for attaching the lock to the stock. The parts are not identical but will all interchange with slight fitting; there is, however, a wide variation in the shape of hammers.

The serial numbers appear on the back of the plates and on all parts, including the hammers.

The serial numbers appearing on these locks offer little or no solution to the riddle concerning the output of this armory for we find an Enfield type undated gun serial number 11 and an Austrian type gun dated 1865 with the same serial number and Satterlee shows an Enfield type dated 1864 with serial number 337.

145

Fig. 1. Serial numbers 46, 679, 472. These are marked Texas Rifle, Tyler, Cal. .57 in three lines forward of the hammer and to the rear of it C. S.

Fig. 2. Serial numbers 409 and 458 are marked Texas Rifle, Tyler in two lines forward of the hammer and to the rear of it C. S.

Fig. 3. Serial number 802 is marked Texas Rifle, Tyler, Cal. .57 in three lines forward of the hammer and to the rear of it C. S. 1865.

Fig. 4. Serial numbers 60, 63, 64, 170, 196, 244, 261, 262 are marked Enfield Rifle, Tyler, Tex., Cal. .57 in four lines forward of the hammer and to the rear of it C. S.

Fig. 5. Serial numbers 460, 462A, 469, 479, 484, 500 are marked Enfield Rifle Tyler, Tex., Cal. .57 in four lines forward of the hammer and to the rear of it C. S. 1865.

Fig. 6. Serial numbers 12 and 301 are marked Hill Rifle, Tyler, Tex., in three lines forward of the hammer and to the rear of it C. S.

Fig. 7. Serial numbers 192 and 229 are marked Hill Rifle, Tyler, Tex., Cal. .54 in four lines forward of the hammer and to the rear of it C. S.

Fig. 8. Serial numbers 26, 42, and 49 are marked Austrian Rifle, Tyler, Tex., Cal. .54 in four lines forward of the hammer and to the rear of it C. S. 1865.

Fig. 9. Serial numbers 133 and 274 are perfectly plain locks except the C. S. to the rear of the hammer.

* * * * *

COOK & BROTHER

This firm was the largest private manufacturer engaged in making arms for the Confederacy. Before a court of inquiry assembled pursuant to the orders of the Adjutant and Inspector Generals' office, February 18, 1863, D. W. Brickell testified that as a member of the committee of public safety of New Orleans prior to April, 1862, that members of the committee had waited upon and urged the governor to have Messrs. Cook & Brothers' factory of small-arms enlarged so as to have 100, instead of 25, Enfield rifles turned out per day, and to this end they induced the governor to appropriate $40,000; but this he would not do until the committee had appropriated a like sum. The establishment at that time was making guns for the State of

Alabama alone. They wanted that contract executed in the shortest time, so that the State of Louisiana might have the benefit of its works . . .

Before the same court F. W. C. Cook testified as follows:

"By the Judge Advocate:

"Question. Were you a resident of New Orleans from October, 1861, to May, 1862? If so, what was your occupation?

"Answer. I was, and, with my brother, engaged in the manufacture of small arms. I have lived in New Orleans for seventeen years.

"Question. Was your machinery removed from the city at the time of its capture, in April, 1862? If so, was it done in pursuance of orders from or with the assistance of General Lovell?

"Answer. I saved all the machinery connected with the armory, except the motive power. I did not save all the work. I left 130 tons of wrought iron, which I could not bring away. We lost the tools and machinery of the machine shop. Afterwards, on or about April 29, I received a schooner laden with steel and iron. At Madisonville, the Yankee sentinel permitted her to pass through the canal for $20. On Thursday morning, April 24, 1862, at 11 o'clock, Major Smith sent for me, and told me the fleet had passed the forts, and to save what I could. I asked him to put it down in writing, which he did; the paper I have not here with me. It was to the effect that, by the wish and consent of the general commanding, Cook & Brother were requested to remove their machinery from New Orleans . . ."

The machinery was moved to Athens, Georgia, where a factory consisting of several brick and stone buildings having a capacity of about 200 arms per week was completed and put into operation early in 1863, where it continued to operate until the close of the war.

The Cooks were real patriots and had their employees organized into a defense battalion that was engaged in opposing Sherman and Major F. W. C. Cook was killed leading his men in the engagement before Savannah, December, 1864.

The report of Chief of Ordnance, A. B. Dyer, to Adjutant General Townsend, dated November 26, 1867, contains the following paragraph in reference to this armory.

"Fourth. Ten acres of land at Athens, Ga., known as the Athens Armory, upon which are several brick and stone buildings. This Athens armory was turned over to and is in charge of the Ordnance Department, but was not the property of the so-called Confederate States, but was used for the manufacture of arms for said Confederacy. The property is in litigation."

The following letter indicates this property was returned to Francis L. Cook in 1868.

UNITED STATES ARSENAL,
Augusta, Ga., August 20, 1868.

Bvt. Maj. Gen. A. B. DYER,
    Chief of Ordnance, U. S. Army, Washington, D. C.:

GENERAL: I have the honor to report that in obedience to instructions from the Adjutant General, U. S. Army, transmitted to me by Maj. Gen. George G. Meade, commanding Third Military District, I have turned over to Francis L. Cook (one of the former owners) the Athens Armory and all the property pertaining thereto which has been in my charge.

I inclose herewith copies of the instructions received from the Adjutant General and General Meade, a copy of the judgment of Judge Erskine, of the United States district court, and Mr. Cook's duplicate receipt. The originals of these papers are on file in this office.

Very respectfully, your obedient servant,
D. W. FLAGLER,
Brevet Lieutenant Colonel, U. S.
Army, Captain Ordnance, Commanding.

The report of Gen. Gorgas to Secretary of War Seddon, of December 31, 1864, indicates that this armory was under the control of his Bureau and that with a full force of workmen it had a capacity of 10,000 rifles per annum.

THE COOK INFANTRY RIFLE
Figure 1, Plate XIV

This is an exceptionally well made arm patterned after the British-Enfield but of caliber .58. The length of the barrel is 33 inches while the over-all length of the arm is 49 inches. The lock plate is 5⅜ inches long and is marked COOK & BROTHER, ATHENS, GA., 1864, with the serial number 5,782 all placed forward of the hammer   and to the rear of it the Confederate flag, a typical marking on all Cook arms. The mountings are all of brass—the bands being of the clamping type—the forward band carrying the sling-swivel while the rear swivel is carried on the butt stock. The butt plate is of the typical Enfield type stamped on the tang with the serial number 5,782. The rear sight is fixed and the front sight is of the regular pattern, acting as a bayonet lug. The barrel is stamped

PLATE XIV

Fig.
1

Fig.
2

Fig. 3

Fig. 4

Fig. 1. Cook Infantry Rifle.
Fig. 2. Cook Artillery Carbine.
Fig. 3. Cook Cavalry Carbine.
Fig. 4. Enlarged View of Lock.

PLATE XV

Fig. 1

Fig. 2

Fig. 1. Tallassee Carbine.
Fig. 2. Enlarged View of Same.

on the side opposite the nipple with the serial number 5,782 and on top the date 1864. The stock appears to be made of cherry and the iron ramrod is provided with a brass cup-shaped end.

THE COOK ARTILLERY RIFLE
Figure 2, Plate XIV

This is a good example of the Cook product, made up in special size as an artillery arm. The barrel is 24 inches long, caliber .58, while the total length of the arm is 40 inches. The lock, which is 5⅜ inches long, is marked COOK & BROTHER, ATHENS, GA., 1863, and numbered 2,379 forward of the hammer and to the rear of it the Confederate flag. The mountings are all of brass, the bands are of the clamping type and carry the number 2,379, the forward band carrying the sling swivel. The trigger guard is of the Enfield type and has a sling swivel at the back end of the guard plate. The butt plate is also of the Enfield pattern and carries the serial number. The barrel is mounted with fixed sights and is marked on top ATHENS— 1863, and on the side opposite the nipple is the word "proved." The stock is of black walnut while the all-iron ramrod has the typical cup-shaped end. This arm probably served as a rabbit gun after the war for upon dismantling it in 1934 it was found to contain a light charge of homemade bird shot, each shot having the tell-tale oblong shape and small teat indicating that they had been dropped but a short distance into the water. The wads were of newspaper and having the very small print used in the early 1870s.

THE COOK MUSKETOON
Figure 3, Plate XIV

This arm is patterned somewhat after the Enfield model 1858 carbine and is an exceptionally well made piece. The mountings are all of brass. The bands are the clamping type, while the trigger guard and butt plate follow the Enfield pattern. The swivel ramrod is attached with very short swivel bars and the end of the ramrod is provided with a large button head. The barrel is 21 inches long. Caliber .58. Total length of arm, 36½ inches. A large fixed rear sight and an Enfield type of front sight is provided. A nipple protector is carried on a chain attached to a small eyebolt on forward part of the trigger guard.

149

The lock plate screws hold in place a bar for attaching a sling ring. Marked on lock plate forward of the hammer, COOK & BROTHER, ATHENS, GA., 1864 and the number 5,278. To the rear of the hammer is engraved a Confederate flag. The numeral 5,278 also appears on the breech of the barrel and the tang of the butt plate.

* * * * *

THE TALLASSEE ARMORY

The report of General Gorgas of December 31, 1864, enumerating the machinery under the control of his bureau for the manufacture of arms, estimated a capacity of 55,000 rifles and carbines per annum and included among these 6,000 carbines from the armory at Tallassee, Ala., indicating that this was to be one of the important armories of the Confederacy, and it is, therefore, entitled to more than passing notice.

The Official Records afford no help as Tallassee does not appear in the index of Volume 3, Series IV, which contains the above referred-to report, nor does it appear in the General Index of the Records, making it necessary to depend on other sources for information.

The buildings of this plant were erected over a period of years, with construction beginning in the early forties of the nineteenth century and finished in 1846. The group of smaller buildings were the first to be completed.

The contractors, Thompson Bros., brought many American, Irish, Scotch, and English workmen from Maryland and other seaboard states, for the construction work. The original purpose of these buildings, was that of a complete cotton-sheeting, thread and yarn mill, and they were located on this particular sight, which is some 27 miles northeast of Montgomery, Ala., on the west bank of the Tallapoosa River, to utilize the very fine waterfalls which provided a head of some forty odd feet for power. Water power was then just coming into its own, and this cotton mill had the distinction of being one of the world's greatest water-power mills of its day.

The buildings were constructed of granite ashlar cut out of the local stone of the building site. The buildings were constructed of native materials as far as possible, because the nearest railroad head was Cowl's Station, a distance of 7 miles, or more.

The location, which was a part of a land grant from the Creek Nation of Indians of some thirty odd thousand acres belonging to Barent DuBois. The water rights were leased to the mill operators for a period of 99 years, with certain specific and definite restrictions made by the owner for the purpose of preserving the natural beauty of the place—he had selected a nearby sight overlooking the waterfall, and built his home there to enjoy the scenery and the music of the falling water. In later years, the violation of many of these restrictions by subsequent operators of the property, were the subject of extended lawsuits brought by heirs of the original owner.

That the enterprise, at the beginning, was of a very substantial character is evidenced by the sturdy construction of the original buildings; the lower walls were several feet thick made of cut granite blocks.

With the excellent water power and a great deal of machinery that could be utilized already available, it was but natural that these buildings were converted into an armory to meet the urgent need for arms existing in the South at the beginning of the war and from present available evidence it is believed that this armory was either a private or State enterprise started sometime in 1862 for the purpose of remodeling sporting arms and repairing battlefield pick-ups for the service. Sometime in 1863 it was taken over by the Confederate authorities and with machinery and personnel from Richmond, the fabrication of completely new arms was commenced.

An order of General Gorgas, dated February 21st, 1865, directed Col. J. H. Burton to assume directive charge of the operations of this armory as well as the armories at Macon, Ga., Athens, Ga., and Columbus, Ga., with authority to transfer employees, materials, machinery, tools and public funds from either armory to the others, when, in his judgment, the public interest would be promoted.

A letter from W. E. Elseberry, Primrose Farm, Montgomery, Ala., to Berkley Bowie dated May 15, 1924, reads in part as follows:

"During 1863 there arrived at Tallassee, Alabama, from Richmond, Va., a very complete lot of gun-making machinery in charge of four officers of the Confederate States Government, and sufficient number of gunsmiths, mechanics, blacksmiths and helpers to turn out in considerable numbers, carbines for cavalry use. The carbines were muzzle-loaders, and the recollection of the writer is that the locks thereon were stamped C. S. A. Tallassee, 1863 or 4, depending on date of completion of the weapon. The stocks and barrels were in the rough, stocks being turned and barrels bored and finished while locks were made entire by the force at Tallassee.

"Before mounting the barrels, they were tested by double loading. Cartridges were also made at Tallassee, for these carbines but revolvers were not made at Tallassee, according to the recollection of the writer. None of these carbines are extant in this territory."

In a letter dated August 24, 1863, by Gen. Gorgas in Richmond, in connection with a report made by John W. R. Chambliss, Jr., a Colonel in Lee's cavalry brigade, complaining of the cavalry arms then in use, and recommending a breech-loading carbine, said "A good breech-loading carbine is now making here in small numbers. No reliable carbines except muzzle-loaders are to be obtained abroad. Cavalry officers are not all agreed as to the value of the breech-loading carbine, and officers of great experience pronounce in favor of the muzzle-loading carbine. As the latter can be produced when the former cannot, I have ordered a model to be prepared, and have had it submitted to General Stuart for the criticism of his officers. As soon as its main features are settled, it will be adopted." In support of this we have this news item:

Tri-Weekly South Carolinian, June 2, 1864:

"A Richmond correspondent says TALLASSEE, Ala., is shortly to be favored, like Columbia, with the advent of some of the Government employees therein. All the hands employed in the carbine factory here are to be transferred to that point, there being quite an amount of the necessary machinery there, and a large cotton factory already engaged as suitable for the operations of this branch of military manufacture. This factory turns out carbines for the cavalry chiefly of the Maynard patent and fully equal in workmanship to the best productions of Yankeedom. At present, the force is chiefly employed on Musketoons, a species of the muzzle-loading firearms."

Among these workmen transferred from Richmond, was a Mr. Shelton, who was made a foreman of one of the Tallassee shops and who boarded with Mrs. Leaena Hairston, whose home was only a bit over a mile East of the plant,—a short walk for exercise before and after working twelve hours at making something out of practically nothing and doing it the hard way.

Composite Photograph of Tallassee Armory

The Elisha Hotchkiss Clock From Tallassee Armory

One of Mr. Shelton's prized possessions which he brought with him from Richmond, Va., to Tallassee, was a Connecticut Shelf Clock made by Elisha Hotchkiss, Burlington, Conn., about 1815. This clock was placed on a shelf high up out of harms way, on the wall of the shop and was used as the official time piece of the entire force.

Mr. William New was also one of the workmen transferred from Richmond to Tallassee and in 1924 he related how, upon the approach of the Federal troops the armory employees destroyed all the guns and parts that were in process of manufacture, much of the machinery, and about 600 completed arms. They then made a quick departure to avoid capture, to find upon their return that the Yankees had completely demolished and thrown into the river all of the machinery but that the sturdy construction of the buildings had defied them as they were practically intact, and, lo and behold!—the old clock had been overlooked and was still in place.

The destruction of the armory, of course, threw the men out of employment, and evidently money was none too plentiful, for Mr. Shelton paid his board bill to Mrs. Hairston with his beloved clock, which is now the prized possession of Mr. J. G. Gauntt, of Chattanooga, Tenn., a grandnephew of Mrs. Hairston.

The accompanying composite photograph, shows the armory buildings as they were during the war, but with the return of peace, when the buildings reverted back to their original use as cotton mills, many changes were made both on the buildings and in the immediate vicinity. A top story was added to the main building and in 1881-2, Lee & Mehaffey constructed the T stem portion of the large building to left. A large weave-shed was built between the river and main building. The old wing race was built of solid granite blocks, laid up in mud and chinked in lead. This wall extended only sixty feet from the West shore, as specifically specified in the lease of 1836 and was part of the original installation for gathering water for the running of the mill.

In 1899-1902 a rock dam was built across the stream at the armory sight, by Hardaway & Watkins, and just South of the armory, a steel railroad bridge was erected in 1897-8 while mill No. 2, including a second mill race from the new dam, was erected across the stream from the original installation about 1902, so that present-day photographs give but a poor conception of the original setting.

Immediately following the construction of the dam, etc., the heirs to this property entered suit on the grounds that the terms of contract and lease had been violated by constructing a dam across the river along with the other structures built on the property of the heirs.

The heirs won their suit before the high court of Montgomery, Ala. The Manufacturing Co. appealed and fought the heirs over a period of several years and thereby kept possession of the property belonging to the heirs. This is another sad story of how the Indian and those of Indian blood have been treated by the white man.

Under "Breech-loading Carbines" will be found additional data on this armory and a description of the breechloader made there.

THE TALLASSEE MUZZLE-LOADING CARBINE
Figure 1, Plate XV

The specimen shown is marked on lock plate forward of the hammer C. S. Tallassee, Ala., in three lines and to the rear of the hammer 1864. The lock plate is of the Enfield type, $5\frac{1}{4}$ inches long. The caliber .58, and the barrel is 25 inches long. Total length of the arm, $40\frac{3}{4}$ inches. The two brass bands are of the clamping type and there is provided a swivel ramrod similar to our 1842 musketoon. The trigger guard is of brass and also similar to our model 1841 guards. Sling swivels are carried on the top band and the brass plate at the butt of the stock. The butt plate of brass has a decided curve and the rear sight is similar to our regular 1861 model. The stock is made of what appears to be maple and the arm as a whole is an exceptionally well made piece. Figure 2 is an enlarged view of this lock.

CHAPTER IV

STATE AND PRIVATE ARMORIES — PRIVATE CON-
TRACTORS AND THE CROSSROADS GUNSMITHS —
ARMORIES WITHOUT ARMS AND UNIDENTIFIED
ARMS — CONVERSION OF SHOTGUNS AND SPORT-
ING RIFLES TO MILITARY USE—BREECH-LOADING
CARBINES.

In THE reports of General Gorgas he refers to the establishments for the manufacture of arms as armories and those
establishments for the storage and issue of arms as arsenals.

Of course an armory would have in connection with it an
arsenal for the storage of its output pending issue and a first
class arsenal would have some shop facilities for the repair and
maintenance of arms.

Some confusion is created by the fact that in much of the
war-time correspondence and reports the terms armory and
arsenal are used to suit the individual and just a few years ago
it was quite common to meet up with an ex-Confederate who
claimed in all good faith that he had worked in a Confederate
armory in some given town and in many of these cases it developed that he merely worked in some repair shop of an arsenal
or one of the many shops devoted to altering and repairing sporting arms.

The foregoing Chapter covers the armories that were
finally taken over by the Confederate Ordnance Department
while the present Chapter attempts to cover the less known
State and Private armories, and because of the very meager information available these present the most fascinating part of
the study of Confederate arms. There are some armories known
to have operated but no arms have been identified as a part of
their output while there are other arms of undoubted Confederate manufacture whose place of origin is still a mystery.

The identification of arms as being of Confederate manufacture provides a good many puzzles for the student collector
as there seems to be no positive "earmarks" to go by where the
markings are obliterated or parts of guns have been inter-
changed.

Most of the contracts with State or private armories specified an arm "of the value and description of the Enfield or
Mississippi rifle" and this obviously left a great many of the
details to suit the maker. The original Mississippi or U. S. Model
1841 was caliber .54, had fixed rear sight, no bayonet lug and
a large brass patch box in the stock. Later many of these rifles
were rebored to .58 caliber and provided with adjustable leaf
rear sight and bayonet lug. The Enfield rifle almost invariably
had an adjustable rear sight soldered to the barrel and was
provided with oval iron bands of the clamping type.

With the exception of Richmond and Fayetteville and in
some cases Tyler and Dickson, Nelson, the fixed rear sight was
adhered to though there are scattered specimens having a U. S.
1861 leaf sight, the latter probably being salvaged material from
captured guns damaged beyond repair.

Almost all kinds of native wood that was suitable for stocks
was used and as the kiln drying of lumber was not in extensive
use at that period and as there was no time for the usual two
or three year air seasoning period the stocks on Confederate-
made arms generally give some indication of the use of this
green timber such as air cracks, warping and in many cases the
sticking of the screws in the wood.

The U. S. model 1841 or the Mississippi rifle had the large
patch box and the U. S. Remington 1863 rifle had a somewhat
smaller patch box. The Dickson Nelson lock plate fits the Remington rifle, the J. P. Murray fits the model 1841 rifle, etc., so that
it is not uncommon to see these U. S. guns equipped with Confederate-made locks and where actual deception is intended the
U. S. markings on the barrels are easily removed but the patch
boxes remain as a telltale as it can safely be assumed that no
patch boxes were put on the Confederate-made arms.

The manufacture of sword bayonets in the Confederacy was
discontinued by an order issued by Adjutant General Samuel
Cooper dated January 14, 1864,[1] so that most of the rifles are
found with saber bayonet lugs though this was not a fixed rule
as many of the State contracts provided for the triangular
socket bayonet and it is fairly safe that the bayonet lug which
was an additional expense was omitted after the above order.

Most Confederate-made arms have serial numbers, and
these are generally low numbers usually put on with individual
dies and showing considerable irregularity. Some manufacturers

[1] Official Records, War of the Rebellion, Series 4, Vol. III, Page 28.

went to the extreme in using serial numbers, as every part of the gun, including the lock parts large enough to take the serial number have it on—the Tyler guns are a good example of these —while other manufacturers use the numbers more sparingly— generally the barrel, lock and butt plate being marked.

There are a number of breech-loading arms of probable Confederate manufacture as yet unidentified and as these were evidently made by individual or very small shops no rules were adhered to except those of the inventor, leaving the present day student very little in the way of gun markings or characteristic to go by. The so-called Confederate Perry was a good example of this and unless—or until—documentary evidence to the contrary is submitted we can reasonably assume that the so-called "rising breechblock carbine" which has puzzled collectors and arms students for years, is the weapon patented by N. T. Read, of Danville, Va., March 20, 1863, and manufactured at the plant of Keen, Walker & Company, Danville.

* * * * *

ALABAMA'S WAR EFFORT

Alabama, which because of its rich coal and iron ore deposits gave promise of being the industrial center of the new south, was extremely active in its war supply efforts and Governor Shorter, apparently, was determined to get arms for the Alabama troops, as in addition to the Alabama firms, his contracts were made with at least three Georgia firms—Greenwood & Gray, John D. Gray and John M. Gray, all of Columbus, Ga. He also made a contract with Lewis G. Sturdivant, of Talladega, Ala., on March 6, 1862, to manufacture "two thousand good army guns, of the value and description of the Mississippi or Enfield rifle, with saber bayonet attached" to be delivered in lots of 100 by May 1, 1863, at a cost of $35 each. Sturdivant and James G. L. Huey, of Talladega, gave bond in the sum of ten thousand dollars for the faithful execution of the contract, and the State advanced Sturdivant $5,000. Sturdivant was a jeweler before the war. He rented a shop from S. D. Watson on the south side of Battle street, West, in Talladega. The shop was a two-story building.

The Sturdivant rifle (See Figure 4, Plate XVIII) is a very small and fragile weapon, 46 inches over-all, with 32-inch barrel, of .54 caliber, with small stock and all brass mountings. It bears no mark except the serial: "130."

Maj. Gen. Lovell H. Rousseau, in his raid from Decatur, Ala., to West Point, Ga., July 10-22, 1864, reported:

"On the 15th (July, 1864) I reached Talladega, where about 100,000 rations of sugar and salt, 20,000 rations of flour and bacon, and a quantity of other stores were captured. The command was supplied with what was required, and the remainder destroyed. Two gun factories, several railroad cars and the railroad depot were destroyed. The latter contained a large quantity of leather, with grain, sacks, flour, wheat, salt and cotton. 143 rebel soldiers were found in the Hospital at Talladega, and were paroled.[2]

The other gun shop reported destroyed by Rousseau at Talladega probably was that of Daniel Wallis. Wallis was given a contract by Governor Shorter on May 9, 1862, to make one thousand Mississippi rifles. Wallis and Samuel F. Rice gave bond for the execution of the contract, and the State advanced Wallis $2,000.

The contract provides that the guns are to be "of the value and description of the Mississippi rifles with bayonets similar to the bayonet commonly used on such rifles or muskets in the United States before the secession of Alabama, excepting the bayonet to be made by said Wallis is not to be grooved, and with regulation tube lock and bore with mountings similar to said Mississippi rifles with the exception of the patch box."

An original report of Duff C. Green, Quartermaster General of Alabama, in the Military Archives of the State of Alabama, contains the following:

Statement of arms and munitions of war received from contractors and purchased by the Quartermaster's Department of Alabama, with the price paid for the same from 1st October, 1863, to 1st November, 1864.

---

[2] Official Records, War of the Rebellion, Vol. 38, Part 2, Page 906.

PLATE XVI

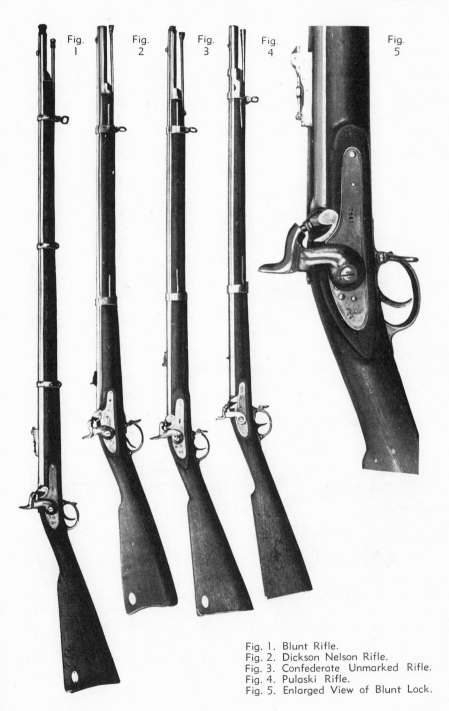

Fig.
1

Fig.
2

Fig.
3

Fig.
4

Fig.
5

Fig. 1. Blunt Rifle.
Fig. 2. Dickson Nelson Rifle.
Fig. 3. Confederate Unmarked Rifle.
Fig. 4. Pulaski Rifle.
Fig. 5. Enlarged View of Blunt Lock.

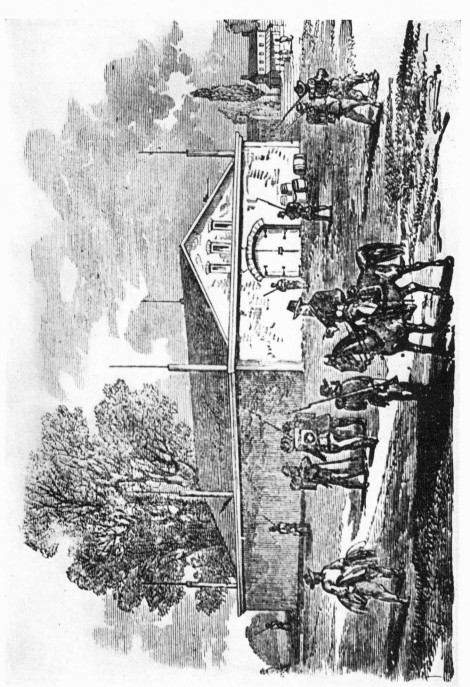

CONFEDERATE ARSENAL AT MILLEDGEVILLE, GA.

Contractors, &c.	Powder lbs.	Lead lbs.	Miss. Rifles	Carb's.	Price	Amount
*C. Kreutner			36		$35.00	$1,260.00
*C. Suter & Co. (P. Lessier)			50		37.50	1,875.00
*Davis & Bozeman			50		27.50	1,375.00
* " "			27		42.50	1,147.50
* " "			56		45.00	2,520.00
* " "			8		35.00	280.00
" "			741	89	60.00	49,800.00
**John M. Gray			96		45.00	405.00
**Greenwood & Gray			253	73	55.00	17,930.00
**John D. Gray				80	45.00	3,600.00
Dickson, Nelson & Co.			645		90.00	58,050.00
**Gwin & Ellsberry	421¾				6.50	2,741.37
**W. H. C. Price		6,000			2.00	12,000.00
	421¾	6,000	1,981	242		$157,303.87

*Contract Expired
**Purchase

Note: Mr. L. G. Sturdivant, by orders of His Excellency Governor
Shorter, turned over direct to Col. H. C. Lockhart two hundred
and eighty guns, which did not pass through the Ordnance
Office; and forwarded other guns which, upon inspection, prov-
ing not equal to standard, were returned to him and not entered
upon the receipts of the Department.

DUFF C. GREEN

* * * * *

DICKSON, NELSON & CO. RIFLE
Figure 2, Plate XVI

This arm is patterned after the U. S. Model 1855 Rifle,
except that the cone seat and lock are of the Model 1842. The
stock is made of what appears to be cherry. The barrel is 33
inches long, caliber .58 and the rifling consists of seven grooves.
The total length is 4 feet, 1 inch and weighs, without bayonet,
9 pounds, 6 oz. Marked on lock plate DICKSON, NELSON & CO.,
C. S. forward of the hammer and to the rear of the hammer,
ALA 1863. The barrel is stamped 1863 and ALA and the tang of
the butt plate is also marked ALA. The barrel is provided with
a two-leaf rear sight and does not have the lug for saber bayonet.
The bands are flat, retained by regular band springs and all the
mountings are of brass.

There are a number of minor variations in this arm and
another specimen by the same makers dated 1865. The bands on
the latter are oval and of the clamping type. The trigger guard
plate is longer and the rear sight is fixed. The stock is of black
walnut and the only markings are on the lock plate. As the plant
was not moved to Dawson, Ga., until late in 1863 it is possible
that the specimen shown was made at Adairsville, Ga.

In 1861, William Dickson, of Dickson, Ala., O. O. Nelson, of Tuscumbia, Ala., and L. H. Sadler, of Leighton, Ala., organized the Shakanoosa Arms Company and were awarded a contract to manufacture "Mississippi rifles" for the State of Alabama. They began to build a plant at Dickson, but before it was completed the tide of war changed, and the firm moved hastily to Rome, Ga.

There they leased a large brick building, but hardly had gotten under way when fire, believed of incendiary origin, wiped out the plant. The harassed firm next moved to Adairsville, Ga., where rifles were manufactured until after the battle of Chicamauga. The next move was to Dawson, Ga., where rifles were made until the end of the war. And so these guns that bear the name of Alabama, all were made in the neighboring State of Georgia.

We are sometimes wont to believe that our present day W. P. B. and other Federal agencies for the control of materials and manpower are children of the present war but the following letters indicate that the Confederates had just such a system.

Selma, (Ala.) July 15, 1862.

SIR: I am instructed by Colonel Gorgas to fill your orders for iron to enable Messrs. Dickson, Nelson & Co. to complete a contract with you for 5,000 rifles and bayonets. Please send an order for the quantity and description of iron wanted and I will have it executed at the Shelby works immediately.

With much respect, your obedient servant,
C. J. McRAE

His Excellency JOHN GILL SHORTER,
Governor of Alabama, Montgomery.

The following letter from Governor Watts of Alabama to Secretary of War Seddon would indicate that they were still working on the Alabama contract in 1864:

EXECUTIVE DEPARTMENT,
Montgomery, Ala., June 7, 1864.

Hon. J. A. SEDDON,
Secretary of War:

The enrolling officer, Colonel Browne, of Macon, Ga., has enrolled several of the hands of the Shakanoosa Arms Manufacturing Company at Dawson, Ga., and threatens to take many more, thus in effect destroying an establishment with which Alabama has a contract for a supply of arms. This establishment is of common and great utility to the Confederate States and the States of Georgia and Alabama. Arms are a necessity, and Alabama has a very inadequate supply. I request, therefore, that no further conscription from that factory be made, or that of those making (arms?) such may be returned or detailed as may under oath by the superintendent be deemed necessary to the successful working of the establishment.

T. H. WATTS,
Governor.

The practice of manufacturing parts of equipment at a number of different plants in order to utilize the facilities and manpower of the scattered locations and then collecting all the parts at one plant for final assembly, which practice is being followed today, is of no new conception as the following letter from Shorter to Pickens concerning the forced movements of the Dickson, Nelson Company and suggesting the policy of manufacturing arms under our present system will show. This letter is also interesting that it shows that there were no arms delivered on the Dickson, Nelson Company contract up to May 2, 1862.

EXECUTIVE DEPARTMENT,
Montgomery, Ala., May 2, 1862.

SIR: I have to apologize for not having replied at an . . .

I have made contracts wherever it was possible to do so, for the manufacture of guns, but the deliveries under these contracts have not yet commenced. One establishment with which I had contracted for the manufacture of 5,000 Mississippi rifles, the first of which were to have been delivered by this date, has been forced to remove its machinery to Georgia, in consequence of the invasion of our northern counties by the enemy, and I shall, on that account, be subjected to a considerable delay in receiving the arms. I have also had made a considerable number of pikes and bowie knives, which are now ready for use. A large factory of arms is about being established under the patronage of the State, which it is probable from the character of those engaged in it, will soon be put in operation. It is probable that the combination of the States in making arms would greatly expedite the equipment of our soldiers. Different parts of a gun could be made from models at different points, and sent to a common armory for the purpose of being fitted together for service. Such a division, could it be accomplished, would be beneficial in the highest degree. To adjust the details of such a scheme would require time and a knowledge of the capabilities of the States in workmen as well as material.

I have the honor to be, with great respect, your most obedient servant,

JOHN GILL SHORTER

To His Excellency, Governor PICKENS

An original report of Duff C. Green, Quartermaster General of Alabama, in the Military Archives of the State of Alabama, shows that from October 1, 1863, to November 1, 1864, Dickson, Nelson & Company delivered 645 Mississippi rifles at a price of $90.00 each.

UNMARKED CONFEDERATE RIFLE

Figure 3, Plate XVI

The specimen shown here is supposed to be of Confederate manufacture but there are no details available in reference to it. The rifled barrel is caliber .58 and is 33 inches long and the cone seat is patterned somewhat after the Enfield type though there is a marked difference in its shape and the nipple threads do not interchange with the regular Enfield nipples. The lock plate is only 4¾ inches long and is marked forward of the hammer in a very deep stamp 1863, and to the rear of the hammer C. S. No other marks appear except the numeral 47 which is carried by all parts. The mountings are all of iron. The two flat bands are retained in place by the conventional band springs. The trigger guard is made similar to our 1861 guard but the trigger plate is somewhat longer and heavier. Sling swivels are carried by the top band and trigger guard. The rear sight is of our regular 1861 model. The butt plate is of iron and resembles the conventional Enfield plate though of somewhat different design. Total length of arm, 49 inches.

The stock is made of American black walnut and while the arm appears to be a very substantial piece the workmanship throughout is rather crude.

*   *   *   *   *

THE SO-CALLED
BLUNT RIFLED MUSKET

Figure 1, Plate XVI

The very small number of these arms that have been found by collectors has but added to the mystery of just who made them.

When the present compiler found a part of a case of these guns, all badly damaged, but not showing any particularly hard wear, and compared them with the arms proposed by Orison Blunt as outlined in the brochure by Norman Wiard of 1863, it was concluded that they were a part of his product; the markings of the lock plate and the fact that the stocks were of American black walnut leading to this belief.

The arm is of the typical Enfield pattern weighing 8¾ pounds and having a total length of 55 inches. The barrel is .58 caliber, 39 inches long, with regular Enfield type sights—the rear sight being soldered on in regular British fashion, and the barrel carries the regular British proof marks—all indicating that the completed barrel was an importation.

The iron bands are regular Enfield type, but have no markings, while the trigger guard and butt plate are both of brass, the tang of the trigger guard being stamped L. S. M. in heavy, crude letters.

The lock plate is of the Enfield type, but will not fit on a regular Enfield gun, nor will a regular Enfield lock fit the present specimen. It is marked forward of the hammer 1862 and to the rear of hammer a shield with the letter M surmounted by a spread eagle.

The fact that Blunt proposed making guns of the Enfield pattern, that he proposed to import some completed arms, and possibly some barrels to be used until his plant was more complete, and the fact that American black walnut stocks were used fitted this arm pretty well to the Blunt output.

An article about this arm in *Hobbies* Magazine of July, 1941, is as follows:

A CONFEDERATE ORDNANCE MYSTERY AND
AN ATTEMPT TO SOLVE IT

A scientific theory does not have to be proven to get wide circulation.

But, not so with an historical theory. Unless an historian be prepared to prove his theory by quoting chapter and verse, there is little chance of its acceptance by anyone.

But there are times when an historical theory may be advanced by one person and proven by another. The theory may blaze a new trail for researchers. It is with some such hope in mind that the following is advanced:

The outbreak of the so-called Civil War in 1861 found the Southern States without a single privately-owned arms factory within their borders. But all the "Yankee" enterprise and ingenuity was not north of the Potomac. Numerous plants for the manufacture of arms were started in the South by individuals, encouraged by State and Confederate governmental subsidies.

Many of these were futile almost to the stage of pathos. Others, like the Enfield gun plant of Cook & Brother and the various industries of the Haimans, of Columbus, Ga., were planned and carried out with so much brains and industry that they were only stopped by one factor—the enemy.

The first privately-owned arms plant to be given a contract by the Confederate War Department was the Marshall Manufacturing Company, of Holly Springs, Miss.; also referred to as W. S. McElwaine & Company and Jones, McElwaine & Company.

The partnership of Jones, McElwaine & Company was formed "by verbal agreement" in the Spring of 1859 "for the purpose of erecting a foundry and carrying on the business of the same." The firm's first product was iron grillwork for which there was a large sale in New Orleans, where grillwork was an architectural gesture of elegance.

The three original partners were W. S. McElwaine, W. A. P. Jones and Capt. E. G. Barney, each having a one-third interest. In 1860 a fourth partner, J. H. Athey, of Louisville, bought half of Jones' holdings. At that time the firm was employing about 200 hands.[20]

By an Act of the Called Session of the Mississippi State Legislature in July, 1861, the firm empowered to buy additional machinery and to "make and enforce any by-law not contrary to the State Constitution." Deciding to convert the plant into an arms factory, the firm obtained a grant of $60,000 from the Confederate Government.

McElwaine, the mechanical genius of the firm, was a native of Pittsfield, Mass., where he learned the trade of machinist. After working in a New York gun factory and in a machine shop at Sandusky, Ohio, his uncle, W. L. Goodman, induced him to go South.[21] Goodman was then building the Mississippi Railroad.

On August 12, 1861, Gen. Josias Gorgas, Chief of Ordnance, C. S. A.; reported that the company had been given a contract to make 20,000 rifles and 10,000 muskets, delivery to begin November 1 and the output to be 2,000 a month.[22]

To shed some light on the output, this newspaper article of March 14, 1862, is quoted:

"The Gun factory at Holly Springs, Miss., is now turning out 40 good muskets per day. It will be able to turn out 100 per day for the government. Muskets are the best weapons for three-fourths of the Army. It shoots strong, far and accurate and seldom gets out of order."[23]

After the battle of Shiloh, April 6 and 7, 1862, the Confederate army fell back to Tupelo. Holly Springs being exposed to capture, the arms plant was sold to the Confederate Government.

On June 6, 1862, Captain Porter sent this message to General Beauregard:

"Head of Yankee column is at Middleburg. It occurred to me that their purpose is to get possession of the Government Armory at this place (Holly Springs). I advised the officer in charge of the Armory to pack up all the guns on hand and be ready to move the machinery at a moment's notice."[24]

On August 3, 1862, W. S. McElwaine wrote to Col. James H. Burton, Superintendent of Armories:

"I have the honor to enclose to you the invoice of ordnance and ordnance stores from Holly Springs Armory that have arrived at the Armory at this place (Macon, Ga.)."[25]

With the absorption by the Government Armory at Macon of the Holly Springs machinery and the burning of the Holly Springs Armory buildings by the Federals after the battle of Corinth, the documentary history of Jones, McElwaine & Company's Holly Springs Armory comes to an end.

But what of the product of the Holly Springs Armory?

In view of the fact that the Holly Springs plant was making guns for about five months, turning out from 25 to 40 stands a day, it is curious that historians and collectors do not know what manner of guns these were and or how they were marked. In common with other collectors and students of Confederate ordnance history, the writer of this article has tried for 20 years to identify a Holly Springs gun, but in vain—unless. Unless this theory be sound.

---

[20] The Story of Coal and Iron in Alabama, by Ethel Ames.

[21] Ibid.

[22] Official Records, War of the Rebellion, Series IV, Vol. I, P. 556.

[23] The Memphis (Tenn.) Appeal.

[24] Official Records, Vol. X, P. 591.

[25] Colonel Burton's papers.

FIREARMS OF THE CONFEDERACY

Ethel Ames, in her admirable *Story of Coal and Iron in Alabama*, says the first gun made at Holly Springs was retained by Mr. McElwaine. This gun passed into the possession of McElwaine's daughter, Mrs. H. J. Miller, of Chattanooga. Years ago this writer had some correspondence with Mrs. Miller about this gun and she said she had sold it to the late Mr. Gunther, Chicago collector. She could not recall how the gun was marked, but she did remember that about three inches of the muzzle had been "shot off."

This particular gun seems to have disappeared. We know that the bulk of the Gunther collection of arms was given to the Chicago Historical Society. In 1933 the writer visited the Society's rooms and asked about the rifle. The files showed a "Holly Springs rifle," in the list of Gunther arms, but it was not on exhibition. Permission was courteously given to examine the arms stored in the basement, but a search revealed no gun that suggested Holly Springs.

All the foregoing is by way of preface to the suggestion the theory that the modified Enfield rifles bearing on the lock plate back of the hammer a shield, with an "M" in the field, surmounted by an eagle with spread wings, and in front of the hammer the date, are the guns made by McElwaine's plant at Holly Springs and later at Macon.

Most collectors will tell you that these rifles are the "Blunt contract rifles" made by Orison Blunt, of New York, and rejected by the War Department at Washington. Bannerman's catalogue, usually so accurate, lists them as "Blunt contract rifles." But are they?

On September 10, 1861, Orison Blunt, 118 Ninth Street, New York, wrote to Gen. James W. Ripley, at Washington, offering to furnish 20,000 Enfield rifled muskets for $18 each and a similar amount "as per sample" at the same price, to be manufactured in this country.

To this General Ripley replied that the Secretary of War would not accept the imported rifled muskets but would take "as many as can be manufactured in this country up to January 1, 1862."

There is nothing to show that this order was accepted by Blunt. But on February 6, 1862, Blunt wrote to the Secretary of War saying that upon receipt of General Ripley's letter he had set to work to prepare a factory building, machinery and tools and had gone "to great expense" in so doing.

He was prepared, he said, to produce 500 to 1,000 guns per month, "like the two I now present, which I have made myself and are like the pattern gun filed in the Ordnance Office."

In a postscript, Mr. Blunt said he would be in Washington in a day or two, and present the two guns in person.[26]

Blunt's own story of his dealings with the War Department at Washington is found in a brochure on "The Manufacture of Small Arms at Home versus Their Purchase Abroad," by Norman Wiard, published in 1863.

Blunt says that on June 11, 1862, he wrote to Maj. W. A. Thornton, at Watervliet Arsenal, New York:

"Sir—Yours of June 9, came to hand. I can only say in answer that I reported to General Ripley, Chief of Ordnance, March 31, 1862, that I had two hundred guns, finished, packed and ready for delivery. I also reported again on April 12, which was answered April 15, stating that when I had five hundred arms ready for delivery, under my order of March 27, 1862, measures would be taken to have them inspected and received.

"I reported May 13 that I had five hundred muskets ready for delivery under my orders of March 27, 1862. I was advised May 15 that you were directed to inspect the arms that I had ready and that my sample was lost. I was advised May 19 that my sample gun had been sent you at No. 55 White Street, care of Captain Crispin, and that

---

[26] This correspondence is found in the House Executive Documents file for the 2nd Session, Thirty-seventh Congress.

you would be advised on that day that the gun was there for your use in making the inspection of my arms. The arms are now ready and have been since May 13, for inspection and delivery under my order of March 27."

On June 15, Major Thornton wrote Blunt saying that he had sent an inspector to examine the arms and that the inspector had reported "he did not think one in ten could pass inspection."

In conclusion, Mr. Blunt says:

"You will see by the foregoing that I received an order and filed a sample in the Ordnance Office to manufacture a rifled musket of the same pattern and size of the English Enfield rifled musket, which is 58-100 bore, 39-inch barrel, brass guard and butt plate, iron bands and 16-inch angular bayonets, and, after correspondence from March 31 to June 17, 1862, it was decided definitely by the Ordnance Department that they would receive no arms of me until the Department had proved and gauged the barrels in the rough state and also in the finished state and gauged and inspected the mountings and locks and other parts in their filed state and also in their finished state, which inspection only applies to the Springfield rifled muskets as referred to in the Ordnance manual. I consequently stopped my works, as I did not undertake to manufacture an arm of that kind."

Now, let us inspect the so-called Blunt rifles, of which three examples have been examined by the writer.

No. 1 is dated 1861, and has a barrel 34½ inches long, with a long knob for saber bayonet on the right hand side.

No. 2 is dated 1862 and has a 31½-inch barrel, with no provision for saber bayonet. On the inside of the lock plate is the number "50."

No. 3, which is in the museum of the Fredericksburg Battlefield National Military Park at Fredericksburg, Va., is dated 1863 and is a rifled musket, with 39-inch barrel. The inside of the lock plate is marked "100."

All three of these guns have brass butt plates, trigger guards and fore-end tips. Bands are of iron, rounded. The rear sights are elevating devices similar to those on the regular English Enfield rifles, but differing in certain details.

The 1863 gun is the only one which answers to the description of the arms made by Blunt, but Blunt says he made no guns after May, 1862. And it is equally certain that he made none in 1861.

And now, consider the lock plate markings:

The shield surmounted by an eagle form the Coat of Arms of Mississippi. And the "M" on the shield can be for Mississippi, for McElwaine, or for the Marshall Manufacturing Company. You can take your choice.

The one weak point in the theory of the Holly Springs or Macon origin of the so-called Blunt contract rifles is the elevating rear sight, a device that is not found on any other Confederate-made rifle.

There is nothing conclusive about this theory, but it may serve as a starting point for another investigator.

* * * * *

TENNESSEE WAR WORK AND
THE PULASKI RIFLE

In reply to the letter of November 20, 1860, addressed to the War Department by Gov. Isham G. Harris, of Tennessee, John B. Floyd wrote:[27]

[27] Vol. I, Series III—Rebellion Records.

FIREARMS OF THE CONFEDERACY

WAR DEPARTMENT,
Washington, November 26, 1860.
His Excellency ISHAM G. HARRIS,
    Governor of Tennessee, Nashville:
    SIR: In reply to the inquiry contained in your letter of the 20th instant, I have the honor to inform you that there are now due Tennessee, on account of her quota for the present and previous years, arms to the value of 892 -12/13 muskets, and that the quota for 1861 will become available on the 1st of January next.
    Very respectfully, your obedient servant,
                            JOHN B. FLOYD,
                            Secretary of War.

John Heriges, keeper of public arms, reported in January, 1861, that the State arsenal contained 8,761 muskets and rifles, 350 carbines, 4 pieces of artillery, and a small lot of pistols and sabers, with 1,815 muskets and rifles, 228 pistols and 220 sabers in the hands of volunteer companies. Of the muskets in the arsenal, 280 were percussion, the balance were flintlock, and over 4,300 of them were badly damaged; the carbines were flintlock and unserviceable, and two of the four pieces of artillery were in the same condition. The governor reported in his message, dated April 2, 1861, that since the date of the report of the keeper of public arms, he had "ordered and received at the arsenal 1,400 rifle muskets." This constituted the armament of the State of Tennessee.

The chief of ordnance, Capt. M. H. Wright, thoroughly educated to the duties of his place, soon organized a force for the repair of arms, the manufacture and preparation of ammunition and the equipments of the soldiers, and for the conversion of the flintlock muskets to percussion; and aided by patriotic citizens like Samuel D. Morgan, established a plant for the manufacture of percussion caps. Thus he was able to supply the troops of Tennessee as they took the field. Shipments of caps were made to the authorities at Richmond, who used them very largely at the first battle of Manassas. About 3,000 pounds of powder were being manufactured daily. Foundries for the manufacture of field guns were constructed at Nashville and Memphis, and by November, guns of good pattern were turned out at both points at the rate of six a week. Capt. W. R. Hunt, of the ordnance department, was the efficient head at Memphis.[28]

Secretary Holt on January 3, 1861 advised Benjamin Stanton, Chairman on Military Affairs that there had been distributed since January 1, 1860, to the State of Tennessee, 701 caliber

---

[28] Vol. VIII—Confederate Military History, Atlanta, 1899.

.58 rifled muskets and 381 caliber .58 Cadet muskets together with some other arms. These were probably included in those reported by Governor Harris as having been received since the report of John Heriges.[29]

Even the repairing and altering of the old arms proved to be something of a task as indicated by the following correspondence:[30]

Memphis, Tenn., November 12, 1861

J. P. BENJAMIN, Secretary of War, Richmond, Va.

SIR: Your telegram of the 11th instant . . . I took measures some weeks prior to my appointment to secure arms sufficient to arm three regiments. These consisted of such guns as were furnished by the recruits themselves, together with others of a similar kind, which I had procured by various means throughout the country. Some two months since I distributed 1,600 rifles among the different armories in the State, viz, Memphis, Nashville, Pulaski and Columbia, where I had supposed they would be rapidly repaired and fitted for use . . . The guns deposited in the armory at this place would have been completed but for the breaking of the armory machinery, which was only repaired a day or two since. The work is now being pushed forward as rapidly as possible. So soon as I ascertained that my arms could not be obtained for some time to come, I set about securing such guns as would answer in the sudden emergency brought about by the recent unfriendly demonstrations made in East Tennessee. With these (shotguns, country rifles, and old muskets) I armed Colonel Looney's regiment, and moved it yesterday.

Very respectfully,

WM. H. CARROLL,
Brigadier General, C. S. Army.

BRIGADE HEADQUARTERS,
Chattanooga, Tenn., November 17, 1861.

Hon. J. P. BENJAMIN, Secretary of War, Richmond: . . .

Regret that arms suitable for service cannot be procured in Tennessee. Have left nothing undone in attempting to obtain them. So far, however, have secured only common rifles, double-barreled shotguns, and flintlock muskets, very few being at all serviceable. The boring and rifling machine in the ordnance department at Memphis failed entirely to meet expectations. Have 600 rifles distributed for repairing at Murfreesborough, Pulaski, and Nashville, but can get no information as to the time it will take to finish them. . .

Very respectfully,

WM. H. CARROLL,
Brigadier General.

ORDNANCE OFFICE AT MEMPHIS,
August 12, 1861.

Major General POLK:

SIR: If this war should unfortunately be prolonged, the valley of the . . . I would also respectfully recommend that contracts be made for 25,000 sword bayonets for Mississippi rifles and 10,000 for double-

---

[29] Vol. I, Series III—Rebellion Records.
[30] Vol. IV, Series I—Rebellion Records.

barreled shotguns. These bayonets complete will cost about $9. each, making a total cost of $315,000 for the 35,000. Bayonet and gun barrels for rifles ready forged out for rifling can be procured in any quantity at $3 each from Hillman Bro., on Tennessee River. The dies for locks and nipples are being made here and can be turned out in large quantities. A foundry and shop in this city can turn out gun stocks at the rate of 100 to 200 per day, and we can thus have a weapon equal in all respects to the Mississippi rifle, while it will not be so heavy . . .

Respectfully,

WM. RICHARDSON HUNT,
Captain of Ordnance.

In July, 1861, Geo. W. Morse, signing himself as Sup. Tennessee Armory, wrote Sec. of War Walker concerning the loan of machinery for use at the proposed gunmaking plant at Nashville, but there are no records available of guns made. (See "The Morse Breechloader")

The Pulaski rifle seems to be the only gun made in any quantity in the State and in order to facilitate its manufacture the authorities commandeered all the gun locks and other gun parts on hand in the hardware stores and in the hands of other merchants in the city of Nashville and other cities where there were dealers with any serviceable stock of this class of material on hand.

Mr. A. C. Cross, from whom this specimen was secured, wrote on November 21, 1941, as follows:

There were many gunsmiths then in the State of Tennessee and he (Gov. Harris) probably had no difficulty in getting a full compliment of labor in his rifle factory at Pulaski. The time was short and they had to have these rifles quickly so the barrel bands and other parts were made of cast brass which was easy to work and finish and did not require the expert workmanship that was required on the same parts made of iron and steel. The gun locks acquired from the hardware and sporting goods stores were all of the sporting type and in most cases too small and unfit for military use. The heels of the hammers were lengthened by brazing on an additional piece of metal and the hammers were refit to the locks. By this method the hammers were given a much longer pitch than they originally had.

According to the old Confederate Soldier from whom I obtained my information regarding the Pulaski rifle in my collection, the rifle factory at Pulaski was in existence for only a short time before it was raided by a company of Northern Soldiers and according to his estimate only about 200 or 400 or possibly 500 of the Pulaski rifles were produced.

The rifle in my collection was obtained by me from Mr. Frank Lebron who inherited it from his maternal grandfather, Johnny Adams, an ex-Confederate soldier who lived at Columbia. Mr. Adams on joining the Army of Tennessee carried his own personal rifle which he considered far superior to any musket or rifle of those days and he considered that he could do more good with the gun he was familiar with than he could with one of the Pulaski military weapons, so when the Pulaski rifle was given him he carried it home and left it and continued to use his own rifle in his military duties. This accounts for this particular rifle being in such excellent condition. It appears to have had little or no use, although it is somewhat rusty from standing around with no care for so many years.

One old Confederate soldier whom I met on a trip to Columbia several years ago, told me that there were a number of Eli Whitney's former gunsmiths at work in the Pulaski factory and that they had quickly accepted the call of Governor Harris for mechanics as they were in sympathy with the Confederacy. This information, I was unable to authenticate and I only had the old soldier's word for it.

A. C. CROSS,
November 21st, 1941.

N. B. Zuccarelle had a gunshop at Pulaski before the war. He was a Northern man, but not averse to working for the South. He was associated with Webb and McLean in the manufacture of guns. McLean was a practical mechanic. Webb, I believe, furnished some of the capital. The plant began operations in the latter part of 1861 and closed up early in 1862. The output must have been very small. In my 25 years of collecting, I have heard of only three of these guns, including the one which I have and another which turned up in Chicago about a year ago. I recall that Boffin—I believe it was—wrote to me about it . . .

THE PULASKI RIFLE
Figure 4, Plate XVI

The specimen shown follows somewhat the U. S. Model 1841 Rifle but the workmanship is very crude. The total length of the arm is 48½ inches and the weight is 9.75 pounds. The .58 caliber round barrel is 32¼ inches long, having a 5-groove rifling. It is provided with fixed front and rear sights and is marked "PULASKI, T. C. S. A. 61." The mountings are of brass, patterned after the 1841 mountings, but are much heavier, probably caused by unskilled workmen. The band retainers, in place of having a round shank in the hole extending through the stock is merely bent to right angle and driven in, making it impossible to remove the retainer without marring the wood. The trigger is swung on a rivet in place of a screw and the trigger guard is riveted to the plate. The butt plate is heavy brass. The lock is of the regular sporting type attached to the stock with but one screw. The original hammer was lengthened to give it the required reach.

FIREARMS OF THE CONFEDERACY

THOMAS RIGGINS

The *Magazine of Antique Firearms* of April, 1911, gives the following account of this gunmaker who was identified with the Confederate arms industry:

Born 1821. Thomas Riggins, of McMinn Co., Tenn., is one of the oldest living gunmakers in the United States, and is probably the only living armorer of the Confederacy. At the age of ten, he entered as apprentice a shop owned by one of his relatives. After studying the armorer's art for several years, he began making sporting rifles. In 1845 he could make a rifle out and out from the raw bulk iron. The unusual excellence of his work attracted attention throughout a section within a radius of a hundred miles. Many a successful contestant at an old-time shooting match owed his luck to a Riggins rifle. The Riggins rifle generally "got the beef."

At the outbreak of the Civil War he contracted to make the rifles for arming the "East Tennessee Squirrel Shooters"—a State cavalry regiment of "rebel" Volunteers. After volunteering in '61 he went to Lynchburg under Col. Vaughn of the Third Tennessee regiment. Before his company saw actual service, he was ordered to Knoxville to instruct about sixty mechanics in the making of cavalry rifles out of fowling pieces. Many a wagonload of long Kentucky flintlock rifles were collected in the South and sent to Knoxville where Mr. Riggins and his assistants converted them into serviceable short percussion lock, large-bore carbines for Confederate cavalry. Mr. Riggins with a natural pride, unconquered by time, states that his picked assistants were fast workers and that they labored strenuously for many months, often working all night to complete the equipment of some waiting troop of cavalry, until the Federal army forced them to destroy the arsenal and retreat.

SELMA, ALABAMA

Despite the fact that ever so often there is offered for sale, and generally at a very high price, a rifle or carbine marked Selma, Alabama, there is very little evidence that any small arms were made there during the war.

Fleming's *Civil War and Reconstruction in Alabama* says:

"The Naval Foundry at Selma, Ala., employed 3,000 hands, the Armory a like number. The plant covered 50 acres and comprised 100 buildings. Manufactured great guns, ordnance stores, rifles, pistols, swords, etc.

This is one of the few accounts of the Selma activities that claims rifles and pistols as a part of the output.

According to Hardy's *History of Selma* the war plants at that place included:

"Naval Iron Foundry, Capt. Jones, 3,000 men.

"Selma Arsenal, which made cartridges, knapsacks, clothing. Col. J. L. White.

"Central City Iron Works, Capt. Henry H. Ware, were made everything from cannon shot to horseshoe nails.

"Central City Iron Foundry, made cannon balls.

"Phelan and McBride Iron Works, made shot and shell.

"Dallas Iron Works."

General Gorgas, in his account of the Confederate Ordnance Department, wrote concerning this establishment as follows:

"Attracted by the deposits of fine ore immediately north of Selma, made accessible by the Selma, Rome & Dalton Railroad, the War Department accepted the proposition of Mr. Colin McRae to undertake the erection at Selma of a large foundry for the casting of cannon of the heaviest caliber. A large contract was made with him and advances of money made from time to time as the work progressed. After a time Mr. McRae was called on by President Davis to go abroad in connection with Confederate finances. He made it a condition that he should be relieved of his works and contract at Selma without pecuniary loss to himself. The works were thereupon assumed by the War and Navy Departments jointly, and placed at first under the charge of Colonel Rains as general superintendent, while an officer of less rank took immediate charge. Subsequently it was agreed by the War Department that the Navy should take sole charge, and use the works for its own purposes. It was here that Commander Brooke made many of his formidable banded and rifled guns.

"The foundry and rolling-mills grew into large proportions, supplied by the iron and coal of that region. Had the Confederacy survived, Selma bid fair to become the Pittsburgh of the South.

"The iron obtained from the brown haematite at the furnaces in Bibb County (Brierfield), and from the Shelby Works, was admirable, the former being of unusual strength."

That the arsenal in charge of Col. White did include facilities for the repair and alteration of arms is indicated by the following:

FIREARMS OF THE CONFEDERACY

O. R. Vol. 24, Part 3 - Pg. 902.

Selma, Arsenal, May 20, 1863.

CHIEF OF STAFF,
General J. E. Johnston's Headquarters, Jackson, Miss.:

SIR: I have this day received from Ordnance Bureau the following . . .

I have about 2,000 muskets and other arms of military pattern, which are being repaired as rapidly as possible with the means at my command. Besides these, I have about 10,000 sporting arms, chiefly rifles, all needing repairs in various degrees . . .

There are now orders from Richmond for the supply of 1,500 country rifles to citizens of Mobile, through General Slaughter. This order is being filled as rapidly as possible. There are also orders for the supply of about 200 arms to two companies of riflemen recently organized at Columbus, Miss. It is impossible to state at what time these orders can be filled, owing to the various degrees of repairs required.

An inquiry has just been received by telegraph from Richmond, to learn whether or not I can supply 1,000 long-range rifles to General Ruggles, at Okolona. There are not so many of that kind of arms on hand, but the order will remove all that may be . . .

The force at my command will enable me to prepare about thirty or forty arms per day, in ordinary or average amount of repairs. I have but few good gunsmiths or machinists, and none are to be had, since those who may be in the army are not detailed.

The laboratory will turn out about 25,000 or 30,000 cartridges per day when supplied with material. If disabled soldiers could be detailed for this latter work, and the supply of lead could be increased, the products of the laboratory would be likewise increased.

I am, very respectfully, your obedient servant,

J. L. WHITE,
Lieutenant General,
Commanding.

The final chapter of the Selma activities in indicated by the following:

O. R. Vol. 49 - Part 2 - Pg. 217.

Selma, Ala., April 4, 1865, 10 a. m.

Major General THOMAS:

GENERAL: My corps took this place by assault late on evening of the 2d. We have captured 20 field guns, 2,000 prisoners, besides over 2,000 in hospitals, and large quantity of military stores of all kinds. Large arsenals and foundries with their machinery are in my possession intact. I shall burn them today, with everything else useful to enemy. I have already destroyed iron-works north of here, eight or ten in all, and very extensive.

J. H. WILSON,
Brevet Major General

*   *   *   *   *

THE DICKSON, NELSON & CO. CARBINE
Figure 1, Plate XVII

As the carbines made by this firm, which operated as the Shakanoosa Arms Co., are much scarcer than their rifles, they probably represent a salvaging operation, to utilize barrels that developed flaws during the process of manufacture that prevented their use as rifle barrels, but which had sufficient good stock to make a shorter barrel.

The report of Quartermaster General Green of Alabama does not include any carbines received from this firm up to November 1, 1864, so there were probably very few of them made. This arm is marked on lock plate Dickson, Nelson & Co. forward of the hammer and to the rear of it Ala. and the date.

The barrel is caliber .58 and is 24 inches long. Total length of arm, 40 inches. The butt plate, trigger guard, one round band and fore-end tip are of brass. It has a fixed rear sight and swivel ramrod. Some of the stocks are stamped "F. ZUNDT."

* * * * *

STOCK BLANK
FOR DICKSON, NELSON CARBINE
Figure 3, Plate XVII

This carbine stock blank which plainly shows that it was cut out and not turned on the lathe is interesting as it indicates the difficulties under which arms were manufactured and as there were quite a number of them recovered from the old Dickson, Nelson plant it might indicate that they intended producing these carbines in quantity.

THE GREENWOOD & GRAY
OR
THE J. P. MURRAY CARBINE
Figure 2, Plate XVII

This carbine or, as it is sometimes called, musketoon comes in two types, with a double or single fore-end band. It has a 24-inch barrel and is all brass mounted. There is no swivel ramrod. The barrel is provided with a brass front sight and a fixed rear sight. The lock plate is stamped "J. P. Murray, Columbus, Ga." and the breech is stamped "Ala. 1864" and the initials of the ordnance officer "F. C. H." who was Major F. C. Humphries,

PLATE XVII

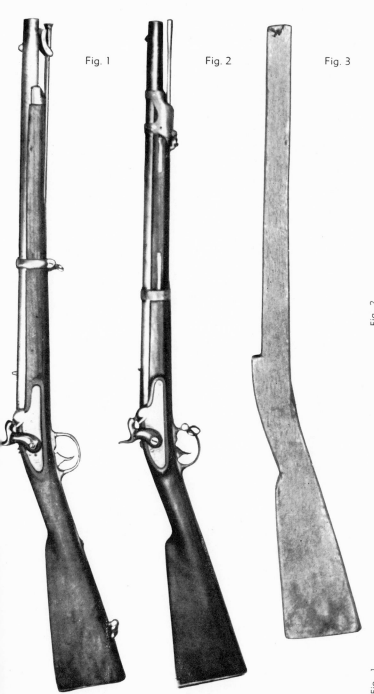

Fig. 1

Fig. 2

Fig. 3

Fig. 2
Greenwood & Gray Carbine or Musketoon. 40 inches over-all, 23-inch barrel, .58 caliber, brass butt plate, trigger guard, one flat band and double front band; fixed rear sight, sling swivels on trigger guard and front band. Made at Greenwood & Gray's factory, Columbus, Ga. On lock plate: J. P. Murray, Columbus, Ga. On barrel: F.C.H. The initials of the Confederate inspector, Maj. F. C. Humphreys. On bolt heads the serial 23.

Fig. 1
Dickson, Nelson & Company Carbine or Musketoon. 40 inches over-all, 24-inch barrel, .58 caliber, brass butt plate, trigger guard, one round band and fore-end tip, swivel ramrod, fixed rear sight. On lock plate: Dickson, Nelson & Company, Ala., 1864. Stamped on stock: F. Zundt. Made at Adairsville, Ga. for the State of Alabama.
Fig. 3
Dickson, Nelson & Company carbine stock blank. From the last plant of the Dickson, Nelson & Company at Dawson, Ga.

PLATE XVIII

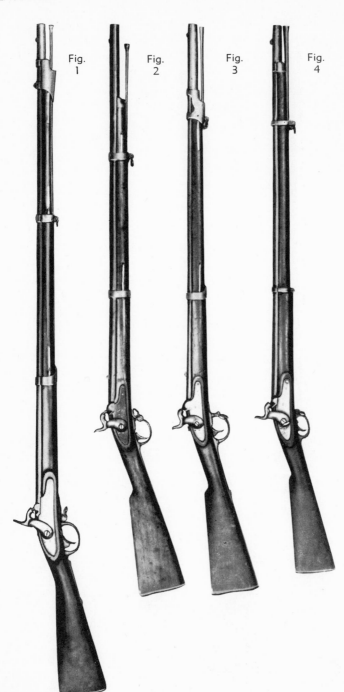

Fig.
1

Fig.
2

Fig.
3

Fig.
4

Fig. 1
Montgomery Arsenal Musket. Originally a Springfield flintlock, 57 inches over-all, 41-inch barrel, .69 caliber, all iron mountings.
On lock plate: Star and C. S. Montgomery Arsenal, 1863.
On barrel: V. P. and Eagle's head. Also 1820.
On butt plate tang: U. S.
On bolt heads and other parts: 3
Fig. 2
Confederate Rifle, 48 inches over-all, 33-inch barrel, .58 caliber, extremely deep grooves, all mountings and trigger of brass.
On lock plate: C. Chapman.
On screw bolt heads and various parts: 4
On ... ... unknown.

Fig. 3
Davis & Bozeman Confederate Rifle. 48 inches over-all, 33-inch barrel, .58 caliber, all brass mountings.
On lock plate: D & B. Ala., 1864. On inside of plate: 406
On side of barrel: Ala., 1864.
Made by Davis & Bozeman of Cousa County, Ala.; who made 900 rifles for the State between October 1863 and November, 1864.
Fig. 4
Unusually small Confederate Rifle, 46 inches over-all, 32-inch barrel, .54 caliber, all brass mountings, small stock. Made by L. G. Sturdivant at Talladega, Ala. for the State of Alabama. No marks except serial 130.

in charge of all inspection work in and around Columbus. The serial number of the gun is stamped on the lock plate screwheads, and, like the rifles, are sometimes found with brass triggers.

* * * * *

THE DAVIS & BOZEMAN RIFLE
Figure 3, Plate XVIII

According to the report of Duff C. Green, Quartermaster General of Alabama, it will be noted that the firm of Davis & Bozeman, whose plant was near Central, Ala., had, by November 1st, 1864 delivered on their contract with the State nearly 900 Mississippi rifles and 89 carbines.

In addition to the manufacture of new arms they were probably employed in repairing and altering old ones for the service as from the Legislative Journal of the State of Alabama this wartime item is culled:

"Resolved, that the Governor be requested to communicate to the Senate the nature of the contract with Davis & Bozeman of Coosa County for the repair of arms; what number of arms have been repaired and delivered to the State and the cost of same August 23, 1863."

The Davis & Bozeman rifle has a 33-inch barrel with brass butt plate, trigger guard, and double top band. The caliber is .58. The lock plate is marked: "D & B. ALA. 1864" and on the breech is stamped: "ALA. 1864." On the rear of the lock plate is the serial.

The price of these arms, according to the report of the Quartermaster General above referred to, ranged from $27.50 up to $60.00 each, a greater portion of them being at the latter price.

* * * * *

THE GEORGIA ARMORY RIFLE
Figure 2, Plate XVIIIa

The Georgia Armory was established in the State Penitentiary at Milledgeville in 1862. Governor Brown reported to the Legislature early in that year that it was turning out 125 "good arms a month."[3]

The Daily Richmond (Va.) *Examiner,* of September 7, 1861, said that a convention of gunsmiths called by Governor Brown was held in Atlanta and it was suggested that the "State

---

[3] Avery's History of Georgia. Page 248.

road shops" were available at once for forging new barrels, caliber .58. Four forges were set aside and each forge could yield 10 barrels a day, it was said. John H. Newton, of Athens, said he and others had raised the funds for an Armory and estimated the cost of the finished rifle, less the barrel in the rough, at $12.50.

On November 6, 1862, Governor Brown reported to the Legislature that $350,000 had been appropriated for the State Armory and that Peter Jones had been made master armorer.[4]

In *The Southern Recorder*, of Milledgeville, for August 12, 1862, is this item:

GEORGIA ARMORY

We have the satisfaction to announce that Georgia is now manufacturing in her State Prison a variety of arms, a specimen of which we examined a few days ago, which was made under the direction of Major McIntosh, Chief of Ordnance. The "Georgia Rifle" with sword bayonet attached, is a beautiful piece of workmanship, not surpassed by any arm manufactured in the United States or in Europe, for actual service. For this triumph in the impliments of war, the public is indebted to the skill of Mr. Peter Jones, who was 18 years head armorer at Harper's Ferry. He made all the machinery, or at least the finer portions of it, which is now employed in the State Armory for the Manufacture of Muskets, rifles, bayonets, swords, &c. The work executed under his inspection is a very great improvement upon the patterns at Harper's Ferry, which used to be considered as near perfection as art would permit. Mr. Jones has no superior in his line of business, and we are gratified that his services are faithfully devoted to the South.

The first musket manufactured in the Penitentiary bears, on a plate inserted in the breech, the inscription—"Presented to his Excellency J. E. Brown, Governor of Georgia" under the Coat of Arms of the State. For the present, until the machinery can be increased, we learn that only 300 muskets and rifles will be completed per month, with the prospect of a much larger delivery. The work has been prosecuted under difficulties which have been entirely surmounted and we feel strengthened in our national arm by the happy success of the Georgia Armory.

The Georgia Armory was burned by Wilson's raiders.[5]

General Sherman reported that the penitentiary at Milledgeville was burned before his arrival, but that he burned the arsenal and the railroad buildings.[6]

A committee of the Legislature was appointed to examine into the feasibility of rebuilding the Armory. On March 2, 1865, Mr. Polk, chairman of that committee, submitted this report of the Master Armorer:

[4] War Records of Georgia. Vol. II, Page 242.
[5] Avery's History of Georgia. Page 308.
[6] Official Records, War of the Rebellion. Vol. XLIV, Page 789.

FIREARMS OF THE CONFEDERACY

To the committee on State Armory and Penitentiary.

GENTLEMEN:—Agreeably to your request, I offer the following hastily prepared report of the condition of the machinery and materials of the State Armory together with rough estimates or supposed cost of repairs, amounts and value of material on hand, suggestions, &c. A short time only was allowed me for its preparation, but it is believed that a more thorough examination would scarcely disclose any very great differences or alter materially my estimates. In the machine department proper, the lathes, drills, presses, planes, and gear cutter, were not burned but broken, yet in a condition to be repaired, with slight cost, in proportion to their actual value. Of the machinery, directly in use upon gun, there is scarcely any of it that could be made useful. Milling, rifling, barrel-boring, and drilling machines were badly burned and broken. A large portion of the main-line and some counter shafting was saved in order. Many of the most important small tools of the machine shops and Armory, together with several complete sets of gun-stockers, tools, components of the gun finished and unfinished, materials, &c. were saved, and would be useful, on the event of the establishment of any ordnance repair shop. In the Smith's department, the tilt, hammer, frames, were destroyed. The irons were unharmed. The fan can be repaired at a cost not exceeding $250.00. Anvils, some ten or twelve in number, together with tongs, sledges, hammers, setts, and component forging tools, generally in good order. The foundry was not burned and with the exception of the loss of a few patterns in perfect condition. The engine and boiler though badly burned I think could be put in thorough order, and housed at a cost not exceeding $1,000 or $1,200. At present we have on hand and in order about 60,000 or 70,000 pounds of bar iron assorted sizes. Of new cast steel about 250 weight; of files present value about $50,000 worth; of bench vises, about 70, 60 in order, nearly new. Sand paper and emory cloth, about one dozen reams; together with carpenters tools, copper, brass, zinc, tin, &c. unnecessary to report useful and valuable. Of cast iron, scraps useful only at the Foundry, estimated weight 300,000 pounds. Wrought scraps say 20,000 pounds, of gun and leather belting in order I would suppose 2,500 feet of widths varying from 1 to 12 inches. I would respectfully suggest the collection and sale of all the condemned cast and wrought scraps. The proceeds to be applied or added to any appropriation of, say $150,000 for the erection of a suitable building, (and repairs of such machinery as may be necessary), for the repairs of State arms, and ordnance generally. In my humble judgment, such an establishment would be, not only useful, but actually necessary. I would farther suggest that there ought to be no connection whatever with the Penitentiary. The past has furnished sufficient evidence of the incalculable injury the State Armory has sustained by its introduction within the walls of that institution. A substantial one-story frame, 50 x 80 or 100 feet would answer a very excellent purpose.[7]

Respectfully submitted,

W. B. WERNAC,
Master Armorer

Milledgeville, Ga., Feby 28, 1863.

The resolution of the Penitentiary Committee was approved March 4, 1865, but the war ended before the Armory could be reestablished.

The Georgia Armory rifle was of .58 caliber, with 33-inch barrel, brass butt plate, trigger guard and bands. The earlier

---

[7] Georgia State Senate Journal. Page 77.

ones were fitted with saber bayonet knob. The earlier saber bayonets had brass handles and hilts; the later ones grips of wood and iron hilts. They resembled the English Enfield saber bayonet.

The rifle was marked on lock plate : "GA. ARMORY" and the date, all in the rear of the hammer.

* * * * *

THE GREENWOOD & GRAY
OR
J. P. MURRAY RIFLE
Figure 1, Plate XVIIIa

J. P. Murray, Columbus, (Ga.) gunsmith, was an Englishman and a skilled mechanic. He entered into partnership with another well-known gunsmith of Columbus before the war. The firm was Happoldt & Murray. The *Columbus Daily Sun* of July 19, 1862, speaks of him as J. P. Murray, successor to Happoldt & Murray, 45 Broad street. Before the war Murray confined his activities to making fine sporting rifles and a few pistols. Eldridge S. Greenwood and William C. Gray were partners in the cotton business. On January 17, 1862, they bought a lot from Abraham H. De Witt and started a rifle factory with J. P. Murray as superintendent.

William C. Gray was a brother of John D. Gray who had a furniture factory at Graysville, Ga. He is believed to have made the gunstocks for Greenwood and Gray.

It is probable, too, that before taking over the superintendency of the Greenwood & Gray plant, J. P. Murray did a little work on his own account for the Confederacy. An advertisement in the *Columbus Times* of July 6, 1861, informs "all persons who have guns or pistols in his shop" to call for them before August 1 or they will be sold.

The *Columbus Times* of August 28, 1861, under the caption "Flint Versus Steel" says:

"We learn that about 200 muskets of the flint and steel pattern reached here yesterday by express over the Muscogee Railroad. They were sent by orders of Governor Brown to J. P. Murray, gunsmith in this city, to be changed to the percussion lock."

And in the *Columbus Sun* of November 9, 1861, Murray advertises for 30 gunsmiths "to whom the best of wages will be paid and steady employment given."

The *Macon Telegraph* of March 29, 1862, says "J. P. Murray is manufacturing the Mississippi rifle in Columbus, Ga."

The *Columbus Sun* of January 30, 1863, refers to "the saber and gun factory of Messrs. Greenwood & Gray." In the same newspaper for March 1, 1863, is an advertisement for four sword grinders, two machinists and ten good gunsmiths.

And on March 31, 1863, the *Columbus Sun* ran this advertisement—"Notice. Wanted 50 good gunsmiths and machinists. None but the best need apply, to whom as good wages as is given in the Southern Confederacy will be paid. Greenwood & Gray."

According to the report of Gen. Duff C. Green, Quartermaster General of the State of Alabama, already quoted, Greenwood & Gray furnished the State of Alabama with 262 rifles and 73 carbines between October 1, 1863, and November 1, 1864.

The Greenwood & Gray factory employed about 150 hands. The plant was about 150 yards from that of Haiman and Brother.

J. P. Murray died about 1910.

The Confederate ordnance officer at Columbus all during the war was Maj. F. C. Humphries, son of Col. Gad Humphries, of St. Augustine, Fla. When the war broke out Major Humphries was a lieutenant in the United States Army in charge of the Augusta Arsenal. After the South took over the Augusta Arsenal, Humphries went to Washington and resigned. He then returned to Georgia. His initials, "F.C.H." appear on all the guns made in or near Columbus.

The Murray rifle is the Mississippi model with 32¾ inch barrel, .58 caliber, with brass butt plate, trigger guard, flat bands and fore-end tip. It has a brass front sight and a fixed rear sight. On the lock plate is stamped "J. P. Murray, Columbus, Ga." On the breech is stamped: "Ala. 1864" and the initials of the ordnance officer, "F. C. H." The serial is stamped on the bolt heads. These rifles are sometimes found with brass triggers, and fitted with a brass saber bayonet adapter invented by Boyle, Gamble and MacFee of Richmond and stamped: "B. G. & M. Richmond, Va., Pat. Sep. 2, 1861."

Figure 4, Plate XVIIIa shows a J. P. Murray sharpshooter's rifle, 45 inches over-all, heavy octagonal barrel, 29 inches long, 50 caliber, with wooden ramrod and an inlaid stock. This is one of six sharpshooter rifles captured by Sherman in his Atlanta Campaign. It was taken home by Quartermaster H. Clay Evans of Chattanooga. Formerly in the Cline Collection.

MENDENHALL, JONES AND GARDNER RIFLES
Figure 3, Plate XXIV

De Bow's Review, for March and April, 1862, contains an article by the editor, J. D. B. De Bow, under the caption: "What we are gaining by the War." And in listing the industries of North Carolina, the writer says:

"Messrs. Mendenhall, Jones and Gardner, of Greensboro, are now engaged in the manufacture of arms for the State of North Carolina. This establishment is just getting under way, and it is the intention of the proprietors to manufacture largely so soon as they can get their machinery in operation."[11]

The firm was made up of Cyrus P. Mendenhall, a lawyer and landowner of Greensboro; Ezekiel P. Jones, tobacco merchant, and Grafton Gardner. Gardner lived at Friendship, a few miles from Jamestown, and is said to have been a mechanic and the superintendent of the plant. Some accounts say the foreman was Frank Cavanaugh and that the superintendent was Shubal Gardner, son of Grafton Gardner.

The gun factory was a frame building on Deep river, about a mile below Jamestown and at what used to be called Old Jamestown. About 75 or 80 men were employed there, and the guns manufactured were of the Mississippi type rifle, with a lug for saber bayonet. The gun factory was under contract with the State of North Carolina, and all the rifles were for the State.

Most of them were marked on the lockplate: "M. J. & G., N. C." with the date and "C. S." Some few also had "Guilford" on the lock plate. The barrels were stamped "N. C." and "P."

That the manufacture of these guns stopped in the Autumn of 1864 is indicated by the following advertisement in the *Greensboro Patriot* of November 24, 1864:

MACHINERY FOR SALE AT PUBLIC AUCTION

On the 15th day of December next, at the Deep River Armory or Cotton Mills ½ mile from Jamestown Depot, we will sell at public auction the following articles of machinery, *viz,* Turning Lathes, Drill Presses, Smoothing Slabbing and Boring Machines, Shafting, Hangers and pulleys of various size and kinds. A large lot of Belting, Blacksmith tools, and about twenty thousands pounds of iron. The sale will continue from day to day until the articles are disposed of. Terms cash.

MENDENHALL, JONES & GARDNER.

---

[11] Ellis-Clark letters, North Carolina in the War.

Confederate and Conservative, Charlotte Bulletin, copy in Daily for two weeks, and send bill to this office.

Greensborough, N. C., March 30th, 1865

The Copartnership heretofore mentioned existing between Cyrus P. Mendenhall, Col. E. P. Jones and Grafton Gardner under the name and style of Mendenhall, Jones and Gardner is this day dissolved by mutual consent of parties.

C. P. MENDENHALL
E. P. JONES
GRAFTON GARDNER

Adjutant General Gatlin of North Carolina, in his report covering the period from September 30, 1862, to March 31, 1864, says that the State of North Carolina had made 3,442 rifles, repaired 4,937 rifles, imported 1,200 and purchased 431. In another report dated November 18, 1864, Adjutant General Gatlin says the manufacture and purchase of arms by the State had been discontinued.

In April, 1865, Federal raiding cavalry passed through Jamestown, and asked some boys where the gun factory was. The frightened boys pointed out the Jamestown Woolen Mills, which employed 40 hands and made goods for the Confederate Government. And the mill was burned. The cavalry then moved up the river, and the Mendenhall, Jones and Gardner gun factory was not destroyed. After the war the frame gun factory was demolished and replaced by a brick woolen mill.

It is curious, perhaps, but every M. J. & G. rifle seen by the writer which carried a bayonet was fitted with the English Lancaster rifle sapper bayonet, model of 1856. It is possible that the Jamestown factory did not manufacture bayonets, but imported the Lancaster bayonets for their rifles.

Lieutenant Breck, of the *U. S. S. Niphon*, reported August 24, 1864, that he landed a boat's crew at Masonboro Inlet and captured nine rifles marked "C. S. 1863, N. C."[12]

* * * * *

LAMB RIFLE
Figure 2, Plate XXIV

Two miles north of Jamestown and near Greensboro, N. C., was the small gun factory of Lamb and Brother, later H. C. Lamb & Company. This firm was given a contract in 1861 to make 10,000 rifles for the State of North Carolina.[13]

---

[12] Official Records of the Union and Confederate Navies. Vol. X, Page 388.
[13] Ellis-Clark letters, North Carolina in the War.

The output was very small. Federal raiders who passed through that section of North Carolina in April, 1865, overlooked the Lamb factory.

The Lamb rifles are crudely made, with stocks of yellow oak, almost as light as hickory. They are of .58 caliber, with 33-inch barrels, about seven inches of which at the breech is octagonal. The butt plate, trigger guard, fore-end tip and two flat bands are of brass. The rear sight is fixed, and there is a knob for saber bayonet. The lock plate is perfectly plain, but the serial appears on the breech and the inside of the hammer. Stamped on the left side of the stock: "H. C. Lamb & Co., N. C." and the serial.

There were several members of the Lamb family who were gunsmiths—William Lamb, H. C. Lamb and Anderson Lamb. Anderson Lamb had a small gun shop on Bull Run creek. The other Lamb factory was on Deep river.

* * * * *

THE HODGKINS CARBINE
Figure 2, Plate XXVI

The firm of D. C. Hodgkins & Sons had a large gun shop in Macon, Georgia, when the war began.

Governor Brown of Georgia in his message to the Georgia Legislature of November 17, 1860, reported that contracts for arms had been made with Northern firms, and he added: "There is a fund of $75,000 to pay for these and to D. C. Hodgkins & Sons and others for arms." Later in the report Governor Brown says that Hodgkins & Sons had not delivered 250 rifles, 700 Colt revolvers and 700 sabers ordered from them.[8]

On February 5, 1861, Governor Brown demanded that the Governor of New York release guns seized in New York, the property of Hodgkins & Sons, of Macon.[9]

On March 2, 1861, the ship *Martha J. Ward* and the schooner *Julia A. Halleck* were offered for sale to indemnify D. C. Hodgkins & Sons for the arms seized in New York.[10]

Later, the firm began the manufacture of muzzle-loading carbines of the U. S. Model 1854. The *Macon Telegraph* of February 12, 1862, says:

---

[8] Confederate Records of Georgia. Vol. II, Page 1.
[9] Official Records, War of the Rebellion. Vol. LIII, Page 120.
[10] Confederate Records of Georgia. Vol. II, Page 30.

182

FIREARMS OF THE CONFEDERACY

We visited yesterday the workshop of D. C. Hodgkins & Sons, and were much pleased with what we saw in them. Messrs. Hodgkins & Sons have manufactured for the State of Georgia over $100,000 worth of munitions of War, and altered over 2,000 of the old flint and steel muskets into good percussion locks. They are now manufacturing for the Confederate Government rifled carbines. They forge the barrels by hand, which is a very tedious and laborious work. We saw the various parts of the guns in process of manufacturing—tubes, locks, ramrods, wipers, plates, mountings, etc., etc., all made by tools manufactured in the shop. The tubes for the guns alone require great labor and many tools to make them correctly. The difficulty in forging gun barrels is, that it requires too much labor, as it is only when the barrel is near complete, that it can be ascertained whether it is perfect or not.

Forging by hand, must, therefore, for practical purposes, in making a large quantity of guns, be considered impracticable. The machinery and arrangements of the establishment are complete. The motive power is an eight horsepower engine, made by Messrs. Schofield & Brother of this city.

Messrs. Hodgkins & Sons think that if they could devote all their energies to the manufacturing of guns, they could turn out over one hundred guns per month, complete, and finely finished. Their works will testify of them in the hour of trial. In Virginia and along the coasts of Georgia are scattered many specimens of their skill and handiwork, which will no doubt demonstrate to the Yankees that even old worn out guns, renovated by them are capable of doing good execution, and their new ones deal out certain death.

We think that Messrs. Hodgkins & Sons deserve the liberal patronage they are receiving from our people and Government. They are now executing an order for one hundred rifled carbines for the Confederate Government.

To judge from the scarcity of these carbines among museums and collectors, it would seem that the first hundred was also the last.

At any rate, less than four months later, this item appeared in the *Macon Telegraph* of June 7, 1862:

D. C. Hodgkins & Sons, having disposed of the Mechanical branch of their business to the Government, (the Junior going into Government employ exclusively) give notice that no more Gun Work can be received.

Persons having work in store are requested to call for the same as early as possible. D. C. Hodgkins will dispose of the Sporting articles and material on hand, and continue to accommodate as far as possible.

We return thanks to the public for the liberal patronage heretofore extended to us, and at the expiration of the present war will renew business with increased efforts, and endeavor to receive a continuation of past favors.

D. C. HODGKINS & SONS

After the war Walter C. Hodgkins went to New York and became associated with the firm of Cooper & Pond, firearms dealers, at 177 Broadway. In 1868 the firm became Cooper, Barris and Hodgkins.

* * * * *

THE READ RIFLE AND/OR CARBINE

This is one of the Confederate "Mystery" arms. The mystery being who made them, where they were made and what became of all of them that are mentioned in the early reports.

The Virginia Armory report covering arms issued from Nov. 1, 1861, to Nov. 1, 1862, shows, among other munitions, 596 Read's cavalry rifles—405 of which were evidently issued to General Floyd's command. From Nov. 1, 1862, to Oct. 1, 1863, there were 220 Read's cavalry rifles issued and there remained in the armory on the latter date 400 of these rifles.

Mr. John B. Read, of Tuscaloosa, Alabama was issued patent No. 17233 dated May 5, 1857, on a Muzzle-Loading Firearm. The patent specifications read in part as follows:

"The nature of my invention consists, in providing the upper part of the chamber or powder space of firearms, with angular or wedge shaped projections, varying in number according to the size of the bore, and running parallel or nearly so with its axis; so that in the act of loading the ball, whether spherical or solid elongated, may rest upon these projections, and being expanded by having them forced into it by a few blows of the ramrod, may completely and accurately fill the bore of the gun, thus saving windage and securing range and accuracy; also, in providing a ball, solid, and conical or conoidal at both extremities, with a cylindrical belt at or near the middle, sufficient to prevent turning in the barrel, with the inner or under part of the rear of the cylindrical portion slightly excavated, so as to favor the expansion of the ball when forced home by the ramrod upon the projections of the chamber or powder space as well as to afford a thin edge to take into the grooves by the force of the charge. The claims of the patent read as follows:

"1. The providing the upper part of the powder space, or chamber of firearms, with angular or wedge shaped projections to be forced into the rear of the projectile in the act of loading as described.

"2. Also the form of ball represented in my drawings, cylindrical at or near its middle portion, with a slight excavation or recess on the inner and under side of the cylindrical part; both ends of the ball to be conoidal or conical."

There is no evidence to indicate that the rifles mentioned in the foregoing armory reports were of this type but since the patented device could be incorporated into any muzzle-loading rifle or smooth-bore arm without any external evidence of its existence, except the joint between the barrel and the powder chamber, which if properly made would be scarcely visible, they could, at a later date be easily overlooked.

That John B. Read of Alabama was active in the Confederate munition effort at an early date is indicated by the following extracts from the Acts of the C. S. Congress:

"Feb. 15, '61—Mr. Fearn—A letter from John B. Read relative to rifled cannon and projectiles. (Vol. I. P. 54)

"March 11, '62—Mr. Clay—That the Com. Mil. Affairs be instructed to inquire what is due Dr. John B. Read of Alabama for his projectile for iron cannon known as the Read Shell. (Vol. II. P. 51)

"May 16, '62—Mr. Sparrow—That the Com. Mil. Affairs be relieved of further consideration of John B. Read's petition for compensation for the use of the improved projectile known as the Read Shell. (Vol. II. P. 174)

"June 4, '64—Mr. Jamison—That the memorial of John B. Read praying for compensation for the use of the Read Shell be transferred from the files and referred to the Com. on Naval Affairs. (Vol. IV. P. 152)"

As an indication of the fact that Mr. Read was fairly well known we have General Polk's report of Oct. 14, 1861, reading:

"Have had a shop put up in Memphis for the alteration and repair of guns. Can we not have Mr. Read of Alabama to show us how to make his shells."

As a part of the riddle concerning the Read arms we find that a Confederate States patent was granted to N. T. Read, of Danville, Va., dated March 20, 1863, covering a breech-loading firearm but unfortunately there is no description or cut of this arm available. In connection with the possibility that this latter arm really was produced for the Confederate service prior to the date of the patent we have the following advertisement from a Richmond paper of June 26, 1862:

GUNSMITH:—We wish to employ 20 to 30 steady gunsmith hands for Keen, Walker & Co.'s Gun Factory in Danville, Va. Liberal wages will be given those who come well recommended. Apply Keen, Walker & Co., Danville, Va., or "Hunt & James" Cary St.

According to the History of Danville, Va., Mr. James M. Walker was the Mayor in 1865 and E. F. Keen was Magistrate of the 5th District and it is quite probable that it was they who were interested in the gun factory in 1862.

The *New York Times* of June 26, 1932, carried an account of the re-election of Capt. Harry Wooding as Mayor of Danville, Va. Capt. Wooding was then 88 years old and had held the office for 40 years. In connection with the manufacture of Read carbines he stated:

"I think there was an old house in which the Read carbines were made, that has been taken down. It stood very near the present ice factory. There were about 50 carbines made in Danville, sent to Co. C, 5th Va. Cavalry (which was the Danville Cavalry). The carbines proved worthless, several bursted when first fired. Sent about Oct. 1862."

To add a bit to the confusion of trying to run down the story of the Read rifle we find there was another Read active in the Confederate ordnance. This was Mr. R. H. Read, who evidently had been connected with the Holly Springs, Mississippi, armory, for at about the time of its forced removal we find him writing from Holly Springs on October 7, 1862, to Secretary of War Randolph as follows:

"I have not yet heard from Atlanta, but received a communication from Col. Gorgas, C. O., some time ago. I have no choice of place so that I could be useful in any of the Arsenals or Armories."

*   *   *   *   *

THE ALABAMA ARMS MANUFACTURING CO.

There is very little known to the present compiler concerning this armory and, so far as is known at this time there has been no gun definitely identified as having been made there. A letter from Mr. John Purifoy, Secretary of State of Alabama, of Montgomery, Ala., of March 4, 1924 to E. Berkley Bowie reads in part as follows:

"The Alabama Arms Manufacturing Company, in Montgomery, Gov. Shorter stated in 1863, 'was the best equipped shop in the Confederacy for the fabrication of the Enfield rifle.' I have found some of the older residents, now living here, who distinctly remember the plant, and can point out its location; they can also remember that the manager was a Major Wagner, that he was what is denoted a Westpointer. This information is conveyed by several, but what I have stated is the extent of the memory of all I have approached.

"I looked up the record for Gov. Shorter's statement, and find it was made in defense of his contention that the workers in it should not be disturbed for field service. If the information I have so far received is reliable, the gun manufactured in that shop was a shorter gun, perhaps the Mississippi or Belgian rifle, and not the Enfield. All my information, so far, agrees that the gun made was a short rifle. My personal knowledge informs me that the Enfield rifle was, and is, a long gun, the longest of the common rifles used at that time, the Belgian shorter, and the Mississippi rifle slightly shorter than the former. It is possible that Governor Shorter made a mistake in his use of Terms. I have failed so far to obtain details concerning the factory."

That the output was very limited is evident from the following:

OFFICE OF ORDERS AND DETAIL,
C. S. NAVY DEPARTMENT, Richmond, November 16, 1863.

SIR: In obedience to your instructions of the 5th ultimo I have the honor . . .

No deliveries have been made on the contract of the War and Navy Departments with the Alabama Arms Manufacturing Co.; they should have commenced in June last, and there is yet no certainty as to the time when they will begin.

I have the honor to be, very respectfully, your obedient servant,
JOHN K. MITCHELL,
Commander in Chief.

To Hon. S. R. MALLORY,
Secretary of the Navy.

From present evidence it appears that Mr. Thomas McNeil was the promotor of this enterprise and was awarded the contract to supply arms to the Confederate Government on May 6, 1862—these arms being referred to as breech-loading carbines in some cases and Enfield rifles in other cases.

On April 25, 1862, Mr. McNeil made a contract with James H. Burton under which, for the consideration of $5,000.00 the latter was to permit copies to be taken of his plans and drawings of machines, fixtures, tools, etc., pertaining to the manufacture of the Enfield rifle. These were to include drawings of the stock machines which had previously been prepared by Mr. Burton for the construction of such machines by the Ames Manufacturing Co. for the Royal Manufactory, Enfield, England. Burton was also to assist in the enterprise with professional advice and other services he could render from time to time.

In October, 1862, Burton wrote to Colonel Gorgas, Chief of Ordnance, setting forth at great detail the very poor progress that had been made by McNeil and while McNeil's partners in the deal had spent $30,000.00 of their private means in addition to the $20,000.00 advanced by the Government on the contract there was little to show for the expenditures and he recommended that General Huger be instructed to investigate the McNeil contract and no further advances be made pending a satisfactory report from General Huger.

Mr. Burton had written to Mr. McNeil shortly before stating his determination to withdraw from their contract of April 25, which McNeil replied to, withholding his consent to a cancellation upon the grounds that he had fulfilled his part of the contract in every way and that he was proceeding on the contract with the Government as rapidly as conditions would permit.

The Arsenal at Montgomery, apparently, was engaged entirely in repairing arms and altering flintlock muskets to percussion. Figure 1, Plate XVIII, shows a Springfield flintlock musket altered to percussion at Montgomery. The barrel bears the U. S. regulation "V. P." and eagle's head and the date, "1820." The tang of the buttplate is stamped: "U. S." The lock plate is marked with a large Star and "C. S. Montgomery Arsenal. 1863."

George H. Todd, who at one time helped to make revolvers in Texas, was also engaged in the manufacture of muskets in a small way at Montgomery in 1864. Figure 1, Plate XXVII, shows a Todd musket, a most remarkable weapon in that the lock plate, hammer, trigger guard, trigger, fore end tip and three bands are ALL of brass. The lockplate is stamped: "Geo. H. Todd, Montgomery, Ala. C. S. A. 1864."

*   *   *   *   *

ATLANTA, GEORGIA

Most students of the Confederate Arms manufacture seem determined to locate an armory at Atlanta, Ga., but from present evidence the activities in this line did not get beyond the local shops which were devoted to the conversion of sporting pieces to military guns and the repairing of battlefield pick-ups.

The *Macon Telegraph* of September 3, 1861, reports a meeting of gunsmiths as follows:

> On Tuesday, at 11 O'Clock, a number of the gunsmiths of this State assembled at the City Hall.
> E. H. Walker, Esq., of Monroe, was chosen Chairman, and W. J. Camp, of Covington, Secretary.

FIREARMS OF THE CONFEDERACY

The following committee was appointed to wait on the Governor and inform him that the meeting was organized, and ready to hear any suggestions he wished to make . . . J. M. Higgins, W. C. Hodgkins, J. H. Newton.

Peck & Bowman, of Atlanta, stated that they had contemplated for some time the establishment of an armory at this place; that they had a sufficient shop and machinery and could manufacture to a considerable extent, with sufficient encouragement.

Several others made remarks, advocating the propriety of each man making written propositions, stating their preparations for making guns, prices, &c.

Gen. Wayne then said: "The purpose in calling the convention was, first, to see if it could render fit for efficient service the common shotguns and rifles of the country; and to see how far the rifles could be reamed out to bring them to the caliber of 58-100 of an inch—the size of the Harper's Ferry Rifle and the Minie Musket. It was desirable to have all the guns of the same size so that all the ammunition—the ball and cartridges—may be of the same size and have the same charge, and no confusion arise from having different sized balls and cartridges prepared." He forcibly showed the terrible consequences of furnishing companies and regiments in a battle with the wrong sized ammunition through any kind of a mistake. The guns should all be of the same length as well as size. Bayonets were not needed on them. In close quarters the bowie knife was the best weapon in the world. The rifles should also have but few grooves—three being preferable.

Mr. Hodgkins had experimented with rifles, with few and many grooves, with 14, 10, 7, 4 and 3; preferably the latter. All Military guns should have the grooves wide apart, on account of those with a great many grooves having often to be wiped. A gun with many grooves might be more accurate, but it was too much trouble to keep clean. He exhibited a specimen of a short rifle of his own make, and stated that the greatest difficulty was to get wood for the stocks; that wood of one or two years was not sufficiently seasoned. It ought to be cut twenty years. The bark should be taken off the tree at once. Some thought best to cut the timber in the summer—others in the fall or winter.

Mr. Newton, of Athens, suggested that we would be under the necessity of adopting some artificial process of seasoning timber for stocks, and called on any gentleman present acquainted with such a process, to respond, etc., etc.

A letter from Mr. C. R. Winship, Continental Gin Co., Atlanta, Ga., to E. Berkley Bowie dated May 19, 1924, reads in part as follows:

"I do not believe any revolvers and rifles were manufactured here. This plant was operated during the war by my father, Robert Winship, and my uncle, George Winship, under the name of Winship and Brother. I have heard them say they both enlisted in the Confederate Army, one of them serving in the cavalry in Virginia. My father was detailed to run the shop and manufacture ammunition, shot and shell it was called in those days, for the Confederate army, while Uncle George was serving in Virginia. He continued operating the shop for that purpose until Sherman's Army bore down on Atlanta, and the family refugeed to Middle Georgia and remained there until the war was over. The shop has been in continuous operation since 1853. It is now operated by the Continental Gin Company.

"J. C. Peck had a planing mill and lumber yard in Atlanta and did not manufacture anything except material for buildings."

Two guns, one of undoubted Georgia origin and the other probably so, have puzzled collectors and students.

Figure 2, Plate XVIII, shows a well-made rifle of .58 caliber and 33-inch barrel, with deep grooves. All the mountings and the trigger are of brass. Various parts, including the bolt heads, bear the serial, "4." On the lock plate is stamped "C. Chapman." Nothing is known of Chapman, but he probably was a master armorer who stamped his name on guns made for someone else, just as did J. P. Murray of Columbus, Ga.

Figure 3, Plate XVIIIa, shows a composite rifle, .58 caliber, with 33-inch barrel and most unmilitary-looking stock. The lock plate is marked: "Tilton, Ga. 1861." Probably made up of old parts by a Tilton gunsmith.

*   *   *   *   *

CARTERSVILLE, GEORGIA

The finding of a number of locks and other gun parts near the wartime site of the Cooper Iron Works some time ago led to considerable speculation as to whether or not guns were made there for the Confederates, and a later discovery of a lot of correspondence indicating that this works supplied steel of a special quality to the Colt Fire Arms Company before the war added to the belief, but recent investigations indicate rather definitely that there were no guns made there.

In a recent letter Mr. Mark A. Cooper, of Rome, Ga., great-grandson of the owner of these works advised that he had no definite information as to what was made there but was of the opinion that there were no guns made.

These iron works were located on Etowah River some six miles from Cartersville, utilizing the power from the falls provided by a dam across the river. The iron ore was obtained from the mines in that immediate vicinity but the coal all had to be shipped from above Chattanooga by water—thence by rail to Etowah and then on a private siding to the Works and as they operated until late in the war they undoubtedly made much of the iron that went into the guns made in the Georgia armories.

Scrap iron was just as essential for producing a high grade product from iron ore during the Civil War as it is in our present war and a good source of their supply would have been the many gun shops that were at work altering and cutting down the country rifle for military use and it is some of this scrap material that probably led to the original idea of this being a gun works.

That it was a plant of considerable importance is indicated by the fact that there were about five hundred employees and that they had a yard engine for handling the materials from the railroad to the plant. This engine, the "Yonah," is of considerable interest to students of the Civil War as it figured in one of the exciting exploits of that time, which was the Andrews raid. When James J. Andrews and his party of Federals, within sight of three thousand Confederate recruits, calmly uncoupled the "General" and three box cars from the balance of the train on the morning of April 12, 1862, and started from Big Shanty, Ga., northward with the intention of burning the bridges along the entire line they started a most interesting race. Captain W. A. Fuller, who was the conductor of the train, together with two other railroad men started in pursuit of the stolen engine on foot for about two miles and then by hand car to Etowah where the Yonah was pressed into service and it made sixty miles per hour to Kingston where the tracks were blocked by other trains and the chase taken up by another locomotive which finally overtook the abandoned General between Ringgold and Graysville. It was the speed of the Yonah covering the distance from Etowah to Kingston that kept Capt. Fuller in the race and finally led to the recapture of the General.

The Iron Works were completely destroyed by a detachment of Federal troops from Sherman's army on his march from Chattanooga to Atlanta; the officer in charge of the detachment being named Cooper and the story is told of how the great grandson of this officer just a few years ago looked up Mr. Mark A. Cooper, great grandson of the proprietor of the Iron Works, and they became very good friends after talking over the wartime activities of their ancestors.

*   *   *   *   *

ASHEVILLE RIFLE

The Asheville (N. C.) Armory was started early in the war by Col. Robert William Pulliam, head of a large wholesale clothing firm, with headquarters in New York, Ephraim Clayton and G. W. Whitson. In the Spring of 1863 the output was 300 rifles a month. In the Fall of 1863, the machinery was removed to Columbia, S. C.

Colonel Pulliam was a member of the wholesale clothing firm of Pulliam, Wills, Rankin & Company. In 1861 the firm was dissolved by mutual consent, and Colonel Pulliam returned from New York to North Carolina, where he had large business interests. Being past 50 years old and unfit for military service, he looked about him for a way by which he could aid the Confederacy and his native State.

He formed a company with Clayton and Whitson and began the manufacture of guns. Colonel Pulliam was in active charge of the arms plant. The total output probably was not more than 1,000.[14]

Clayton was a native of Buncombe county, N. C., and was a builder. He erected Wofford College, Spartanburg, S. C., and the Buncombe County Courthouse, which was burned in 1865.

The gun factory was in Clayton's shop adjoining his home. Iron for the guns was obtained at Cranberry. After the war Clayton became a railroad contractor and died at his home in Asheville in 1892. At its peak some 120 men were employed in the gun factory.[15]

Maj. Benjamin Sloan, of the Confederate Ordnance Department, was sent from Richmond in the Fall of 1862 to develop the Asheville Armory.[16] He says the superintendent was "Mr. King, a Harper's Ferry man" and that Thomas Clayton was the outdoor manager. He also says that by the Spring of 1863 about 300 "beautiful and efficient muzzle-loading rifles" were being turned out monthly.[17]

Colonel Gorgas reported September 23, 1863, that two hundred or more rifles might be had from the Asheville Armory.[18] Colonel McRae also mentions the Asheville Armory.[19]

The building which housed the armory was burned by Stoneman's cavalry on April 28, 1865.

---

[14] Letter of Lawrence Pulliam, son of Colonel Pulliam, to E. Berkley Bowie, Sept. 29, 1931.
[15] Asheville and Buncombe County, by F. A. Sondley, 1922. Page 184.
[16] Maj. Benjamin Sloan in the Asheville Citizen, December, 1922.
[17] Maj. Benjamin Sloan was later president of the University of South Carolina and died February 19, 1923, at the age of 87.
[18] Official Records, War of the Rebellion, Series I, Vol. XXIX, Part II, Page 740.
[19] Ibid. Series IV, Page 733.

The Asheville Armory rifle is a modified Enfield model. It is of .58 caliber, with a barrel 32 and five-eights inches long, with all brass mountings. The bands have no springs and there is a fixed rear sight. On the right side of the barrel, near the muzzle is a saber bayonet knob. The lock plate is marked: "Asheville, N. C."

* * * * *

J. B. BARRETT

A great many of the damaged guns and gun parts secured at Harper's Ferry were shipped to the shops of J. B. Barrett at Wytheville, Va., and as early as August 12, 1861, General Gorgas reported that from eight to ten rifles per day were being furnished to General Floyd's troops from there.

The so-called Hall muzzle-loading rifle is thought to be a product of this shop and also Model 1855 rifles made up without a patch box in the stock and minus the primer lock mechanism are usually considered as part of his output. In addition to reconditioning these arms he also altered many flintlocks to percussion and converted sporting guns into Military arms, but so far as is known he did not make any completely new arms.

* * * * *

BREECH-LOADING CARBINES

Except for the few breech-loading arms that had been tested and purchased in limited quantities for field trials by the U. S. Government prior to 1861 there were no arms of this class in the service except the Hall's, Sharp's and Colt's and a few of these were distributed to the States on their quota for 1860.

In Major Gorgas' report of May 7, 1861, he shows 735 carbines of various patterns at Baton Rouge when it was taken possession of and probably part of these were breechloaders.

As the war progressed and more and more of the Federal troops were armed with one of the "57" varieties of breechloaders that came out during that period, captures by the Confederates increased so that towards the end of the war whole regiments could be armed with breechloaders.

The practice, however, was limited by the fact that most of the arms required special ammunition and as the Confederates were in no shape to provide this, when the little that was captured along with the arms was exhausted, the arm became useless.

The habit of the Confederate soldier exchanging his own gun for a better one on the battlefield, which was a practice encouraged early in the war, was finally forbidden by general orders because of the disastrous effects of running out of special ammunition that could not be replenished.

The only breechloader made to any extent for the Confederates was the so-called Richmond carbine, and because of the lack of skilled workmen and proper facilities, they were never very satisfactory. Many complaints were made of its "spitting fire" at the breech, and on numerous cases actually bursting at the breech.

Despite this, continual calls were made for breechloaders by officers in the field whose men were armed with the comparatively slow muzzle-loader and pitted against the much faster breechloader, and towards the end even repeaters such as the Henry and Spencer which could, as one soldier put it, "be loaded on Sunday and shot all week." The few breechloaders that did make an appearance were in response to this crying need, but lack of facilities and skilled mechanics was a barrier that could not be overcome.

*   *   *   *   *

CONFEDERATE SHARPS CARBINE
Figure 3, Plate XIX

This arm is a copy of the regular Sharp's carbine but is made up without the priming magazine, as the Confederates had great difficulty of supplying copper caps alone, without attempting the special primers.

Marked on lock plate and barrel, S. C. Robinson Arms Mfg. Co., Richmond, Va., 1862, with serial number 816.

Made with a block movement perpendicular to the barrel axis. Brass butt plate and band. Fixed rear sight. Before the war Samuel C. Robinson operated the Belvidere Planing Mills. He first was awarded a contract to manufacture revolvers. Then he formed the S. C. Robinson Arms Manufactory and began the manufacture of carbines on the Sharps model.

General Gorgas, the Confederate Chief of Ordnance, reported on September 30, 1863, that 3,000 carbines had been made there since September, 1862. But the carbines were so poorly made that many of them burst. The arms were not gas-tight and spat fire at every discharge, so that the men were afraid of them. General Lee, in a letter to Gorgas in June, 1863, said the carbines were "so defective as to be demoralizing to our men."

PLATE XVIII (a)

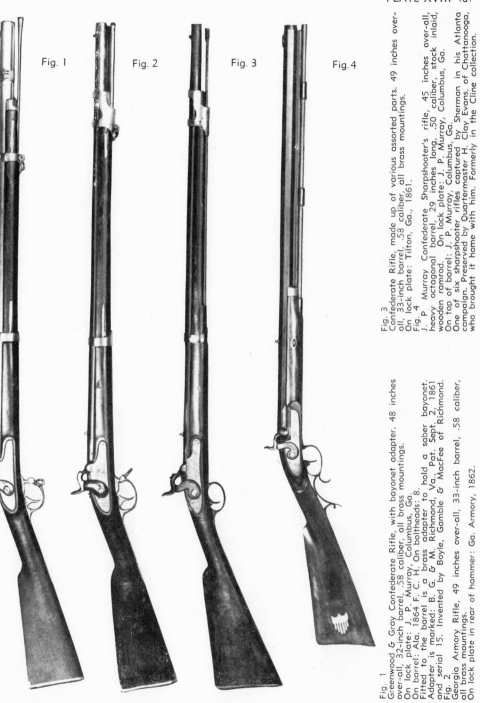

Fig. 1

Fig. 2

Fig. 3

Fig. 4

Fig. 1
Greenwood & Gray Confederate Rifle, with bayonet adapter. 48 inches over-all, 32-inch barrel, .58 caliber, all brass mountings.
On lock plate: J. P. Murray, Columbus, Ga.
On barrel: Ala. 1864 F. C. H. On boltheads: 8.
Fitted to the barrel is a brass adapter to hold a saber bayonet. Adapter is marked: B. G., & M. Richmond, Va., Pat. Sept. 2, 1861 and serial 15. Invented by Boyle, Gamble & MacFee of Richmond.

Fig. 2
Georgia Armory Rifle, 49 inches over-all, 33-inch barrel, .58 caliber, all brass mountings.
On lock plate in rear of hammer: Ga. Armory, 1862.

Fig. 3
Confederate Rifle, made up of various assorted parts. 49 inches over-all, 33-inch barrel, .58 caliber, all brass mountings.
On lock plate: Tilton, Ga., 1861.

Fig. 4
J. P. Murray Confederate Sharpshooter's rifle, 45 inches over-all, heavy octagonal barrel, 29 inches long, .50 caliber, stock inlaid, wooden ramrod. On lock plate: J. P. Murray, Columbus, Ga.
On top of barrel: J. P. Murray, Columbus, Ga.
One of six sharpshooter rifles captured by Sherman in his Atlanta campaign. Preserved by Quartermaster H. Clay Evans, of Chattanooga, who brought it home with him. Formerly in the Cline collection.

PLATE XIX

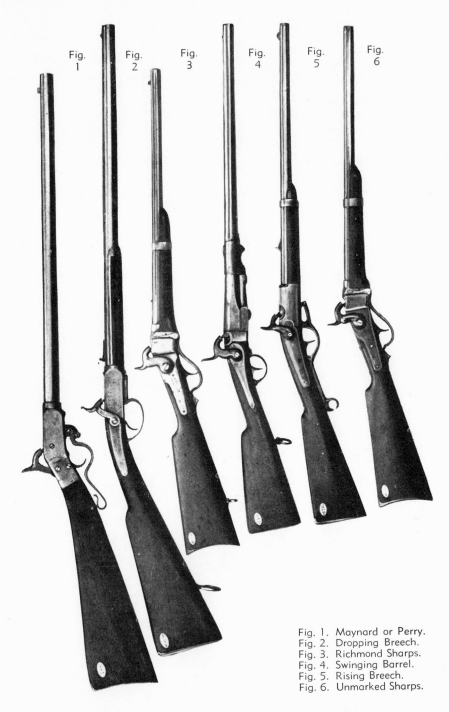

Fig.
1

Fig.
2

Fig.
3

Fig.
4

Fig.
5

Fig.
6

Fig. 1. Maynard or Perry.
Fig. 2. Dropping Breech.
Fig. 3. Richmond Sharps.
Fig. 4. Swinging Barrel.
Fig. 5. Rising Breech.
Fig. 6. Unmarked Sharps.

Under the caption "An Outrage," the *Richmond Whig* of March 30, 1863, says in an editorial: "A correspondent, a Lieutenant of Cavalry, writes us from Culpepper, C. H., March 23 as follows: "Forty new Sharp's rifles with Richmond stamp on them were handed yesterday to my company. The men were ordered to test them. Nine were fired, and seven of the nine burst. The Lieutenant suggested that the manufacturers of these arms be sent to the field, where they can be furnished Yankee sabers, while the iron they are wasting can be used for farming implements."

The Government finally bought out the Robinson carbine plant and converted it into a factory for the manufacture of muzzle-loading carbines.

CONFEDERATE SHARP'S CARBINE
Figure 6, Plate XIX

This arm is a copy of the one above described except that there are no markings of any kind upon it and the sling swivel in the butt stock, and the bar and swivel ring on the left side of the gun are omitted, as are also the sights. These parts, which are common on the regular output, have not been removed as there is no trace of them ever having been on the arm.

CONFEDERATE RISING-BREECH CARBINE
Figure 5, Plate XIX

Percussion, breech-loading, caliber .54. Length of barrel 21 inches. Total length, 39½ inches. Marked on barrel and also on breechblock, C. S. and P. Pulling down the trigger guard causes the breechblock to rise vertically.

A very well made arm, the history of which is unknown as there are but two or three of them in present collections and none carry the maker's name. The serial number 22 appears on different parts of the arm.

An article appearing in Army Ordnance, September, 1938, entitled "Historic Military Firearms, said: "Mr. Bowie had an interesting theory about these carbines, but one which he never was able to support by documentary evidence. He believed this carbine was the "Read rifle" mentioned frequently in Confederate ordnance reports. N. T. Read, of Danville, obtained a patent for a breech-loading firearm on March 20, 1863. The manufacture of these carbines was begun, and it is on record that fifty were completed and sent to the 5th Virginia Cavalry. They proved worthless, many of them bursting on the first shot, and were discarded.

"Unfortunately for Mr. Bowie's theory, however, there is a mention of "Read's cavalry rifles" in the early part of the war. The report of the Virginia Armory at Richmond shows that 596 Read's rifles were issued to troops in the year ending November 1, 1862, and 220 more in the year ending October 1, 1863. Also, that the armory had on hand October 1, 1863, 400 of these rifles."

THE CONFEDERATE "PERRY" OR "MAYNARD" CARBINE

Figure 1, Plate XIX

An exceptionally well made arm of .52 caliber, having a 22½ inch barrel and total length of 40 inches. Weight 7¾ pounds. The frame is of bronze, while the breechblock is of iron, having a bronze lining—this lining has a deep groove cut in a spiral and on about ¼ inch pitch so that a slight twisting motion to the cartridge when loading would tend to seat it more firmly. The combination of bronze lining and deep groove was quite probably an attempt to take advantage of the expansion to make a gastight joint. Fixed sights. There are no markings of any kind on this arm except the letter "P" on the barrel and also on the breechblock.

That generally reliable handbook of all early collectors, The United States Cartridge Co.'s catalogue has this item:

> 231 - "Perry Confederate Breech-loading Rifled Carbine, cal. .52. Paper cartridge, brass breechblock, similar construction as the "Burnside" heavy barrel.

From that time on collectors and cataloguers generally referred to it as the "Confederate Perry," some even going so far as to say they were made for the Confederates by the Perry Arms Co., of Newark, N. J.

The similarity to the regular Perry carbine lies in the manner the breechblock is pivoted in the frame but there all resemblance ceases—in the regular Perry the breechblock is actuated by a rigid lever terminating in the trigger guard, while in the present specimen the block is actuated by a toggle lever of the same design as the Maynard—in the Maynard, however, the toggle lever moves the pivoted barrel and not the breech

196

block. A further resemblance to the Maynard lies in the extremely thin stock, and absence of the usual fore-stock.

The present specimen undoubtedly used a combustible cartridge loaded into the forward end of the breechblock while the Maynard loads directly into the barrel, using a special metallic cartridge having an extra wide flanged head, and perforated to take the fire of a regular musket cap. Of special interest in connection with this arm is an item from:

> *Camden* (S. C.) *Journal*, May 31, 1861—G. B. Schriver, gunsmith, has built a breech-loading rifle upon the same principle as the Maynard but is an improvement thereon.

With this bit of source material to start with the following news items take on a special significance:

> *Daily Clarion*, Meridian, Miss., June 6, 1864—The carbine factory at Richmond has been removed to Tallassee, Ala. The factory is engaged in making carbines for the cavalry, chiefly of the Maynard patent and fully equal in workmanship to the best product of Yankeedom.

> The *Augusta Constitutionalist* says all the hands employed at the carbine factory at Richmond are transferred to Tallassee, Ala. There is a quantity of the necessary machinery and a large cotton factory there already engaged for the purpose. This factory turns out carbines for the cavalry chiefly of the Maynard pattern and fully equal in workmanship to the best Yankee product.
> —*Daily Richmond Examiner*, June 11, 1864.

> *Daily Advertiser*, Montgomery, Ala., June 25, 1864—Twenty to thirty carpenters, white or black, can get constant employment with liberal wages by applying to C. P. Bolles, Capt. in charge of C. S. Armory, Tallassee, Ala; or Maj. C. G. Wagner, C. S. Arsenal, Montgomery, Ala.

For later day evidence we have a copy of a letter from John Purifoy, Secretary of State of Alabama, Montgomery, Ala., to E. Berkley Bowie, dated March 4, 1924, reading in part as follows:

"Fortunately I met Mr. William New, a member of our local camp, U. C. V., and sooned learned from him that he is a native Virginian and was enlisted as a Confederate soldier during the last one and a half years or two years of the War of the Sixties. That soon after his enlistment, being but 17 years of age, he was detailed as an operator or helper, in a carbine factory at Richmond, Va. He further stated that the authorities, becoming apprehensive that Richmond would fall into the hands of the Federals, shipped the machinery to Alabama, he accompanying it, in 1864, early part, and was set up in a building at Tallassee where breech-loading carbines were manufactured; that when the Federal troops reached Alabama and took possession of everything, the machinery was destroyed, together with all completed guns and material. He states that 600 of the guns were destroyed in the streets of this city. Under his statement the machinery was the property of the Confederate Government."

Taking all in all for what it is worth it would appear that neither PERRY nor MAYNARD is the proper designation of this arm but that it should be referred to as THE TALLASSEE BREECH-LOADING CARBINE.

CONFEDERATE DROPPING-BREECH CARBINE
Figure 2, Plate XIX

Percussion, breech-loading, caliber .52. The rear of the trigger guard is hinged and the forward part of the trigger guard provides a slidable attachment for the breechblock. A spring catch locks the trigger guard in place or permits it to swing downward, for loading, or if desired the block can be removed, it evidently being the intention of the inventor to provide a number of breechblocks ready loaded to save time. A single leaf elevating rear sight is provided and the butt stock has the swivel ring attached with a regular swivel plate.

Marked on barrel and tang of butt plate, "C. S.," otherwise there are no marks of any kind on this arm. This carbine was purchased some thirty years ago from an ex-Confederate soldier who claimed he had used it in the war.

CONFEDERATE SWINGING-BARREL CARBINE
Figure 4, Plate XIX

Smooth-bore, caliber .61, percussion breech-loading carbine. The barrel is pivoted to the frame and swings sideways for loading. Locked into position by a brass sleeve sliding on the barrel. Brass butt plate and trigger guard. Sling ring attached to extended trigger-guard plate. Small brass front sight and the sliding sleeve on the barrel also acts as a rear sight.

There are no marks on the arm except the serial number 44. An exceptionally well made piece of heavy construction and using a back-action lock. In the cheek recess on the left side of the stock is cut the initials A. H. B., below which is 4th Tex.

There is no data as to the manufacture of this arm but from its general appearance it is believed to be of Confederate make as the stock is of American black walnut not usually found in European-made arms.

THE TARPLEY CARBINE
Plate XXI

Through the courtesy of Mr. Edwin Pugsley, of New Haven, Conn., we have a photograph of the Tarpley, which of the few breech-loading carbines invented and actually manufactured in the Confederacy was the best advertised. Apparently, this weapon was the only Confederate breechloader "offered to the public" both in newspaper advertisements and broadsides. The Tarpley broadside (see page 211) is believed to be unique.

Jere H. Tarpley, of North Carolina, was granted a Confederate States patent for his breech-loading carbine, February 14, 1863. He then associated himself with J. and F. Garrett, of Greensboro, who seem to have been men of enterprise. *De Bow's Review* of March-April, 1862, already referred to, says that the Garretts had started a sewing machine factory at Greensboro and were to undertake the manufacture of pistols. The *Greensboro Patriot* of January 21, 1862, says the Messrs. Garrett had established a hat factory at that place "on a large scale."

The Garrett factory, where the breech-loading carbines were made, was in what had been the Pioneer Foundry. The carbines were made for the State of North Carolina and the total output is believed to have been only a few hundred. The Tarpley carbine in the National Museum collection, Washington, bears the serial 143.

In the *Greensboro Patriot* of January 14, 1864, appears this advertisement:

JERE H. TARPLEY

Tarpley's Breech-Loading Gun—This gun has been tested by the Armory at Richmond and Raleigh, N. C., and has stood the test finely, making a favorable impression wherever it has been exhibited. We say, without fear of contradiction, that it is the best Breech-loading gun in the Southern Confederacy. It can be shot with perfect safety when loaded either from the breech or the muzzle. This gun is less complicated and easier kept in order than any gun that has been invented in this county. The Gun was invented in Guilford County, N. C., and we are now manufacturing it for the State of North Carolina, at our shop in Greensboro. We are ready to sell shop rights to Manufacturers in the gun business in any states in the Confederacy.
(Signed)   TARPLEY, GARRETT & CO.

That the production of Tarpley carbines was limited to about a year is evident from this advertisement which appeared in the *Greensboro Patriot* of March 23, 1865:

Greensboro Foundry—Sixteen horse power engine steam, apperten-ances, stocks of fixtures consisting of four iron lathes, one entirely new of superior finish, two wood lathes, two drills, a lot of shafting pulleys and belting, sets blacksmiths tools, fifteen hundred bushels of coal and coke, one ton of lassom pig iron, Ten Thousand (10,000) pounds scrap iron, Four Thousand (4,000) pounds wrought iron, a lot plow stuff, over one hundred plows and plow castings, a lot hollow ware, a sorghum boiler, a lot pine lumber, patterns, flasks, and many other articles for sale at auction, at Greensboro, N. C., on Tuesday 4th of April, being compelled to close our concern on account of Military status.
(Signed)   TARPLEY & YARBOUGH

The Yarbough mentioned in the advertisement evidently was George Yarbough, a capitalist, with whom Tarpley associated himself.

The Tarpley carbine is .52 caliber, using paper ammunition. The breechblock swings to the left when the catch spring on the right is opened. There is no provision for a gas check. It has a 23-inch barrel, an iron butt plate and a brass breech. On the metal tang is stamped: "J. H. Tarpley's Patent Feb. 14, 1863." Stamped on the stock is "Manufactured by J & F Garrett & Co., Greensboro, N. C." and "C. S. A."

It is of interest to note that considerable ingenuity was used in the design of the Tarpley carbine so that it could be made with a file. The cuts are so designed that there is file clearance in all of them, thereby reducing the machine require-ments to a minimum.

* * * * *

THE ALEXANDER BREECH-LOADING CARBINE

While this carbine was probably never used by any Con-federate force, the fact that the Richmond Armory made at least one of them at the expense of the Government entitles it to a place in Confederate arms.

The U. S. patent on the arm was number 20,315, dated May 25, 1858; granted to Chas. Wm. Alexander, of Moorefield, Hardy County, Virginia, and the specifications read in part as follows:

"The nature of my invention consists in providing a rifled cylinder, E, containing load and cap, and which is forced laterally to a point corresponding exactly with the rifled bore of the barrel, by being introduced at the front of a revolving chamber, D, in which chamber it is kept from turnng by means of the point of a screw fitting exactly into a notch in the hinder end of the cylinder E, and to which revolving chamber D is attached a lever or handle, by which it is forced to revolve, and is kept in its place by means of a spring, H.

"To enable others to understand and use my invention, place the thumb of the right hand on the cock of the gun, drawing it to half-cock; then with forefinger of same hand draw back the spring H until it releases itself from the notch in the revolving chamber D; then with the fingers of the left hand grasp the handle of the revolving chamber D, and, by pulling it, cause the revolving chamber to revolve until the now released spring H catches in the second notch of revolving chamber D, then push the now freed cylinder E forward out of the revolving chamber D, and introduce another loaded cylinder E, and return revolving chamber to its original place, where the spring H will hold it secure.

"The merits of my invention are, first, accuracy of shooting, gained by using a patched ball, which my rifled cylinder enables me to do successfully without danger of stripping the patch from the ball in its passage through the barrel, as the rifles in both the barrels and cylinder correspond exactly; the patch gives the rotary motion to the ball without indenting it, and keeps the bore free from leading; secondly, facility of loading, as a number of cylinders may be carried loaded, and which cylinders are again loaded with facility; thirdly, no escape of gas, as the fit between the end of the cylinder E and the barrel A is perfect. Its simplicity is such that it cannot easily get out of order.

"What I claim as new in my invention, and desire to secure by Letters Patent, is—

"The replaceable rifled cylinder with its dovetail for cap, and notch for holding it in its place, in combination with the revolving chamber that bears it and holds it to its place."

The following statement, made before a Notary Public by Jas. H. Burton on February 4, 1863, provides a case history of the Confederate interest in this arm, and as Mr. Alexander was granted a Confederate States patent No. 163, dated April 18, 1863, this new patent probably covered the changes in construction as outlined by Col. Burton.

FIREARMS OF THE CONFEDERACY

Georgia
Bibb County.
Personally came James H. Burton, of Macon, Ga., formerly of Richmond, Va., who being duly sworn says, That during the early Spring of 1861 being then in the employ of Jas. R. Anderson & Co., of Richmond, Va., as Engineer having charge of their contract with the State of Va. for the supply of machinery, etc. required for the Va. State Armory and occupying an office in the State Armory Building in Richmond—Mr. C. W. Alexander, of Hardy Co., Va., called upon him and expressed a desire to have him examine a breech-loading rifle which the said Alexander claimed to have invented with a view to an expression of his (deponents) opinion in regard to its merits and requesting that he (deponent) would make any suggestions which might be of service in perfecting the weapon, remarking at the same time substantially that he came to deponent for his opinion because of his (deponents) acknowledged reputation as a military gun maker. Acquiescing (?) in Mr. Alexander's request he submitted then and there his weapon saying that it was a rough specimen having been made in a blacksmith's shop in the mountains much of it by himself. The weapon then submitted was a small-bored rifle with a short barrel (about 30″ in length) and fitted with a breech-loading arrangement of which Mr. Alexander claimed to be the inventor. The breech-loading device consisted of a breech piece which moved or revolved at right angles to the axis of the bore of the barrel on a stout axis pin below the axis of the bore of the barrel and parallel with it: said breech piece being of sufficient length to contain a chamber in which the cartridge, or powder and bullet was to be placed in loading for which purpose the breech piece was to be moved by a hand lever attached to its lower extremity about one fourth of a revolution so as to expose the mouth of the chamber in the breech piece on the right hand side of the barrel. The charge being inserted, the breech piece was to be again moved by the aforesaid lever so as to bring the chamber in a position coincident with the line of the axis of the bore of barrel for which purpose a stop-screw was provided. The chamber was enlarged at its mouth in order to receive a ring of copper wire slightly flattened which ring, the inventor stated, was driven forward against the breech end of the barrel by the expansion force of the gas when the arm was fired and thus a gas-tight joint was secured. Said ring of copper fitted loosely in the mouth of the chamber and could be, and was several times in the deponents presence removed by the insertion of the inventor's little finger nail. The aforesaid breech piece also contained a cone or nipple from which a communication was formed in the rear end of the chamber. Deponent states that he objected to the breech arrangement as then submitted as not being adapted to military service as cartridges would have to be used in such service and there would most probably be an accumulation of paper resulting from continued firing and which would constitute a serious difficulty for several reasons which must be obvious.

Deponent states further that he also objected to the use of the copper ring in the mouth of the chamber on the ground of its great liability to be lost. Having raised these objections deponent also states that he then suggested the use of a shorter breech piece without any chamber for the cartridge and to be used simply for the purpose of closing the breech of the barrel, the cartridges to be inserted into the breech of the barrel instead of into the chamber of the breech piece as originally proposed by the inventor.

Upon the occasion of this interview with Mr. Alexander and subsequent ones about the same time deponent states that he gave him (Alexander) a free and unreserved expression of opinion in regard to the general requirements of a breech-loading carbine, or rifle, for military use and for which opinion and advice he seemed grateful and expressed his thanks.

202

About six or eight months after having submitted his arm as above described Mr. Alexander again called upon deponent at his office in the Va. State Armory building in Richmond, and submitted for his deponent's examination and criticism another rifle which he (Alexander) had in the meantime made, and which was fitted with a solid revolving breech piece with some device not clearly recollected by the deponent for closing the joint of the breech piece and barrel gas tight, but which was deemed insufficient by deponent. Deponent then and there suggested to Mr. Alexander the application to his arm of a gas check similar in construction and application to that patented a year or two before in the U. States by R. S. Lawrence of Hartford, Ct., and applied by him to Sharp's patent Breech-loading carbines and rifles with which arms deponent had been familiar from their first conception. And deponent further suggested that the use of this gas check would afford a means of providing a better knife edge for cutting off the rear end of the cartridge than could otherwise be provided: the knife edge for this purpose being formed of the solid substance of the breech piece, in the arm as submitted by Mr. Alexander and consequently more difficult to harden and temper properly and to renew when required. At this time Mr. Alexander seemed to be ignorant of the construction of the Lawrence gas check until it was explained by deponent. Deponent being of the opinion that by the addition of this gas check the arm might be made efficient brought it to the notice of Col. J. Gorgas, Chief of Ordnance, and recommended that a Carbine be made at the Govt. expense at the Govt. Armory at Richmond under the Superintendence of the deponent who was then filling the position of Superintendent of Armories C. S. A. Authority was granted by Col. Gorgas to have the Carbine made as suggested by deponent and the work was commenced immediately thereafter. Mr. Alexander being provided with a room and other facilities for preparing his drawings and also a Sharp's carbine with the Lawrence gas check from which to copy after and make the application to his arm. The carbine was ultimately completed in the Govt. Armory under superintendence of deponent at considerable cost to the Govt. and was understood to be Govt. property although Mr. Alexander retained the possession of it against the orders of Col. Gorgas.

Deponent states that from that time to the present he has not seen the arm last referred to; and further states that the application of the solid revolving breech was suggested by him to Mr. Alexander in the Spring of 1861 and the application of the Lawrence gas check about six or eight months thereafter, and that the Carbine in the form it was gotten up in the Armory at Richmond under deponent's superintendence was the result in its valuable features of deponents suggestions at various times and for which deponent has no desire or intentions of making application for Letters Patent.

Deponent further states that a reference to the three several arms herein referred to will fully illustrate the improvements which have been the result of his (deponent's) suggestions.

Deponent further states that, when in England in 1857 he saw a breech-loading carbine patented in England Sept. 23d, 1853, by James Leetch with whom deponent was acquainted personally and which embraced substantially the same breech-loading arrangement as that originally submitted to deponent by Mr. C. W. Alexander in the Spring of 1861.

Sworn and subscribed to before G. S. Obear, Notary Public, Macon, Ga., Feb. 4th, 1863.

*   *   *   *   *

FIREARMS OF THE CONFEDERACY

THE SIBERT MAGAZINE RIFLE

While this arm has no direct connection with the Confederacy it is mentioned in Colonel Burton's wartime papers and is included here as an illustration of the brainstorm occasioned by impending war or the talk of war.

The U. S. patent covering this arm was number 32,316, dated May 14, 1861, and was granted to Lorenzo Sibert, of Mount Solon, Virginia, and assigned to himself and John M. McCue and in all likelihood there were never any of them manufactured. Had they been able to get in production and if the thing would have worked it would have been a "Yankee Killer" of the first magnitude and might well have rated with some of the "secret weapons" of our present war.

Too bad the inventor did not furnish some computation on the weight of the arm when fully loaded with cartridges heavy enough to withstand the force of the explosion without any outside support, and the ballistic experts could well have pondered the effects upon the firing of a fully loaded arm as compared with the last shot from it.

The description of the arm as given in the patent specifications follows:

My invention relates to that class of single-barrelled breech-loading repeating firearms in which a series of cartridges are successively automatically brought into line with the bore of the gun, fired, and the exploded cases removed, and has for its object the production of a more simple, rapid, and effective firearm than any heretofore known; and to this end my invention consists, first, in arranging a magazine composed of separate tubes to carry complete ball-cartridge concentrically around the barrel of the gun in such manner that the magazine may readily be revolved upon the barrel, and the tubes be caused successively to occupy such a relation to the loading mechanism that the cartridges may regularly and readily be fed one at a time into the discharging mechanism by their own gravity alone, whereby I am enabled to feed the cartridge to the discharge-chamber as rapidly as the gun can be cocked and fired; secondly, in a conveyer which depresses the cartridge into its place between the fluted rollers, and at the same time prevents the escape of another cartridge from the magazine; thirdly, in dividing the breech by a vertical slot passing entirely through it, to permit the passage of the cartridge through the same with only the detention necessary for its explosion; fourthly, in the combination of two fluted rollers, or their equivalent, arranged to constitute an open receiving-chamber for the loaded cartridge, and in which it is securely held until expelled therefrom by the succeeding cartridge; fifthly, in arranging the mechanism for discharging the gun in such manner that the cartridge is received from the magazine by its own gravity, brought into line with the bore of the gun in the act of cocking, driven forward by the hammer, at the moment of igniting the charge, into the conical part of the breech to pack the joint, and held in this position by the hammer until the gun is cocked, while the conveyer rises at the moment of explosion to admit of the entrance of a fresh cartridge, whereby the ability to fire rapidly

PLATE XIX (a)

C. W. ALEXANDER.
Breech-Loading Fire-Arm.

No. 20,315.

Patented May 25, 1858.

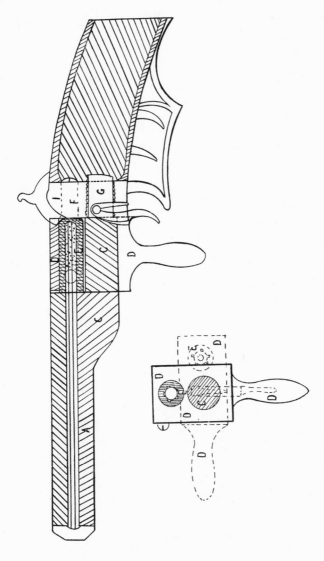

PLATE XX

2 Sheets—Sheet 1.

L. SIBERT.

Magazine Fire-Arm.

No. $\left\{ \begin{array}{l} 1,312, \\ 32,316. \end{array} \right.$

Patented May 14, 1861.

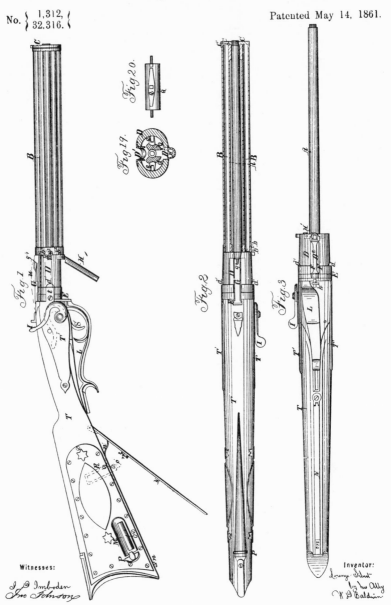

Fig 20.

Fig 19.

Fig 1.

Fig 2.

Fig 3.

Witnesses:

Inventor:

is greatly augmented; sixthly, in a combination of parts whereby the loaded cartridge which is being brought into line with the bore of the barrel by the act of cocking is made to expel the cartridge previously exploded; seventhly, in discharging the cases of the exploded cartridges automatically into a secure receptacle in the stock of the gun or into the hand at pleasure; eighthly, in arranging the discharging mechanism in such manner that the cartridge shall be exploded in an open chamber and form a continuation of the barrel of the gun, in contradistinction to those devices in which the cartridge is either inserted into the barrel itself or into a tight breech-chamber, or into both combined; ninthly, is such an arrangement of the parts which receive the loaded cartridge and convey it to the discharge-chamber that the semi-diameter of the cartridge which slides into the breech shall project above the line of the magazine tube and prevent the escape of more than one cartridge at a time; tenthly, in combining with the lock a conveyer which brings the loaded cartridge into line with the bore of the barrel, so that cocking the lock shall cause the conveyer to act upon the cartridge, while the act of firing shall release the conveyer and cause it to ascend preparatory to the admission of another cartridge; eleventhly, in the combination of the conducting-tube, which receives the spent cartridges and conveys them into the chamber in the stock, with the fluted rollers, so that the exploded cartridges may pass from thence directly into the tube by their gravity alone; twelfthly, in arranging two guides in the breech in such relation to the fluted rollers that the cartridge, when forced below the level of the guides, occupies such a relation to the rollers that it cannot fail to enter between them in a proper manner.

The cartridges which I design to use in connection with my improved gun are of a peculiar construction. They are composed of a strong cylindrical case, O, of metal, of a length sufficient to pass easily through the openings in the breech, their internal bore being exactly coincident with that of the gun, while externally they are sufficiently large to withstand the force of the explosion of the charge. A nipple, o, is screwed into the rear end of this case, the rear edge of which projects slightly beyond the nipple, in order to prevent accidental explosions by a blow upon the cap when placed upon the nipple..

The ball used by me is also of a peculiar form, being of a cylindro-conoidal shape, having a sharp tapering point in front, and being provided with two angular wings or tails in the rear, which are expanded by the force of the explosion to fill the bore of the gun, and thus to prevent windage.

The ordinary percussion-cap may be used upon this cartridge.

The accompanying estimate covering the cost of providing 3,000 of these rifles per annum gives some idea of the magnitude of the job of manufacturing arms in quantity and while the complicated mechanism of this particular piece probably called for some additional machines over that required for the ordinary musket, the difference for this reason would be but slight.

It will be remembered that the James R. Anderson & Co. (also referred to as The Tredegar Iron Works) Richmond, Va., had the contract for building the new machinery for the Virginia State Armory and that James H. Burton was in their employ as engineer having charge of that particular work, so it was natural that they would be interested in supplying the machinery for any other gun manufactures.

It will be noted that the estimate amounting to $41,405.00 covers only the machinery required for fabricating the arm from barrels obtained in an advanced stage of finish from some barrel maker and does not include the cost of motive power, shafting, pulleys, etc., nor the cost of the buildings so that the completed plant would represent a large investment.

An interesting feature of this patent is that it was issued by the U. S. Patent Office to a citizen of the Confederacy on May 14, 1861, almost a month after the opening of hostilities, and is believed to be the only patent on firearms thus issued during the war.

Estimate of Cost of Machinery etc. for making 3,000 Sibert's patent repeating Rifles per annum, prepared at the request of Col. McCue, of Staunton, Va., March 11, 1861.

2 Machines for Rifling Barrels, H. F. Pattern	@	$600	$1,200.00
2 Drill Presses, 3 spindles each	@	250	500.00
1 do 4 do	@	260	260.00
15 Straight Milling Machines	@	310	4,650.00
2 Profiling Machines, 2 spindles each	@	400	800.00
1 Set of 4 Machines for making Cones			1,300.00
2 Clamp Milling Machines	@	330	660.00
2 Screw Macking Machines	@	300	600.00
1 Machine for threading wood screws (Hand)			125.00
1 do for cutting screws to length			340.00
1 do for polishing exterior of Barrels			600.00
1 do for finishing boring Barrels			400.00
1 Lathe for cutting screws on do			250.00
1 Machine for milling barrel to length			275.00
1 do for 1st boring bayonet-socket			500.00
1 do for turning do			350.00
1 do for 2nd boring do			340.00
2 Iron Frames for large Grindstones & spindles	@	150	300.00
1 Punching & trimming Press			600.00
3 Iron Stands for straightening Barrels	@	25	75.00
5 Iron Polishing Frames	@	50	250.00
2 Machines for Buffing Bayonets	@	250	500.00
1 do for slitting screw heads			200.00
1 Fan Blower			50.00
1 Swedge Drop Hammer, double drop			500.00
1 Small Iron Tilt Hammer for forging screws			500.00
1 Double Frame do for Bayonet blades			900.00
1 Machine for boring cartridge cylinders			325.00
1 Lathe for turning do			200.00
2 Machines for threading Lock Screws etc. (Hand) @		75	150.00
5 Machines for making Stocks @ $1,000 each			5,000.00
Carried Forward			$22,500.00
Amount brought forward			22,500.00

Machines for Tool & Machine Shop

1 Planing Machine 7 foot bed					$500.00
1 do 5 " "					400.00
2 Slide Lathes 6 " "		@	250		500.00
2 Hand Lathes 6 " "		@	140		280.00
1 Shaping Machine 7-inch stroke					500.00
1 Drill Press, 3 spindles					250.00
1 Drilling Machine, 1 spindle					175.00
1 Profiling Machine for Tool Making					450.00
1 Universal Milling Machine					850.00
					$26,405.00
Small tools, Gauges, fixtures, etc., etc. estimated at					15,000.00
			Total estimate		$41,405.00

The above estimate is based upon the supposition that barrels will be obtained in an advance stage of finish from some barrel maker, to be finished-bored, rifled, screwed and finished complete in Staunton, Va. Some few additional special machines for lock work may be ultimately required. The machines for the Stock will have to be specially adapted to the peculiar stock of the arm, and the estimate for this item is only approximative. The estimated cost of the other machines is based upon the prices at which they can be obtained at the North, delivered at the shops of the makers. The cost of motive power, shafting, pulleys, gearing, forges, furnaces, etc. and cost of transportation of machinery and erection, as also the adaptation and alteration of buildings, is not estimated for, in the absence of special information on these points.

JAS. H. BURTON, Engineer

Richmond, Va. March 11th, 1861.

* * * * *

CONVERSION OF SHOTGUNS AND SPORTING RIFLES TO MILITARY USE

To supply the urgent need of firearms, the South early in the war resorted to the use of the privately owned shotguns, sporting rifles and pistols of the country, and shops were established all over the Confederacy to repair and alter these arms and make them suitable for the use of troops in the field. The Sutherland shops at Richmond were one of the largest establishments devoted to this work and the arms that they worked on were generally marked. Other large shops were at Nashville, Pulaski, Memphis and Murfreesboro, but so far as known Memphis is the only one of these outfits that marked their output.

This work consisted of making them of uniform length, boring them out and sometimes rifling them for the regulation .58 caliber ammunition and fitting them for either regular triangular bayonets or saber bayonets.

The Governors of the various States appealed to the people to turn over all such arms to the Ordnance officers and later by proclamation called upon them to deliver all surplus firearms, shotguns and rifles of every description.

The Confederate Government officers also undertook to collect such arms for the general service and appointed officers to visit the various communities in search of them and as many of the people were averse to turning their weapons of defense over to the authorities, controversy arose between the general government and the different State authorities, as indicated by the notice of Gov. Clark, of North Carolina, published in the *Raleigh Standard* of April 26, 1862, saying in part:

> These agents have no lawful authority to seize your private arms, and you will be protected in preserving this means of self defense.

The records indicate, however, despite this reluctance to part with their arms, many thousands of them were put into the service and the large shop of Samuel Sutherland at Richmond was employed throughout the war in the alteration and repair of the many arms thus secured.

Figure 4, Plate XXVI, shows a flintlock hunting rifle hastily cut down to carbine size for cavalry use, but with the flintlock unaltered, by Samuel Sutherland, of Richmond. The barrel is 17 inches long and the caliber about 50. On the barrel is stamped: "C. S. A.   S. S.   1861" and on the brass counterplate is stamped: "Rep. No. 941. S. Sutherland."

The firm of Jones, McElwaine & Co., of Holly Springs, Miss., also did a great deal of this work, as indicated by the letter of July 8, 1861, from W. Goodman to Sec. Walker, which reads in part as follows:

> Mr. McElwaine informs me he will soon have in readiness a machine of his own make for boring and rifling barrels, and can readily change old rifles to a larger caliber. Could he obtain one of the rifling machines that General Polk informed me he had procured he could greatly facilitate the General's desire to change the country rifle into one suitable for the Army."

On July 12, 1861, Mr. Goodman wrote to General Polk, of Memphis, on this subject, saying in part as follows:

> They will in a few days have a machine in readiness to rebore and rerifle the common rifle and make bayonets therefor, and if you could supply them with a machine for this purpose they could put it into immediate operation.
>
> I think you would facilitate the consummation of your wishes to change the common rifle by supplying them with one of the machines for that purpose.

FIREARMS OF THE CONFEDERACY

As early as May 18, 1861, double-barreled shotguns were used in the service as indicated by the following correspondence of that date:

Montgomery, May 18, 1861.

Governor PETTUS,
Jackson, Miss.:

Can you give me two regiments for twelve months, armed with heavy double-barreled shotguns?

L. P. WALKER,

Jackson, Miss., May 18, 1861.

L. P. WALKER:

Two regiments at Corinth have arms and ammunition. I think we can send you two regiments with double-barreled guns, and know I could send you five regiments armed with muskets and rifles in ten days.

JOHN J. PETTUS

The correspondence between General Hardee, at Memphis, to General Cooper, which reads in part as follows indicates that battalions armed with sporting rifles and shotguns were received into the service:

The letter of Mr. Sharp, with your indorsement, of June 30, to the Secretary of War, making the same tender and offering to increase the battalion to 500, is just received, and you are authorized to muster in the additional companies of the battalion as they are presented. The arms with which the battalion is now supplied (common country rifles and shotguns, &c.) will be used until others are supplied, if that be possible. After a report from you that the battalion has been mustered into service and organized, a field officer will be appointed by the Department, doubtless Major Sharp.

Very respectfully, your obedient servant,

S. S. COOPER,
Adjutant and Inspector General.

That the double-barreled shotgun was considered an efficient weapon, especially for the cavalry, is indicated by the letter of March 3, 1862, from W. R. Hunt to Secretary Benjamin which follows:

ORDNANCE OFFICE,
Memphis, March 3, 1862.

Hon. J. P. BENJAMIN,
Secretary of War:

SIR: Requisitions are daily made upon me for pistols for cavalry service in the department, but I can now find none for sale at any point in the Confederacy. Many have been bought up by the infantry (officers and privates), and I respectfully suggest that you disarm the infantry and let the cavalry get the pistols now in the hands of the former. In this way enough pistols could be obtained for all the cavalry in this section and the infantry could get money for an arm that is of no service to them. Colonel Forrest, the most efficient cavalry officer in this department, informs me that the double-barrel shotgun is the best gun which cavalry can be armed, and that at Fort Donelson one discharge of his shotguns, at close quarters, scattered 400 of the enemy whom three of our regiments had vainly tried to dislodge from the stronghold in a ravine.

Respectfully,

WM. RICHARDSON HUNT,
Ordnance Officer.

On April 7, 1862, Colonel Johnson, reporting to General Cooper in reference to raising cavalry regiments in the State of Texas writes as follows:

Although I had some hesitation in receiving the fifth regiment, yet in doing so I feel sure that I did not exceed my authority. The men of the command are mostly armed with good double-barreled shotguns. Those not so armed have good common hunting rifles.

A large majority are provided with good pistols and nearly all with large knives, well mounted on good serviceable horses, and equipments which, together with the arms, have been procured without expense to the Government.

The use of privately owned sporting rifles and shotguns became so prevalent that on April 28, 1862, the Confederate Congress passed, and the President approved, the following:

SEC. 8. Be it further enacted, That each man who may be mustered into service, and who shall arm himself with a musket, shotgun, rifle or carbine, accepted as an efficient weapon, shall be paid the value thereof, to be ascertained by the mustering officer under such regulations as may be prescribed by the Secretary of War, if he is willing to sell the same, and if he is not, then he shall be entitled to receive $1 a month for the use of said received and approved musket, rifle, shotgun or carbine.

It is, of course, to be very much regretted that the shops doing this repair and alteration work did not put some distinguishing mark upon the arms but so far as now known they did not and the present day collector is compelled to rely upon tradition or private markings to distinguish these arms as having been in the service.

The privately owned weapon could, of course, be marked in any way to suit the owner's fancy which probably accounts for much of the crudely worked ornamentations found upon them, especially the revolvers thus brought into the service.

A Kentucky-type rifle with a barrel cut down to about 33 inches, bored to a caliber .58 and rifled in conformity with the prevailing military rifling and equipped to take a bayonet can safely be judged as having been in the service and many of these arms will be found to have been provided with nipples of musket size as the furnishing of caps for the sporting arm-size nipple presented somewhat of a problem.

PLATE XXI

Fig. 1

Fig. 2

Fig. 3

Gun at extreme left:
Tarpley Confederate Breech-
loading carbine. Collection of
Edwin Pugsley, New Haven,
Conn.
Fig. 1. Converted Country Rifle.
Fig. 2. Homemade Confederate
Pistol.
Fig. 3. Converted Double-barrel
Shotgun.

PLATE XXI (a)

THE
TARPLEY RIFLE.

We now offer the public one of the best breech-loading Rifles that has been introduced in the country. This gun was invented by J. H. TARPLEY, in the town of Greensboro, North Carolina, and was patented the 14th of February, 1863.

The Gun has been tested at the Armory in Richmond, and the Armory at Raleigh, North Carolina, and it stood the test fully at each place.

The barrel screws in the breech, and each gun may have a rifle and a shot gun barrel. It is the simplest and safest gun now in use.

We are now manufacturing this gun for the use of the army, and as there is a much greater demand for it where it has been exhibited and tried, than we can supply from our Factory, we propose to sell rights of all the States in the Confederacy except North Carolina. Persons wishing to make an investment in a gun that will give perfect satisfaction when tried, will do well to avail themselves of this opportunity, before the territory of States is disposed of.

Tarpley, Garrett & Co.

F. A. GARRETT, General Agent.

Greensboro, N. C., April 11th, 1863.

Confederate Conversion of the Country Rifle

Figure 1, Plate XXI

A typical specimen of the so-called Country Rifle (the type now usually referred to as a Hog Rifle) that was converted to a military arm during the first years of the war by the Confederates. Many small gun shops were established and hundreds of these rifles were collected throughout the country and reworked for military use and from the numerous records it would appear that on account of the poor workmanship many very good rifles were made practically worthless by the necessity of boring them out to musket caliber. The specimen shown was originally a typical full-stock, .40 caliber, octagon barrel having open sights, set triggers and curly maple stock. The alteration consisted of cutting the barrel down to 33 inches, boring it out to .58 caliber smooth-bore, turning down the end of the octagon barrel to fit a model 1822 bayonet, adding the bayonet lug and providing a musket-size nipple in place of the original sporting size. An iron ramrod cupped at the end to fit the bullet and sling strap swivels; the lower swivel attached to the butt stock, the top swivel attached to a lug on the barrel completed the work. Despite the fact that there were hundreds of these rifles reworked and put into the military service they are today probably the scarcest of any of the Confederate arms due to the fact that as fast as they were replaced by better arms by the Confederates or captured by the Federals, they were destroyed and the few that survived were worn out as rabbit guns after the war.

Confederate Pistol

Figure 2, Plate XXI

A typical example of a homemade pistol as brought into service by many Confederate volunteers. The octagon barrel is 17 inches long, rifled and caliber .40. Apparently made from an old rifle barrel, as it is provided with a rear sight similar to those used on sporting rifles.

The lock is well made and nicely engraved and marked, "Hyde, Gregg & Day, Charleston." On top of the barrel is cut in script the name "I. Carper." The trigger guard and butt plate are of light crude design of brass and set into the stock, as an ornament a U. S. flying eagle penny dated 1858.

The fore-stock has been badly broken and repaired and a piece of leather used for holding the barrel to the stock, the leather being badly worn through, probably from jostling against the saddle while being carried by the soldier. Total length, 22½ inches. Weight, 4 pounds, 6 ounces.

CONFEDERATE DOUBLE-BARREL SHOTGUN
Figure 3, Plate XXI

An exceptionally heavy and well made double-barrel ten gauge shotgun with nicely engraved front action locks. The barrels are 21½ inches long and the total length 37½ inches. Weight, 10 pounds. Marked on top rib, "Fine twist."

This arm is believed to be a typical specimen of the better grade of shotguns remodeled and adapted to army use for the Confederate service. The barrels, besides being cut off, have been equipped with regular musket-size nipples and a large forward sight made from a coin bearing the date 1858 and a sling swivel has been added to the butt stock. Set into the right hand side of the stock with small brass nails is FIFTH TEXAS C. S. A. and on the left hand side of the stock the letters B. C. L. and Co. D.

CHAPTER V

CORRESPONDENCE AND REPORTS OF CONFEDERATE AGENTS ABROAD — CONTRACTS FOR FOREIGN ARMS — IMPORTATIONS AND BLOCKADE RUNNING — DESCRIPTION OF THE VARIOUS ARMS IMPORTED.

WHILE the arms imported by the Confederates are of lesser interest to collectors, the story of their agents' activities, both in making the purchase abroad, and running the blockade here, comprises a chapter in the story of the arms used in this country that is very important.

A few letters and reports included here give but a glimpse of the magnitude of the undertaking, but they serve to show that the agents of the Confederacy were in most cases very capable men.

Capt. Caleb Huse was ordered to Europe by President Davis on April 15, 1861, and his first report from London was dated May 21, indicating the difficulties occasioned by the slowness of travel.

On May 18, 1861 Major Anderson was ordered to Europe to work with or supercede Huse, and their reports indicate that they were extremely active, and it will be noted from the correspondence that in the early days of the war they had plenty of money, and were only hampered by the fact that they could not secure, ready for delivery, arms of the quality they desired.

As the magnitude of the struggle developed, the need for arms became more pressing and as early as August 30, 1861, Secretary Walker recommended the purchase of flintlocks if nothing better was to be had. This was after he had received the letter of August 11, 1861 reporting the failure to make a contract with the London Armory Company and the arrangement to purchase arms to be made by the smaller contractors, principally those of the Birmingham district.

On December 5, 1862, Col. Gorgas reported to the Secretary of War that funds to the extent of $3,095,139.18 had been sent to Huse, but that this amount had been wholly inadequate to meet the needs of the department, and that Huse was then in debt to the amount of 444,850 pounds, the equivalent to $5,925,402 Confederate currency.

Other agents acting for the Confederate government were sent abroad and to Cuba, Mexico, etc., while private interests seeing the chance to profit by speculating sent their agents out to purchase any kind of war munitions, the result being that the price of all materials advanced rapidly, since the North was also very active with its agents in all fields where munitions of any kind could be secured.

As the blockade of the Confederate ports became more effective, the reports of cargoes lost increases, and the proposals to offset the blockade more numerous. The fact that most of the ships in the blockade traffic were under British colors, and with the British base at Nassau, New Providence, available for their use, made it necessary for the Union Blockading Squadron to confine its seizure to vessels entering the Southern ports, after there could be no question as to their destination or intention. The law protecting neutral vessels clearing from one neutral port to another neutral port gave the runners a great advantage, and as practically all the vessels clearing from Nassau carried papers for some other neutral port, they could not be taken until their destination was beyond dispute a Confederate port.

However, the blockading fleet finally became so numerous, and efficient that this source of supply was almost cut off, the cost well nigh prohibitive, the freight from Nassau to a Confederate port being $500 per ton Confederate currency, and at the last, cargoes were only taken on the basis of freight prepaid in sterling.

The report of Col. Gorgas showing the receipt of 48,510 stand of arms from April 27th to August 16th, 1862 indicates the extent of the activities, which made it necessary for the Union Government to exert every effort to curtail it.

The letter of August 13, 1861 from Bulloch to Mallory refers to the thousand sea service rifles and cutlasses he contracted for and it will be noted that the cutlasses were identical with those used in the British Navy and could be shipped upon the end of the rifle as a bayonet.

A letter included here from Captain Huse to Major Gorgas dated April 1, 1862 refers to a contract for Enfield rifles and discusses the merits of this arm as compared with the Austrian rifles and it will be noted that he favors the small bore of the latter.

An item of interest to collectors of Confederate arms is the letter of April 23, 1863 from Commander North to G. B. Tennent where he refers to the Wilson rifle which was a breech-loading arm and it appears that some of these were used, as he ordered two hundred rounds of ball cartridges for each rifle.

There were probably other arms than those mentioned in the correspondence shipped to the Confederates as it is known that they used a small number of Whitworth and Kerr rifles in their sharpshooter service.

With depreciation of the Confederate currency and bonds which finally became almost worthless, the purchase of arms abroad was seriously hampered, and it was only by exchanging cotton, which of course, was badly needed by all of Europe, especially England, that any at all could be secured.

London, England, May 21, 1861

OFFICER OF ARTILLERY IN CHARGE OF ORDNANCE BUREAU, C. S. A.:

SIR: In compliance with instructions from the War Department I left Montgomery on the . . .

A very short time sufficed to satisfy me that of small arms there were none in market of the character and quality required by the Department. There were muskets to be purchased in a quantity, called by different names. I heard of not a few Enfield rifles. These, when I came to examine them, I found, to be for most part altogether worthless. I could have purchased a few, perhaps 500, short Enfields of good quality. To ship so small a quantity as that, however, after the proclamation of the British Government, would have been an impossibility.

After fully satisfying myself that small arms that I was willing to send to the Confederacy were not to be had either in England or Belgium, I made inquiries at the London Armory Company for Enfield rifles to be manufactured by them. This establishment is in some respects superior to every other musket manufactory in the world, and in every respect is equal to the Government works at Enfield. Since it was first put in operation it has been constantly employed by the British Government, and they have work on hand for this Government which will require eighteen months to complete. The rifles made at this establishment interchange in every part and with perfect accuracy. The importance of the principle of interchange of parts I need not dwell upon. It is fully recognized by the war departments of every civilized nation. The London Armory Company is the only establishment in Europe, excepting the Government armories, that works upon this principle. It seems to me highly important to obtain rifles from this company, if possible. I found that they were willing to entertain a proposition for 10,000, but not for anything less than that number. After conferring freely with the commissioners and receiving from them an entire approval of my action, I proposed to take from the London Armory Company 10,000 Enfield rifles of the Government pattern, with bayonet, scabbard, extra nipple, snap-cap, and stopper complete for £3 16s. 6d. This price is somewhat above the limit given in my instructions from Major Gorgas, and I engaged to take 10,000 instead of 8,000. Under all the circumstances, I believed myself not only justified, but required, to go beyond my orders . . .

I am, very respectfully, your obedient servant,
C. HUSE,
Captain, C. S. Army.

CONFEDERATE STATES OF AMERICA, WAR DEPARTMENT,
Richmond, July 22, 1861.
Capt. CALEB HUSE and Maj. EDWARD C. ANDERSON,
London:

GENTLEMEN: A complete and brilliant victory has crowned our arms. A battle was fought yesterday near Manassas, Va. . . . You will purchase at the earliest possible moment all the arms suitable for our purposes which can be obtained, from whatever places and at whatever price; and if a sufficient quantity of arms cannot be purchased at once, you are authorized to enter into contracts at your discretion with manufacturers and to spare no expense or risk which may be necessary to secure the largest quantity of arms, of the best quality, at the earliest possible moment, sufficient to arm, if need be, not less than 500 regiments. To this end increased sums of money, to whatever amount may be necessary, will be placed at your disposal . . .

The Secretary of the Navy has placed at the disposal of this Department the armed vessel the *McRae.* This vessel will proceed at once to England to cooperate with you. A duplicate of this letter will be forwarded by her. It is suggested that if a number of smaller vessels could be secured under British colors and with British clearances and laden with our arms the *McRae* could convoy and protect them upon their voyage. These vessels might make the port at Nassau, New Providence, or some other port equally favorably situated. There might clear with probable safety for the coast of Honduras or of Yucatan, and enter . . .

Pressing once more the supreme importance of this subject upon your earnest attention and confiding in your unremitting efforts,

I am, very respectfully,
L. P. WALKER,
Secretary of War.

Havana, July 24, 1861.
The Honorable President of the Confederate States of America the Hon. JEFFERSON DAVIS and the MEMBERS OF HIS RESPECTIVE CABINET:

In compliance with the terms of a contract made and entered into on May 18, 1861, in Montgomery, Ala., we left New Orleans on the . . .

He desired a list of goods and their prices, which we gave to him on the eve of Friday, July 19, in the following communication, which is a true copy of the original:

Havana, July 19, 1861
Col. THEO. LEWIS,
Confidential Agent of Confederate States of America:

SIR: It is in our power to procure, in accordance with our contract of May 18, 1861, with Maj. J. Gorgas, for and in behalf of the Confederate States, at the request of the Hon. Jefferson Davis, President thereof, viz. 6,500 infantry muskets, Spanish pattern, at $13 each;

FIREARMS OF THE CONFEDERACY

500 minie rifles, with bayonets, at $26 each; 500 sabers (cavalry), complete, at $12 each; 500 sabers (cavalry), without belt, at $10.50 each; 5,000 kegs cannon-powder, 25 pounds each, at $6.50 each; 2,000 kegs HFg rifle-powder, 25 pounds each, at $6.50 each; 50,000 pounds lead, at 9 cents per pound; 10,000,000 percussion-caps, at $5 per thousand; 500 artillery muskets, with bayonets, at $12 each; 1,000 cavalry sabers, without belts, at $8 each; 500 artillery sabers, at $5 each; 500 cavalry revolvers, American pattern, latest improved, at $35 each; 100 dozen 12-inch bowie knives, at $9 per dozen; 2,500 Enfield rifles, new and complete, in transit, at $32.50 each.

If the foregoing prices meet your views samples of everything can be seen, and subject to your approval or rejection. If the prices do not meet your approbation there is no use negotiating further. Should purchases be made to any extent we desire to know positively whether you will make a deposit of the amount of freight which will have to be paid, as we can make no arrangements except on this basis. And we desire to further know if in case it becomes necessary to fee any officials to let the vessel or vessels depart in peace, you will pay such amount as may be necessary. As we informed you a few days ago that we should return to Richmond as soon as we know what your final disposition was, we desire an answer before or by 8 o'clock this p. m., July 19, as it is our intention to take the first opportunity to return that presents itself.

Yours, respectfully,

W. G. BETTERTON, *Agent*
J. E. CHALARD, *Agent*

Upon which the following freight would have to be paid: Per musket, 50 cents; per rifle, 50 cents; per keg of powder, 3 shillings; per pistol, 25 cents; per ton of lead, $7; seventy cases C caps, each $2, with 5 per cent primage, amounting in all to $5,859. Not despairing of being able to make some understanding with Colonel Lewis, we reopened the whole negotiations, and found up to date, July 20, his . . .

We have the honor to be, your most and very obedient servants,

W. G. BETTERTON.

CONFEDERATE STATES OF AMERICA, WAR DEPARTMENT,
Richmond, January 28, 1862.

B. FALLON, Esq.,
New Orleans, La.:

SIR: In reply to your communication of 28th instant (ultimo) I inform you that I cannot accept your propositions, but will enter into contract with you as follows, viz:

First. You are to introduce into some port of the Confederate States east of the Trinity River, Tex., the articles (or as many thereof as you can) embraced in the list inclosed and signed by me. Your deliveries are to commence as promptly as possible . . .

Fourth. Payment to be made to you on arrival and delivery of cargo in a Confederate port in good order. This Government assumes no risk whatever, but will pay on delivery for the articles received at the rates agreed on, in cotton, at current market prices, which cotton you shall be at once at liberty to export for your own account and risk: If you bring your cargo into a port where there is no cotton market, the cotton will be delivered to you at the nearest cotton port to the one you enter . . .

Seventh. This contract shall cease upon the restoration of peace between the United States and the Confederate States, but this Government will receive and pay for all articles that may be actually shipped under its terms before it shall be publicly announced in the newspapers

217

of France and England that peace has been made. The articles referred to are as follows: Two hundred tons of saltpeter; 200 tons cannon powder; 100 tons rifle or musket powder; 20,000 rifles or rifled muskets, with bayonets; 5,000 carbines; 5,000 revolving pistols for cavalry; 5,000 sabers for cavalry, with belts; 1,000 sabers for artillerists, with belts; 50 tons of bar steel, assorted sizes, from 1-inch square upward, chiefly smaller sizes; 100 gross of files, assorted sizes, for armorers and finishing purposes: 400 gross assorted screws from 1¼ inches to 2½ inches; 40 carboys nitric acid; 100 carboys sulphuric acid; 50,000 pounds of leather suitable for harness and bridles.

Respectfully,

J. P. BENJAMIN,
Secretary of War.

Nassau, New Providence, January 30, 1862.

Hon. J. P. BENJAMIN,
Secretary of War, Richmond, Va.:

DEAR SIR: The steamer *Kate* arrived here on the 18th and brought ... *Gladiator's* cargo, now on board of the Kate, as per bill of lading inclosed:

Blankets and serge	32 bales
Rifles, Enfield (6,000)	300 cases
Surgical instruments	2 cases
Mess tins, pouches, serge, &c.	94 boxes
Medicines	15 boxes
Lint	2 boxes
Medicine	1 barrel
Gunpowder (all cannon with the exception of some 5 or 6)	500 barrels
Cartridges	514 boxes
Caps	90 boxes
Surgical instruments	2 cases

Having no invoice of the cargo I had to take the contents as marked on the packages. Total number of packages, 1,552. We completed loading this morning, and the *Kate* proceeds to sea this evening with fine weather and a good prospect of reaching her destination in forty hours. You will perceive that I have filled out the bill of lading for Saint John, New Brunswick. This is to cover in case the *Kate* should be overhauled on the voyage. Since the *Trent* affair Federal cruisers will hesitate to interfere with British vessels, unless caught in the very act of violating the blockade. By the transhipment of this portion ...

I am, very respectfully, your obedient servant,
L. HEYLIGER

New Orleans, La., January 31, 1862

Hon. J. P. BENJAMIN,
Secretary of War, Richmond, Va.:

SIR: I have in Havana some eighteen hundred and odd Enfield and Brunswick rifles; on board the *Gladiator* at Nassau about 500, and about 800 at Cardenas, if the *Stephen Hart*, that left Liverpool early in November for that port, has arrived. You have a valuable cargo of arms, &c., on the *Gladiator* at Nassau and arms at Cardenas, for which Mr. Heyliger was sent. The difficulty thus far in getting these arms to the Confederate States has proven insuperable. In order to obtain them, as they are so greatly needed, I am willing to incur a heavy risk to get those belonging to this State if you will join in the adventure and the risk in proportion to the amount of arms, &c., which you have at the places referred to, I propose to take up a fast steamer (we have many here), send her out with or without cotton, as you prefer, and bring home the arms. I will take care that she is properly officered, with competent river and coast pilots on board. There are a number of steamers here that can outrun anything in the Navy of the United States, and I feel great confidence in the success of the enterprise. If you will share in the risk on the terms proposed, telegraph immediately,

Very respectfully, your obedient servant,

THO. O. MOORE,
Governor

No. 58, Jermyn Street, London,
March 15, 1862.

Maj. J. GORGAS,
Confederate States War Department:

MAJOR: I have the honor to inform you that the owners of the *Stephen Hart* have taken steps for the recovery of their property . . .

The rifles of the London Armory Company are so greatly superior to all others that I have made an effort to obtain the control of all that they can make within the next three years. The contract of the company with the British Government is about expiring, and I have requested the managing director not to apply for a renewal of it until I can receive instructions from the War Department, and have also requested him to tender to me a proposal for supplying 50,000. I have not received his formal reply, but it will be in substance as follows: The price to be the same as to the British Government, which I think is 60 shillings, say $15; rifles to be delivered in London, payment on delivery . . .

The steamer *Minna* will leave in a few days, probably on the 19th. There will be on board of this vessel for the Government 5,000 rifles, 1,500 cavalry sabers, 1,500 cavalry belts, 10,000 friction tubes and 500 barrels of cannon powder. The steamer *Bahama* is expected to arrive today at Hamburg, where she will take on board the Austrian field . . . I am quite at a loss what destination to give to the *Bahama*. My conviction is that York River is the point for which she should run, but I do not think that the master of the ship will be willing to attempt the blockade, at any rate, and I shall be obliged to send her to Bermuda or Nassau. I beg to suggest to the Department the importance of everything relating to these shipments being kept entirely secret. From the evidence given in the case of the *Stephen Hart*, I am confident that, no matter what may be the character of the flag, munitions of war belonging to the Confederate Government will be held by U. S. officers liable to capture, no matter where they may be found. My next shipment of arms I shall endeavor to make by the Havana mail steamer from Southhampton. My steps are so narrowly watched by the agents of the United States wherever I may go, and such efforts are made by the . . .

I have the honor to be, very respectfully, your obedient servant,

CALEB HUSE.

FIREARMS OF THE CONFEDERACY

List of steamers which have arrived since April 27, 1862, with the date and place of arrival, and a statement of the arms on board of each one.

Date.	Names.	Place of arrival.	Number stand of arms.
Apr. 27	Cecile.........	Charleston.........	3,000
27	Nashville.........	Wilmington.........	6,420
May 24	Kate and Cecile.........	Charleston.........	5,000
25	Minho.........	....do.........	5,010
June 24	Memphis.........	do.........	11,000
25	Kate.........	Savannah.........	2,060
28	Modern Greece.........	Wilmington.........	7,000
July 3	Herald.........	Charleston.........	1,280
6	Nashville.........	Savannah.........	2,600
25	Hero.........	Charleston.........	140
Aug. 3	Leopard.........	....do.........	4,000
	Cuba.........		500
	Ann.........		500
	Total.........		48,510

J. GORGAS,
Colonel.

[August 16, 1862.]

ORDNANCE BUREAU,
Richmond, December 5, 1862.

Hon. JAMES A. SEDDON,
Secretary of War:

SIR: The purchases of ordnance and ordnance stores in foreign markets on Government account are made by Maj. Caleb Huse, C. S. artillery, who resides in London, and whose address is No. 38 Clarendon Road, Notting Hill, London West. Major Huse was detailed for this duty in April, 1861.

His instructions directed his attention chiefly to the purchase of small arms, but his list embraced all the most necessary supplies. Under these instructions he has purchased arms to the number of 157,-000 and large quantities of gunpowder, some artillery, infantry equipments, harness, swords, percussion caps, saltpeter, lead, &c.

In addition to ordnance stores, using a rare forecast, he has purchased and shipped large supplies of clothing, blankets, cloth, and shoes for the Quartermaster's Department without special orders to . . .

Of course a large proportion of his purchases have fallen into the hands of the enemy.

To pay for these purchases funds have been from time to time sent to him by the Treasury Department, on requisitions from the War Department, amounting in the aggregate to $3,095,139.18. These have been wholly inadequate to his wants and have fallen far short of our requisition. He was consequently in debt at latest advices to the amount of £444,850, a sum equivalent, when the value of exchange is considered, to $5,925,402 of our currency.

While this capacity for running in debt is the best evidence of the ability of Major Huse, the debt is a matter that calls for immediate attention . . .

Very respectfully, your obedient servant,
J. GORGAS,
Colonel and Chief of Ordnance.

220

FIREARMS OF THE CONFEDERACY

Abstract of summary statement showing quantity and value of army supplies purchased and shipped by Maj. C. Huse on account Confederate State Government.

One hundred and thirty-one thousand one hundred and twenty-nine stand of arms, as follows: Seventy thousand nine hundred and eighty long Enfield rifles, 9,715 short Enfield rifles, 354 carbine Enfield rifles, 27,000 Austrian rifles, 21,040 British muskets, 20 small-bore Enfield, 2,020 Brunswick rifles, at a cost, including cases, molds, kegs, screw-drivers, &c., of £417,263 9s. 11d.

One hundred and twenty-nine cannon, as follows: Fifty-four 6-pounder bronze guns, smooth; 18 howitzer bronze guns, smooth; 6 12-pounder iron guns, rifled; 2 howitzers, iron; carriages and caissons for same; 6 rifled Blakely cannon; 6 3.10-inch carriages for same; 18,000 shells for same; 2,000 fuses; 3 rifled cannon, 8-inch Blakely; 600 shells for same; 12 rifled steel guns, 12-pounders; shot, shell, &c., for same; 32 bronze guns, rifled (Austrian), with caissons, &c. complete; 10,000 shrapnel shells and fuses for same; 2 bronze guns, rifled; 200 shells and fuses; 756 shrapnel shell, round; 9,820 wooden fuses; 4 steel cannon, rifled, 9-pounders; 1,008 shells and fuses for same; 220 sets harness; spare parts artillery, harness, &c.; all costing £96,746 1s. 8d.

One thousand two hundred and twenty-six cavalry equipments, 16,178 cavalry sabers, 5,392 cavalry saber belts, 5,392 cavalry saber knots, 1,360 cavalry Humnals (sic), 1,386 cavalry surcingles and pads; total expended for cavalry, £20,321 12s. 3d.

SUPPLIES THAT HAVE BEEN SHIPPED

	£	s.	d.
For small arms	417,262	9	11
Artillery and harness	96,746	1	8
Accouterments, &c.	54,873	16	3
Ammunition	47,010	10	3
Leather	9,717	11	0
Clothing	110,525	3	9
Medical supplies	13,432	10	7
Ordnance stores, &c.	19,616	15	5
Freight, railway carriage, &c.	19,732	7	8
Insurance, &c.	29,951	11	9
Total	818,869	18	3

SUPPLIES NOW IN LONDON READY FOR SHIPMENT

	£	s.	d.
23,000 rifles to be delivered at Nassau (value at Nassau)	87,950	0	0
20,000 scabbards	1,500	0	0
46 casks saddler's material	631	5	0
11 cases nitric acid	38	4	8
2,012,000 cartridges	5,533	0	0
3,000,000 percussion caps	681	0	0
10,000 pouch tins, prepared for accouterments, order (illegible)	250	0	0
286 ingots tin	628	2	6
931 pigs lead	1,252	17	9
3 cases thread, &c.	240	17	3
1 bale serge	60	19	6
13,750 pair trousers, Quartermaster's Department	8,565	2	1
14,250 greatcoats, Quartermaster's Dept.	23,835	13	17
1,804 pair boots, Quartermaster's Dept.	887	11	6
4 chests tea, Medical Department	48	7	6
Total value	249,853	1	0

IN VIENNA AWAITING PAYMENT

	£	s.	d.
20,000 rifles	115,500	0	0
30,000 scabbards	2,250	0	0
Total expended and under order	117,750	0	0
Shipped up to date	818,869	18	3
Ready for shipment in London, to be shipped by December 15	249,853	1	0
In Vienna waiting payment	117,750	0	0
	1,186,472	19	3
Received by Fraser, Trenholm & Co.	613,589	0	0
Total required	572,883	19	3

[INDORSEMENT]
February 3, 1863
Respectfully referred to the Secretary of War for information as to purchases made by Major Huse.

J. GORGAS,
Colonel, Chief of Ordnance.

Houston, December 16, 1862.
Maj. S. HART:

DEAR SIR: I am willing to proceed to Europe at once and use my means and my best exertions to procure 20,000 stand of muskets or Enfield rifles, with all appurtenances, 5,000 revolvers complete, 5,000 sabers, French army shoes, blankets, gray cloth and trimmings, twilled flannel, twilled flannel shirts, and felt hats, the whole invoice not to exceed $1,000,000. If the 20,000 stand or Enfield rifles cannot be obtained, 10,000 I agree to furnish, and as many of the other articles as I can obtain, and commence to deliver to you at Matamoras within four months from the 1st of January, 1863, with the agreement and understanding that you pay me on delivery of said invoice 100 per cent upon invoice cost and charges in cotton on shipboard at the port where said goods are delivered, at 30 cents per pound. It is also agreed that there shall be no delay in furnishing the cotton. The arms are subject to proper inspection.

Very respectfully, yours,

NELSON CLEMENTS

I accept above proposition to furnish the above-enumerated public stores.

S. HART,
Major and Quartermaster, C. S. Army.

Approved.

J. B. MAGRUDER, Major Gen.

BRITISH TOWER MUSKET

Figure 1, Plate XXII

British Tower Musket which was selected by the Army Board appointed at Woolwich in 1836, it being the first percussion musket in the British service and remained in the hands of the troops until the beginning of the Crimean war when it was superseded to some extent by the musket rifled on the Minie system.

This arm is generally referred to as the Model 1842 and is caliber .753 and used a charge of 70 grains of powder with a bullet .670 inches in diameter weighing 490 grains.

The barrel is 39 inches long. Total length of arm 54½ inches. Weight with bayonet, 11 pounds, 6 ounces.

The general construction of this arm follows very closely that of the Brown Bess flintlock, it being a pin fastened barrel with the ramrod carried in three brass pipes and having brass trigger guard, butt plate and stock tip.

In place of the pins fastening the barrel used on the older arms this one is provided with flat keys. The lock plate is marked Tower with the usual crown and the barrel has the usual Birmingham proof marks.

This arm was, of course, obsolete at the beginning of the Civil War but owing to the scarcity of arms a good many of them were purchased.

Major Huse's report of February 3, 1863 shows that he had shipped to the Confederacy 21,040 of these.

THE BRUNSWICK RIFLE
Figure 4, Plate XXII

The Brunswick rifle adopted in the British service on the recommendation of the board appointed at Woolwich in 1836 was the first percussion rifle of the British army and known as the Brunswick Rifle of 1835.

The rifling consists of two grooves making one turn in thirty inches and shooting a belted bullet weighing 557 grains. The caliber is .704 and the charge of powder 124 grains. The length, 45½ inches and weight with sword bayonet, 11 pounds, 5 ounces.

The heavy twist barrel is fastened to the stock with three keys and the ramrod is carried in two brass pipes. The mountings including the large patch box in the stock are of brass and the stock extends to the end of the barrel; the bayonet being carried on a special attachment. The back-action lock is marked R1. Manufactory Enfield V.R. surmounted by a crown and dated 1842. The barrel has the usual British proof marks and is provided with a special leaf sight graduated to 250 yards.

The Confederates used a number of these rifles. Governor Moore of Louisiana writing to Secretary of War Benjamin, January 31, 1862 reported that he had a number of them at Havana and also at Nassau, and Major Huse's report of February 3, 1863 indicates that he had shipped to the Confederacy 2,020 of these Brunswick rifles.

THE MODEL 1858 ENFIELD RIFLE
Figure 2, Plate XXII

The Model 1858 Enfield rifled musket was undoubtedly the best military arm purchased abroad for the Confederate service and despite the blockade many thousands of them were used and the records indicate that besides those made at Enfield and the London Armory Co., the smaller contractors of the Birmingham district supplied large quantities of them.

The caliber is .577 but the regulation U. S. caliber charge could be used without difficulty. The rifling of three grooves makes one turn in six feet, six inches. The regular Pritchett bullet was .568 inch diameter and weighs 530 grains, the powder charge being 70 grains.

Length of barrel is 39 inches. Total length of arm 54 inches and weight with triangular bayonet 8 pounds, 14½ ounces. The lock is marked Tower 1862 with the usual crown and the barrel has the customary British proof marks.

A rear sight graduated to 900 yards is provided and the arm is brass mounted except for the bands which are of iron and held in place by clamping.

Major Huse's report of February 3, 1863 indicates that he had shipped 70,980 of these to the Confederacy and many more were undoubtedly secured after that date.

ENFIELD SHORT PATTERN RIFLE
Figure 3, Plate XXII

Enfield Short Pattern Rifle, caliber .577, powder charge 85 grains, shooting a 538 grain bullet of .550 diameter. Length of barrel 33 inches. Total length 48¾ inches. Weight without bayonet, 8 pounds, 7 ounces.

PLATE XXII

Fig. 1. Fig. 2. Fig. 3. Fig. 4. Fig. 5. Fig. 6.

Fig. 1. British Tower Musket.
Fig. 2. Enfield Rifle.
Fig. 3. Short Enfield Rifle.
Fig. 4. Brunswick Rifle.
Fig. 5. Enfield Musketoon.
Fig. 6. Enfield Carbine.

PLATE XXIII

Fig.
1

Fig.
2

Fig.
3

Fig.
4

Fig.
5

Fig. 1. Jeff Davis Enfield.
Fig. 2. Sharpshooter Enfield.
Fig. 3. Whitworth Rifle.
Fig. 4. Austrian Rifle.
Fig. 5. Enlarged View of Whitworth
Lock, Bore and Bullet.

The barrel is provided with a lug for a saber bayonet. The trigger guard, butt plate and stock tip are of brass. The bands of the regular clamping type are of iron, blued as also is the barrel, the lock being case hardened. Stamped on lock plate Tower 1861 with Crown over V. R.

This was a popular arm with the Confederate rifle companies and are repeatedly referred to in the various reports and correspondence; the report of Major Huse, February 3, 1863 indicates a shipment of 9,715 of them and further records indicate the receipt of many more.

ENFIELD RIFLED MUSKETOON

Figure 5, Plate XXII

Enfield Rifled Musketoon, caliber .577 shooting the regulation bullet and powder charge. Length of barrel 23 inches. Total length 39 inches. Weight 6½ pounds.

The trigger guard, butt plate and stock tip are brass, while the two bands are the regulation iron clamping type. The barrel is blued and provided with a two-leaf sight. The sling swivels are carried on the front band and in the butt stock. The lock plate is marked Barnett, London. The stock has the oval stamp reading Barnett Gun Makers London.

ENFIELD CARBINE

Figure 6, Plate XXII

Enfield carbine, caliber .577. Length of barrel 21 inches. Total length 37 inches. Weight 7¼ pounds. Marked on lock plate Barnett, London and Tower surmounted by a crown. The barrel has the usual London Gun Makers proof marks and is provided with a two-leaf rear sight. The sling swivels are carried on the top band and on the trigger guard; the ramrod has a swivel attachment and a nipple protector attached to the rear sling swivel with a brass chain is also provided. The mountings are brass except the bands which are iron of the regular clamping type.

Three hundred and fifty-four of these are included in the report of arms shipped by Major Huse of Feb. 3, 1863 and numerous mention is found of them throughout the correspondence.

OFFICERS MODEL ENFIELD RIFLE
Figure 1, Plate XXIII

Officers Model of the Enfield Rifled Musket known to collectors as the Jefferson Davis rifle, it being facsimile of one now in the Government collection at Springfield said to have been captured with that gentleman. This is the regular Enfield rifled musket as described under Figure 2, Plate XXII, but having an especially fine stock beautifully checkered and the finish throughout showing the best of workmanship.

The trigger guard, butt plate and stock tip are of brass— the bands of the regular clamping type are of iron and the rear sight is of the regular Enfield type. The barrel and bands are finished blue while the lock plate and hammer are case hardened. The nipple protector attached to the rear sling swivel with a chain is provided. The lock plate is marked L. A. Co. 1861 with V. R. below the crown. The barrel is stamped L. A. C. with the usual proof marks. The stock is stamped London Armory Bermondsey 1861.

BRITISH SHARPSHOOTER'S RIFLE
Figure 2, Plate XXIII

This small-bore Enfield type rifle was used to a small extent in the Confederate service as an arm for their sharpshooters and besides the report of February 3, 1863 by Major Huse which shows shipment of twenty of them frequent mention is found of their use.

The length of the barrel is 36 inches. Total length of arm, 52 inches. Weight 9¾ pounds, and it was probably one of the finest military arms of its day. The heavily checkered stock extends almost to the end of the barrel; the arm not being intended for use of the bayonet, and the mountings all of iron are beautifully engraved. The bands are the clamping type with countersunk recesses for the screw heads, and in place of the customary sling swivels rings are provided for attaching snap hooks. The trigger guard has a spur extension forming a grip and the lock is provided with a half cock safety.

The barrel which is of the patent breech type, is octagon for the first three inches, the balance round and the brown finish shows the decided twist of the barrel. A special rear sight is graduated to 1,200 yards while the front sight provides for side adjustment. The caliber is .45 and the rifling is upon Henry's principle, consisting of seven grooves, .03 inch of the original bore being left between each groove as lands. The twist is right handed, uniform, one turn in 22 inches, the grooves .009 deep at breech and .007 at muzzle. This is the rifling used in the famous Martini-Henry arm which was the standard of the British service for many years after its adoption in 1871.

The bottom side of the barrel carries the Gunmaker's Company (London) proof marks, the provisional proof being the letters G. P. in script interlaced in a cipher surmounted by a lion rampant and the definite proof mark of G. P. surmounted by a crown and the view mark being the letter V surmounted by a crown. The top of the barrel is marked, Henry's Patent Rifling.

WHITWORTH RIFLE
Figure 3, Plate XXIII

This rifle is of particular interest to students of Confederate arms as it is believed to be the only one of the imported arms that was used exclusively by the South who used them in small numbers for arming sharpshooters. They were an accurate and powerful weapon—good for a range of half a mile and were responsible for the taking off of many a Federal officer.

The specimen shown is marked on the lock plate Whitworth Rifle Co., Manchester and on top of the barrel Whitworth Patent. Length of barrel, 33 inches. Total length of arm, 49 inches. The bore is hexagonal. Caliber .45, using an elongated bullet weighing 530 grains. The twist is one in twenty inches. The arm is an exceptionally well made piece—iron mounted throughout and besides the regular sight equipment, is provided with attachments for a telescope sight to be mounted on the left side of the gun. The stock is nicely checkered and the arm has all of the characteristics of the highest type sporting piece. All parts bear the serial number 554.

In the year 1852 when the British Ordnance department conducted extensive experiments to test the comparative merits of various rifles submitted to the Government they found a wide variation in the accuracy obtainable. Whitworth, one of the leading technicians of the day, was commissioned to make exhaustive experiments at the cost of the Government in order to discover the best form of rifling.

This gentleman had devoted a great deal of time and study to the design and manufacture of cannon and had adopted the polygonal bore as giving the best results and decided to use this type of rifling for his small arms. The advantage of the elongated bullet had long been demonstrated but in attempting to use it in connection with polygonal bore considerable trouble was experienced from the ball "capsizing" or "turning over." He became convinced that this action was due to the slow spiral and eventually after testing every graduation from one turn in seventy-eight inches to one turn in five inches found that the necessary rotation to impart the required steadiness to the ball and cause it to maintain a flight parallel to its axis was best obtained at a pitch of one turn in twenty inches.

On tests before the Minister of War and many distinguished officers the Whitworth rifle of .45 caliber beat the Enfield of Government factories by three to one. The mean deviation at five hundred yards was four and one-half while the recorded best of any rifle previously tried was twenty-seven.

The rifle was never adopted into the Government service but forty of them were made for the competitive shoot of 1860 for the Queen's prize at the meeting of the National Rifle Association. Plate XXIII also shows an enlarged view of the bore of this arm and the machine-made bullet used with it.

While the original Whitworth bullet was hexagonal to fit the rifle bore, those used by the Confederates were for the most part cylindrical.

The late Walter M. Cline, who made a study of ammunition used in the opposing armies in the Atlanta campaign, said he never found any hexagonal bullets from the Whitworth on the battlefields, but he found many Whitworth cylindrical bullets. He said the Confederates used this bullet with a hollow base and wood to lengthen the missile.

Twenty or thirty of these Whitworth rifles were run through the blockade to the Confederacy in 1862. They were divided between the army in Virginia and that in the West. The guns were issued to men specially selected because of their marksmanship.

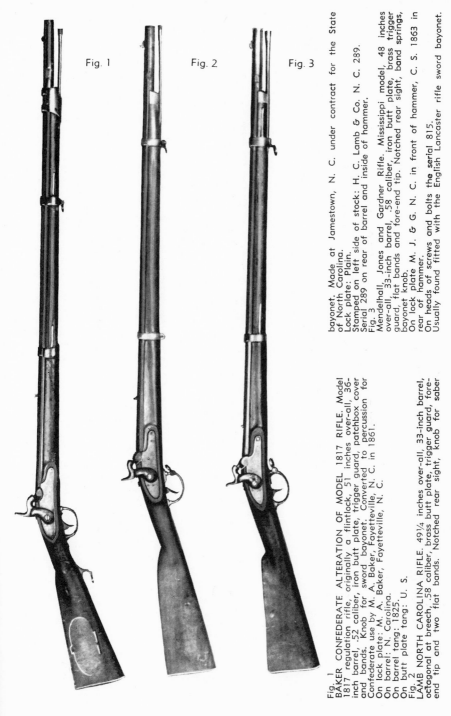

PLATE XXIV

Fig. 1

Fig. 2

Fig. 3

Fig. 1
BAKER CONFEDERATE ALTERATION OF MODEL 1817 RIFLE. Model 1817 regulation rifle, originally a flintlock, 51 inches over-all, 36-inch barrel, .52 caliber, iron butt plate, trigger guard, patchbox cover and bands. Knob for sword bayonet. Converted to percussion for Confederate use by M. A. Baker, Fayetteville, N. C. in 1861.
On lock plate: M. A. Baker, Fayetteville, N. C.
On barrel: N. Carolina.
On barrel tang: 1825.
On butt plate tang: U. S.
Fig. 2
LAMB NORTH CAROLINA RIFLE. 49¼ inches over-all, 33-inch barrel, octagonal at breech, .58 caliber, brass butt plate, trigger guard, fore-end tip and two flat bands. Notched rear sight, knob for saber bayonet. Made at Jamestown, N. C. under contract for the State of North Carolina.
Lock plate: Plain.
Stamped on left side of stock: H. C. Lamb & Co. N. C. 289.
Serial 289 on rear of barrel and inside of hammer.
Fig. 3
Mendelhall, Jones and Gardner Rifle. Mississippi model, 48 inches over-all, 33-inch barrel, .58 caliber, iron butt plate, brass trigger guard, flat bands and fore-end tip. Notched rear sight, band springs, bayonet knob.
On lock plate M. J. & G. N. C. in front of hammer, C. S. 1863 in rear of hammer.
On heads of screws and bolts the serial 815.
Usually found fitted with the English Lancaster rifle sword bayonet.

PLATE XXV

Fig. 1
Fig. 2
Fig. 3
Fig. 4

Fig. 3
Virginia Manufactory flintlock musket, 57 inches over-all, 42-inch barrel, all iron mountings. Thousands of them issued to Virginia regiments in 1861.
On lock plate: Virginia Manufactory and Richmond, 1808.
On barrel: 74 Va. G. Regt.
Fig. 4
Virginia Manufactory Musket, altered and cut off for Confederate use in 1861, 30-inch barrel.
On lock plate: Virginia Manufactory and Richmond 1812.
From White House, the home of Gen. W. H. F. Lee, on the Pamunkey

Fig. 1
Virginia Manufactory flintlock rifle, 58 inches long, 44-inch octagonal barrel, about .45 caliber, all iron mountings except two brass thimbles
Issued to Virginia troops in 1861.
and front sight.
On lock plate: Virginia Manufactory and Richmond 1806.
Fig. 2
Virginia Manufactory Rifle, altered to percussion for Confederate use.
Ornamental iron patch box bears the legend: Don't tread on me and
the image of a snake.
On lock plate Virginia Manufactory and Richmond 1806.

The *Richmond Daily Examiner* of November 10, 1863, says:
"We have a wonderful gun in our Army, the Whitworth rifle. It kills at 2,000 yards, more than a mile. It is no bigger than the Mississippi rifle. With a few of these rifles Longstreet shot across the Tennessee river, killing the Yankees and completely blocking the river road."

Evidently more of the Whitworths were received in the Confederacy, because in Thomas' *History of the Doles-Cook Brigade* it is said that "Capt. Joseph I. Carson, Company I, Fourth Georgia Regiment, commanded the Sharpshooters of Gordon's Brigade, one hundred strong, armed with Whitworth rifles of the latest pattern with a range of 1,800 yards."[1]

The same author makes the statement that Sergeant Grace, of the Fourth Georgia killed General Sedgwick of the Union Army with a Whitworth rifle at a range of 800 yards.[2]

Sergeant Grace used a globe sight. Most of the Whitworths were equipped with telescope sights, but these were easily lost.

Whitworth rifles are said to have done terrible execution at Fort Wagner, Charleston.[3]

General Cleburne, writing in 1863, said: "The fire of five Whitworth rifles appeared to do good service. Mounted men were struck at distances ranging from 700 to 1,300 yards."[4]

Twenty men of Company F, Eighth North Carolina Regiment, were armed with Whitworth rifles with globe sights at Morris Island.[5] South Carolina sharpshooters also had Whitworths[6] and General Lytle is said to have been killed at Chickamauga with a bullet from a Whitworth rifle.[7]

All the Whitworths used in the South in the war were not of the same model, the one in the Steuart collection has a 33-inch barrel, .45 caliber, with half stock, iron butt plate and trigger guard, brass fore-end and brass thimbles and no swivels. The Davidson telescope is 14½ inches long and on the left side of the stock.

The lock plate is marked "Whitworth Rifle Co., Manchester." On the breech is "Whitworth's Patent" and "52.C 619." The trigger-guard tang is stamped: "2nd Quality."

---

[1] Thomas' History of the Doles-Cook Brigade, Page 38.
[2] Thomas' History of the Doles-Cook Brigade, Page 76.
[3] The Confederate Veteran, Vol. XXXV, No. 7, Page 255.
[4] Official Records, War of the Rebellion, Vol. XXIII, Part II, Page 587.
[5] North Carolina Regimental Histories, Vol. I, Page 394.
[6] Memoirs of Gen. Johnson Hagood, Page 207.
[7] Shelby and His Men, Page 191.

THE KERR RIFLE

Figure 2, Plate XXVII

The Kerr rifle is another of the very fine British arms imported by the Confederates for their sharpshooters service, and it is of .44 caliber and is frequently referred to in the Confederate reports and records as the Enfield .44. It resembles the Enfield in appearance.

Cleburne's sharpshooters in February, 1864, were armed with 20 Whitworth and 10 Kerr rifles.[8]

Mr. Cline said he found the Kerr bullets first on the battlefield of Resaca, Ga.

The Kerr rifle is 53 inches over all, with a 37-inch barrel, all iron mountings, folding front sight and elevated rear sight. The lock plate is marked "L. A. Co." and "1863." On the breech is stamped "Kerr's Patent" and "L. A. Co." They were made by the London Armory Company.

The rifling is six grooves, Ratchett form, without angles. As the deeper part of the groove is on the side from which the bullet turns, the resistance to the air is reduced to a minimum; the other side of the groove verges into the cylinder bore, thus leaving lands which are mechanically true.

The bullet weighed 530 grains.

The rifle shown in the illustration was taken from a Confederate sharpshooter killed at Resaca, Ga.

Compare this weapon with the sharpshooter rifle shown in Figure 2, Plate XXIII.

AUSTRIAN RIFLE

Figure 4, Plate XXIII

The piece shown illustrates one of the many examples of European arms purchased by both the North and South during the war and while not as well finished an arm as the Enfield it was a good serviceable piece.

The specimen shown is a two-band gun, caliber .54. Back-action lock. Barrel fitted with a lug for saber bayonet. Sling strap swivels on bottom band and butt of stock. Length of barrel, 33 inches. Total length, 48½ inches. Weight, 7¾ pounds.

Captain Huse, reporting to Gorgas from Liverpool, England, April 1, 1862, writes as follows:

---

[8] Cleburne and His Command, by Buck. Pages 107 and 224.

PLATE XXVI

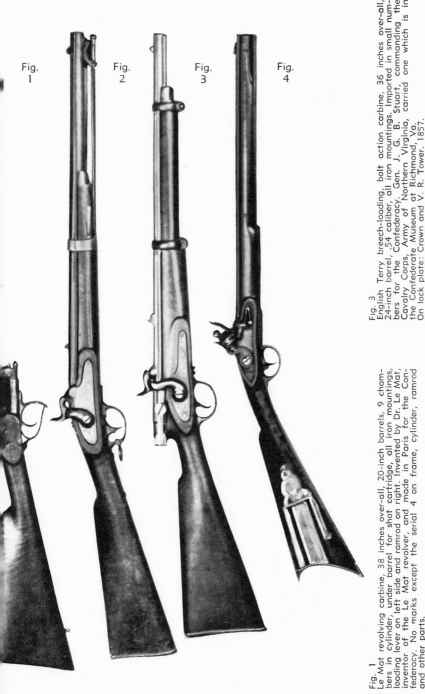

Fig. 1

Fig. 2

Fig. 3

Fig. 4

Fig. 1
Le Mat revolving carbine, 38 inches over-all, 20-inch barrels, 9 chambers in cylinder, under barrel for shot cartridge, all iron mountings, loading lever on left side and ramrod on right. Invented by Dr. Le Mat, inventor of the Le Mat revolver, and made in Paris for the Confederacy. No marks except the serial 4 on frame, cylinder, ramrod and other parts.

Fig. 2
Confederate carbine, U. S. Model 1854, 37 inches over-all, 22-inch barrel, .58 caliber, all iron mountings except brass fore-end tip, swivel ramrod.
Stamped on barrel: P. C.S.A.
Inside of lock marked: C 44.
Made by D. C. Hodgkins & Son, Macon, Ga.

Fig. 3
English Terry breech-loading, bolt action carbine, 36 inches over-all, 24-inch barrel, .54 caliber, all iron mountings. Imported in small numbers for the Confederacy, Gen. J. G. B. Stuart, commanding the Cavalry Corps, Army of Northern Virginia, carried one which is in the Confederate Museum at Richmond, Va.
On lock plate: Crown and V. R. Tower. 1857.
On barrel: Terry's Patent.
Confederate inspector's mark, C. S. on breech, barrel and top of stock.

Fig. 4
Flintlock sporting rifle, converted for cavalry use in 1861 by Samuel Sutherland of Richmond, 34 inches over-all, 17½-inch barrel, about .50 caliber, brass mountings.
On left side of barrel: C.S.A. S.S. 1861.
On brass strap: Rep. No. 941. S. Sutherland.

PLATE XXVII

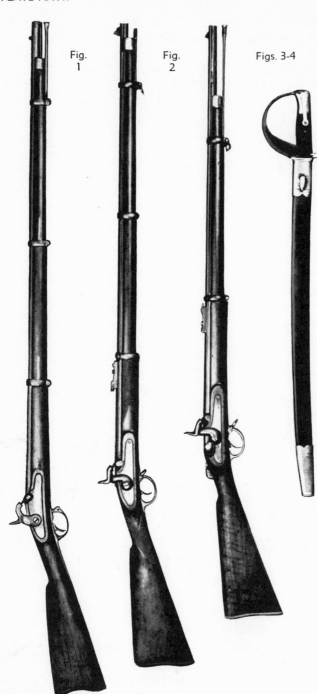

Fig.
1

Fig.
2

Figs. 3-4

Fig. 1
TODD RIFLED MUSKET, 56 inches over-all, 40-inch barrel, .58 caliber, lock plate and hammer, trigger guard, trigger, butt plate, fore-end tip and three round bands ALL of brass, sling swivels, folding rear sight, U. S. proof marks on barrel.
Stamped on the lock plate: Geo. H. Todd, Montgomery, Ala., and in the rear of the hammer: C.S.A. 1864.
Fig. 2
KERR'S BRITISH Sharpshooter's rifle, 53 inches over-all, 37-inch barrel, .45 caliber, all iron mountings, elevated rear sight, folding front sight. Imported for the use of Confederate sharpshooters. This

particular rifle taken from a Confederate sharpshooter at Resaca, Ga. who refused to surrender and was killed.
On lock plate: Crown and V.R. LA. Co. 1863.
Figs. 3-4
WILSON BREECH-LOADING ENGLISH RIFLE and bayonet, 49 inches over-all, 33-inch barrel, about .56 caliber, brass butt plate, trigger guard and fore-end tip; iron bands, elevated rear sight. Fitted with cutlass bayonet. A few of these guns were imported for the Confederate Navy.
On lock plate: Crown and 1863.
On breech block: T. Wilson's Patent.
British proofmarks on barrel.

"The Austrian bore is slightly smaller than the English; but almost every other European Government rifle is of a larger bore. The Austrian rifle is a very serviceable weapon, but to one accustomed to Enfield and Springfield arms they have a very rough appearance. I am in position to purchase 20,000 to 30,000 Austrian rifles at about 40 shillings each, say about $10.00."

The report of Col. Gorgas to the Secretary of War, of February 3, 1863, shows that Major Huse had shipped 27,000 Austrian rifles to the Confederate Government.

THE TERRY BOLT-ACTION CARBINE
Figure 3, Plate XXVI

Among the long arms imported by the Confederacy in almost infinite variety was the Terry bolt-action carbine.

The Terry carbine was patented in 1856 by Terry and Calisher, of Birmingham. It was issued experimentally to the British cavalry in 1858. With a range of 1,000 yards, it could be fired ten times a minute by an expert marksman.

Maj. H. B. C. Pollard, in his *History of Firearms,* says many of them were sent to the Confederacy, where they were known as the "door bolt breechloader." Gen. J. E. B. Stuart, famous cavalry leader of the Army of Northern Virginia, carried a Terry carbine, which is preserved with other relics of "Jeb" in the Confederate Museum in Richmond.

Two variations of the Terry have been noted. The one carried by General Stuart has a 25-inch barrel, is iron mounted, with cap box in stock, ramrod and sling swivels. The breech is marked: "Terry's Patent .30 bore." The lock plate is marked: "Thomas Blissett," and on the barrel is "Thomas Blissett, Liverpool." The other type has a 24-inch barrel, no ramrod, no sling swivels and no cap box. The lock plate is marked with the Crown and "V. R. Tower, 1857." The barrel is marked "Terry's Patent." The "C. S." ordnance officer's mark is on breech, barrel and stock. The Terry rifle appears to be the first British bolt action to have symmetrical lugs, but they were placed close to the rear end of the bolt; the cartridge had a thick felt wad at the base, which was pushed forward by the bullet of the next cartridge after firing, and a very close joint was effected. The ball for this rifle was larger than the bore into which it was forced on firing. This type of cartridge and method of loading resembles that of the U. S. Green Oval Bore rifle, some of which were used by Union troops during the war.

THE LEMAT REVOLVING CARBINE
Figure 1, Plate XXVI

Dr. Jean Alexander Francois LeMat, inventor and maker of the LeMat revolver, also made a percussion, revolving carbine, which is particularly interesting because many of the parts are interchangeable with those of the LeMat revolver. A few of these carbines were brought through the blockade to the Confederacy.

The LeMat carbine is 38 inches over-all, with 20½-inch barrels, part octagonal. There are nine shots of .42 caliber in the cylinder, and the shot barrel takes about a .60 caliber cartridge. The loading lever is on the left side, a ramrod on the right and there is an elevated rear sight and places for sling swivels. The serial appears on the frame, cylinder, rear sight, ramrod and other parts.

The U. S. patents covering this arm were No. 15,925 of October 21, 1856, and No. 16,124 of November 25, 1856. Another patent to L. LeMat of New Orleans is No. 22,958 of June 7, 1859, and a post war patent on a breech-loading revolver was granted to F. A. LeMat, of New Orleans, December 14, 1869, being No. 97,780. In addition to these U. S. Patents, four British patents were taken out covering this mechanism. See the LeMat Revolver for these and other details of this most interesting arm.

THE WILSON BREECH-LOADING RIFLE WITH CUTLASS BAYONET
Figures 3 and 4, Plate XXVII

A British breech-loading rifle imported by the Confederates was the Wilson, which was fitted with a cutlass bayonet. Invented by T. Wilson, the rifle has a 33-inch barrel, brass butt plate, trigger guard and fore-end tip, iron bands and elevated rear sight. The use of a cutlass which could be fitted to the end of a rifle like a sword bayonet was noticed early in the war. Commander Drayton, of the U. S. Navy, reported from Port Royal, S. C., in November, 1861, that there was a British frigate off the port. And the observing officer noted that the crew were armed with short Enfield rifles, fitted with cutlass bayonets.[9]

Commander Bulloch, C. S. Navy, reported that the necessary number of revolvers and short Enfield rifles with cutlass bayonets for 150 men were purchased for the crew of the cruiser *Alabama*.[10]

And on August 13, 1861, Bulloch reported to Secretary of the Navy Mallory that 100 "sea service rifles" and cutlasses would be ready in three weeks. And he adds: "The cutlasses are identical with those in use in the British Navy and can be shipped on the end of the rifle as a bayonet."[11]

Two companies of the Twenty-first Mississippi infantry were armed with "Marine Enfields" in 1861, the rifles with cutlass bayonets.[12]

In 1862 Archibald McLaurin, agent for J. Schofield Sons & Goodman, speaks of "a pattern rifle, called the Wilson rifle breech-loading rifle."[13]

Commander North, C. S. Navy agent in England, in a letter to G. B. Tennent, dated April 23, 1863, says: "Let me call your attention to the bayonet of the Wilson rifle as too close a fit. Will require 200 rounds for each rifle, which please order."[14]

The Wilson rifle was in use at Charleston, S. C., in 1864.

---

[9] Records of the Union and Confederate Navies, Vol. XII, page 274.
[10] Secret Service of the Confederate States in Europe, by Commander Bulloch, page 236.
[11] Records of the Union and Confederate Navies, Series II, Page 65.
[12] Letter from J. Downs, former member, Twenty-first Miss. Infantry, to E. Berkley Bowie, June 1923.
[13] Official Record War of the Rebellion, Vol. II, Page 220.
[14] Records of the Union and Confederate Navies, Series II, Vol. II, Page 409.

All photographs of hand arms in Part II are by Woodward Burkhart, of Baltimore

PART II

CHAPTER I

THE PISTOLS AND REVOLVERS OF THE CONFEDER-
ATES, INCLUDING THE REGULAR U. S. MODELS,
IMPORTATIONS AND THOSE MANUFACTURED
WITHIN THE CONFEDERACY.

THE War of the States was the first major conflict in which revolvers were used extensively.

The Mexican War had established the efficiency of the Colt revolver and the superiority of that type of weapon over the old, single-shot pistol. And in the 15 years which intervened between the Mexican War and the outbreak of hostilities in 1861, revolvers had been patented and produced in almost infinite variety, many of them infringements on the Colt patents and most of them borrowed from the Colt idea.

Next to a good horse, the mounted Confederate soldier wanted most and pinned his highest hopes to "a pair of Navy sixes," as the .36 caliber Colt was called. The young Southerner took naturally to the cavalry service. He was accustomed to horses and to firearms from early boyhood. At the outbreak of the War virtually every Southerner wished to enlist in the mounted service. It was a great disappointment to many of them when forced into the infantry.

While the Confederate cavalryman did a lot of fighting on foot with carbine and rifle, he much preferred to fight astride a good steed, with a "pair of Navy sixes." The saber was a strange weapon to him. The very fact that he spent so much time making grotesque gestures with it for the edification of the drillmaster gave him a deep-rooted prejudice against it as a weapon. It was all right for a parade or guard mount, perhaps, but he simply could not see its use in a fight.

The revolver was much more to his liking. The manual was simple—to draw and open fire. He understood and liked it. That is why when he "jined the cavalry" his first thought was to get himself a brace of revolvers, Colts preferred.

But the acquisition of any kind of a revolver was difficult in the South in 1861. Officers returning from the Mexican War had brought their big Colt Dragoons back with them and they were treasured as heirlooms. But the popularity of the weapon

236

among army officers on frontier service, Texas Rangers and cowboys was so widespread that the Colt factory could not supply the demand. Prices jumped to $500 for a single weapon.

Before the War, the Southerner, when he went armed, usually carried a Deringer, a small but powerful, single-shot pocket pistol. Some were so small as to be carried in the vest pocket, hence were much in demand by young gallants. The pepperbox pistol, so popular in the West in the Eighteen Fifties, was not much used in the South.

In the arsenals taken over by the various Southern States when they seceded were only a few hundred horse pistols, of the type used in the United States Army up to and including the Mexican War. Many of them were clumsy, big-bore weapons which had been converted from flintlock to percussion. Nowhere in the South was there a revolver factory, except the plant of Shawk and McLanahan, at St. Louis, of which more later.

Thousands of Confederate troops went to the front in 1861 carrying flintlock pistols. The Virginia Armory issued Harpers Ferry and Model 1836 pistols, flintlock and altered, and the Model 1842 percussion to its volunteers, and other States did the same. Plate XXVIII shows the Virginia Manufactory pistol, early model, altered to percussion for Confederate use.

Figure 2, Plate XXIX, shows the Rappahannock Forge pistol, probably the first military pistol manufactured in this country. The Rappahannock Forge was set up BEFORE 1776 by James Hunter and made both pistols and muskets for the Virginia Convention. The pistol bears on the lock plate, in rear of the cock: "Rapa Forge" and on the barrel: "J. Hunter." On the brass counterplate: "A. L. D. No. 50. 5 T" (Albemarle Light Dragoons. No. 50 Fifth Troop). On the buttplate: "3 Rgt" (Third Regiment) Issued in 1861.

In 1864 a South Carolina trooper captured by the Fifth Ohio Cavalry carried a breech-loading carbine and a flintlock pistol, probably a family heirloom. The pistol is shown in Figure 3, Plate XXIX, and has a nine-inch brass barrel, silver mountings, rosewood stock and is marked on lock plate and barrel: "H. Nock, London."

The South had many fine gunsmiths, but they devoted their time and talents to the manufacture of sporting rifles, fowling pieces and duelling pistols. Also in the South before the War were many firms which sold guns and pistols. They were im-

Virginia Manufactory Pistol, early model, originally a flintlock converted to percussion for Confederate use. Length over-all 18½ inches, 12½-inch barrel, .70 caliber, iron mountings. Lock plate marked: Richmond, 1807 in rear of hammer.

PLATE XXVIII

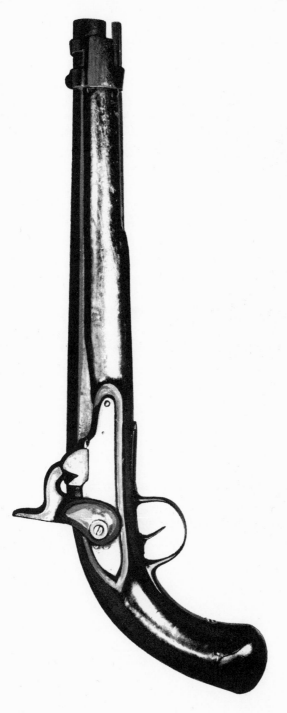

PLATE XXIX

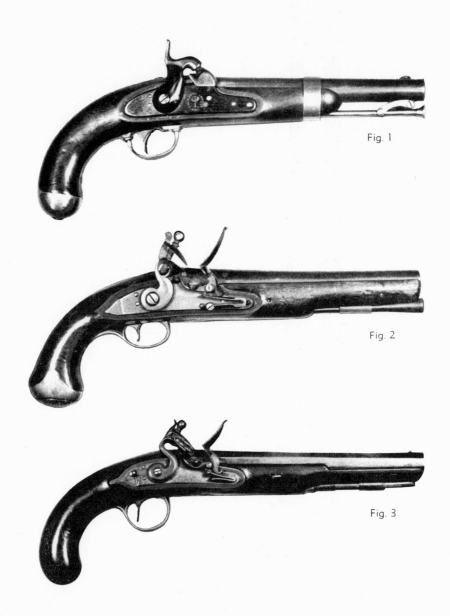

Fig. 1

Fig. 2

Fig. 3

Palmetto Armory Pistol, U. S. Model 1842: made by William Glaze & Company, of Columbia, S. C. by order of the Legislature of South Carolina in 1852, 8½-inch barrel, .54 caliber, brass handle strap, butt plate and bend. Stamped on lock plate: Palmetto Armory and Columbia, S. C. 1852 with Palmetto tree. On top of barrel: 1852. On side of barrel: Wm. Glaze & Co. V. P.

Rappahannock Forge Flintlock Pistol, 13 inches over-all, 8¾-inch barrel, about .65 caliber brass butt plate, trigger guard and thimble, iron ramrod. Stamped on lock plate: Rapa Forge. On barrel: J. Hunter. On counter-plate: A. L. D. No. 50 5 T. (Albemarle Light Dragoons). Stamped on butt plate: 3 Rgt. (Third Regiment). Made by James Hunter at his forge on the Rappahannock River, about 1775, and issued to a member of the First Virginia Cavalry in 1861.

Nock English Flintlock Pistol, nine-inch barrel of brass, silver mountings, rosewood handle. Marked on lock plate: H. Nock. On barrel: H. Nock, London. Captured from a Confederate Cavalryman in South Carolina in 1865 by a member of the Fifth Ohio Cavalry. The Confederate trooper was armed with a Morse breech-loading carbine and this pistol.

porters and repairers, rather than manufacturers. Both British and Northern arms makers were accustomed to make guns and pistols for these dealers and stamp them with the dealers' names. That explains the large number of Tranter and Adams revolvers, and Allen and other single-shot pistols made in the North, bearing the names of Southern firms.

Among the better known of these Southern firms, which should be classed as military goods importers rather than gunsmiths, were Samuel Sutherland, Mitchell & Tyler and Kent, Paine & Company, all of Richmond; Hyde & Goodrich, of New Orleans, which firm became later Thomas, Griswold & Company; T. W. Radcliffe, of Columbia, S. C.; Courtney & Tennent, Charleston, S. C.; Halfmann & Taylor, Montgomery, Ala.; Schneider & Glassick, Memphis, Tenn.; W. B. & C. Fisher, Lynchburg, Va.;[1] and Canfield Brothers & Company, of Baltimore. The last named firm had extensive Southern connections.

When war seemed inevitable and, in some instances after the secession of the States, the South sent agents to the North to purchase arms. They had no difficulty in making contracts with Northern manufacturers. Through its business connections with the North, the Tredegar Iron Works, of Richmond, placed orders for revolvers with the Colt Company at Hartford and other firms.[2]

The State of North Carolina bought 500 Navy revolvers from Colt in March, 1861, for $8,454.

Delivery of the weapons, after the outbreak of the war, was sometimes a difficult task. Probably more than half the shipments of arms from Northern to Southern ports were seized.

As late as Christmas Eve, 1863, newspapers report the seizure of the steamer *George Cromwell* as it was about to sail from New York. In her cargo, according to the newspaper account, were 50 kegs labeled "lard." When opened the kegs were found to be filled with "Navy revolvers."[3]

The eagerness of some Northern manufacturers to do business with the seceding States became so much of a public scandal in the North that Secretary of War Cameron took action. In May, 1861, he authorized his brother, Col. James Cameron, to

---

[1] The Fishers were of a family of old Shenandoah Valley gunsmiths. The father had a gunshop in Strasburg. Four of the sons—Levy, William B., Cyrus and George went to Lynchburg and opened a gun business there before the War, S. O. Fisher, the youngest brother, worked at a bench in the shop. The firm did not make guns for the Confederacy, but manufactured percussion caps. From a letter of Mrs. S. O. Fisher, Lynchburg, in 1925.

[2] Bruce's History of Iron Manufacture in Virginia in the Slave Era, page 346.

[3] The Baltimore Sun.

go to Baltimore, Philadelphia, New York, Providence, Boston, New Haven and Hartford to investigate the sale of arms to the South.

To judge from advertisements in Southern newspapers in 1861, there were plenty of Colt and other revolvers in the hands of Confederate dealers.

C. Leonard, agent, 56 Sycamore street, Petersburg Va., advertised on May 27, 1861, that he had received Colt's pistols, army, navy and belt size, which were for sale.[4]

James Walsh, gun importer, 60 Main street, Richmond, advertised March 25, 1861, "I have received from the manufacturer a further supply of Colt's celebrated five-shooters in Navy and pocket sizes."[5]

And on July 8, 1861, Walsh again advertised: "Forty Colt's Navy pistols, 20 Colt's pocket size, 4 Colt's army pistols and 30,000 caps."[6]

One of the principal sources of arms supply to the South was by capture. For that reason a glance at the hand weapons used in the Union armies is of interest, because the various types fell into the hands of Confederate ordnance officers and were reissued to the Southern troops.

General Ripley, Union Chief of Ordnance, reported June 30, 1862, that since the outbreak of the War the Federal War Department had purchased the following:

Colt Holster Revolvers	39,368
Colt Belt Revolvers	14,816
Remington Revolvers	10,640
Savage Revolvers	11,274
Whitney Revolvers	3,288
Beal Revolvers	1,346
Joslyn Revolvers	975
Starr Revolvers	4,900
Horse Pistols	1,977
Total	88,585

The report does not so state, but it is probable that the Colt holster, Remingtons and Joslyns were of .44 caliber and the Colt belt, Savage and Whitney were .36 caliber. The Starr and the Beal were made in both sizes.

[4] The Richmond Dispatch.
[5] Ibid.
[6] Ibid.

Three pedigreed Confederate revolvers made in the North—

Colt's Army Revolver, six shots, .44 caliber, 8-inch barrel. Captured from a Union trooper in 1864 by Capt. Richard D. Murphy, adjutant, First Virginia Cavalry, and given to his brother, Private James Buchanan Murphy, Company B, First Virginia, and used by the latter until he was killed in a charge at Rude's Hill, Va.; November 22, 1864. Serial 120,888.

Remington Revolver, six shots, .44 caliber, 8-inch barrel. Carried by John M. Heighe, Company K, First Maryland Cavalry, C.S.A.; which cut its way through the Union lines at Appomattox and did not surrender. Heighe loaded the revolver April 9, 1865, the day of Lee's surrender and the loads are still in it.

Whitney Revolver, six shots, .36 caliber. Engraved on trigger guard: Lt. Col. Sam T. Harison, C.S.A. Serial 1599.

PLATE XXX

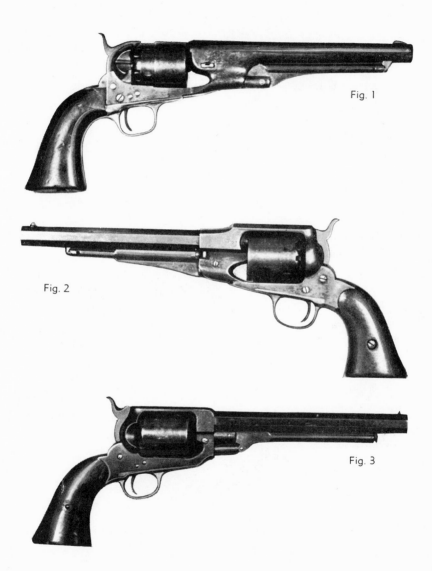

Fig. 1

Fig. 2

Fig. 3

PLATE XXXI

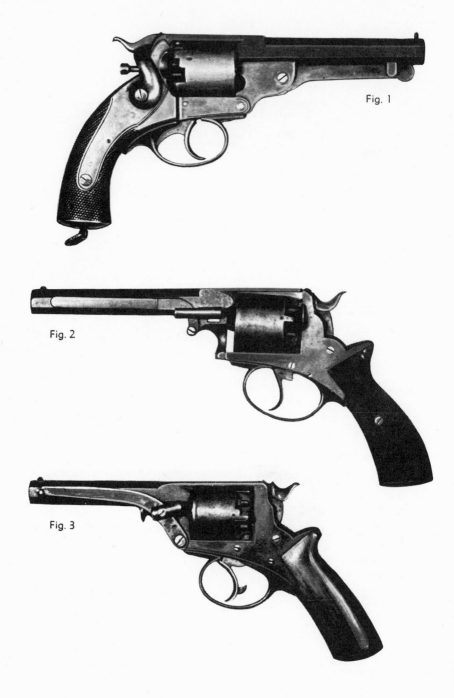

Fig. 1

Fig. 2

Fig. 3

Kerr English Revolver, five shots, .44 caliber, 5½-inch barrel. Used in the Confederate Army. On lock plate and left side of frame: London Armoury Co. On right side of frame: Kerr's Patent, 9224.

Deane, English Revolver, five shots, .44 caliber, 6-inch barrel. Carried for three years by Capt. George Russell, Forty-seventh Tennessee Infantry, C.S.A. On top of barrel: F. Barnes, London. On left side of frame: Patent No. 5553.

Tranter English Revolver, six shots, .36 caliber, double-action, 4½-inch barrel. On top of barrel: T. W. Radcliffe, Columbia, S. C. On frame: Tranter Patents. Made for Radcliffe.

It is interesting to note that while the .44 caliber became the regulation bore of the Union army revolver, the Confederates preferred the .36 caliber.[7]

The following table from the Official Records shows the revolvers (other than Colts) purchased for the Union Army during the four years of war:

Starr, .44	47,952
Whitney Navy	11,214
Savage (for Navy)	11,284
Rogers & Spencer	5,000
Pettingill	2,001
Remington .44 & .36 cal's.	5,000
Beals, .44	2,814
Allen & Wheelock	500
Joslyn	1,100
Raphael (French)	978
Perrin (French)	200
Lefaucheaux (French)	12,000

Some of the revolvers in the foregoing list were not a success. They could not stand the hard wear of army service. The Starr revolver was said to be "too delicate for service." The Savage was another weapon which was soon discarded.

In a letter to his distinguished father, Hon. Howell Cobb, John H. Cobb, of Macon, Ga., under date of March 4, 1861, wrote:

DEAR FATHER:

A package came by express today from Washington containing the presents from Colonel Colt, the revolver man; one for mother and one for you. Mother's is a book. On the back it has "Colt on the Constitution, dedicated by the Author to Mrs. Howell Cobb." On the inside is a pistol case containing a fine, ivory-handled revolver and on the handle is engraved "To Mrs. Howell Cobb from Col. Colt." Yours is a large horseman's revolver in a fine case.[8]

More than two years later—March 11, 1863—General Bee reported:

"I am informed that carbines and pistols can be had; bought in New York and shipped to Brownsville (Texas) without trouble. Am offered 5,000 Colt's revolvers at $25 for the Navy size and $38 Army size."[9]

---

[7] In the Field Manual for the Use of the Officers on Ordnance Duty, prepared by the Confederate Ordnance Department and published by Ritchie & Dunnavant of Richmond in 1862, is this note on hand arms in the Confederate service:

"Colt's pistol is used in our service and is constructed on the revolving principle, with a cylinder containing six chambers and a rifled barrel. There are two kinds in use; Colt's Army pistol of .44 inch caliber, the Navy pistol of .33 inch caliber."

The .33 is undoubtedly a misprint.

[8] American Historical Association Report, Vol. II, Page 547.

[9] Official Records, Vol. XV, Page 1014.

Plate XXX shows three "pedigreed" Confederate revolvers of Northern origin. Figure 1 shows a Colt Army revolver, six shots, .44 caliber, with eight-inch barrel. Serial 120,888. It was captured from a Union trooper in 1864 by Captain Richard D. Murphy, Adjutant, First Virginia Cavalry, and given to his brother, Private James Buchanan Murphy, Company B, First Virginia, and used by the latter until he was killed in a charge at Rude's Hill, Va., November 22, 1864.

Figure 2 is a Remington Revolver, Army size, .44 caliber, eight-inch barrel. It was carried by Private John M. Heighe, Company K, First Maryland Cavalry, C. S. A.; which cut its way through the Union lines at Appomattox and did not surrender. Heighe loaded the weapon April 9, 1865, the day of Lee's surrender, and the loads are still in it.

Figure 3 is a Whitney Revolver, six shots, 36 caliber, Serial 1,599. Engraved on the trigger guard is: "Lt. Col. Samuel T. Harison, C. S. A."

Also shown in Plate XXXIII, Figure 1, is a Colt Navy Revolver, six shots, 36 caliber, 7½-inch, octagonal barrel. Serial 100,260. Captured on the Confederate ironclad Atlanta by the Union monitor Weehawken, June 17, 1863.

It may surprise some collectors and historians to learn that the Smith & Wesson revolver, using a .32 caliber, copper-cased cartridge, jumped into great popularity in the Confederate armies at the outbreak of the war. But the cartridges were difficult to get, and their popularity was short-lived.

There is a Smith & Wesson revolver of Confederate service in the Florida Room of the Confederate Museum, in Richmond. One of these weapons was carried by Capt. A. C. Watkins of A Company, Twenty-first Georgia.[10]

P. W. Kraft, 184 Main street, Columbia, S. C., advertised in the *Richmond Daily Examiner* of January 3, 1861: "Colts, Smith & Wesson, Allen & Wheelocks and Adams English repeaters."

In the *Richmond Dispatch* of May 27, 1861, C. Leonard, of Petersburg, advertised Smith & Wesson cartridges, and E. Feuchtwanger, of Macon, Ga., advertised in the Macon Telegraph of January 1, 1862: "Just received 10,000 pistol cartridges for No. 1 Smith & Wesson."

But when these cartridges were exhausted, no more were to be had, and the weapons became useless.

---

[10] History of Doles-Cook Brigade, by H. W. Thomas, Page 374.

Figure 3, Plate XXXIII, shows a Smith & Wesson revolver, six shots, 32 caliber, rim fire, metallic cartridge, six-inch barrel. Serial 366. Used in the Confederate Army in 1861.

General Gorgas, Confederate chief of ordnance, in a special report under date of October 13, 1864, gives figures which shed light on the relative value to the South of the three sources of small arms—capture, manufacture and importation. These figures show that in the year ending September 30, 1864, the Confederacy imported 30,000 small arms, manufactured 20,000 and captured 45,000. The number captured was almost equal to the number manufactured and imported.[11]

As purchases abroad, despite the strict blockade, provided the Confederacy with its second largest source of supply, an examination of that source and the quantity and quality of the weapons sent through the blockade is interesting.

The most interesting of the hand firearms imported was the LeMat revolver, the invention of a Southerner, which, however, will be treated in detail later.

The English Adams revolver, a .44 caliber, double-action weapon, patented by John Adams, of Dalston, England, in 1857, ranked next to the Colt in the estimation of Southern ordnance officers. On January 21, 1861, the Virginia State Ordnance Department received 999 "new Adams revolvers" to equip its militia.[12]

Col. William Couper, in his book *One Hundred Years of the V. M. I.*, says the State purchased "1,000 Deane and Adams revolvers" in 1861. This reference undoubtedly is to the same purchase.

Col. John M. Payne, Collector of the Port of Wilmington, N. C., in 1864-65, notes in his record book that on October 31, 1864, the blockade runner *Hope*, landed 900 Kerr revolvers "with extra parts and 900 Kerr revolver flasks."

Again on May 13, 1864, according to Colonel Payne, the steamer *Index* landed 30 cases of revolvers (type not named) and on May 21, 1864, the steamer *Helen* landed, among other things, 17 cases of revolvers and two cases of pistols. It would be interesting to know what these pistols were.

The Kerr, also popular in the South, was patented by J. Kerr, of Southwark, England, April 14, 1857, and August 4, 1863. Maj. Caleb Huse, who was sent to England by the Confederate

---

[11] Southern Historical Society Papers, Vol. II, Page 59.
[12] Original document in the Virginia State Library, Richmond.

War Department, made a contract with the London Armory Company to furnish Kerr revolvers for the South.

Figure 1, Plate XXXI, shows a Kerr Revolver, five shots, .44 caliber. Used in the Confederate Army. On lock plate and left side of frame: "London Armoury Co." On right side of frame: "Kerr's Patent. 9224."

Figure 2, Plate XXXI, shows a Deane Revolver, five shots, .44 caliber, six-inch barrel. Carried for three years by Captain George Russell, Forty-seventh Tennessee Regiment, C. S. A. On top of barrel: "F. Barnes, London." On left side of frame: "Patent No. 5553."

Before the War the Tranter revolver, patented by William Tranter, of Birmingham, England, had quite a vogue in the South. Most of these imported revolvers were stamped with the names of the firms importing them, which explains the Tranter revolvers bearing the names of Hyde & Goodrich, New Orleans; T. W. Radcliffe, Columbia, S. C.; and others.

Figure 3, Plate XXXI, shows a Tranter Revolver, six shots, .36 caliber, double-action. On top of barrel: T. W. Radcliffe, Columbia, S. C." On frame: "Tranter Patent."

In his report of December 31, 1864, to Secretary of War Seddon, General Gorgas said the importations for the fiscal year included 1,716 "pistols." General Gorgas frequently used the generic word "pistol" to designate all kinds of hand firearms, but the reference in Colonel Payne's notebook of the receipt of both revolvers and pistols in 1864 tends to confuse as to just what Gorgas means.

In the early part of the War, Confederate agents in England were in keen competition with representatives of the Union cause. In some instances, the Northerners beat the Southerners to it. Secretary of the Confederate Navy Mallory wrote to Commodore J. D. Bulloch, the Navy's representative in England, under date of May 9, 1861, directing him to purchase 1,000 Navy revolvers.[13]

And on August 13, 1861, Bulloch answered saying, in part: "The revolvers are not to be had at any price. I contracted for 1,000 of them with a large factory and hope to forward them with the great guns."[14] Bulloch does not say so, but this "large factory" probably was the London Armory Company.

---

[13] Record of the Union and Confederate Navies, Vol. II, Series II, Page 65.
[14] Ibid., page 84.

Le Mat Revolver, first model, cylinder holds nine .42 caliber cartridges. Under barrel for buckshot cartridge, .50 caliber, loading lever on right side, spur trigger guard, ring in butt. Made in Paris. Marked on top of barrel: Col. Le Mat's Patent. Serial 168 on cylinder, side of frame, barrel and other parts.

Le Mat Revolver, last war model; loading lever on left side, no spur on trigger guard. Marked on top of barrel: Syst. Le Mat, Bte, s.g.d.g. Paris. Serial 1824 on various parts.

French pin fire model, six shots, 11 mm caliber, 6½-inch round barrel. Carried by Col. Clement Sulivane, who commanded the rear guard of the Army of Northern Virginia in the evacuation of Richmond.

PLATE XXXII

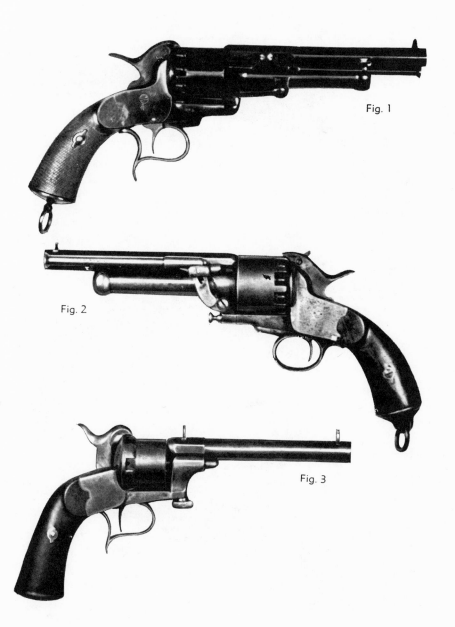

Fig. 1

Fig. 2

Fig. 3

PLATE XXXIII

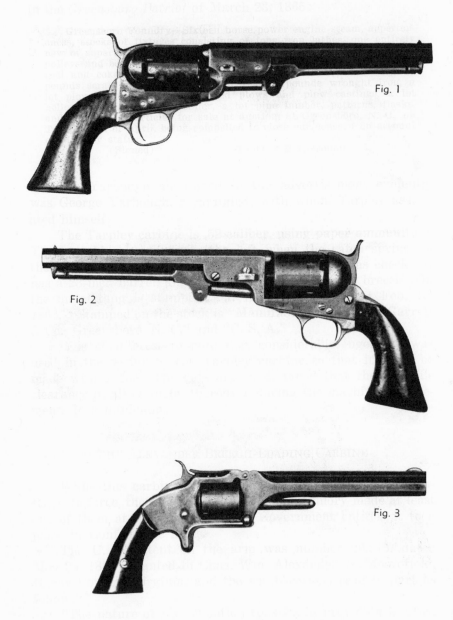

Fig. 1

Fig. 2

Fig. 3

Colt Navy Revolver, Model 1851, six shots, 7½-inch barrel, octagonal barrel. Captured on the Confederate iron-clad ram Atlanta by the Weehawken, June 17, 1863. In walnut case with all accessories. Serial 100,-260.

Dimick "Colt" Revolver, 14 inches over-all, six shots, .36 caliber, 7½-inch barrel, rifled seven grooves right, brass handle strap, trigger guard and front sight. Engraved on top of barrel: Made for H. E. Dimick, St. Louis. Serial 1470 on various parts. Probably made for Dimick by the Manhattan Fire Arms Company.

Smith & Wesson Revolver, six shots, .32 caliber, rim fire, metallic cartridge; six-inch barrel. Serial 366. This type of revolver was popular with Confederate officers in 1861 but was soon discarded because of the difficulty of getting cartridges.

Many of the volunteer companies, made up of the sons of wealthy planters, in 1861 armed and equipped themselves, and often their arms were the best obtainable. The Liberty Independent Troop (Company G) Fifth Georgia Cavalry, went to war in '61 armed with Sharp's carbines and English holster revolvers.[15]

Prices were apt to be high in Confederate money, as witness this advertisement of 1863:

FINE ENGLISH REVOLVERS

Just received from England six Tranter's fine revolving pistols, 80 and 120 bore. Price $220 each. H. E. Nichols, Columbia, S. C.[16]

Large quantities of the Lefaucheaux, a French pin-fire revolver of 12 millimeters, or about .42 caliber, were purchased by Northern agents. Gen. John C. Fremont bought thousands on his own account, and Col. George Schuyler bought 10,000 more. Ripley's report of June, 1862, shows 11,940 Lefaucheaux revolvers imported since the beginning of the war. Southern agents probably bought some, too, because the weapon was not uncommon in the South.

Figure 3, Plate XXXII, shows a French pinfire revolver, six shots, II millimeter, 6½-inch round barrel. Carried by Colonel Clement A. Sulivane, who commanded the rear guard of the Army of Northern Virginia in the evacuation of Richmond.

Other French revolvers imported by the North and probably by the South were: Devisme, six-shot, .36 caliber, percussion. Raphael, six-shot, .42 caliber, double-action, center fire metallic cartridge. Perrin, six-shot, .44 caliber, double-action, metallic cartridge. Houllier & Blanchard, six-shot, .44 caliber, percussion.

The Devisme was an ingenious weapon, but hardly suited for army service. The Houllier & Blanchard was, perhaps, the most practical of all, but seems to have been used little. The Raphael and Perrin were good, but required special cartridges, which was the principal objection to the Lefaucheaux and other pistols using the pin-fire cartridge.

One of the first steps taken by the Confederate Government to obtain arms was to encourage home industries by subsidies. On January 13, 1862, Congress passed an Act providing for an advance of 50 per cent of the capital of any firearms manufac-

---

[15] The Confederate Veteran, Vol. 9, Page 340.
[16] The Times Dispatch, Richmond, March 10, 1863.

turing company. President Davis vetoed the measure because he considered some of its features objectionable and because, he said, power to advance one-third of the capital already existed.[17] On April 19, 1862, however, another measure of similar import was signed by President Davis.[18]

Throughout the South many companies were organized in an effort to obtain the Government subsidy. Many of them never got beyond the paper stage. In some instances patents were obtained. In some instances model revolvers were painstakingly turned out by hand for submission to the ordnance officers, but they failed to pass the test. Schneider & Glassick, of Memphis, probably belong in the last-mentioned class, as witness this news item:

> Memphis Manufacture. We were yesterday shown by Messrs. Schneider & Glassick, of Jefferson street, between Front and Main streets, a six-shooter Navy pistol of their own manufacture. It is a beautiful weapon, not inferior to the Colt's make in any particular. The finish of the whole, the accuracy of the parts and the excellent working of the mechanism are admirable. Iron, brass work and wood work are all specimens of skill. We are proud that Memphis can turn out such splendid workmanship.[19]

But Schneider & Glassick were never heard of after the fall of Memphis, so their pistol-making activities must have been short-lived.

And in the *Macon* (Ga.) *Telegraph* of June 26, 1861, we find this item:

> Thomas Godwin, an ingenious mechanic of Portsmouth, Virginia, has invented a revolver which fires nine times, each barrel discharging separately at intervals. The machinery is much more simple than that in Colt's repeater. A Bowie knife is also attached, which may be unshipped or retained in service at pleasure.

This "ingenious mechanic" was of the firm of Thomas W. Godwin & Company, which operated the Virginia Iron Works at Norfolk.

Also in the *Florence* (Ala.) *Gazette* of September 4, 1861, there is this announcement:

> A Homemade Colt's Repeater. On Saturday last we had the pleasure of examining a Colt's repeater which was made by the Rev. Felix Johnson. This weapon was complete in all its details and appointments and as well calculated to do damage as Mr. Colt's best. Every

---

[17] Acts of the Confederate Congress, Vol. I, pp. 477, 753, et al.
[18] Acts of the Confederate Congress, Vol. II, p. 147.
[19] Memphis Daily Appeal, Dec. 8, 1861.

calculation necessary to a perfect fitting of all the parts were made with the utmost nicety. The Reverend inventor of this valuable weapon was on a mission from the Governor and Military Board of Tennessee to make arrangements with Messrs. Wright and Brice, of this vicinity, for the procurement of suitable machinery to aid in the manufacturing of this weapon. We earnestly hope this enterprise may be a success.

Which merely calls attention to the fact that both the North and South had reverend gentlemen in 1861 who were eager to contribute to the general blood-letting.

The earliest record of pistol making in the Confederacy is found in the report of General Gorgas of August 12, 1861, wherein he says that a contract had been awarded for 5,000 LeMat revolvers, already mentioned, and that another contract for 5,000 "pistols" had been given to Edward Want, of Newberne, N. C.; delivery to begin in three months.[20] Newberne was captured by the enemy on March 14, 1862, and the writer can find no record of any actual manufacture by Want, who seems to have disappeared completely. It should be noted that Gorgas, in speaking of the LeMat contract, refers to "revolvers" and, in the next paragraph, in mentioning the Want contract he calls them "pistols." While Gorgas often used the word pistol to designate a revolver, it is evident that in this case he meant just what he said—single-shot pistols.

With the exception of the flintlock pistols made at Harper's Ferry, there was only one plant in the South where pistols—not revolvers—were made on a large scale before the war. That was the factory of William Glaze & Co., known as the Palmetto Armory, at Columbia, S. C. When the first secession convention was held in South Carolina in 1852, the convention awarded the Palmetto Armory a contract to make arms, including the U. S. model 1842 pistol. These weapons were well made, brass mounted, and stamped: "Palmetto Armory, S. C. Columbia," and a palmetto tree. There is no record showing how many were made. During the war the Palmetto Armory seems to have been used entirely for repairing arms. There is no record of any arm being made there originally between the outbreak of the War and the destruction of the plant by Sherman in 1865.

Figure 1, Plate XXIX, shows the Palmetto Armory pistol of 1852, U. S. Army Model 1842, made by William Glaze & Co. Stamped on the lock plate: Palmetto Tree and "Palmetto Armory," "Columbia, S. C. 1852." On barrel: "Wm. Glaze &

---

[20] Official Records War of the Rebellion, Part IV, Vol. I, Page 556.

Co., V. P. 1852." Palmetto pistols are never found bearing any date other than 1852.

Mention has been made of the pistol contract given Edward Want, of North Carolina, but it is evident that Want never made a single pistol. And this suggests the question: Were any pistols (single-shot hand weapons) made in or for the Confederacy?

There is a pistol, made on the 1842 model and with many characteristics of the Palmetto Armory pistol, but without the Palmetto proof marks on the barrel. It is unmarked except that the lock plate has "C. S. Richmond."

Figure 1, Plate XXXIV shows the Richmond pistol.

And another unanswered question is: What became of the pistol-making machinery used by William Glaze & Company at the Palmetto Armory in Columbia, S. C.?

There is no evidence, documentary or otherwise, to indicate that pistols were made on a large scale anywhere within the limits of the Confederacy. The shoulder-stocked pistols, Model 1855, bearing Fayetteville, N. C., and Richmond rifle lock plates may be remade arms such as were turned out by Samuel Sutherland, of Richmond, and other gunsmiths in the early days of the Confederacy.

Figure 3, Plate XXXVI, shows a deringer, with six-inch octagonal barrel, about .45 caliber, with swivel ramrod and belt hook. Stamped on tang of lock plate: "S. Sutherland, Richmond, Va." Probably made BY or FOR Sutherland BEFORE the war.

However, the collector should look with suspicion on pistols with lock plates marked with the names of rifle makers and bearing 1863 and later dates. At that time the Confederacy had neither the mechanics nor the material to waste on the manufacture of single-shot pistols, when their revolver factories were short of both.

The Confederate Ordnance Manual of 1863, prepared under the direction of Colonel Gorgas, Chief of Ordnance, and published by West & Johnston, of Richmond, shows on plate No. 26 a sketch of a pistol-carbine similar to the Springfield Armory shoulder stock pistol, Model 1855. But it is quite obvious that this and other plates in the book were lifted bodily from the United States Ordnance Manual of 1860.

THE LEMAT REVOLVER

The most unusual—and since the War the most famous—of all Confederate revolvers was the LeMat, the invention of a Southerner, but the product of a French factory.

Dr. Jean Alexander Francois LeMat was a Creole physician of New Orleans before the War. Being of a mechanical turn of mind, he was granted a patent by the United States Patent Office under date of October 21, 1856, for his revolving pistol.

The weapon had a revolving cylinder containing nine shots of .42 caliber and an under barrel of .60 caliber for a shot cartridge. This last was fired by a small movable head on the end of the hammer.

When the War began, Dr. LeMat lost no time in offering his invention to the Confederate Government. About this time Le Mat made a connection with the Edward Guatherin Company, of New Orleans, which was engaged in buying tobacco for the French government. The firm began the manufacture of military clothing, the goods being imported from France.

There is no evidence that any LeMat revolvers were manufactured in this country. The only suggestion to that effect is an article in the *Richmond Daily Examiner* of June 28, 1861, which quotes the *New Orleans Daily Delta* as saying:

"F. W. C. Cook, of the firm of Cook and Brother, manufacturers of Enfield model guns, contemplates the manufacture of Dr. LeMat's grapeshot revolver, one of the most formidable weapons of the pistol kind ever invented."

But this never materialized, and LeMat ran the blockade and took passage for Europe on the English mail liner *Trent* with Mason and Slidell. He escaped capture when the *Trent* was stopped by a Federal warship, and Mason and Slidell were taken prisoner. LeMat continued to Paris and entered into partnership with Girard & Son to make the revolvers.

General Gorgas reported on August 12, 1861, that he had given LeMat a contract to make 5,000 revolvers for the War Department.[21] Later the Confederate Navy Department gave LeMat a contract for 2,000 (or 3,000) to be delivered for inspection in London.

Under date of July 30, 1862, Secretary Mallory of the Navy Department wrote to Commander James D. Bulloch, C. S. Navy, in Liverpool, saying in part:

---

[21] Official Records, Series IV, Vol. I.

"You will observe by the terms of the contract with Mr. LeMat that the pistols are to be delivered and inspected in London and you will inspect them or designate an officer of the Navy in England to do so and receive them, after which you will pay for them out of any funds in your hands and forward them to the Confederate States. Two hundred pistols have been delivered and paid for here."[22]

To this the Secretary received the following reply from Commander Bulloch, dated Liverpool, September 24:

"Immediately upon receipt of your letter of July 30, in which you direct me to carry out the terms of this contract, I wrote to Messrs. C. Girard & Company informing them of the fact and stating that I would make arrangements for the inspection of the pistols as soon as they could deliver them, at stated periods and in sufficient numbers to make it advisable. I was obliged to inform them at the same time that I had no available funds from which to make the prescribed payments, but, to avoid, if possible, any delay in forwarding the arms, I requested them to suggest some means by which I could give them security for ultimate payment, and am now awaiting their reply."[23]

On October 25, Bulloch again wrote the Secretary of the Navy:

"Messrs. C. Girard and Company have agreed to deliver the revolvers without payment being made here. No sample of the pistol furnished the War Department has been sent me, and it is therefore impossible to judge of the relative character of those the contractors are making for the Navy."[24]

Under date of November 7, 1862, Bulloch again wrote to Mallory and had this to say about the LeMat Navy revolvers:

First, contract for revolvers.—This contract, whether regularly made over by Colonel LeMat or not, is in the hands of Messrs. C. Girard & Co., of Paris. When these gentlemen, after some correspondence, declared their willingness to deliver the revolvers upon a simple receipt with or without payment, I directed the inspecting officer, Lieutenant Chapman, since relieved in this duty by Lieutenant Evans, to ask for a sample of the pistols already delivered to the War Department and to get a written certificate from the manufacturer that the one furnished him was identical with those previously accepted. He was then to see that the revolvers offered for the Navy came fully up to the sample. One hundred have been accepted by Lieutenant Evans, and I hope they will be here in time to send by Lieutenant Wilkinson. Lieutenant Evans reports that these hundred are quite as well furnished in every way

[22] Records of the Union and Confederate Navies, Series II, Vol. II, Page 230.
[23] Ibid., Series II, Vol. II, Page 274.
[24] Records of the Union and Confederate Navies, Series II, Vol. II, Page 282.

as the sample, but adds that the barrels, lock frames, and hammers are of cast iron; that the contact between the barrels and cylinders is so loose as to permit much escape of gas; and that the cylinders, not being provided with springs, as in other repeating arms, are apt to revolve too far when the pistols are rapidly cocked, so that the hammers are likely to fall upon the divisions between the nipples when the firing is quick. These are such serious defects that I shall decline receiving any more of the revolvers under this contract unconditionally, but will write Lieutenant Evans to say to Messrs. Girard & Co. that he will forward the balance subject to inspection upon arrival in the Confederate States. I presume you have not seen any of the pistols already sent forward, but I beg that you will have them inspected and instruct me what to do in the matter as soon as possible. The ordinary revolver costs in England about 63s. and the grapeshot revolver Messrs. C. Girard & Co. are now supplying can be manufactured by the London Armory Co. for something less than £5 each.[25]

There is an unexplained interval of some 16 months between the foregoing correspondence and the next letters on the subject in the records, as witness the following:

CONFEDERATE STATES, NAVY DEPARTMENT,
Office of Ordnance and Hydrography, Richmond, April 7, 1864.

SIR: Herewith you will receive a copy of a contract with Messrs. C. Girard & Co., for 2,000 "grapeshot revolvers," for the use of the Navy, to be delivered and inspected in England.

Commodore Barron has been requested by this office to select an officer to inspect and receive the pistols, and upon the presentation of bills properly certified by such officer, you will please direct Messrs. Fraser, Trenholm & Co. to pay them according to the terms of the contract, chargeable to the appropriation for the ordnance for the Navy.

When the pistols are received for service with 10 rounds of ammunition for each (percussion caps to be included) please have them shipped by first favorable opportunity to Nassau, New Providence, consigned to L. Heyliger, Esq., agent, Navy Department, with instructions to him to ship them to a Confederate port in lots of 250 each,

marked ⚓ accompanied by invoices and letters of advice,

or they may be shipped in lots of 500, if favorable opportunities offer, direct.

Respectfully, your obedient servant,
JOHN M. BROOKE,
Commander in Charge.

Commander J. D. BULLOCH, C. S. Navy,
Liverpool, England[26]

Paris, June 13, 1864

SIR: Under a contract made by the Confederate States Navy Department with Messrs. C. Girard & Co., for 2,000 grapeshot revolvers, with 10 rounds of ammunition for each, to be delivered in England for use of Confederate States Navy, you are hereby appointed the officer to attend to the inspection and reception of the pistols. You

---

[25] Ibid., Page 295.
[26] Records of the Union and Confederate Navies, Series II, Vol. II, Page 620.

will certify bills for all that may pass a satisfactory inspection, and forward them to Commander J. D. Bulloch, who is authorized to direct the payment according to the terms of the contract.
Respectfully etc.,

S. BARRON,
Flag Officer.

Lieutenant W. H. MURDAUGH, C. S. Navy,
Paris[27]

Lieutenant Murdaugh evidently took his assignment seriously, for under date of Paris, June 23, 1864, he reported to Barron:

Paris, June 23, 1864.

SIR: In obedience to your order of the 13th instant, I have inspected the pistols made by C. Girard & Co. under contract with the Navy Department and have the honor to report that from the general bad character of the workmanship I have declined to receive those which they had on hand ready for delivery. As a specimen of the workmanship, I would state that of the first seven examined six had defects, as follows, viz: In one the grapeshot barrel went off at the fourth or fifth fire of the revolving cylinder from a defect in the hammer. In the next the cylinder would not revolve from defect in spring of revolving apparatus. In the next the hammer at times would miss striking the nipple altogether, seriously damaging it. In the other three the fixed and revolving barrels were not true with one another when in position for firing, and in one of these the hammer did not strike fair.

Of all those examined, none appeared to be reliable, and almost all of them had serious defects, such as those enumerated. In all the metal of which the faces of the hammers were made was too soft.

Very respectfully, your obedient servant,

W. H. MURDAUGH.

Flag Officer S. BARRON,
Paris.[28]

The result of Murdaugh's report was that Barron promptly annulled the Navy Department's contract, as shown in the following letters:

Paris, February 6, 1865.

GENTLEMEN: Your letter of the 5th, asking "for a copy of the order from the Navy Department of the Confederate States giving you (me) authority to send us such notice," viz, "to annul our contract with the Navy Department for revolvers" is received. In reply to your request I have to state that the contract made by you with the Navy Department has been sent to me for my guidance, and in it you agree that "500 of said revolvers are to be delivered per month, the first delivery of 500 to be made before the 1st of November next," 1863. The terms stipulated in this agreement have by no means been complied with by you up to this day; nevertheless, so long as there was a chance of getting these arms into the Confederacy and cotton out to pay for them,

27 Ibid., Page 670.
28 Records of the Union and Confederate Navies, Series II, Vol. II, Page 676.

I did not hesitate to take upon myself the responsibility of ordering the inspection and payment of such as were received, but now, the aspect of things is so changed by the closing of our ports that I do not feel myself authorized to continue the inspection and payment without further orders from the department.
Respectfully, etc.,

S. BARRON,
Flag Officer.

Messrs. C. GIRARD & CO.,
No. 9, Passage Joinville.[29]

Paris, February 7, 1865.

SIR: According to the terms of the contract made by Messrs. Girard & Co. with the Ordnance Bureau, the first 500 pistols were to have been delivered on the 1st of November, 1863. They have not been delivered up to this date, but 100 are now reported ready for inspection. I have directed these to be inspected, and such as are reported worthy of being received, to be paid for; and have notified Messrs. Girard & Co. that I do not feel myself authorized to continue the inspection and receiving under the present condition of affairs until I learn the views of the department. The closing up of our ports by the blockade and the fall of Fort Fisher, thus rendering it quite impossible to get arms into the Confederacy and cotton out, together with a report from Commander Bulloch, financial agent of the department, of the shortness of money to meet all the engagements made under bona fide contracts and faithfully complied with and the noncompliance by these contractors with their agreement, have induced me to notify these gentlemen in order that they may not run into any further expense on account of this contract. They shall lose nothing by what they have already manufactured so far as they are reported favorably on. I do not think these gentlemen will have any just grounds of complaint after the indulgence that has been shown to them. They complain of my decision, and are about to make a formal protest, which I shall forward to the bureau when it is received by me.
I am, most respectfully, your obedient servant,

S. BARRON,
Flag Officer.

Commander JNO. M. BROOKE,
Chief of the Bureau of Ordnance and Hydrography.[30]

It is apparent from the foregoing that few of the LeMats made for the Navy Department ever reached the Confederacy. Supposedly these Navy LeMats were the smaller type, with rifled barrel of .35 caliber and shot barrel of about .50 caliber. These small LeMats are exceedingly rare. There is a fine one in the Nunnemacher Collection in the Milwaukee Public Museum. There is, however, no documentary evidence to indicate that the Navy LeMats differed in size from those furnished the Army.

The War Department seems to have fared better than the Navy Department in its contract for LeMat revolvers.

[29] Ibid., Page 795.
[30] Records of the Union and Confederate Navies, Series II, Vol. II, Page 795.

"The Field Manual for the Use of the Officers on Ordnance Duty," prepared by the Confederate Ordnance Department and printed by Ritchie & Dunnavant, of Richmond, in 1862, contains in the chapter on small arms in use in the Confederate armies this paragraph:

"Grapeshot pistol—This pistol is manufactured by M. Le-Mat, of Paris. It has a cylinder which revolves, containing nine chambers, a rifled barrel and a smooth-bore barrel. The latter receives a charge of buckshot, and is fired by a slight change in the hammer. Some are in our service."

Col. John M. Payne, detailed as ordnance officer in charge of imported munitions of war at Wilmington, N. C., reports the receipt of 150 LeMat revolvers in July, 1863, which were "not approved." Colonel Payne's record book, which is preserved in the Museum at Richmond, shows that LeMat revolvers came through the blockade with some regularity in 1864. The following excerpts are from this record book:

"On June 17, 1864, the steamer *Lynx* arrived with four cases of LeMat revolvers, which were forwarded to Richmond.

"On July 27, 1864, the *Lynx* again landed four cases of LeMat revolvers.

"On May 16, 1864, the steamer *Pevensey* landed five cases of LeMat revolvers."

Among the arms found on the Confederate ironclad *Atlanta*, captured June 30, 1863, were three LeMat revolvers and 32 Colt revolvers.[31]

When Lieut. John Taylor Wood and a party of picked men from the *C. S. S. Patrick Henry* burned the steamship *Alleganian* in November, 1862, it is recorded that the men were armed with LeMat revolvers.[32] Kent, Paine & Company, Richmond arms dealers, advertised LeMat revolvers for sale in December, 1862.[33]

LeMat revolvers were recognized for use in the army. "The Field Manual for the Use of Confederate Officers on Ordnance Duty" refers to them on page 54. In the Confederate Museum in Richmond are LeMat revolvers used by Gen. J. E. B. Stuart, General Beauregard and Gen. Patton Anderson. The Chicago Historical Society has the LeMat revolver carried by Maj. Henry Wirz.

There were many changes in the LeMat models. The earliest ones had round barrels, spur trigger guards, loading

---

[31] Records of the Union and Confederate Navies, Vol. XIV, Page 696.
[32] Official Records, Vol. V, Page 141.
[33] The Richmond Whig, December 4, 1862.

Richmond pistol, U. S. Model 1842; 14½ inches over-
all, .54 caliber, brass band and butt plate, swivel
ramrod. Marked on lock plate: C. S. Richmond.

Shawk & McLanahan Revolver, brass frame, 8-inch
round barrel, six shots, .36 caliber, rifled seven grooves
right. Made at Carondelet, St. Louis, Mo. about
1858-59. Marked on back strap: Shawk & McLanahan, St. Louis, Carondelet, Mo. Serial 16 on inside of
trigger guard frame.

Cofer Revolver, 7-inch barrel, six shots, .36 caliber,
rifled seven grooves right, brass frame. Marked on
top of barrel: T. W. Cofer's Patent, Portsmouth, Va.
W.I.H. stamped on back strap. E. B. Georgia stamped
on frame in two places. Thomas W. Cofer was granted
a patent for this revolver by the Confederate Patent
Office, August 12, 1861.

PLATE XXXIV

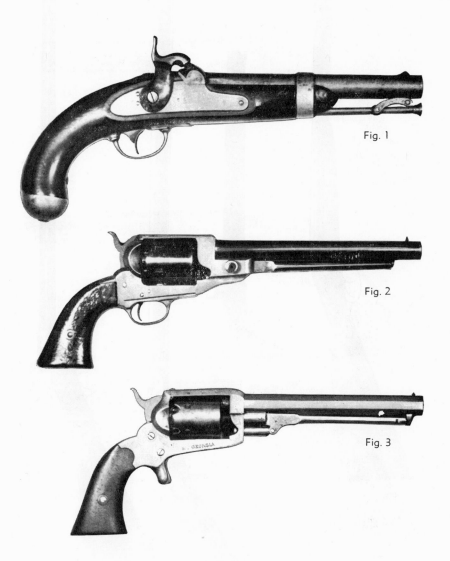

Fig. 1

Fig. 2

Fig. 3

PLATE XXXV

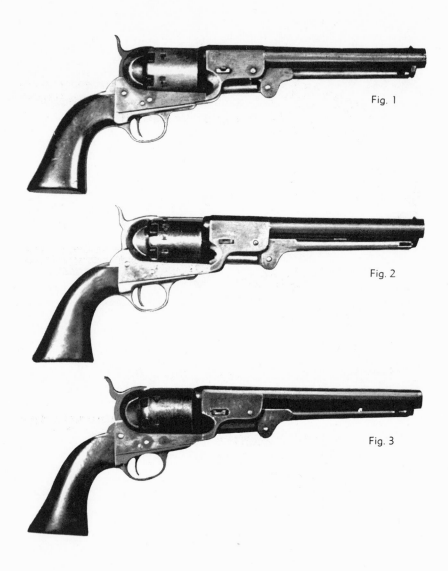

Fig. 1

Fig. 2

Fig. 3

Leech & Rigdon Revolver, 7½-inch barrel, .36 caliber, six shots, rifled 7 grooves left, trigger guard, handle strap and front sight of brass. Made at Greensboro, Ga. 1863. Marked on top of barrel: Leech & Rigdon, C.S.A. Serial 899 on cylinder, handle strap, trigger guard frame, key and loading lever. Carried by Col. Harry Gilmor, Second Maryland Confederate Cavalry.

Rigdon & Ansley Revolver, 7½-inch barrel, .36 caliber, six shots, rifled 7 grooves left, 12 cylinder stops, trigger guard, handle strap and front sight of brass. Made at Augusta, Ga. 1864. Marked on top of barrel: Augusta, Ga. C.S.A. Serial 1582 on cylinder, handle strap, trigger guard frame, barrel lug and ramrod.

Columbus Fire Arms Manufacturing Company Revolver (L. Haiman & Brother), 7½-inch barrel, six shots, .36 caliber, rifled seven grooves right, brass handle strap, trigger guard and front sight. Made at Columbus, Ga.; 1864. Marked on top of barrel: Columbus Fire Arms Manuf. Co., Columbus. On trigger guard plate: C. S. Serial 46 on side of frame, under barrel lug and cylinder.

levers on right side and were marked "LeMat's Patent." Later the marking was changed to "Col. LeMat's Patent." The loading lever was shifted from the right to the left side, and the spur was removed from the trigger guard. The markings were changed to "Col. LeMat, bte.s.g.d.g. Paris."[34]

Plate XXXII shows two models of the LeMat Army Revolver. Figure 1 is the first model, with loading lever on right side, spur trigger guard and ring in butt. On top of barrel: "Col. LeMat's Patent," Serial 168. Figure 2 shows the last war model, with loading lever on the left side and no trigger guard spur. On top of barrel: "Syst LeMat, Bte, s.g.d.g., Paris." Serial 1824.

All these references are to the percussion LeMat. The pinfire LeMat was a post-war model and was not used in the Confederacy.

There are also LeMat revolvers marked "LeMat & Girard's Patent, London." Often these are found with Birmingham and other English proof marks, indicating that they were imported to England "in the white," that is, unfinished, and were finished and proved in England.

The first patent issued to LeMat by the British Patent Office was in 1859, and is applicable to both muzzle and breechloader. His second patent, No. 1,081, issued in 1862, shows the ramrod on the left side and merely claims a new kind of cylinder stop. There is a third patent of 1868 for breechloader and a fourth of 1871 with a new type of hammer, but these latter patents were issued after the end of the War.

The LeMat revolver had serious defects other than those found by the inspector. The most notable of these was the small, movable tip on the end of the hammer. When this tip was turned down, it fired the shot cartridge. But when it was broken off, as was frequently the case, the weapon was useless.

Another and even more serious defect was that the LeMat revolver would not take the regulation .44 caliber revolver cartridge.

THE COFER REVOLVER

According to the records of the Confederate Patent Office the first—and probably the only—revolver patented and made in the Confederacy was the Cofer. The other revolvers manufactured there were "captured" models.

---

[34] Manufactured for the inventor.

FIREARMS OF THE CONFEDERACY

Thomas W. Cofer was granted a patent on August 12, 1861, for a brass-frame revolver, the most conspicuous feature of which was a sheath trigger, rather unusual for a military revolver. Cofer was a resident of Portsmouth, Va., just across the river from Norfolk, and he promptly set up a little shop there, employing less than a dozen hands. The Richmond *Daily Examiner* of July 17, 1861, says:

> Mr. T. W. Cofer, of Portsmouth, Va., has just completed an improvement in revolving firearms whereby the process of loading is so much facilitated that a Colt or other revolver may be loaded and discharged with fourfold rapidity. Mr. Cofer, says the Portsmouth *Transcript*, has left for Richmond to secure a patent for his invention." And the Richmond *Examiner* of October 17, 1861, says: "A citizen of Portsmouth, T. W. Cofer, has made and patented a revolving pistol which seems to possess very many advantages over that of Colt's, so general in use and from which in the manner of loading it differs in sundry important aspects while it is of long range and equal accuracy. It is fired with a prepared Minie cartridge and about these times must be considered not only a useful invention, but a decided evidence of the inventive genius of the Southern people." In *De Bow's Review* for March-April, 1862, we find this note (page 327): "Thomas W. Cofer, inventor of a revolving pistol pronounced by judges to be superior to the Colt pistol. At present he is engaged in manufacturing them on a small scale at Portsmouth, Va."

But by the time the *Review* came off the press, Norfolk had fallen, and the Cofer plant closed. The writer can find no record of the manufacture of these revolvers elsewhere, so there must have been very few made—certainly fewer than a hundred. In the report of the Confederate Commissioner of Patents, for 1864, there is a list of patents expiring that year and among them is this: "T. W. Cofer, Portsmouth, Va., revolving pistol, August 12, 1864."

In the famous arms collection of Charles Noe Daly, which was sold at auction in Toronto, Canada, in June, 1935, was a huge duck gun, nearly 10 feet long, bearing the name "Cofer, Portsmouth, Va." Cofer was a well-known gunsmith of Portsmouth before the War, but it is not known what became of him after the fall of Norfolk in the Spring of 1862, which must have closed his pistol factory.

Figure 3, Plate XXXIV, shows the Cofer revolver, which has a brass frame, seven-inch barrel, six shots, .36 caliber, rifled seven grooves right. On top of barrel: "T. W. Cofer's Patent, Portsmouth, Va." Stamped on the frame in two places is "E. B. Georgia."

One of the first firms we have to consider in studying the revolver-making industry in the Confederacy is that of Robin-

Griswold & Grier Revolver, brass frame, 7½-inch barrel, .36 caliber, six shots, rifled six grooves right. Made at Griswoldville, Ga., 1862-64. No marks except serial 2419 on cylinder and left side of frame and barrel lug.

Spiller & Burr Revolver. Whitney model, 7-inch octagonal barrel, six shots, .36 caliber, rifled seven grooves left. Made at Atlanta, Ga., 1863-64. Stamped on top of barrel: Spiller & Burr. On left side of frame C. S. Serial 150 on cylinder, under side of frame, brass handle strap, loading lever and under side of barrel.

Samuel Sutherland Pistol, six-inch octagonal barrel, about .45 caliber, swivel ramrod, 2½-inch belt hook on left side. Stamped on tang of lock plate: S. Sutherland, Richmond, Va.

PLATE XXXVI

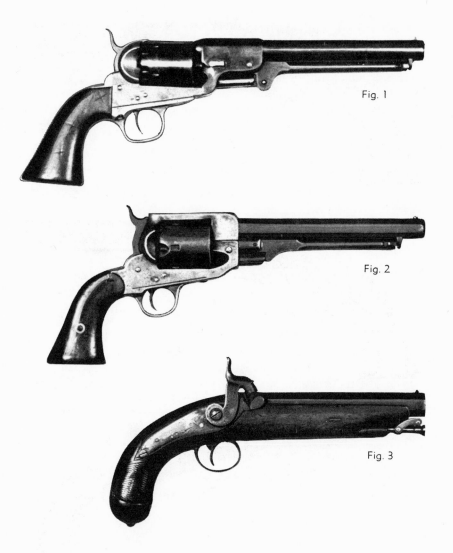

Fig. 1

Fig. 2

Fig. 3

PLATE XXXVII

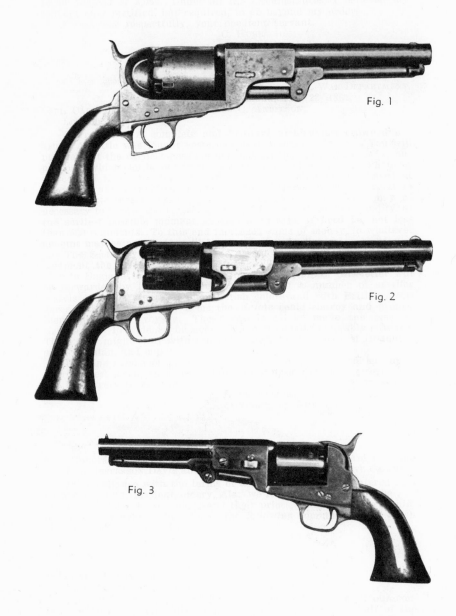

Fig. 1

Fig. 2

Fig. 3

Tucker & Sherrod Revolver, Colt dragoon model, 7½-inch barrel, part octagonal; .44 caliber, no loading aperture on right side of frame; rifled seven grooves right. Made at Lancaster, Texas, 1863-64. No marks except serial 103 on various parts.

Dance Brothers & Park Revolver, 8-inch barrel, part octagonal, .44 caliber, brass back strap, trigger guard and front blade sight. No rear sight, flat frame, no recoil shield. Made at Columbia, Texas, 1863-64. No marks except serial 95 on various parts.

Dance Brothers & Park Revolver, Navy size, 6-inch barrel, .36 caliber, part octagonal, flat frame, no recoil shield. Made at Columbia, Texas 1863-64. No marks except serial 83 on various parts.

son & Lester of Richmond. Samuel C. Robinson in 1860 owned and operated the Belvidere Planing Mills, in Richmond. Early in 1861 Robinson and Lester got together to start a revolver plant. A building was leased on the south bank of the canal near the Petersburg railroad bridge. Robinson seems to have been the purse and brains of the enterprise. Lester was the practical mechanic and foreman.

The *Richmond Daily Examiner* of June 9, 1861, said the factory had been started and "good revolvers are soon to be made there." Nowhere, however, do we find the statement that revolvers have been made. On September 23, 1862, there was an alarm of fire at "the pistol manufactory of Robinson & Lester under the Petersburg railroad bridge," but the loss was said to be slight.[35] On April 27, 1861, Robinson wrote the Advisory Council withdrawing his proposal to furnish 3,000 army or navy pistols of Whitney pattern to be delivered in 60 to 120 days at $18 each and proposed to make them at $20 each. This offer was accepted.[36]

Early in 1862, Robinson turned his attention from revolvers to carbines and organized the S. C. Robinson Arms Manufactory for making carbines on the Sharps model. If Robinson & Lester ever made any revolvers, both the records and the weapons have disappeared.

THE SHAWK & McLANAHAN REVOLVER

To find the background of most of the Confederate Navy revolvers made on the Colts model, we must go back to a Northern city several years before the War.

In Cincinnati were two men—Abel Shawk, of Pennsylvania Quaker parentage, and Charles H. Rigdon. Both were engaged in peaceful pursuits. Shawk was an inventor and maker of steam fire engines. Rigdon was a member of the firm of Rigdon and Harmsted, scale manufacturers. Both were mechanics of a high order.

Shawk sold one of his fire engines to St. Louis in 1855 and went there to demonstrate it. Rigdon had preceded him and started a scale factory in North Main street—the St. Louis Scale Manufactory. Rigdon was employed as engineer of the fire engine when occasion demanded.

---

[35] Richmond Daily Examiner, Sept. 24, 1861
[36] Official Records, Vol. LI, Part II, Page 48.

In 1858 Shawk petitioned the authorities of Carondelet, a suburb of St. Louis, to help him establish a factory for the manufacture of locks and fire engines. A plant was established there under the firm name of Shawk & McLanahan,[37] and it was while there that Shawk invented a rifling machine and started out to manufacture revolvers on a small scale. The result was the Shawk & McLanahan revolver.

The Shawk & McLanahan revolver is shown in Figure 2, Plate XXXIV. It has a brass frame, with eight-inch round barrel, .36 caliber, six shots, rifled seven grooves right. Marked on backstrap: "Shawk & McLanahan, St. Louis, Carondelet, Mo." and Serial 16.

It is entirely possible that Rigdon had a hand in the manufacture of these weapons, as he and Shawk were friendly. In any case, it is likely that both Shawk and Rigdon were largely influenced by the popularity of the imitation Colt revolvers sold by H. E. Dimick, noted gunsmith of St. Louis. These revolvers bear Dimick's name, but they probably were made for him by the Manhattan Arms Company, which made imitation Colts until the Colt firm stopped them.

Figure 2, Plate XXXIII, shows the Dimick Revolver, .36 caliber, six shots, 7½-inch barrel, rifled seven grooves right. Engraved on top of barrel is "Made for H. E. Dimick, St. Louis." and Serial 1470. Probably made for Dimick by the Manhattan Arms Company.

In 1863, Shawk, after failing to get a contract for the manufacture of muskets for the Union army (he was no Confederate sympathizer) sold his plant in St. Louis and returned to Cincinnati, and thus he passes out of our picture.[38] The plant, it is said, was used for the repair of Army muskets. Dimick, being more fortunate, got a Union contract.[39]

THE LEECH & RIGDON REVOLVER

Charles H. Rigdon became the ace revolver manufacturer of the Confederacy. His revolvers were the best made within the borders of the Confederacy. And if he did not manufacture more revolvers for the Confederacy than any other Southern maker, he was a close second in the quantity of his products.

---

[37] J. K. McLanahan was also a Cincinnati man.
[38] He died in 1873.
[39] Dimick was given a contract to make 1,000 sharpshooter rifles with saber bayonets.

This seems all the more remarkable when it is learned that the fortunes of war kept Rigdon and his plant always on the jump. From Memphis, he moved to Columbus, Miss.; thence to Greensboro, Ga., and finally to Augusta, Ga. He never was able to continue operations in one place as long as a year.

And he must have been an excellent executive and organizer, as well as a first-class mechanic, because many of his hands followed him from place to place.

In 1860 Rigdon went to Memphis and opened a scale shop. It is probable that he took his revolver-making machinery with him. In Memphis Rigdon met Thomas Leech, a former cotton broker, who had gotten the war fever and had started the Memphis Novelty Works to make swords for the Confederacy.[40]

Just about that time, according to newspaper reports, they were setting up machinery in the Eagle Foundry of Streeter, Chamberlain and McDaniel for the manufacture of Colt revolvers.[41] This may have been Rigdon's machinery.

It was in the Spring of 1862 that Leech and Rigdon entered into partnership . . . At first, apparently, their endeavors seem to have been devoted exclusively to the manufacture of swords. On May 1, 1862, the firm advertised a number of infantry and field officer's swords for sale at the Memphis Novelty Works, Main and McCall streets.[42]

On Thursday, May 8, Leech & Rigdon announced: "All persons having swords left here for repairs are hereby notified to call for them today, as we are going to start for Columbus, Miss., Friday morning" (next day).[43]

This was because of the advance of the Federal Army and the order of General Beauregard directing arms makers to leave the city, which put an abrupt end to the manufacture of arms in Memphis for the Confederacy.

When Leech & Rigdon moved to Columbus, Miss., they took their machinery with them. They settled on a tract of an acre and a quarter of land, which they had purchased in March from Thomas B. Bailey. The real estate transaction is recorded in Deed Book No. 33, page 48, Chancery Clerk's Office for Lowndes county, Miss.

---

[40] In the writer's collection is a long, straight, double-edged cavalry sword marked "Memphis Novelty Works, Thomas Leech & Co."
[41] Memphis Daily Appeal, Nov. 15, 1861.
[42] Memphis Daily Appeal.
[43] Memphis Daily Appeal.

There Leech & Rigdon remained until December, making swords, and maybe revolvers. In December the exigencies of war compelled them to move again. As the Federal cordon around the Confederacy began to tighten, Southern officials ordered all arms plants removed to the interior, where they would be safe from enemy raids. And so Leech & Rigdon packed up again and moved to Greensboro, Ga., about December 15.

They began operations in Greensboro and on February 2, 1863, they purchased from John Cunningham the Greensboro Steam Factory, more recently known as the Greensboro Mills, and from Edward T. Richter a triangular piece of land at Bush and South streets running west to the tracks of the Georgia Railroad. They paid $20,000 for the factory and $1,000 for the tract of land. Both sales are on record in the Deed Book of the Office of the Clerk of Greene County, Ga.

On March 6, 1863, Leech & Rigdon received a contract to manufacture revolvers on the Colt model for the Confederate War Department. But in December of that year, Leech & Rigdon dissolved partnership, the agreement of dissolution being dated December 13.

Thus the Leech & Rigdon revolvers, assuming that they were all made in Greensboro, were all products of 1863. It is entirely possible, however, that some of them, particularly those bearing the name "Leech & Rigdon" without the "C. S. A.," were made at Columbus, Miss.

It is apparent that Leech & Rigdon discontinued the manufacture of swords when they moved to Greensboro, because in an advertisement of April 21, 1863, Leech & Rigdon offer for sale sheet steel, solder, iron, brass and copper wire and leather belts, all material for the manufacture of swords.

Some of the first revolvers made by Leech & Rigdon were sent to Rigdon's old friends of the First Missouri (Confederate) Infantry, composed almost entirely of St. Louis boys.[44]

See Figure 1, Plate XXXV, for Leech & Rigdon revolver, .36 caliber, six shots, rifled seven grooves left. On top of barrel: "Leech & Rigdon, C. S. A." Serial 899. Carried by Col. Harry Gilmor, Second Maryland Confederate Cavalry.

Leech remained in Greensboro after the dissolution of the firm, but Rigdon moved on to Augusta, Ga.; probably taking his revolver-making machinery with him. In January, 1864,

---

[44] From letter of Capt. Joseph Boyce, of St. Louis, veteran of the First Missouri, and friend of Rigdon.

Rigdon organized a new firm, his partners being Jesse A. Ansley, A. J. Smythe and C. R. Keen, operating under the firm name of Rigdon, Ansley & Company.

The firm leased a building in Marbury street, at second canal level, and on March 13, signed a water-power lease with the Augusta Canal Company. And there were made the iron frame Confederate "Colts" which have the twelve cylinder stops, instead of the usual six. The earlier ones were marked "Augusta, Ga." but later they bore simply the letters "C. S. A." on top of the barrels and the serial numbers.

See Figure 2, Plate XXXV, for Rigdon revolver made at Augusta, Ga., in 1864. .36 caliber, six shots, rifled seven grooves left and with 12 cylinder stops. Marked on top of barrel: "Augusta, Ga. C. S. A." Serial 1582.

The firm had its troubles in Augusta, too. Ansley was conscripted for military service early in 1864. He was brought before the court on a writ of habeas corpus on April 19, but the court refused to exempt him. He appealed to the Georgia Supreme Court but again lost his case.[45] At the hearing on the writ, Captain Hudgins, ordnance inspector, testified that Rigdon, Ansley and Company were carrying out faithfully the terms of their contract with the War Department. Rigdon testified that the firm employed 60 hands and that Ansley's presence was indispensable to the business, but his plea was of no avail.

The mechanics of the Rigdon plant were organized into a defense battalion, for the munition makers of the South had to fight as well as work. They were known as the Rigdon Guards and were enrolled among the home defense troops of Augusta as Company C under A. J. Smythe as captain and Lieut. J. W. Poor. The Rigdon Guards took part in the battle of Griswold-ville, Ga., on November 22, 1864, when they were called upon to help defend another revolver factory, and Captain Smythe and several of the revolver-makers were wounded. However, there must have been some fight left in them, because in the Augusta *Constitutionalist* of December 2, 1864, we find this notice: "Attention, Rigdon Guards! The members of this company who are cut off from their command, whether furloughed or detailed, will meet at the pistol factory on Friday morning at 9 o'clock to be organized for immediate home defense. By order of J. R. W. Poor, First Lieutenant, Company C, Augusta (Ga.) Battalion. J. M. Wood, brevet sergeant."

---

[45] See Ansley vs. Starr, Laws of Georgia, November term, 1864, page 21.

Meanwhile, the pistol-making industry of Rigdon and Ansley must have lapsed. It is possible that the machinery was boxed and shipped to Macon late in November, when the powder works and machine shops were dismantled.[46] However, as late as February 21, 1865, we find an order of General Gorgas directing Colonel Burton to assume supervision over the operations at the Macon, Athens, Columbus and Tallassee armories, "including the contract establishment of Rigdon & Ansley at Augusta.[47]

And on January 24, 1865, Ansley advertised in *The Daily Constitutionalist*: For sale—One-fourth interest in the pistol factory; a very desirable paying investment. J. A. Ansley, 306 Broad street, Augusta, Ga.

The 12 stops on the cylinder which distinguish the Rigdon and Ansley revolvers was the application of an improved safety device brought out by the Manhattan Arms Company of Newark, N. J., in 1859. The original Colt safety consisted of a hole in the hammer face which engaged a pin projecting from the rear face of the cylinder between the cones. Later the hole in the hammer face was changed to a slot. These pins were easily damaged, and the constant strain on the cylinder bolt stop spring when the hammer was down on the pin usually resulted in a fracture after a short period. The extra slot in the periphery of the cylinder did away with the pins, released the strain on the spring and provided a positive safety by locking the cylinder with the hammer down between the capped cones.

The Leech & Rigdon contract, which was taken over by Rigdon, Ansley & Company, to manufacture revolvers for the War Department, is dated March 6, 1863, but the firm made revolvers before that. There is no documentary evidence to show how many revolvers they made, but we can get some idea by considering the serial numbers.

A check of all the Leech & Rigdon in private collections and museums shows that a few of them bear no name; others the name, but no "C. S. A." The highest serial noted on a Leech & Rigdon revolver bearing the firm name is No. 1393.

The Rigdon, Ansley & Company revolvers are, as said before, easily noticeable because of the 12 cylinder stops. Of all those checked, only one bears "Augusta, Ga." and the "C. S. A.," and that is No. 1582. The lowest serial with the "C. S. A." is

---

[46] The Augusta (Ga.) Chronicle, November 24, 1864.

[47] Rigdon returned to Memphis after the War and died there October 8, 1866, at the age of 43 years. It is said he intended to return to St. Louis, but was warned that Colonel Colt intended to prosecute him for using Colt patents.

No. 1,742 and the highest serial found is No. 2,330, which is in the Milwaukee Public Museum.

If these serials mean anything, they indicate a total output by Rigdon and his associates of at least 2,330 revolvers.

Apparently, the "C. S. A." on the Leech & Rigdon revolvers and the "C. S. A." on the Rigdon, Ansley & Company revolvers were made with the same die. And it is equally apparent that Rigdon numbered all his products consecutively, there being no overlapping of numbers in changing from one factory or firm to another.

THE SPILLER & BURR REVOLVER

One of the first revolver-making enterprises to get under way in the Confederacy was that of Spiller & Burr. The close connection of Col. James H. Burton with this firm adds to the interest in its career.

Edward N. Spiller was a commission merchant in Baltimore before the war. Being a strong Southern sympathizer, he went to Richmond before hostilities opened. There he formed a partnership with David J. Burr, a Richmond machinist and capitalist.[48] Their plan originally was to incorporate as the Richmond Small Arms Manufactory, but this name does not seem to have been used.

Much of the correspondence relating to the early days of the Spiller & Burr firm and its contracts with the Government are preserved in the private papers of Colonel Burton, and is reproduced here:

Early in November, 1861, Colonel Burton wrote to Colonel Gorgas, Chief of Ordnance, as follows:

COLONEL:

I have the honor to inform you that at your suggestion I have duly considered the subject of erecting a manufactory of revolving pistols of a model adapted to the requirements of the War Department and that I have decided to embark in the business provided the Department affords sufficient encouragement to me to do so, feeling confident that if I undertake such an enterprise with the mechanical skill and ability for its development and management now at my disposal, its success will be certain, and creditable to all concerned.

I have been induced to arrive at this conclusion in the expectation that the C. S. Government desires not only to supply their own wants at the present time, but also to foster and encourage the development of manufacturing enterprizes generally within the limits of the Southern Confederacy but particularly such as are essential to the

---

[48] David J. Burr was head of the David J. Burr Machine Company of Richmond and later of the Burr & Ettinger Locomotive Works. See Bruce's "Iron Industry in Virginia."

military defense of the Confederacy; and as there is not at the present time any establishment in the South prepared to supply revolving pistols in quantity, I look with confidence to the support of the C. S. Government in my proposed effort to inaugurate the manufacture of this much needed weapon on our own soil.

I propose to establish the manufactory in or near to the City of Richmond and have made arrangements to secure the most experienced talent to Engineer the mechanical requirements of the enterprize. I beg to enclose herewith a draft of the conditions and terms on which I propose to embark in the business and contract with the War Department for the supply of revolving pistols, to which draft I respectfully invite your attention and if consistent with your views, your favorable consideration.

Under a more favorable condition of surrounding circumstances I would be glad to propose more liberal terms, but in view of the present very high prices of materials and the almost impossibility of obtaining them of suitable good quality at any prices, together with the high rates of wages now demanded by mechanics, I feel that I would not be justified in embarking in the business on a Government contract for a less number than 15,000 pistols at the sliding scale of prices proposed: my expectation being that this Government order will reimburse me for my outlay in developing the enterprize without subjecting me to positive loss should I receive no further orders. I propose to build and erect all the necessary machinery myself and will have to provide the means for doing so from Southern sources so that the whole establishment will be purely Southern in its character and the result of Southern enterprize exclusively. Should the War Department be willing to award me a contract for pistols on substantially the terms and conditions I propose, I am prepared to commence making the necessary arrangements at once. A reply at your earliest convenience will oblige.

Very Respectfully, your obt. Servt.,

JAMES H. BURTON

Lt. Col. J. GORGAS,
Chief of Ordnance.

The conditions proposed by Burton provided that the War Department should aid the contractors by advancing $20,000 on the signing of the contract, $20,000 at the end of three months and a further $20,000 at the expiration of six months, making $60,000 in all. This sum, or a maximum of $100,000 if necessary, was to be returned to the War Department in two years by deducting 20 per cent of the value of each delivery of pistols. The pistols were to be paid for at the rate of $30 for the first 5,000, $27 for the second 5,000 and $25 for the final 5,000.

On their part the contractors agreed to supply the pistols at the rate of 4,000 by December 1, 1862; 7,000 by December 1, 1863; and 4,000 by June 1, 1864. The frames were to be of "good, tough brass properly electroplated with silver." Nothing is said about the model to be supplied.

Burton had selected Charles G. Morriss as the contractor, and Morriss' name appeared on the original document. Meanwhile, however, on November 20, 1861, Burton entered into an agreement with Spiller and Burr in which Burton agreed to obtain for Spiller & Burr a Confederate contract for 15,000 Navy revolvers. Burton also agreed to superintend the preparation of plans for machinery, the erection of buildings and the manufacture of the weapons.

And ten days later, November 30, 1861, the War Department made a contract with Spiller & Burr substantially the same as that proposed by Burton in his letter to Gorgas, with the exception that the contract specifies the revolvers are to be "Navy size of a pattern substantially the same as that known as Colts, the model of which will be supplied by the said War Department."

This contract is presented here in full because it is a typical Confederate arms contract:

Articles of Agreement made and entered into this 30th day of November in the year 1861 between the War Department of the Confederate States of America and Edward N. Spiller and David J. Burr, of the City of Richmond, State of Virginia.

Whereas

The said Edward N. Spiller and David J. Burr propose to erect and put in operation a Manufactory for the fabrication of Revolving Pistols with a view of supplying the same to the War Department of the Confederate States: and it is hereby agreed between the said Department and the said Edward N. Spiller and David J. Burr as follows.

1st. The War Department guarantees an order for fifteen thousand (15,000) Revolving Pistols (Navy size) of a pattern substantially the same as that known as "Colts" the model of which will be supplied by the said War Department.

2nd. The War Department agrees to aid the said Spiller and Burr by advancing to them the sum of twenty thousand (20,000) dollars immediately on the conclusion of the contract, the further sum of twenty thousand (20,000) dollars at the end of three months, the further sum of twenty thousand (20,000) at the end of six months from the date of this contract; in all sixty thousand ($60,000) dollars; the said Spiller and Burr to give satisfactory personal security in the sum of One hundred and twenty thousand (120,000) previous to any advance being made to them by the said War Department. The money so advanced to be free of interest provided the said Spiller and Burr comply substantially with their obligations under this contract, but in case they fail from causes within their contract, to comply with their obligations, they, (or their sureties) will be required to refund all the money advanced to them by the said War Department with interest at the rate of eight (8) per centum per annum to be calculated on the time the said Spiller and Burr may have had the use of the money so advanced. The money advanced by the said War Department to be refunded by the said Spiller and Burr by deducting not less than twenty (20) per cent of the value of each delivery of Pistols until the whole amount advanced is paid back which must be by the end of two years from date of this agreement.

3rd. The War Department agrees to pay for all the Pistols delivered under this contract that may be proved and accepted by the authorized Agent of the said War Department at the following sliding scale of prices viz:

For the first 5,000 Pistols the sum of $30.00 each.
For the next 5,000 Pistols the sum of $27.00 each.
For the last 5,000   ”   the sum of $25.00 each.

Payment to be made in bankable funds at the end of each calendar month for all the Pistols approved and accepted during the month less twenty (20) per cent for the full value thereof until all the money advanced the said Spiller and Burr has been refunded, after which payment will be made in full.

4th. The War Department agrees to give the said Spiller and Burr the preference over all others in case the said War Department may desire to increase their orders for Pistols of the pattern herein contracted for provided that the said Spiller and Burr may be prepared to execute such increased orders and that no other parties offer to supply Pistols of the same pattern at prices materially less than those herein specified, it being understood that the War Department desires to encourage and sanction as far as it can consistently the said Spiller and Burr in their proposed enterprize.

5th. The War Department agrees to cause to be inspected all Pistols presented by the said contractors for inspection as hereinafter provided for within two weeks from the date of presentation for that purpose.

1st. The said Edward N. Spiller and David J. Burr undertake to erect and put in operation at some favorable point within the present limits of the Confederate States of America a manufactory capable of producing not less than (7,000) seven thousand revolving Pistols per annum of the pattern previously agreed upon and of the model supplied to the contractors, the said Spiller and Burr, for the purpose of governing the supply.

2nd. The said Spiller and Burr undertake to supply the said War Department the 15,000 pistols herein contracted for, as follows viz:

4,000 Pistols by the 1st of December 1862.
7,000   ”   ”   ”   ”   ” December, 1863.
4,000   ”   ”   ”   ”   ” June, 1864. Or at an earlier period if convenient to the said Spiller and Burr.

3rd. The said Spiller and Burr undertake to employ none but the best and most suitable materials that can be obtained in the manufacture of all pistols for the said War Department but in the event of the impossibility of obtaining steel for the cylinders and barrels of the pistols herein contracted for, it is agreed that iron of suitable good quality may be substituted for steel provided that the efficiency and serviceableness of the weapon is not impaired by this substitution. It is further agreed that the Lock frames of said Pistols may be made of good tough brass if properly electroplated with silver.

4th. The said Spiller and Burr undertake to furnish the said War Department pistols of the best quality in accordance with the model arm supplied to them by the said War Department and to which model reference will be made in all cases of dispute that may arise between the Government Inspector and the said Spiller and Burr with respect to dimensions, quality of workmanship or other supposed deviation from the approved model weapon.

5th. The said Spiller and Burr undertake to submit all the finished Pistols manufactured for the said War Department for inspection and approval in accordance with special instructions defining the system of inspection and the tests to be applied in the examination of the finished arms the nature of which will be previously agreed upon and reduced to writing in duplicate. One copy of which will be placed in the hands of the said Spiller and Burr and the other copy to be retained by the said War Department.

6th. The said Spiller and Burr undertake to present the pistols herein contracted for at such point in the City of Richmond as the said War Department may designate in lots of not less than one hundred (100) at one time unless otherwise desired by the said War Department.

275

7th. The said Spiller and Burr undertake to supply at fair and reasonable prices such implements as the said War Department may hereafter require to accompany the pistols herein contracted for; also such spare parts as may be required for the repair of said pistols.

8th. As a means of securing the mechanical success of the proposed enterprize the said Spiller and Burr undertake with the consent of the said War Department to avail themselves of the practical skill of Mr. James H. Burton, Superintendent of the Confederate States Armory, Richmond, Virginia, who will give his valuable assistance to the engineering of the mechanical arrangements and details to such extent as will not interfere with his public duties and obligations.

In testimony whereof the Secretary of War of the Confederate States of America has signed his name and caused to be affixed thereto the Seal of his Department and the said Spiller and Burr have hereunto set their hands and seals the day and year first herein mentioned.

(signed)   J. P. BENJAMIN,
                       Secretary of War

(signed)   EDWARD N. SPILLER

(signed)   DAVID J. BURR

Certified twin copy

A building was leased in Richmond, but before the factory could be started it was decided to move it to Atlanta, Ga. Meanwhile, the project had met with difficulties. On April 20 there was severe criticism of Colonel Burton on the floor of the Confederate House. It was insinuated that Colonel Burton was neglecting the Government's business for his own.

Burton was a man of spirit and the first thing he did was to send his resignation to Gorgas. Gorgas was not the type of man to desert a friend in an emergency, and he promptly wrote to the member of Congress responsible for the attack and assumed all responsibility for Burton's connection with Spiller and Burr. And he added:

"I do not hesitate to pronounce him (Burton) the most competent and valuable officer we have connected with the Bureau and you will find that my high opinion of him is fully endorsed by the head of the Bureau of Ordnance of the Navy, Captain Minor."[49]

Gorgas also protested to the Secretary of War, George W. Randolph, who wrote to Colonel Burton declining to receive his resignation and saying:

"Your qualifications and services are too well known and too highly appreciated by this Department to permit its acceptance upon such grounds."[50]

---

[49] Burton's papers.
[50] Burton's papers.

FIREARMS OF THE CONFEDERACY

In June, 1862, Burton went to Atlanta to arrange for the removal of the Spiller & Burr plant to that place. There is no evidence that a single revolver was produced before that time in Richmond. The move was made in the Autumn of 1862, probably in September, if an item in a Richmond newspaper can be accepted as a hint.[51]

On October 21, Spiller had an advertisement in the Atlanta *Constitution* for a "comfortable dwelling" and the advertisement was signed: "Address through Postoffice or call E. N. Spiller at the Pistol Factory." Burr, apparently, remained in Richmond.

Writing on the official stationery of the Confederate States Armory at Macon, Ga., November 20, 1862, Colonel Burton accused Spiller of permitting drawings he had made for Spiller and Burr to get into the hands of the Haiman brothers of Columbus, Ga. His letter, about which more will appear later, was as follows:

> DEAR SIR: During one of my interviews with you at this place you consulted me with reference to your undertaking to manufacture and supply to other parties duplicate machines of those you have constructed from my drawings and plans for the purposes of your pistol factory. You will recollect that I objected to your doing so on the ground that it would be prejudicial to your own interests and unfair to me, as those drawings apart from your right to use them for the purposes of your own factory, are my property. It has come to my knowledge that copies of some of the drawings I furnished you have been made for the use of Messrs. Haiman Bros. & Co., of Columbus, Ga., who now have the copies in their possession.
>
> You will much oblige me by informing me at your earliest convenience whether or not those copies were taken with your knowledge and consent and if not who is the party guilty of this impropriety.
> Very truly yours,
>
> JAS. H. BURTON

On December 17, 1862, Colonel Burton wrote from Macon to Colonel Gorgas telling him that Spiller would arrive in Richmond shortly with a sample of their revolvers. "Whilst the sample is, in my opinion, the best that has been produced in the Confederacy, yet it is not quite up to my standard of excellence in several minor particulars," he wrote. This letter of Burton's is a lengthy and frank one, in which he tells of the trouble he is having in keeping Spiller "on the right track." Spiller, according to Burton, was a man "bred to purely commercial pursuits" and "at sea in manufacturing operations." In conclusion, Burton writes: "The pistols submitted by Mr. Spiller have been made after a pistol obtained from the U. S. which has

[51] Richmond Dispatch, September 29, 1862—Burr advertises for a brass moulder to go to Atlanta.

so far served as a model, but I think it will be well for Spiller and Burr now to get up a model pistol to serve as a standard of reference, the cost of which the Government should defray, as also that of a set of inspection gauges. All this I intend to do if you will authorize me. I have some doubt as to the caliber of these pistols being the same as that of the Colts Navy Pistol which I think is a trifle larger. As I have no means of testing this exactly I mention it in order that you may direct the point to be determined. I think the calibers should be the same and now is the time to make the correction if required."[52]

On January 1, 1863, Spiller wrote to Burton that he had returned from Richmond, where his pistols "were very favorably received" and that "Col. Gorgas seemed very well pleased with them." Spiller also said that upon examination his pistols were found to be a trifle smaller than the Colt's Navy and that he would have to change this, although it would give him trouble to do so.

Spiller also reported that his request for an increased price for the pistols had been favorably received by Gorgas.

This request of Spiller's had the endorsement of Colonel Burton, who, on January 6, wrote from Macon to his chief, Colonel Gorgas, as follows:

COLONEL:

I have the honor to acknowledge the receipt of your letter of the 29th Dec. on yesterday, on the subject of Messrs. Spiller and Burr's contract to supply pistols. In compliance with your instructions I shall at once proceed to draw up such scheme of inspection for this arm as may be necessary to secure the proper quality and which I will submit for your approval as soon as completed. With reference to increasing the price for this arm I think it would be well to consider the cost of removal of Spiller and Burr's Factory from Richmond to Atlanta and to include a just and fair indemnity for this outlay in fixing the new prices. The original prices as per contract were $30, $27 and $25: 5,000 pistols to be delivered at each of these prices.

I am informed by Major Cuyler that the Ordnance Department is now paying for revolvers made at Griswoldville, near the city, $50 each and from my own observations I know these pistols to be inferior to Spiller and Burr's. Taking into consideration all the circumstances and facts in connection with Spiller and Burr's enterprize, I think the following would be fair and just prices to be specified in the new contract you propose to enter into with them.

For the first 5,000 Pistols, $50 each.
For additional 5000 Pistols, $45 each.
For last 5,000 Pistols, $43 each and 20 per cent reduction on these prices on all pistols made and delivered after the raising of the blockade. I am aware that S and B purchased a quantity of steel and spalter when prices were much lower than at present but apart from this they have to purchase all other materials at present enhanced prices. It will be borne in mind that they are bound by their contract

52 Burton's papers.

to deliver pistols by specified periods and therefore it would be highly impolitic for them to rely upon the raising of the blockade with a view to purchasing materials at cheaper rates. They must secure materials at every opportunity and at the ruling prices. I will at once instruct Messrs. Spiller and Burr to prepare a Model Pistol to become the property of the C. S. Govt.
I have the honor to be Col.

This second contract made by Spiller & Burr with the Confederate War Department, a copy of which is in the Burton papers, is presented here in full because of the light it sheds on the difficulties the Confederacy had in manufacturing revolvers.

This Article of agreement made and entered into this the third day of March, 1863, between Col. J. Gorgas, Chief of Ordnance, in behalf of the Confederate States of the first part; and Edward N. Spiller and David J. Burr, of the City of Richmond, State of Virginia, of the second part

Witnesseth

1st. That whereas the said Edward N. Spiller and David J. Burr did on the 30th day of November, 1861, covenant and agree to deliver to the Ordnance Bureau of the Confederate States, Fifteen Thousand revolving pistols of the Colt's pattern Navy size at the following rates:

for the first 5,000 $30 each
for the second 5,000 $27 each
for the third 5,000 $25 each

to be delivered as follows:
4,000 pistols by the 1st December, 1862.
7,000 additional by the 1st December, 1863.
The 4,000 remaining by the 1st June, 1864.

2nd. And Whereas an advance of $60,000 was made to the said parties of the second part in sums and at dates as follows:
$20,000 on the 11th day of January, 1862
20,000 on the 3rd day of March, 1862
20,000 on the 22nd day of May, 1862
for which a penal bond in $120,000 was executed by the parties of the second part.

3rd. And Whereas the said party of the second part agreed and bound themselves to use in the Manufacture of the said pistols only the best materials, making the cylinders and barrels of steel if possible to be obtained and the lock frames of good tough brass electroplated with silver:

4th. And Whereas the said parties of the second part bound themselves to deliver an arm every way equal to the model arm supplied them by the War Department and subject to a system of inspection sufficient for the purpose to be mutually agreed upon between the contracting parties:

5th. And Whereas the professional services of J. H. Burton, Superintendent of Armories, was secured to the parties of the second part by authority of the Secretary of War to assist them in the successful prosecution of their contract as far as his official duties might permit:

6th. And Whereas it has become manifestly impossible in consequence of the great rise in prices of material and labor since the said contract was made, to carry out its provisions without loss which in a short time would entail pecuniary ruin upon the parties of the second part and whereas it is the policy of the Confederate Government to pay such rates as will enable the said parties of the second part to deliver the arms stipulated for under said contract within the time specified:

279

7th. Now therefore, it is agreed by and between the parties hereto that the execution of said contract is hereby suspended and the delivery of the 15,000 arms provided for shall be made on the following terms and conditions to wit:

600 pistols shall be delivered in the month of February, 1863, and thereafter 1,000 pistols per month until the deliveries are completed and the pistols shall be paid for at the following rates to wit: For the first 5,000, $43 each, being $13 advance over the price previously agreed upon, which advance includes reimbursement for expenses of removal of the factory of the parties of the second part from Richmond to Atlanta (sic) Ga.

For the next 5,000, $37.00 each, and for the last 5,000, $35 each.

Provided, that a reduction of thirty per cent shall be made on the price of all Pistols delivered after the raising of the existing Blockade of the Confederate ports on ninety days notice thereof except in the case of the first five thousand pistols delivered under this contract, on the price of which the reduction shall be twenty per cent.

8th. It is further agreed that payments shall be made on delivery, inspection and approval of the pistols one half in Confederate Bonds if the Government desire: that deliveries shall be made in lots of not less than 100 pistols at a time, that the amounts advanced as set forth in paragraph 2 of this contract shall bear interest at eight per cent per annum from the respective dates therein named and repaid: that the provisions of the former contract as recited in paragraphs 3, 4, and 5 of this contract shall remain in full force and virtue, except that the lock frames need not be electroplated. In witness whereof we have hereunto set out names and affixed our seals this third day of March, 1863.

Signed:

J. GORGAS, Col.   L S
  Chief of Ordnance
EDWARD N. SPILLER   L S
DAVID J. BURR   L S

I certify the above to be a true copy of the original contract.

JNO. P. MANICO, Clerk Ordnance Bureau

Approved.

March 5th, 1863

Signed: J. A. SEDDON, Secretary of War.

Writing to Burton about this new contract, Spiller calls attention to the fact that his firm had not agreed to make "Colt's Navy Pistol," as quoted in Gorgas' draft of the contract. He also expresses pleasure that the electroplating is left out. The pistol is described as the "Whitney model." Again, on February 14, in a letter to Burton, Spiller says in part: "We have no pistols yet, but I think will get some hundred together by the end of February." Later on, in the same letter, he says: "I enclose you a draft of what I have determined to adopt as to the loading lever. It is an improvement I have lately seen on a new pistol taken from the Yankees and the most complete I have seen. Works as well or better than Colt's, is handsomer and can be much more easily made than Colt's."[53]

---

[53] Probably the Starr revolver. This catch was also used on the Leech & Rigdon revolvers, but rejected when the 12-stop revolvers were made by Rigdon, Ansley & Company.

According to the terms of the second contract, Spiller & Burr were to deliver 600 revolvers in February, 1863 and 1,000 a month thereafter.

But again there was delay, and on March 5 Burton wrote to Spiller complaining about the delay in the first delivery of pistols. Burton said that Gorgas held him responsible for the prompt delivery of the pistols and that he thought the factory was in condition to produce them as per contract. But the progress was slow and it is hardly likely that more than 600 of the Spiller & Burr revolvers were produced. Finally, on January 7, 1864, the Government bought the Spiller & Burr plant, lock, stock and barrel, for $125,000.

In Colonel Burton's papers is this receipt:

C. S. ARMORY,
Macon, Ga., February 29th, 1864.

Received from Col. James H. Burton, Superintendent of Armories, one hundred and twenty-five thousand dollars to complete the purchase of machinery, tools, fixtures and materials belonging to what is known as the Spiller and Burr Pistol Factory at Atlanta, Ga., for which I am accountable under the Appropriation Ordnance Service in all its Branches $125,000.00.

CHARLES SELDEN, JR.,
1st Lieut. Artillery, Paymaster.

The brass frame, "Whitney model" Confederate revolvers are found both with and without the name of the firm on the barrel, "Spiller & Burr." Some of them have "C. S." marked on the right or on the left side of the frame. All bear the serial number, and the fact that the serials of those stamped "Spiller & Burr" and those not so stamped do not overlap indicates that all the Confederate "Whitney model" revolvers were made by Spiller & Burr.

Of these Confederate "Whitneys" in museums and private collections, there is no record of a "Spiller & Burr" revolver with a serial above 600 and no record of an unmarked one with serial above 1,400.

See Figure 2, Plate XXXVI, for Spiller & Burr revolver, seven-inch barrel, six shots, .36 caliber, rifled seven grooves left. On top of barrel: "Spiller & Burr." On left side of frame: "C. S." Serial 150.

It has been assumed that the unmarked revolvers were made by the Government after the purchase of the Spiller & Burr plant in February, 1864, but that is only conjecture.

The brass frames for the revolvers were cast by John Weigel, who lived many years after the war in Augusta.

THE HAIMAN REVOLVER

Almost identical with the Leech & Rigdon revolvers in form and design and mechanism, but of inferior workmanship are those revolvers made by the Haimans of Columbus, Ga. Despite the complaint of Colonel Burton that his plans for machinery for making the "Whitney model" revolver had gotten into the hands of Haiman, the Haiman revolver was a Colt model. It resembles the Leech and Rigdon in so many details that it is more than likely Rigdon supplied plans for the machinery.

The Haiman revolver is 13½ inches over-all, with a 7½ inch barrel, one third of which is octagonal. The barrel is rifled seven grooves right. The cylinder holds six shots of 36 caliber. The weapon has a brass handle strap, brass trigger guard and brass front sight.

See Figure 3, Plate XXXV, for Columbus Fire Arms Company revolver, rifled seven grooves right. On top of barrel in two lines: "Columbus Fire Arms Manuf. Co. Columbus." On trigger guard "C. S." Serial 46.

There were two of the Haimans—Louis and Elias— and they were brothers. They were natives of Prussia and settled in Columbus, Ga., when that place was a small village. At the outbreak of the war Louis Haiman was a tinner and owner of a small hardware shop.

In 1861, under the firm name of L. Haiman & Brother, they opened a sword factory. This factory was so successful that at the end of a year it covered an entire block. The first sword made at the plant was presented to Col. Peyton H. Colquitt, who was killed at Chicamauga. At its peak the factory is said to have had an output of 150 swords daily. Some of them were handsomely mounted with elaborately etched blades.

Later the firm made saddles, bridles, wagon covers, bayonets, tin cups and mess plates. As the war advanced, the firm undertook the manufacture of rifles and revolvers.

On August 26, 1862, the Haimans were given a contract by the Confederate War Department to make 10,000 Colt Navy revolvers. The contract was made with the Columbus Fire Arms Manufacturing Company, and the Government advanced $50,000 on the contract.

On April 1, 1862, the Haimans bought the Muscogee Iron Works, at Franklin and Oglethorpe streets, from the Columbus

Iron Works. And on a lot to the north of the iron works they erected a three-story brick building, 65 x 85 feet, which became the pistol factory.

On August 18, 1862, the Haimans advertised in the Columbus *Daily Sun*:

"Twenty-five good machinists wanted. Good wages and steady employment given. Apply to L. Haiman, Brother and Company."

And in the same issue of the paper appeared this notice:

PISTOL FACTORY

We intimated a few days since that there was a good prospect for the establishment in our city of a manufactory of Colt's celebrated repeaters. From the advertisement of Messrs. Haiman & Bro. & Co. in another column for Machinists, we are glad to chronicle the enterprise as a fact soon to be put in operation.

We hail this additional branch of industry to our busy little city as an omen of coming wealth, an extension of mechanical ingenuity and enterprise. It gladdened our hearts sometime since to learn that Colt's repeaters were being manufactured at Griswoldville, Ga., on the Central railroad. But we are more glad that now so enterprizing a firm as Messrs. Haiman, Bro. & Co. have brought this branch of industry nearer home. The establishment of this enterprize in connection with others in our City, suggests a thought for parents who have sons, and particularly widowed mothers. Place your sons in some one of these shops, and let them learn how to be useful to themselves, the community, and a blessing to you. There are now openings for industrious boys and youths through the length and breadth of the land which parents should not permit to pass unimproved.

On March 20, 1863, the Haimans advertised in the Columbus (Ga.) *Daily Sun*:

One hundred gunsmiths and machinists wanted. Wanted at our pistol factory in Columbus, Ga., good machinists and gunsmiths. Piece work will be given and all who remain with us over three months will have their traveling expenses refunded. Haiman, Brother & Company.

David Wolfson, of Columbus, Ga., in a letter to the late E. Berkley Bowie, of Baltimore, dated May 22, 1924, wrote that he was employed by the Haimans during the War and that—
"They made swords, sabers and army revolvers. We employed over 500 people. The first sabers made were for Clanton's regiment of cavalry of Alabama. We also made swords for officers. We had two people from Virginia who were experts in the manufacture of Colt's revolvers or pistols, they built machinery to make the several parts of these pistols and we made quite a large number of them in exact imitation of the Colt army pistol . . . The proprietors of the establishment were

Louis and Elias Haiman. Both are now dead. Elias Haiman went to Europe and sent material over here through the blockade. These works were carried on until the close of the War, when the Federals came in, as the last battle of the War was fought just across the river at what is called Alabama Heights, and they destroyed the works at that time—April 16, 1865."

In a later letter, Mr. Wolfson wrote to Mr. Bowie: "The pistol was made with round barrel and every part was made by machinery. The inspecting officer was a man in Captain Humphrey's office. I do not remember his name."

The Montgomery *Weekly Advertiser* of May 6, 1863, says:

> The Columbus papers state that Mr. Haiman, of that city, is now engaged in the manufacture of repeating pistols equal in every respect to the now celebrated Colt pistols.

And on May 11, 1863, the firm advertised in the Columbus *Daily Sun*:

> Wanted—a couple of boiler flues, 12 to 14 inches in diameter. Columbus Firearms Manufacturing Company.

That is the name which appears on the revolvers made by the Haimans. The lettering is on top of the barrel, near the breech and is in two lines, as follows:

"Columbus Fire Arms Manufacturing Co.

"Columbus."

The brass trigger guard plate is marked "C. S.," and the serial appears on various parts.

Col. James H. Burton says that he was in Columbus on January 19, 1864, to report upon the expediency of purchasing the revolver plant for the Confederate Government. He reported to General Gorgas and estimated the value of the plant at $80,000.

But, apparently, the plant was still being operated by the Haimans when the Federals destroyed it.

THE GRISWOLD & GRIER REVOLVER

In supporting the appeal of Spiller & Burr to the War Department for a higher price for the brass-frame "Whitney" model revolvers made by that firm, Colonel Burton, in his letter dated January 6, 1863, (see page 278) referred to the fact that the Government was paying "for revolvers made at Griswoldville, near this city, $50 each, and from my own observations, I know these pistols to be inferior to Spiller and Burr's."

These Griswoldville revolvers are those known to collectors as the brass-frame Confederate Colts. They are the commonest of all Confederate-made revolvers and, in many ways, the most interesting.

See Figure 1, Plate XXXVI, for Griswold & Grier Revolver, rifled six grooves right. No marks except Serial 2419.

For years collectors held the theory that the brass-frame Colts were the products of several firms. But the late E. Berkley Bowie, after an exhaustive investigation and study of these pistols, concluded that they were all the product of the same plant, the Griswold and Grier factory, on the outskirts of Macon.

Mr. Bowie at one time had probably had more of these brass-frame Colts than any museum or individual. He found that the brass in them was of the same quality and texture, that the rifling—six grooves right—was done with the same machine and that there was no overlapping of serial numbers.

The Griswoldville pistol factory was set up in the old Griswold Cotton Gin Company's plant. At the outbreak of the war, Giles G. Griswold went to Montgomery, Ala., where the Confederate Government was established before its removal to Richmond, and arranged for a loan under the Confederate law to encourage arms making. On his return trip, Mr. Griswold was taken ill and died in Columbus, Ga.

Mr. Griswold's brother-in-law, Col. E. C. Grier, then took over the business and managed the factory successfully. The pistol factory began operations about July, 1862, and continued until November 20, 1864, when the factory was burned by Kilpatrick's cavalry. The output at peak was five finished revolvers a day. The total number made was about 3,500, if the serials are indicative.

The Macon (Ga.) *Telegraph* of Tuesday, August 5, 1862, contained this article:

MANUFACTURE OF COLT'S REVOLVERS

We were equally surprised and gratified on Saturday last, at the sight of a Colt's Navy Repeater, made at the machine shops of Messrs. Griswold, at Griswoldville, about 12 miles from Macon.

The weapon had just passed the inspection of the Confederate Superintendent of Armories at this place, and a contract had been made for as many as the manufacturers could produce, which they thought would be, for the present, about 5 a day. The pistol, to our inexperienced eyes, was as well finished as those made by the patentee himself, and we have no doubt equally as efficient. These weapons are designed for the cavalry service.

The specimen before us was the first fruit of the skill and inventive ingenuity in elaborating machinery and tools for the purpose of men who had never seen a pistol shop, or a single tool or piece of machinery for making them. The machines now in use have all been contrived and built since last March, and the force of the establishment diverted from the manufacture of cotton gins to the making of Colt's revolvers, with the well-known resources and enterprize of this concern. We need not say the business under their hands will grow to meet any demand likely to be made upon them. . . . This is a strong illustration of the power of the South to supply her own wants. We certainly had no idea that a manufactory of Colt's pistols would spring up near Macon in 1862.

In an official report to the War Department dated November 15, 1863, Gorgas said in part:

"Revolving pistols are fabricated under contract at Macon, Columbus and Atlanta, Ga. The number produced is about 500 per month now."

Gorgas' references were to Macon (Griswold & Grier), Columbus (L. Haiman & Brother, trading as the Columbus Fire Arms Manufacturing Company), and Atlanta (Spiller & Burr).

On February 21, 1865, General Gorgas ordered Colonel Burton to assume supervision over the Griswoldville plant in the following order:

WAR DEPARTMENT, ORDNANCE BUREAU,
Richmond, Va., February 21st, 1865.

SIR:

Until further orders you are hereby assigned to the duty of directing the operations of the following named C. S. Armories, and you will be held responsible for the number of arms produced at each of them, viz:

C. S. Armory at Macon, Ga.
"   "   " Athens, Ga.
"   "   " Columbus, Ga.
"   "   " Tallassee, Ala.

In order that you may be placed in a position to properly assume such responsibility, the officers in command of the above named Armories have been instructed to receive and carry into effect your orders and instructions in all that relates to the conduct thereof, and they will be regarded as the orders and instructions of this Bureau, when not in conflict with previously received instructions therefrom.

You are hereby authorized to transfer employees, materials, machinery, tools and public funds from either Armory to the others, whenever, in your judgment, the public interest may be promoted thereby; reporting the same in each instance, to the Chief of Ordnance.

The contract establishments of Rigdon & Ansley, at Augusta, Ga., and of Griswold & Gunnison, at Griswoldville, Ga., for the manufacture of revolving pistols, are also hereby placed under your supervision, and you are authorized to make any arrangements with, or to render any assistance to the above named contractors, consistent with the public interests, which will contribute to the production of the largest possible number of arms at each of these establishments, always reporting, in each instance, to this Bureau.

The object desired to be attained in conferring these powers upon you is, the largest possible product in arms at the several Armories hereby placed under your control, and you will bring all your judgment

286

and energies to bear towards the accomplishment of this much-desired end. All orders for the officer in immediate charge of the Columbus Armory must pass thro Col. M. H. Wright.
Respectfully, your obedient servant,
                                        J. GORGAS, Brig. Genl.
                                        Chief of Ordnance.
Col. J. H. BURTON, Sup't & Inspr. of Armories,
     Macon, Ga.
Approved by order
     J. A. CAMPBELL, A. S. W.
22 d F 65

It will be noticed that Gorgas calls the Griswoldville firm Griswold and Gunnison, but it is usually referred to as Griswold and Grier.

Mrs. Ellen Griswold Hardeman, granddaughter of the elder Griswold who started the cotton gin foundry, in a letter to Mr. Bowie dated Macon, March 13, 1923, said the entire town of Griswoldville, including the factory, was burned by the Federals, excepting the Griswold and Grier homes.

General Kilpatrick reported that the pistol factory he destroyed was a very large and valuable one.[54]

THE TUCKER & SHERROD REVOLVER

The great State of Texas, far removed from the industrial centers of the South, made an earnest effort to supply its men with arms, including revolvers.

In the report of the Military Board of Texas to the State Legislature, dated November 4, 1863, it is stated that Tucker, Sherrod & Company, of Lancaster, Dallas county, had been awarded a contract for 3,000 revolvers "after the pattern known as Colt's, one-half army, remainder navy size."

The samples submitted, however, were not approved by the Board, and the contract was cancelled.

The firm went ahead, however, and made hundreds of these revolvers, as the following article in the *Texas Almanac*, Austin, February 28, 1863, bears witness:

SIX SHOOTERS

We were shown the other day a beautiful specimen of a six-shooter, manufactured in Dallas by Colonel Crockett, who has a large armory now in successful operation. The pistol appears in every respect quite equal to the famous Colt's six-shooter, of which it is an exact copy, with the exception of an extra sight on the barrel which we think is a decided improvement. We learn that Colonel Crockett has now

---

[54] Official Records, War of the Rebellion, Vol. XLIV, page 508.

400 of these pistols on hand, which he has manufactured within the last six months, and which he has offered to the Governor at remarkable low figures—not one-third of what they could be sold at by retail. We hope they will not be allowed to go out of the State, as it is notorious how deficient we are in arms for home defense.

The Tucker & Sherrod revolver is interesting because of its close resemblance to the Dragoon Colt. It had one peculiarity, however, in the absence of a loading aperture on the right side of the frame.

Figure 1, Plate XXXVII, shows the Confederate Texas Dragoon, made by Tucker & Sherrod. .44 caliber, 7½-inch barrel, rifled seven grooves right. No marks except the Serial 105.

The manager of the Tucker & Sherrod plant was Col. John Clannahan Crockett, an early-day Mayor of Dallas and at one time Lieutenant Governor of Texas. Colonel Crockett was of Irish stock and came from South Carolina. His grandfather was John Crockett, a soldier of the Revolutionary War.

Left an orphan when he was 14, Crockett studied law in South Carolina. He met with financial reverses and in 1847, with his wife, moved to Texas. He settled in Dallas in 1848, when it consisted of half a dozen rude houses and a saloon.

In 1857 Colonel Crockett was elected the second Mayor of Dallas. He was re-elected several times, but resigned in 1861 when he was elected Lieutenant Governor of Texas. His friends wished him to run for the Governorship, but he decided to devote his time and his energy to managing the pistol factory.

The Tucker & Sherrod revolvers, as is characteristic of many Texas hand pistols, are frequently found with stars and other devices in silver set in the wooden grips. Some of this work was done at the factory, evidently to make them sell more rapidly.

A. B. Rawlins, pioneer furniture dealer of Oklahoma, who was born in Lancaster, wrote an interesting account of his boyhood recollections of the Tucker and Sherrod pistol factory, the manuscript of which is in possession of the author.

In part, Mr. Rawlins said:

I was born in the town of Lancaster, Texas, in 1855, and at the beginning of the Civil War was probably six years old. Among the things that first impressed my mind was the erection of what we called the pistol factory on the banks of the branch on the west side of Lancaster, about two stones throw west of the public square. In later years I became aware that this pistol factory belonged to the Confederate States of America. My chief interest in boyhood days was the workmen. First in my memory was A. S. Clark, who was reputed by our community to be a Yankee. Next was a man named Fitzsimmons, not a native Texan, but a fine pattern maker; likewise Jim Cary, a scientific blacksmith, and another blacksmith, whose name was Sherrod. Both these men were native Texans. There was also employed in the factory a cousin of mine named Virgil Kellar, a young man about 16, who became very expert as a pattern maker.

My mother and two sisters lived some two years during the war at his father's home in Lancaster, and Virgil Kellar often brought his work at night and worked on it, and I recall his having exhibited a pattern of a six-shooter which he had made out of cedar. Virgil Kellar worked with the factory about two years and was called to the colors in Ross' brigade in the Trans-Mississippi division and never returned, having been killed in battle.

Fitzsimmons died in Lancaster. Cary moved to Dallas after the war and put up a carriage shop and factory and made carriages for years after the war. He served probably two years in my father's company, F, Ross' brigade.

A. S. Clark never left Lancaster to go into the Army and remained a resident of Lancaster until his death about 1905. In later years of my life, being related to him by marriage, I became intimately acquainted with him and have often heard him relate his connection with the pistols factory.

It seems he was brought to Lancaster from Michigan, or some other Northern State, by the Confederate States authorities and placed in charge as superintendent of the factory, was furnished all the money he could spend in its operation, with instructions to make all the guns he could, which he proceeded to do, and in carrying out these plans often recited to me trips he would make to Galveston for the purpose of purchasing steel and other supplies and necessary tools for the making of guns. I recall one item, files, of which he had difficulty in finding a sufficient number having bought the entire supply at Galveston.

When the war ended, of course the pistol factory ended, and who fell heir to it I am unaware. I can still see in mind's eye that old factory with its old melting furnace, filled with charcoal and scraps of all kinds of iron and pouring its liquid metal through a spout into a ladle to be carried by laborers to moulds.

All kinds of camp equipment, such skillets and lids, pots and kettles for army equipment as well as for the inhabitants of Lancaster at that time, who almost without exception had to cook on fireplaces, indeed I can remember when there were only one or two stoves in Lancaster.

As to the service rendered to the Confederacy by the factory I have no knowledge, but inasmuch as some 30 men were employed there and considerable machinery was necessary for the employment of such a force—considerable output must have resulted.

As to who fell heir to this machinery, I have no knowledge, but naturally suppose it fell into the hands of Mr. Clark. As to the ground on which it was located, I only know that four of the Rawlins family have owned the land at various times; first having belonged to Uncle King Rawlins, succeeding him was A. H. Rawlins, who sold it to A. B. Rawlins in 1892 and it was later owned by Henry C. (Stoker) Rawlins.

The old factory building stood for many years used for warehouse and storage purposes, and little by little fell into disrepair. There were for years parts of machinery, in particular a portion of the track upon which the molten metal was conveyed from one part of the building to another lying about the building. There were also many parts of old pistols, barrels, cylinders and parts of frames having the appearance of having been discarded by reason of imperfections in manufacture.

These reminders of grim realities were to be found for many years and the frame of the building was finally torn down about 1906 and used to make a barn on the same location and it is recalled in this connection that the original builders of the factory had built so well that great difficulty was experienced in tearing down the oak framing timbers which were mortised and tenoned at the corners with draw board pins, and when the foundation of stones were laid upon which the barn was to rest, there was found on the ground a heavy piece of cast metal bearing the form of the ladle in which it was cast, perhaps the last from the furnace, who knows. It was the size of a half bushel, and was used as a corner stone upon which to rest the barn.

THE DANCE BROS. & PARK REVOLVERS

Another Texas revolver, something like the Colt, but conspicuous because of its flat frame, without recoil shield, was made by the firm of Dance Brothers and Park, which started operations at Columbia, Texas. Near the close of the war the firm moved its factory to Anderson, about 70 miles northwest of Columbia.

The Dance Brothers & Park revolvers were made in both Army and Navy sizes.

Plate XXXVII shows the two types of the Dance Brothers and Park revolvers. Figure two is the Army size, with eight-inch barrel, part octagonal; .44 caliber, no rear sight and no recoil shield. No marks except the serial 95. Figure 3 shows the Navy size, .36 caliber, with six-inch barrel, part octagonal. No marks except the Serial 83.

The Dance brothers, George and William, are believed to have moved to Texas from Virginia and are said to have established the first machine shop in Texas. They began the manufacture of revolvers in 1863 at Columbia and the factory was burned by the Federals after the battle of Velasco, which enabled the Union gunboats to go up the Brazos river to Columbia.

It was to escape the Federals that the firm moved to Anderson, but it is not believed that any weapons were made at the latter place.

Not more than a dozen Dance Brothers and Park revolvers are known to be in museums and private collections, so that it ranks among the very rare Confederate hand weapons.

THE MANUAL OF ARMS FOR THE REVOLVER

There were a number of cavalry manuals published in the Confederacy and some of these included a manual of the revolver.

A Manual for Colt's Revolver was published by the War Department at Washington, being known as General Orders No. 8, June 25, 1855. This was included in *Cooper's Cavalry Tactics for the Use of Volunteers*, by Gen. Samuel Cooper, published in New Orleans in 1861.

Another Confederate cavalry textbook which had wide use in the Confederacy was *Cavalry Drill and Saber Exercise*, by George Patten, published by West & Johnston, of Richmond, in 1862.

Of all the great cavalry leaders of the Confederacy, only one—Gen. Joseph Wheeler—had the time and inclination to write a book of cavalry tactics. His *Revised System of Cavalry Tactics for the Use of the Cavalry and Mounted Infantry, C. S. A.*, was published in a small, cheap, paper-backed edition by Goetzel, of Mobile, in 1863.

The Trooper's Manual, Or Tactics for Light Dragoons and Mounted Riflemen, compiled by Col. J. Lucius F. Davis, and published by Morris, of Richmond, in 1861, contains the following "Manual for Colt's Revolver":

The preliminary instruction in the use of the Revolver should always be given on foot, but the following Manual will apply equally well either on foot or mounted. In the instruction on foot the trooper should be brought to the position of Guard in the saber exercise, so as to assimilate his motions to those he will execute when mounted.

In the following Manual for Colt's revolver, the term "holster" is applied equally to the holster of the saddle or its substitute on the belt.

The trooper being in position, the instructor will command:

"DRAW PISTOL."

1 time, 2 motions.

1. At the command, unbuckle the holster, seize the pistol by the handle with the last three fingers and the palm of the hand, the forefinger extended outside the holster, so as to be placed on the guard when the pistol is partially drawn, the thumb on the back of the handle.

2. At the command, "two" draw the pistol from the holster, placing the forefinger on the guard; raise it, placing the right wrist at the height and six inches from in front of the right shoulder; the barrel of the pistol perpendicular, guard to the front.

To load the pistol the instructor will command:

"LOAD IN SIX TIMES"—1 Load.

1. Place the pistol in the left hand, the little finger on the point of the key, the muzzle inclined to the left and front and upwards at an angle of sixty degrees to the horizon, half cock the pistol with right thumb, the right hand grasping the handle.

2. Let go the pistol with the left hand, turn it with the right and seize it with the left; the hammer between the thumb and fore-finger, the middle finger on the guard, the last two fingers and palm of the hand grasping the handle, and carry the right hand to the cartridge box and open it.

2—"HANDLE CARTRIDGE."

1 time, 1 motion.

Take a cartridge from the box with the thumb and first two fingers and carry it to the mouth.

3.—"TEAR CARTRIDGE."

Tear off the end of the cartridge with the teeth and carry it opposite the chamber nearest the lever and on the side next the trooper.

4—"CHARGE CARTRIDGE."

1 time, 1 motion.

Empty the powder into the chamber and press the ball in with the forefinger, seize the end of the lever with the thumb and two first fingers of the right hand.

5—"RAM CARTRIDGE."

1 time, 1 motion.

Bring down the lever with the right hand, at the same time turning the cylinder with the thumb and forefinger of the left, until the charged chamber comes in prolongation of the lever, ram home the charge and carry the right hand to the cartridge box, leaving the lever in the charged chamber.

Repeat as above until all the chambers are charged, and after charging the last one return the lever, the thumb and two first fingers remaining on the end of it.

6—"PRIME."

1 time, 2 motions.

1. Seize the handle of the pistol with the right hand below the left, turn it with the guard to the right, muzzle to the left and front and elevated sixty degrees above the horizon, and place it in the left hand, the little finger on the right point of the key; turn the cylinder to the right with the right hand until it clicks, and carry the right hand to the cap box and open it.

2. Take a cap, press it on the exposed cone, turn the cylinder again until it clicks, and carry the right hand again to the cap box.

Repeat the second motion until the priming is completed; then seize the pistol at the handle with the right hand, let down the hammer and bring the pistol to the second position of Draw Pistol.

To fire the pistol the instructor will command:

"READY."

1 time, 2 motions.

1. Place the pistol in the left hand, the little finger touching the key, the muzzle to the left and front, and elevated at an angle of sixty degrees to the horizon, the guard under, the thumb on the cock, the forefinger on the guard.

2. Cock the pistol with the thumb and return to the second position of Draw Pistol.

"AIM."

1 time, 1 motion.

Lower the muzzle and carry the right hand to the front of the neck, half extending the right arm, place the forefinger lightly on the trigger, close the left eye and aim horizontally.

292

"FIRE."

1 time, 1 motion.

Press the forefinger gradually, but quickly, on the trigger, fire and return to the second position of "Draw Pistol."

Should the instructor desire to have all the charges fired, he will give an intimation to that effect, and after bringing the trooper to the position of "Ready," he will command:

1—"AIM." 2—"FIRE."

Which will be executed as prescribed. After firing the first charge, the troopers will go through the motions of "Ready," "Aim" and "Fire," and so continue until the last charge is fired, when they will return to the second position of "Draw Pistol."

To load without observing the times and motions, the instructor will command:

1—"LOAD AT WILL." 2—"LOAD."

Load the pistol as prescribed. Prime and return to the second position of "Draw Pistol."

When the troopers execute the manual well, they will be instructed to come to the position of "Ready" as follows:

The instructor will command:

"READY."

1 time, 1 motion.

Move the right hand six inches to the front, at the same time lowering the muzzle to an angle of sixty degrees with the horizon, cock the pistol with the right thumb and return to the second position of "Draw Pistol."

The trooper having been well instructed in the manual on foot, should be made to repeat it mounted, first at a halt and afterwards at the different gaits, but the progress of instruction should be slow. Every trooper should be made to execute all the motions well at each gait before passing to a more rapid gait.

Aiming, and especially at rapid gaits, requires some remark. Aiming should be practiced to the right, left, front and rear. In aiming to the right, left or front at a gallop, or at speed, the trooper should rise a little in the stirrups and incline the body a little to the front; the arm should be half extended, and the body turned in the direction of the object aimed at. In aiming to the rear, the right shoulder should be well thrown back and the right arm extended to its full length.

Firing should, at first, be executed with the greatest care and deliberation. The target should be 8 feet high and 3 feet wide, with a vertical and a horizontal line, each an inch wide, intersecting at the height of 5 feet. The vertical line should pass through the center of the target. The troopers should be formed in front of, facing, and at a distance of 100 paces from the target. The firing should, at first, be executed at a distance of ten paces, but the distance should be gradually increased to 40 paces. A peg in front of the target will mark the point from which the trooper is to fire.

To commence the firing, the instructor will cause the trooper on the right to move five paces to the front, turn to the right, move 30 paces to the front, turn to the left, move to the front until he arrives abreast the peg in front of the target, then turn to the left and move to the front until he comes opposite the target, turn towards it, cock the pistol, aim and fire deliberately; then turn to the left, move 30 paces to the front, turn to the left again and pass to the rear of the troop, reload and take his place on the left of the rank.

To fire to the right the trooper executes what he did in firing to the front, except that he does not turn towards the target when he comes in front of it. To fire to the left the instructor causes the trooper on the left to execute, inversely, what the trooper on the right executed in firing to the right. To fire to the rear, the trooper on the right executes what he did in firing to the front, except that he turns from the target instead of towards it, and aims to the rear. The points where the troopers are required to turn in the exercise will be marked by pegs.

At first but one chamber of the pistol should be discharged by each trooper, and great care should be taken to guard against frightening the horses. The troopers should be cautioned to be gentle with them and soothe them when excited. When a young horse is very timid, he should be accompanied by one which has courage. When the troopers are sufficiently instructed in the exercise, and control their horses well, three or more targets should be used. They should at first be placed on the same line, and 100 paces apart; but the distance should be gradually reduced to 50 paces.

CHAPTER II

GENERAL CORRESPONDENCE COVERING THE ACTIVI-
TIES OF THE CONFEDERATE AND STATE GOVERN-
MENTS, AS THEY TOUCHED UPON THE SUPPLY
OF MUNITIONS OF WAR—FEDERAL REPORTS ON
THE CAPTURE OF ARMS & ARMORIES. LIST OF
CONFEDERATE ARMS MAKERS AND CONFEDERATE
FIREARMS PATENTS.

THE following correspondence is included here, as it not only gives a first hand account of many interesting events, but there is also a great deal of information for the student of the Confederate arms and collectors in general.

While the percussion system had superceded the flint in 1842 the early State reports indicate that there were many flintlock arms in store in the South, and that at the opening of hostilities many of the troops were armed with them.

Wm. H. Richardson's report to Governor Letcher of Virginia dated December 15, 1860, shows a total of 53,988 flintlock muskets and 3,293 flintlock rifles in that state's possession at that time, and while active steps were taken to convert these to percussion, owing to the urgent need of arms many original flints were issued in the early days of the struggle.

The report of W. L. Sykes, Adjutant General of Mississippi, to Governor John J. Pettus, dated Jan. 18, 1861, gives some interesting data and mentions the flintlock arms on hand belonging to that State. This report is also of particular interest as it includes an account of the so-called Whitney contract, under which Whitney was to furnish 1,500 Mississippi rifles to that State, but the arms when ready for delivery were found to be "old guns fixed up."

Governor A. B. Moore's letter of March 4, 1861 to Secretary of War Walker reports the number of arms in possession of the State of Alabama, but evidently includes only the modern arms purchased the previous year.

Double barreled shotguns early became a favorite weapon where the improved rifles or muskets were not available. The communications of May 18, 1861, between Walker and Gov. Pettus mentions these and they are referred to in subsequent correspondence a number of times.

This early correspondence also indicates the conflict that soon arose between the State and Confederate Government over the supply of arms and the raising of troops—Governor Joseph E. Brown, of Georgia, seems to have had more differences than any of them, but the need of arms and the confusion incident to calling the army into service gave rise to a number of arguments.

The letter of July 15, 1861, from Governor Pickens, of South Carolina to Secretary Walker reports that all of his arms have been issued except a number of flint muskets which he is having altered to percussion and rifled for service, and the letter of Governor Clark, of North Carolina, indicates the preparations under way for boring out, altering and otherwise making the ordinary hunting rifle as nearly uniform as possible.

An item of much interest to collectors of Civil War arms is the report of Governor Clark, of Texas, to the Senate and House of Representatives, dated Nov. 1, 1861. In this he states that Major Ben McCulloch had been appointed to purchase for the State of Texas 1,000 Colt revolvers and 1,000 Morse rifles but found it impossible to procure the rifles.

The letter of W. R. Hunt, Ordnance officer, to Secretary of War Benjamin, of March 3, 1862, again mentions double barrel shotguns and it will be noted that he reports Colonel Forrest, one of their most efficient cavalry officers, recommending it as the best gun with which cavalry can be armed, and cites the engagement at Fort Donelson where one discharge of his shotguns at close quarters scattered 400 of the enemy.

Secretary Benjamin's report to the President of February, 1862, gives a fairly complete history of the activities and accomplishments of the War Department in providing munitions of war and it will be noted that while the deliveries by the various contractors abroad amount to 91,000 stand of arms to be completed within two months, but 15,000 had reached the Confederacy. At the same time he reports contracts with home manufacturers to the extent of 66,500 muskets and rifles as being in the process of execution, and that the government armories at Richmond and Fayetteville were supplying muskets and rifles at the rate of 1,500 per month which number could be doubled but for the deficiency of labor.

The Act of April 21, 1862, covering the organization of the Partisan Rangers, as set forth in the General Order No. 30 indicates that all arms and supplies captured from the enemy by them were to be paid for when turned in, which was a great advantage to this class of troops, as the regular soldier was allowed nothing for captures made by him. General Order No. 9 of January 22, 1863, fixes the allowance of $1.00 per month to be paid to men enlisting into the service and bringing with them their own arms.

ADJUTANT GENERAL'S OFFICE,
Richmond, December 15, 1860.

His Excellency JOHN LETCHER,
 Governor of Virginia:
SIR: This report, which was due on the 1st day of November last, . . .
The armory buildings are now in course of preparation to receive the machinery for the manufacture of arms. As the buildings will all be required for manufacturing operations, the State will have to build quarters for the officers and soldiers, and probably an arsenal, without delay. The ground adjacent, now under lease to R. Archer & Co., would be sufficient and is appropriate, being a portion of the original armory property . . .
These companies have been armed as follows:
CAVALRY—Twenty-four troops have been armed with sabers and pistols; twenty-six with sabers only.
ARTILLERY—Eleven companies with 6-pounder field guns, mounted (in all twenty-four pieces), with implements and artillery swords; one company with six 12-pounder howitzers, mounted, and with horse artillery sabers.
LIGHT INFANTRY—Six companies with rifled muskets; fifty-six companies with smooth-bore percussion muskets; twenty-six companies with flintlock muskets.
RIFLEMEN—Three companies with long-range rifles and sword bayonets; twenty-three companies with percussion rifles; seven companies with flintlock rifles . . .
Arms, accouterments, and ammunition for the year ending September 30, 1860 . . .
TOTAL—62 gun carriages, 46 sponges and rammers, 6 ladles and worms, 4 bricoles and drag-ropes, 36 trail hand-spikes, 2 lead aprons, 38 ammunition boxes, 2 6-pounder caissons, 20 linstocks, 38 sets of harness, 50,000 pounds of powder in magazines, 226,917 ball cartridges of all kinds, 422 muskets, rifled; 2,659 muskets, percussioned; 53,988 muskets, flintlocks; 56,014 bayonets, 4,885 cartridge boxes and belts, 3,609 bayonet scabbards and belts, 72 brushes and picks, 416 ball screws and worms, 80 cavalry musketoons, 90 artillery musketoons, 31 sappers' and miners' musketoons, 725 carbines, 1,020 rifles, percussioned: 3,293 rifles, flintlocks; 94 rifles, Sharps; 246 rifles, Colt; 185 rifles (sword bayonets); 500 powderhorns and flasks, 111 pouches, 123 bulletmolds, 498 wipers, 698 screwdrivers, 1,317 pistols, revolvers; 1,347 horseman's pistols, 993 holsters, 3,675 cavalry swords, 236 cavalry cartridge-boxes, 703 artillery swords, 3,524 sword scabbards and belts, 3 bugles and trumpets, 31 drums and fifes, 6 colors.
Purchased since 1st of October, 5,000 percussioned muskets and 13 rifled 6-pounder cannon.

WM. H. RICHARDSON,
Adjutant General.

December 15, 1860.

FIREARMS OF THE CONFEDERACY

Montgomery, May 18, 1861.
Governor PETTUS,
   Jackson, Miss.:
   Can you give me two regiments for twelve months, armed with heavy double-barreled shotguns?

            L. P. WALKER.

Jackson, Miss., May 18, 1861.
L. P. WALKER:
   Two regiments at Corinth have arms and ammunition. I think we can send you two regiments with double-barreled guns, and know I could send you five regiments armed with muskets and rifles in ten days.

            JOHN J. PETTUS.

EXECUTIVE DEPARTMENT,
Montgomery, Ala., March 4, 1861.
Hon. L. P. WALKER,
   Secretary of War:
   SIR: Your communication of the 1st instant, inclosing an act . . . I am not prepared to say what course the state convention will take with regard to the arms purchased by the State under a late act of the Legislature, but am inclined to the opinion that they should be retained by the State, to enable her to meet any emergency and to protect and defend her citizens. The State has purchased within the last eight months about 9,500 stand of small arms, consisting of muskets, rifles, carbines, pistols, and sabers; also 700 kegs of powder of 28 pounds each, and 20,000 pounds of lead and 8,000 pounds of minie-balls; also 1,500,000 percussion caps and 100,000 fixed cartridges . . .
   Very respectfully, your obedient servant,

            A. B. MOORE.

EXECUTIVE DEPARTMENT,
Montgomery, Ala., January 14, 1861.
GENTLEMEN OF THE HOUSE OF REPRESENTATIVES:
   Events of the utmost moment have rendered it necessary that . . .
   At your last session the General Assembly made an appropriation for the purchase of arms and ammunition, under the direction of this department. I have purchased about 9,000 stand of small arms, 10 brass rifled cannon (6-pounders) and 2 columbiads, 20,000 pounds of lead, 700 kegs of powder of 28 pounds each, and 1,500,000 caps. The cannon have not yet arrived, but I am expecting them daily . . .
   The dispatch was sent from this place at 9 p. m., and the forts, forty miles from Mobile, were taken possession of on the next night, and the arsenal, some fifty miles from Mobile, was seized about daylight next morning, and they are now held in the name of this State by her volunteer troops. In the forts were some hundred cannon—32 and 24 pounder guns—and in the arsenal about 22,000 stand of small arms and 150,000 pounds of powder. Of the small arms about 2,000 were Mississippi rifles and the remainder muskets . . .

            A. B. MOORE.

FIREARMS OF THE CONFEDERACY

GENERAL HEADQUARTERS, STATE OF MISSISSIPPI,
ADJUTANT GENERAL'S OFFICE,
Jackson, January 18, 1861.

His Excellency JOHN J. PETTUS,
Governor and Commander-in-Chief Mississippi Militia:

SIR: Pursuant to an act of the Legislature prescribing the duties of . . .

The following is a list of the arms, etc., examined at the general overhauling that are in tolerable order and fit for use, viz:

Bayonet scabbards, 229, 75 of which were issued to the Enterprise Guards; cartridge boxes, pistol and musket, 315; rifle pouch and flask belts, 214; waist belts, 56; saber belts, 106; saber knots, 107; gun slings, 119; dragoon shoulder belts, 276; holsters, 60; rifle pouches, 116; powder flasks, 88; flintlock muskets, browned barrel, 160; flintlock muskets, bright barrel, 72; sabers, 106. Most of the cartridge boxes, sabers, belts, holsters, pouches, flasks, etc., have been distributed. The arsenal is in bad condition, the floor being worthless from dry rot, and the building totally insecure . . .

Fortunately for the State the quota for 1861, amounting to 319 muskets, was advanced by the Secretary of War in May, 1860, and was taken in U. S. long-range rifles with Maynard primer and saber bayonets, and amounted to 212 . . .

W. L. SYKES,
Adjutant General.

DIVISION HEADQUARTERS,
Harper's Ferry, Va., May 6, 1861.

General LEE, Commander-in-Chief:

GENERAL: I assumed command of this post on Monday last, . . .

As four thousand flints have been found here, I have taken the responsibility of ordering the one thousand flintlock rifles from the Lexington Arsenal, and also ten barrels of musket and ten barrels of rifle powder, as in my opinion the emergency justified the order. Should the Federal troops advance in this direction, I shall no longer stand on ceremony . . .

I am, general, very respectfully, your obedient servant,

T. J. JACKSON,
Virginia Volunteers, Commanding.

DIVISION HEADQUARTERS,
Harper's Ferry, Va., May 7, 1861.

Major General LEE, Commanding Virginia Forces:

GENERAL: I forward herewith a statement of the strength of my command at this post, . . .

Mr. Burkhart, who is in charge of the rifle factory, reports that he can finish fifteen hundred rifle-muskets in thirty days. I have, in obedience to the orders of Governor Letcher, directed the rifle-factory machinery to be removed immediately after that of the musket factory. My object is to keep the former factory working as long as practicable without interfering with its rapid removal . . .

I am, general, very respectfully, your obedient servant,

T. J. JACKSON,
Colonel, Virginia Volunteers, Commanding.

FIREARMS OF THE CONFEDERACY

HEADQUARTERS VIRGINIA FORCES,
Richmond, Va., May 12, 1861.

Col. J. A. EARLY,
Virginia Volunteers, Commanding, &c., Lynchburg, Va.:

COLONEL: Yours of the 9th instant is at hand . . . To the cavalry companies, which may offer themselves unarmed, it is recommended to provide themselves with double-barreled shotguns, buckshot cartridges, and pistols. The supply of cavalry arms and equipments here is nearly exhausted . . .
I am, &c.,

R. S. GARNETT,
Adjutant General.

RICHMOND ARMORY,
April 30, 1861.

General J. E. JOHNSTON, Virginia Volunteers:

SIR: On inquiry from the armorer here, I find we have on hand the following arms: Altered muskets, 1,500; U. S. flint-muskets, 6,000; English muskets, 300; Virginia altered rifles, 250; flint-rifles, 300; U. S. altered rifles, 50; Sharp's carbines (rifled), 93; Harper's Ferry rifles (sword-bayonets), 300; revolvers of all kinds, 170; flint pistols, 400.

I have the honor to remain, general, your obedient servant,

JNO. S. SAUNDERS,
Captain, Virginia Volunteers.

HEADQUARTERS VIRGINIA FORCES,
Richmond, Va., April 30, 1861.

Col. C. DIMMOCK, Ordnance Department:

Major General Lee directs that, with the knowledge of General Richardson, you will forward, in addition to the two hundred flintlock muskets for the volunteers of Kanawha Valley . . .
Very respectfully,

JOHN M. BROOKE,
Lieutenant, Virginia Navy.

HEADQUARTERS VIRGINIA FORCES,
Richmond, Va., May 27, 1861.

Col. J. A. EARLY,
Virginia Volunteers, Commanding, &c., Lynchburg, Va.:

COLONEL: The commanding general instructs me to acknowledge the receipt of your letter . . .
There are no cavalry arms here to issue, unless your companies would be willing to accept flintlock pistols, of which we have only two hundred and ten.
Very respectfully, your obedient servant,

R. S. GARNETT,
Adjutant General.

Richmond, May 24, 1861.

Hon. L. P. WALKER,
We can arm 5,000 troops with flintlock muskets.

JOHN LETCHER.

FIREARMS OF THE CONFEDERACY

Montgomery, April 20, 1861.

Armaments of Forts Moultrie, Sumter, and Castle Pickney (to which must be added the purchase made since by South Carolina) . . .

Small arms in hands of troops and at arsenals.—Rifled muskets, 1,765; percussion muskets, 60,886; muskets altered to percussion, 19,556; muskets (flintlock), 8,283; percussion rifles, 6,990; Hall rifles, 5,001; Colt rifles, 73; carbines, 735; percussion pistols, 2,408, and Colt pistols, 468; total, 106, 165.

The foregoing statements do not, therefore, exhibit the entire quantity of material on hand.

J. GORGAS,
Major and Chief of Ordnance, C. S. Army.

Lynchburg, Va., June 8, 1861.

Col. R. S. GARNETT, Adjutant General Virginia Forces:

COLONEL: I received your dispatch today, and answered it in the same way, . . .

Two companies have double-barreled shotguns, bought by their counties, but no sabers, and are but beginning to drill. There are two companies tolerably well drilled, with forty or fifty sabers each. One has ho guns, and the other a few. There are two other companies, one of which has about forty sabers and a few guns, just commencing to drill. There are about a hundred flintlock pistols, which have been gathered from old companies, a number of sabers, of old patterns . . .

Very respectfully, your obedient servant,

J. A. EARLY,
Colonel, Commanding.

Richmond, Va., July 4, 1861.

Governor J. E. BROWN:

SIR: Can you furnish a volunteer regiment—five companies mounted and five on foot? The mounted companies to be armed with breech-loading carbines, the foot companies to be armed with rifles. If agreeable and consistent, I wish you to give this regiment priority in the issue of arms and equipments.

JEFF'N DAVIS.

EXECUTIVE DEPARTMENT,
Austin, Tex., November 1, 1861.

GENTLEMEN OF THE SENATE AND HOUSE OF REPRESENTATIVES:

Your presence at the seat of government is at all times . . .

An ordnance of the convention appointed Maj. Ben. McCulloch to purchase or otherwise obtain for the State of Texas 1,000 Colt revolvers and 1,000 Morse rifles, or a like number of such other weapons of a similar character as he might approve and obtain. He entered promptly upon his mission, but found it impossible to procure the rifles. The pistols, however, were secured, and have been of great service in arming the regiment called out by the convention. The claim for these arms, which is about $25,000, is due to a citizen of the Government with which we are at war, and it will devolve upon the Legislature to determine upon its adjustment . . .

EDWARD CLARK.

FIREARMS OF THE CONFEDERACY

EXECUTIVE DEPARTMENT,
November 18, 1861.

GENTLEMEN OF THE CONVENTION:

On the 17th day of June last I transmitted to you a communication, accompanied . . .

Respectfully,

JOHN LETCHER.

[INCLOSURE]

Of the articles enumerated in Statement A there were issued from the 14th of June, to 1st of November, 1861, the following:

Flint muskets	9,905
Percussion muskets	4,514
Bayonets	14,682
Hall rifles	620
Flintlock rifles	74
Percussion rifles	56
Musketoons	7

Richmond, Va., March (April) 7, 1862.

General S. COOPER,
Adjutant and Inspector General:

SIR: I have the honor to report that under the authority . . .

I have no doubt they were organized into a regiment on or about the 1st of this month and are now enroute for the seat of war. Although I had some hesitation in receiving the fifth regiment, yet in doing so I feel sure that I did not exceed my authority. The men of the command are mostly armed with good double-barreled shotguns. Those not so armed have good common hunting rifles. A large majority are provided with good pistols and nearly all with large knives, well mounted on good, serviceable horses, and equipments which, together with the arms, have been procured without expense to the Government . . .

Respectfully submitted.

M. T. JOHNSON,
Senior Colonel, Commanding.

ORDNANCE OFFICE,
Richmond, Va., October 13, 1864.

Hon. JAMES A. SEDDON,
Secretary of War:

SIR: I have the honor to present the following general view of the operations of my department for the year ending September 30, and of its present condition and prospects. I refer briefly to the more important branches of supply:

SMALL ARMS—The chief supply has been from importations, which, since the loss of the vessels belonging to this Bureau, have been very light, not to exceed, say, on this side of the Mississippi, 30,000 during the year included in this report. The number manufactured is about 20,000 instead of 50,000 or 60,000, as I anticipated. This reduced product is due to the interference of military operations, both of the enemy and our own. The captures have been about 45,000 and the losses about 30,000, leaving a gain of 15,000. The stock of arms in the arsenals is about the same as it was one year ago. If we place the diminution of our military force at 50,000 men (including reserves, local forces, militia, &c.). the aggregate of their figures (30,000 improved plus 20,000 made plus 15,000 captured plus 50,000 less troops) 115,000 will represent the waste of arms during the year. About 20,000

FIREARMS OF THE CONFEDERACY

are now on the way from Europe and 50,000 more have been ordered purchased. A further purchase of at least 50,000 will be necessary for the coming year unless the operations of the armories can be placed on a permanent footing by declaring all skilled mechanics engaged on them absolutely exempt from military duty, attaching them permanently to the Ordnance Department, and encouraging in every way the growth of this class of workmen. I cannot lay too much stress on the necessity for legislative action on this point in order to give assurance to the workmen . . .

CAVALRY—Good cavalry arms are much needed. Here again the removal of an armory (for military reasons) and the want of work-men have crippled the Bureau . . .

Respectfully, your obedient servant,
J. GORGAS,
Chief of Ordnance.

CORRESPONDENCE AND REPORTS TOUCHING ON CONFEDERATE ARMS AND ARMORIES FROM SERIES I., OFFICIAL RECORDS OF THE REBELLION.

Vol. 6. Pg. 807

HEADQUARTERS DEPARTMENT No. 1,
New Orleans, La., January 15, 1862.

Hon. J. P. BENJAMIN,
Secretary of War:

SIR: I have the honor to acknowledge the receipt of your two letters . . . Through Mr. Dunn and other sources I have collected (by purchase mainly) about 900 small arms, half of which are double-barreled shotguns. After perfecting as far as possible the arming of the war men, I should propose to exchange the shotguns for some miserable muskets and carbines in the hands of twelve-months' troops. It would look badly to go into action with poor guns, while better ones were in our possession, merely because the men were not enlisted for the war. Besides, the war men generally are an inferior class of shots, while the twelve-months' men are nearly all well skilled in the use of arms, and should be intrusted with the best weapons. The rifles that I have collected have been cut off to equal lengths and bored out to the caliber of the old United States rifle (54th of an inch). (.54.)

Respectfully, your obedient servant,
M. LOVELL,
Major General, Commanding.

Vol. 7. Pg. 815.

HEADQUARTERS, Knoxville, January 1, 1862.
S. COOPER, Adjutant General, Richmond, Va.:

SIR: My brigade is . . .

When I organized these regiments I advised the War Department that I had 1,620 Tennessee rifles, and requested an order upon the ordnance departments of Nashville and Memphis to have these weapons remodeled. Of these guns, upon the orders issued in September last, I have received 520 with the saber bayonet attached. I have in addition to the above 200 muskets . . .

The Government shops in this place are now actively employed in repairing the guns collected at this post.

Very respectfully, your obedient servant,
WM. H. CARROLL,
Brigadier General.

FIREARMS OF THE CONFEDERACY

Vol. 8, Pg. 753.

New Madrid, Mo., February 20, 1862.

His Excellency, C. F. JACKSON, Memphis, Tenn.:

DEAR GOVERNOR: Colonel Pheelan took down 500 of your guns to be altered, and, with 100 taken down by Major Rapley some time ago, we have 600 now in Memphis or New Orleans. If these guns are to be repaired as badly as those which were repaired for the Arkansas troops I would prefer them as they are, even without bayonets. Those of the Arkansians have nearly all burst, the cylinder has blown out, or something else has happened, which has left them entirely useless. I hope you will state these facts to those superintending the work, as they are only making traps for our men.

Yours, most respectfully,

M. JEFF THOMPSON,
Brigadier General, Commanding.

Vol. 9. Pg. 461-462.

HEADQUARTERS,
Richmond, Va., April 20, 1862.

Maj. Gen. T. H. HOLMES,
Commanding, &c., Goldsborough, N. C.:

GENERAL: The demand for arms from all sides is so great and their scarcity so keenly felt, that I deem it proper to call your attention to the importance of making a judicious distribution of the rifles recently sent you. By a letter from General Martin to you, of the 16th instant, I am advised of the inability of the State of North Carolina to arm the regiments now in camp at Raleigh. I have written to him, urging that the State make all possible efforts by procuring private arms, &c., to arm them. The rifles sent you were of a very fine quality, and I suggest that you place them in the hands of the flanking companies of the regiments, and give the balance muskets or such private arms as can be procured. The rifles will thus be made to do much towards enhancing the efficiency of each regiment. If you can use them and desire it, I can order a number of pikes to be sent you. Owing to the lack of firearms some of these have been sent to nearly every army in the field, and, if well handled and wisely distributed, will undoubtedly do good service.

I am, very respectfully, your obedient servant,

R. E. LEE,
General.

Vol. 9. Pg. 426.

WAR DEPARTMENT, C. S. A.,
Richmond, Va., February 3, 1862.

Gov. HENRY T. CLARK, Raleigh, N. C.:

SIR: I have received your favor of the 1st instant . . .

I was compelled by stress of occasion to send 1,000 flintlocks to your last two regiments, but will immediately replace them by better arms.

I am, your obedient servant,

J. P. BENJAMIN,
Secretary of War

FIREARMS OF THE CONFEDERACY

Vol. 10. Pg. 413.

Richmond, Va., April 11, 1862.

Governor BROWN,
Milledgeville, Ga.:
Your dispatch received. Thank you for the promptitude with which you have responded to my request. Pikes and knives will be acceptable. Please send them to Chattanooga.

JEFFERSON DAVIS.

Vol. 13. Pg. 28.
Reports of Maj. Gen. Thomas C. Hindman, C. S. Army, of operations May 31, November 3, 1862.

Machinery was made for manufacturing percussion caps and small arms, and both were turned out in small quantity, but of excellent quality. Lead mines were opened and worked, a chemical laboratory was established and successfully operated in aid of the Ordnance Department, and in the manufacture of calomel, castor oil, spirits of niter, the various tinctures of iron, and other valuable medicines. Most of these works were located at and near Arkadelphia, on the Ouachita River, 75 miles south from Little Rock. The tools, machinery and material were gathered piecemeal or else made by hand labor. Nothing of this sort had been before attempted on Government account in Arkansas to my knowledge, except the manufacture of small arms, the machinery for which was taken away by General VanDorn, and there was neither capital nor sufficient enterprise among the citizens to engage in such undertakings . . .

A further supply, together with lead and caps, was procured from the citizens of Little Rock and vicinity by donations, purchases, and impressments. This ammunition, and that which I had brought with me was rapidly prepared for use at the laboratory established at the Little Rock Arsenal for the purpose. As illustrating the pitiable scarcity of material in the country, the fact may be stated that it was found necessary to use public documents of the State library for cartridge paper. Gunsmiths were employed or conscribed, tools purchased or impressed, and the repair of the damaged guns I brought with me and about an equal number found at Little Rock was commenced at once. But after inspecting the work and observing the spirit of the men I decided that a garrison 500 strong could hold out against Fitch, and that I would lead the remainder—about 1,500—to General Rust, as soon as shotguns and rifles could be obtained from Little Rock, instead of pikes and lances, with which most of them were armed. Two days elapsed before the change could be effected.

Vol. 13. Pg. 683.

Helena, Ark., September 28, 1862.

Maj. Gen. H. W. HALLECK,
Commanding Army of the United States:
GENERAL: For more than three weeks . . .
The rebels manufacture gunpowder, caps, and ammunition at Arkadelphia, on the Washita, about 60 miles from Little Rock . . .
I am, with respect, your obedient servant,
JNO. S. PHELPS,
Military Governor of Arkansas.

FIREARMS OF THE CONFEDERACY

Vol. 17—Part 1—Pg. 598.
Report of Col. James Deshler, C. S. Army, commanding Brigade.

UNITED STATES MILITARY PRISON,
Camp Chase, Ohio, March 25, 1863.

CAPTAIN: In compliance with instructions from the general . . .
These numbers I can only give approximately, as all of my papers,
returns &c., as well as those appertaining to the regiments, were
pilfered after the surrender; but I give these numbers from my general
recollection of the strength for duty in my brigade. A large portion
of my men were armed with double-barreled shotguns, rifles of mis-
cellaneous caliber, &c., there being only 315 Enfield rifles in the four
regiments.

Very respectfully, your obedient servant,
JAMES DESHLER,
Colonel, Commanding Second Brigade, Churchill's Division.
Capt. B. S. JOHNSON,
Assistant Adjutant General.

Vol. 17—Part 2—Pg. 18.
Corinth, June 20, 1862.
Hon. E. M. STANTON,
Secretary of War, Washington, D. C.:

Our forces under Major General Sherman have occupied Holly
Springs pushing his cavalry as far south as the Tallahatchie River and
destroying several railroad bridges. The enemy having appeared in
considerable force he fell back to Holly Springs. From captured tele-
grams it was ascertained that the machinery for manufacturing arms
at that place has been removed to Atlanta, Ga. Railroad will be opened
to Memphis by Monday and to Columbus by Wednesday of next week . . .
H. W. HALLECK,
Major General.

Vol. 17—Part 2—Pg. 388.
HDQRS. THIRTEENTH A. C., DEPT. OF THE TENN.
Oxford, Miss., December 6, 1862.
Col. T. LYLE DICKEY,
Commanding Cavalry Division:

Rest your horses and men where you are, and when sufficiently
recruited strike to the east and destroy the Mobile and Ohio Railroad
as much as possible. As stated by me in a previous dispatch it would
be a great strike to reach Columbus and destroy armories and machine
shops there . . .
U. S. GRANT,
Major General.

Vol. 17—Part 2—Pg. 622.
Richmond, Va., June 24, 1862.
Gov. JOHN J. PETTUS, Jackson, Miss.:

Your letter of 11th received. Your request for arms and buckshot had been complied with to the extent of our power. Have just
received some long-range rifles, from which a further supply will be
sent. Buck-shot might be supplied from Columbus; to be made if not
on hand.
JEFFERSON DAVIS.

306

FIREARMS OF THE CONFEDERACY

Vol. 17—Part 2—Pg. 627.

HEADQUARTERS WESTERN ARMY,
Near Tupelo, Miss., June 28, 1862.

Maj. GEORGE G. GARNER,
Assistant Adjutant General:

MAJOR: I have the honor to transmit to you (herewith inclosed) the consolidated statement of ordnance and ordnance stores at Confederate States Arsenal at Columbus and at ordnance depots at Tupelo, Verona, and Okolona, Miss.

The arsenal at Columbus being in its infancy the work necessary for public service is not at present prosecuted with the result adequate to emergency. At armory shop is employed 32 gunsmiths, 16 stockers, and 8 machinists for boring barrels and making and repairing tools; with this force, 50 arms a day can be repaired fit for service. At saddlery, 40 saddlers and harness-makers are employed; they are occupied in repairing artillery harness and in making new. At laboratory, 70 hands are employed; with this force can be manufactured about 20,000 cartridges for small arms and 500 rounds of ammunition, fixed in one day. The machinery for making percussion caps was at the time of my inspection in bad order, undergoing repairs, and in a short time the making of caps will be satisfactory, if only a supply of nitric acid can be procured . . .

H. OLADOWSKI.

Vol. 17—Part 2—Pg. 678.

HEADQUARTERS DEPARTMENT No. 2,
Chattanooga, Tenn., August 14, 1862.

Col. J. GORGAS,
Chief of Ordnance, Richmond, Va.:

SIR: I beg to call your attention to the arsenal at Columbus, Miss., and suggest a thorough inspection and overhauling. It is being expanded into proportions too gigantic for my notions of its importance, and thus far the results from the labors there have been insignificant compared with the means furnished. I am certainly indisposed to make any additions to the very large number of operatives now detailed from my command unless some results are to follow.

I am, colonel, very respectfully, your obedient servant,

BRAXTON BRAGG,
General, Commanding.

Vol. 17—Part 2—Pg. 723.

HDQRS. CHIEF OF ORDNANCE, DIS. OF THE TENN.,
Tupelo, Miss., October 7, 1862.

Maj. Gen. STERLING PRICE,
Commanding Army of the West:

GENERAL: I have the honor to report that in pursuance of your orders I have delivered over 8,000 stand of arms to Brigadier General Tilghman's ordnance officer at Jackson, Miss. Out of the whole lot on hand at present I think I can assort 500 or 1,000 stand of serviceable arms, mostly flintlock muskets, which I will retain for the present, having heard of your late desperate battle and fearing that you may need them to replace such arms as may have been lost on the field.

Believe me, very respectfully, your obedient servant,

THOS. H. PRICE,
Chief of Ordnance, District of the Tenn.

FIREARMS OF THE CONFEDERACY

Vol. 17—Part 2—Pg. 775.

ORDNANCE BUREAU,
Richmond, December 2, 1862.

Hon. JAMES A. SEDDON,
Secretary of War:

SIR: I respectfully return herewith telegram from Maj. G. U. Mayo, chief of ordnance for General Pemberton, to His Excellency the President, with your indorsement thereon . . .

There is a large number of arms at Columbus, Miss., needing repairs, and some time since I directed the commanding officer there to repair these as rapidly as possible and send them. This morning I have a telegram from him in which he says, "Am sending about 600 arms per week to General Pemberton."

In a letter just received from Lieutenant Colonel Oladowski, chief of ordnance for General Bragg's army (dated November 23, 1862), he says:

"To Atlanta, in addition to 2,220 arms sent previously, I forwarded 800 more, and by order of General Bragg I instructed Major Wright as soon as these will be repaired to issue them to General Pemberton, 500 of which are already forwarded.

Very respectfully, your obedient servant,

J. GORGAS,
Colonel, Chief of Ordnance.

Vol. 17—Part 2—Pg. 797.

December 16, 1862—3:30 p. m.

Lieutenant General PEMBERTON, Grenada:
The following telegram just received:

Columbus, December 16, 1862.

Captain HOOE:

Enemy fired on railroad train . . . No ammunition here at arsenal; must have 20,000 rounds musket and shotgun ammunition; also an additional force from Jackson or some point; cannot hold this place against 5,000 of enemy. My effective force only about 600 strong. All machinery is still at arsenal. Large amount of quartermaster and commissary stores here.

JOHN ADAMS,
Colonel, C. S. Army, Commanding.

I am about commencing a movement of troops from the point.

DANIEL RUGGLES,
Brigadier General.

Vol. 17—Part 2—Pg. 799.

Columbus, December 17, 1862.

Captain HOOE:

Copy of dispatch from Barteau forwarded; consider Barteau more reliable; hope to hear from him tomorrow. Arsenal machinery taken down and work stopped. Enemy not nearer than Okolona. All prepared for defense.

JOHN ADAMS,
Colonel, &c.

FIREARMS OF THE CONFEDERACY

Vol. 17—Part 2—Pg. 817.

Jackson (Columbus), Miss., January 1, 1863.

The inclosed is a report of all the troops at this post, except the ... Maj. W. A. Hewlett's battalion Partisan Rangers is stationed at Buttahatchee Bridge, 12 miles north of Columbus, on the Aberdeen road. They have 307 double-barrel guns and accouterments, 320 sabers and belts, 45 flintlock pistols, 8,320 rounds of cartridges, 4,320 percussion caps; all in good condition.

The arsenal, with all its machinery, works, stores, &c., is being removed from this post by direction of authorities at Richmond.

JOHN ADAMS,
Colonel, C. S. Army, Commanding.

Vol. 17—Part 2—Pg. 841.

INSPECTOR GENERAL'S OFFICE,
Jackson, Miss., January 18, 1863.

Col. CHARLES M. FAUNTLEROY,
Inspector General, Jackson, Miss.:

COLONEL: I have the honor to submit the following . . .

The small arms, all of which are in the hands of the troops, number 11,438; bayonets for same, 5,854. You will observe the great deficiency in bayonets. There is also a limited deficiency in the various commands occasioned by the recent arrival of troops and return of convalescents. The arms in use are of various calibers, embracing the Mississippi rifle, caliber .54; Enfield, caliber .57; Minie, caliber .58; the musket, caliber .69, and the Belgian rifle and British musket, caliber .70.

I am, Colonel, with much respect, your obedient servant,

E. J. HARVIE,
Lieutenant Colonel, Assistant Inspector General.

Vol. 18—Pg. 868.

HEADQUARTERS,
Wilmington, N. C., February 3, 1863.

Maj. Gen. (S. G.) FRENCH,
Goldsborough, N. C.:

MY DEAR GENERAL: The question of traverse against reverse fire . . . The bluffs in the city from old Robert Brown's house, near the shipyard, down to Frolick's sword factory, below the foundry, are occupied by several strong batteries.

Very respectfully,

W. H. C. WHITING,
Brigadier General, Commanding.

Vol. 21—Pg. 1040.

HEADQUARTERS DEPARTMENT OF NORTHERN VIRGINIA,
December 1, 1862.

Hon. JAMES A. SEDDON,

Secretary of War, Richmond, Va.:

SIR: About three thousand arms are required for this army. They . . .

I had hoped to supply the deficiency from captured arms sent to Staunton for repair, and many have been supplied from that source. There are now there 1,500 under repair, and 400 that were fit for service have been . . .

I have the honor to be, with great respect, your obedient servant,

R. E. LEE,
General.

FIREARMS OF THE CONFEDERACY

Vol. 22—Part 2—Pg. 871.

HEADQUARTERS TRANS-MISSISSIPPI DEPT.
Shreveport, La., June 16, 1863.
His Excellency the PRESIDENT: •
I have just received your letter . . .
My chief of ordnance has rented, with the right of purchase within two years by the Government, a tract of land in the suburbs of the town as the site for an arsenal. Machinery has been erected, a foundry established . . .
I am, with sincere respect and esteem, your obedient servant,
E. KIRBY SMITH,
Lieutenant General, Commanding.

Vol. 22—Part 2—Pg. 931.

Richmond, July 15, 1863.
His Excellency H. FLANAGIN,
Governor of Arkansas:
SIR: I have the honor to acknowledge yours . . .
You cannot regret more than I do the injury which has resulted from the removal of the machinery for the manufacture of small arms. It had been sent from Little Rock to Napoleon before I heard of its removal. Directions were given to send it back to Little Rock; and afterward, learning that it had been removed from Napoleon before the order was received, though it was promptly given, further directions were given to have it returned, and efforts were being made to do so when, by interruption of communication across the Mississippi, the last information I had of it was that it was on the 9th of this month at Jackson, Miss., and the ordnance officer said he should probably be compelled to send it back to Alabama.
I beg you to accept assurances of the regard and esteem with which I am, very respectfully and truly, yours,
JEFFERSON DAVIS.

Vol. 22—Part 2—Pg. 1003.

HEADQUARTERS TRANS-MISSISSIPPI DEPT.
Shreveport, La., September 11, 1863.
His Excellency JEFFERSON DAVIS,
President of the Confederate States:
SIR: I have the honor to inclose Your Excellency a copy of the proceedings of a conference called by me at Marshall, Tex., on the 15th ultimo.
Immediately on the fall of Vicksburg and Port Hudson, I felt that . . .
It is thought that Texas can and will put into the field from 15,000 to 20,000 men; has grain, bacon, and beef enough to feed the army and her people for at least two years; has four gun factories, making eight hundred guns per month; has metal (copper and tin) to make one hundred cannon, and gun wagons for like number completed and in course of construction; is making percussion caps; has two powder mills; has 30,703 pounds common powder, 28,635 pounds lead, 90,000 rounds fixed ammunition, and 6,232 pounds buckshot.
THOS. C. REYNOLDS,
Chairman.

FIREARMS OF THE CONFEDERACY

Vol. 22—Part 2—Pg. 1098.

Marshall, Tex., August 23, 1863.

According to the request of Lieutenant General Smith . . .
Extract from ordnance report of Cooper's Brigade.

Common rifles, old and worn	460
Shotguns, old and worn	1,078
Mississippi rifles	76
Sharps' rifles	42
Belgian rifles	12
Texas rifles	450
Maynard rifles	2
Muskets, old and worn	416
Enfield rifles, good	265
Minie rifles	20
Hall's carbines	4
Minie muskets	25
Colt's rifles	4

A large proportion of these guns are old, worn, and scarcely serviceable.

Respectfully submitted to the President. ,

J. A. SEDDON,
Secretary of War

Vol. 22—Part 2—Pg. 1140.

OFFICE OF CHIEF OF ORDNANCE AND ARTILLERY,
TRANS-MISSISSIPPI DEPARTMENT,
Shreveport, La., January 19, 1864.

Maj. J. P. JOHNSON,
Assistant Adjutant and Inspector General:

MAJOR: I am unable, from the absence of most of my officers . . .
I am putting up at Marshall, Tex., powder-mills and cap machines
which, when finished, will supply all that can be used; and the other
works, such as gunsmiths' and machine shops, foundries, &c., are being
put up at Marshall and Tyler, Tex., and also at this point . . .
The removal of the works from Camden, Arkadelphia, and Little
Rock, and putting up the necessary buildings and foundries, has
caused me to be very backward in my ability to meet . . .
I am, sir, very respectfully, your obedient servant,

THOS. G. RHETT,
Major and Chief of Ordnance and Artillery, Trans.-Miss., Dept.

Vol. 23—Part 2—Pg. 706.

CONFEDERATE STATES ARSENAL,
Atlanta, Ga., March 18, 1863.

Lieut. S. A. MORENO,
Acting Assistant Adjutant General:

SIR: In answer to the inquiries made . . . I have on hand here
about 2,071 flint-muskets, 2,086 per (cussion) muskets, 123 rifle
muskets, assorted, and 1,217 assorted arms, shotguns, sporting rifles,
old muskets, &c., in bad condition.
I received yesterday 168 damaged arms from army in Tennessee,
muskets chiefly. I am prepared to put in order from 500 to 600 per
week . . .
Very respectfully, your obedient servant,

M. H. WRIGHT,
Major, Commanding.

FIREARMS OF THE CONFEDERACY

Vol. 24—Part 3—Pg. 71.

La Grange, Tenn., February 27, 1863.

Maj. Gen. J. B. McPHERSON,
Seventh Army Corps, Mississippi River:

GENERAL: A Mr. S. Ruggles, with papers from you . . . He says that Jeff Davis is in Jackson, at the Railroad House, and has stopped the manufacture of arms at Columbus, stating that if they could "whip Grant they would have all the guns they wanted, and if they couldn't they would want no more made there."
Very respectfully, your obedient servant,

J. W. DENVER.

Vol. 24—Part 3—Pg. 219.
Statement of Wright, a refugee.

Corinth, Miss., ..., 1863.

General Ruggles and staff came north from Columbus to Verona . . . No troops to speak of at Selma, the largest arsenal in the South, except one in Georgia (Atlanta.)

Making all sorts of ammunition at Selma, but have made no guns. They are now sinking a pit for making guns of a large caliber; they have very large furnaces; hot-air furnaces, too, for brass pieces. Have any amount of iron; it comes from Montevallo, Talladega, and other places on Alabama and Tennessee Railroad. No powder-mill at Selma now in operation. They are making niter all along that railroad. Don't manufacture small arms at Selma, but are repairing many. Are doing nothing in way of manufacture at Columbus; only a sort of barracks. Heard of no movements toward Tennessee now.

Vol. 24—Part 3—Pg. 788.

C. S. ARSENAL,
Jackson, Miss., April 25, '63.

Maj. R. W. MEMMINGER,
Asst. Adjt. Gen., Dept. of Miss. and Eastern La.:

MAJOR: I am expecting a large quantity of heavy projectiles, field ammunition, small arms ammunition, 700,000 musket percussion caps, and 30,000 pounds powder from the Confederate States Arsenals at Charleston, S. C., Augusta and Atlanta, Ga., Montgomery, Selma, and Mobile, Ala., and have the honor to request . . .
Very respectfully,

PHIL STOCKTON,
Colonel, Commanding.

Vol. 27—Part 2—Pg. 859
Report of Maj. Gen. John G. Foster, U. S. Army, commanding Department of North Carolina.

HDQRS. EIGHTEENTH ARMY CORPS, DEPT. OF N. C.
New Berne, July 7, 1863.

GENERAL: I have the honor to report . . .
At this place (Kenansville) an armory was destroyed which contained some 2,500 sabers and large quantities of saber bayonets, bowie knives, and other small arms, a steam engine and implements for manufacturing arms . . .

FIREARMS OF THE CONFEDERACY

Vol. 27—Part 3—Pg. 872.

HEADQUARTERS ARMY OF NORTHERN VIRGINIA,
June 8, 1863.
Col. J. GORGAS,
Chief of Ordnance, &c.:

COLONEL: I reviewed today the five brigades of cavalry in this army, forming the division commanded by General Stuart.

My attention was thus called to a subject which I have previously brought to your notice, viz. the saddles and carbines manufactured in Richmond. I could not examine them myself, but was assured by officers that the former ruined the horses' backs, and the latter were so defective as to be demoralizing to the men.

I am aware of the difficulties attending the manufacture of arms and equipments, but I suggest that you have the matter inquired into by your ordnance officers, and see if they cannot rectify the evils complained of.

I am, most respectfully, your obedient servant,

R. E. LEE,
General.

Vol. 28—Part 1—Pg. 477.

HEADQUARTERS MORRIS ISLAND,
Battery Wagner, August 21, 1863, 2 a. m.

CAPTAIN: I have the honor to report . . .

My Whitworth rifle sharpshooters were comparatively inactive yesterday. I had intended to give special attention to them today, and made arrangements to have a large number of Enfield rifles firing upon the sap-roller . . .

LAWRENCE M. KEITT,
Colonel, Commanding.

Capt. W. F. NANCE,
Assistant Adjutant General.

Vol. 28—Part 2—Pg. 232.

Charleston, S. C., July 26, 1863.
Col. D. B. HARRIS,
Chief Engineer, Charleston, S. C.

COLONEL: It is desirable . . .

There are at the arsenal several thousand (about 3,000) lances or pikes, which could be advantageously used as Chevaux-de-frise in front of Battery Wagner, or palisades in the ditch; they could be obtained on a requisition. Please have the matter attended to at once.

Respectfully, your obedient servant,

G. T. BEAUREGARD,
General, Commanding.

Vol. 29—Part 2—Pg. 740.

September 23, 1863.

I will send 600 muskets to Captain Brenizer, Salisbury, and 200 or more rifles may be obtained at Asheville Armory, N. C.

J. GORGAS,
Colonel.

FIREARMS OF THE CONFEDERACY

Vol. 30—Part 2—Pg. 276.
Report of Lieut. John C. Harrison, Acting Ordnance Officer.

HEADQUARTERS WALTHALL'S BRIGADE,
Near Chattanooga, Tenn., October 15, 1863.
MAJOR: I have the honor to report that during the battle of
Chickamauga . . .
I would state that this brigade is mostly armed with Enfield rifles,
using ammunition caliber Nos. .57 and .58; that the caliber .57 was loose
and never choked the guns, while No. .58, after the first few rounds, was
found too large, and frequently choking the guns to that extent that
they could not be forced down, thereby creating some uneasiness among
the men using that number of ammunition.
Respectfully, your obedient servant,
JNO. C. HARRISON,
Lieutenant and Acting Ordnance
Officer, Walthall's Brigade
Maj. E. B. D. Riley,
Chief of Ordnance, Hindman's Division.

Vol. 30—Part 2—Pg. 571.
Report of Capt. William H. Harris, U. S. Ordnance Department,
Senior Ordnance Officer.

ORDNANCE OFFICE,
Cincinnati, January 1, 1864.
SIR: I have the honor to submit the following report in the relation . . .
The Knoxville Arsenal, established by the rebels, and commanded
by the rebel Major Reynolds, of the rebel ordnance department, consisted of a fine brick building, with storehouse, blacksmith's and car-
riage-maker's shops detached.
The engine and stores had been removed, but about 2,000 pikes or
spears and 2,500 pounds of crude niter were abandoned by them . . .
The machine for the manufacture of percussion caps at present in
use in the rebel army was invented by a citizen of Knoxville, and the
manufacture of this article was carried on to a great extent at the
Knoxville Arsenal before our forces took possession of the place. All of
these machines that were completed were taken away by the rebels . . .
I have the honor to be, very respectfully, your obedient servant,
WM. H. HARRIS,
Capt. of Ord., Senior Ord. Officer,
Dept. of the Ohio.
Maj. Gen. AMBROSE E. BURNSIDE,
U. S. Volunteers.

Vol. 30—Part 4—Pg. 494.
HDQRS. ARMY OF TENNESSEE, ORDNANCE OFFICE,
Chattanooga, August 13, 1863
Col. M. H. WRIGHT,
Commanding C. S. Arsenal. Atlanta:
COLONEL: Your telegraphic communication of yesterday having
been submitted to General Bragg . . .
It will be necessary to have ammunition of small arms of different
calibers for 40,000, being 10,500 caliber .577, 3,600 caliber .58; 12,000
caliber .69; 2,000 caliber .54; 3,000 caliber .53; 900 caliber .70; and for
cavalry arms as Sharps, Maynard, shotgun, Hall, Smith, musketoon, &c.
Very respectfully, &c.,
H. OLADOWSKI.

FIREARMS OF THE CONFEDERACY

Vol. 35—Part 1—Pg. 424.

HDQRS. DIST. OF WEST FLA.,
Barrancas, Aug. 12, 1864.

MAJOR: I have the honor to submit, in connection with my report...

At Columbus, Ga., all the machinery from the arsenal and Government workshops was, on the 25th of July, packed and sent via Macon and Millen to Augusta, where the extensive powder-mills are, and it is generally believed that Hood's army, if forced to abandon Atlanta ...

Very respectfully, Major, your obedient servant,

ASBOTH,
Brigadier General,

Maj. GEORGE B. DRAKE,
Assistant Adjutant General.

Vol. 38—Part 4—Pg. 782.

ARMAMENT AND AMMUNITION REPORT OF THE ARMY OF TENNESSEE, COMMANDED BY GENERAL JOSEPH E. JOHNSTON, for the week ending June 19, 1864.

ARMAMENT

Small Arms:

Caliber .69	5,369	
Caliber .58, .57	27,107	
Caliber .70	64	
Caliber .54	15,841	
Caliber .52	779	
Caliber .56	4	
Caliber .44	29	
Caliber .37	6	
Caliber .51	20	
Spencer rifles	58	
WHITWORTH rifles	26	
TOTAL	49,303	

Ammunition:

Rounds in cartridge-boxes
of men...........1,932,638

In wagons:	
Caliber .70	2,550
Caliber .69	250,941
Caliber .58, .57	893,757
Caliber .56	2,840
Caliber .54	625,993
Caliber .52	3,500
Caliber .37	630
Caliber .44	1,010
WHITWORTH	3,313
TOTAL	3,717,172

Pistols:

Navy	1,673
Army	1,248
Total	2,921

H. OLADOWSKI,
Lieutenant Colonel.

Vol. 39—Part 2—Pg. 774.

SELMA ARSENAL,
August 13, 1864.

Maj. Gen. D. H. MAURY,
Commanding, &c., Mobile:

GENERAL: Your telegram of this date has been received. There are no arms on hand excepting those which are being repaired. From twenty to forty of these, according to condition, are daily rendered serviceable; these will be all held subject to your order. All of the ammunition is so held, and is in quantity as follows:

315

FIREARMS OF THE CONFEDERACY

For rifles: *Cartridges.*

Caliber .57 and .58..ball.... 59,000
Caliber .56 (Colt patent, breech-loading)............do...... 7,000
Caliber .54...do...... 88,000
Caliber .52 (Sharps patent, breech-loading)........do...... 63,000
For dragoon pistol, single barrel, smooth-
   bore, caliber .54...do...... 21,000
For Colt army pistol...do...... 12,000
For Colt Navy..do...... 13,284
For Maynard rifle, caliber .52.............................do...... 7,100
For Maynard, caliber .37.......................................do...... 6,000
For French pistol (leFauchaux) caliber .472......do...... 52,800
For pistol, caliber .40...do...... 4,600
For musket, caliber .69..do...... 145,000
For musket or shotgun...............................buckshot.... 78,900
Very respectfully,

J. L. WHITE,
Lieutenant Colonel, Commanding.

Vol. 44. Pg. 63.
Report of Capt. Thomas G. Baylor, U. S. Army, Chief Ordnance Officer.
Memorandum list of ordnance and ordnance stores captured from the enemy in the campaign from Atlanta to Savannah, ending December 21, 1864:
   Ordnance and ordnance stores destroyed at Milledgeville:
      Muskets (smooth-bore, caliber .69) burned................ 2,300
      Ammunition for the same burned................rounds....... 10,000
      Infantry accouterments burned............................sets........ 300
      Lances, or John Brown pikes, burned....................... 5,000
      Cutlasses burned... 1,500

Vol. 44. Pg. 507.

HEADQUARTERS CAVALRY COMMAND,
Griswold, Ga., November 21, 1864.

Capt. L. M. DAYTON,
   A. D. C. and A. A. A. G., Mil. Div. of the Mississippi:
   CAPTAIN: This is the first time I have deemed it necessary to send . . . We have destroyed at this point a pistol factory and a soap and candle factory, both large and valuable.
   I am, Captain, very respectfully, your obedient servant,

J. KILPATRICK,
Brigadier General, U. S. Volunteers.

Vol. 46—Part 1—Pg. 1315.

Danville, Va., April 27, 1865—7.35 p. m.
(Received 8.25 p. m.)

   The captures at this place are, as far as reported, as follows: About 500 prisoners, 4 locomotives, 67 box and platform cars, 2 cannon, dismounted and mostly disabled; 3,000 shell, the iron work for 10,000 stand of arms, and the machinery for manufacturing muskets, &c., taken from Harper's Ferry and subsequently from Richmond. Of the prisoners captured 132 are sick and wounded in hospital.

H. G. WRIGHT,
Major General, Commanding.

Major General Webb,
   Chief of Staff.

FIREARMS OF THE CONFEDERACY

Vol. 47—Part 1—Pg. 180.
Reports of Bvt. Col. Thomas G. Baylor, U. S. Army, Chief Ordnance Officer.

HDQRS. MILITARY DIVISION OF THE MISSISSIPPI,
ORDNANCE OFFICE,
Goldsborough, N. C., April 7, 1865.

Maj. Gen. W. T. SHERMAN,
Comdg. Mil. Div. of the Mississippi, Goldsborough, N. C.:

SIR: I have the honor to inclose herewith a report of all ordnance and ordnance stores captured from the enemy in the campaign commencing February 1, 1865, and ending March 23, 1865. All of these stores were thoroughly destroyed except two Blakely guns, one 20-pounder Parrott, and one 12-pounder mountain howitzer, which were brought along by the army as trophies. I inclose also a list of the expenditures of ammunition by the army during the campaign.

Very respectfully, your obedient servant,
T. G. BAYLOR,
Captain of Ordnance and Bvt. Lieut. Col., U. S. Army,
Chief of Ordnance, Military Division of the Miss.

Yager muskets	960
Palmetto rifles	500
Remington rifles	100
Mississippi rifles	200
U. S. Muskets, caliber .69	3,440
Enfield rifled muskets	1,900
Enfield rifles (short sword bayo.)	2,000
Austrian rifled muskets (old)	500
Whitney rifles (old)	50
Springfield rifled muskets	100
Morse rifles (South Carolina)	400

Total rifle and muskets, serviceable	10,210
Musket barrels & stocks........unfinished	6,000
Pikes	4,000

Vol. 47—Part 3—Pg. 520.
HDQRS. DEPT. OF NORTH CAROLINA, ARMY OF THE OHIO.
Raleigh, May 17, 1865.

Major General HALLECK,
Richmond, Va.:

I have recovered a large amount of the machinery which was stolen from the Harper's Ferry Arsenal in 1861 and removed from the Fayetteville Arsenal before General Sherman arrived there last March. Where shall I send it?

J. M. SCHOFIELD,
Major General.

Vol. 49—Part 1—Pg. 323.
HEADQUARTERS DISTRICT OF EAST TENNESSEE,
In the Field, Camp at Statesville, N. C., April 13, 1865

I have the honor to report the following as the result of our . . ,

In addition to the arsenal at Salisbury, the military prison was being fitted up and was filled with machinery sent from Raleigh and Richmond, all of which was destroyed.

GEO. STONEMAN,
Major General, Commanding.

Maj. Gen. GEO. H. THOMAS,
Commanding Department of the
Cumberland, Nashville, Tenn.

317

FIREARMS OF THE CONFEDERACY

Vol. 49—Part 1—Pg. 350.
Reports of Bvt. Maj. Gen. James H. Wilson, U. S. Army, commanding Cavalry Corps, Military Division of the Mississippi.

HDQRS. CAVALRY CORPS, MIL. DIV. OF THE MISSISSIPPI,
Macon, Ga., May 3, 1865.

GENERAL: I have the honor to submit, for the information of the
. . . April 17, General Winslow destroyed the iron clad ram *Jackson*,
mounting six 7-inch rifles nearly ready for sea; burned the navy-yard,
arsenal, foundry, armory, sword and pistol factory, accouterment shops,
paper mills, four cotton factories, all the bridges on the river, 15 locomotives, and 200 cars, besides 100,000 bales of cotton and an immense
quantity of artillery ammunition.

J. H. WILSON,
Brevet Major General.

Brig. Gen. WILLIAM D. WHIPPLE,
Assistant Adjutant General,
Department of the Cumberland.

Vol. 49—Part 1—Pg. 484.
Columbus, Ga., April 18, 1865.

MAJOR: Having been assigned to the command of this city, I
have . . .
Niter-Works: Two hundred hands were here employed.
Muscogee Iron-Works: Consisting of foundry, machine-shop, small-
arms manufactory, blacksmith shop (30 forges), a large saddler's
shop, with tools, and 100 sets of flasks; one engine, 30-horsepower.
Columbus Iron-Works: Sabers, bayonets, and trace-chains were
here made; 1,000 stand of arms found.
Haiman's Pistol Factory: This establishment repaired small arms,
made locks, and was about ready to commence making revolvers
similar to Colt army.
Respectfully submitted.

E. F. WINSLOW,
Brevet Brigadier General,
Commanding Post.

Maj. E. B. BEAUMONT,
Asst. Maj. Gen.,
Cavalry Corps, Mil. Div. of the Mississippi.

Vol. 49—Part 2—Pg. 383.
Columbus, Ga., April 17, 1865—10 a. m.
Maj. Gen. E. R. S. CANBY, Mobile:
My forces captured this place by a most gallant attack 10 O'clock
last night . . .
General Winslow is burning navy-yard, foundries, arsenals, fac-
tories, armory, railroad stock, depots, and cotton warehouses today.

J. H. WILSON,
Brevet Major General.

ARMORIES, ARSENALS, GUNSMITHS, A PARTIAL LIST OF THE ARMORERS, AND ARMS DEALERS, IMPORTERS AND MANUFACTURERS OF THE SOUTH IN THE CIVIL WAR PERIOD.

ADAMS, Solomon—Master armorer at Virginia Manufactory and Richmond Armory.

ALABAMA ARMS MANUFACTURING CO., Montgomery, Ala., —Made Enfield rifles.

ALEXANDER, C. W., Moorfield, Va.—Invented breech-loading gun.

ALLEN & DIAL, Columbia, S. C.—Arms dealers.

AMES, J. T.—Purchased 1,000 altered muskets from U. S. Gov.

ANDERSON, Joseph R.—Head of the Tredegar Iron Works, Richmond, manufacturers of cannon and machinery for making small arms.

APALACHICOLA ARSENAL, Florida.

ARKADELPHIA, (Ark.) ARMORY—Machinery removed to Tyler, Texas.

ASHEVILLE ARMORY, N. C.—Made rifles for the State of North Carolina.

ATHENS, Ga.—Cook & Brother Armory.

AUGUSTA, Ga.—Confederate Arsenal.

BAKER, M. A., Fayetteville, N. C.—Altered a large number of Model 1817 flintlock rifles with lock plates bearing his name.

BALL, A. M.—Master Armorer at Harper's Ferry and Fayetteville.

BARBOUR, A. M.—Superintendent of Harper's Ferry.

BARKER—Name found on Confederate rifle lock plates.

BARRETT, J. B., Wytheville, Va.—Altered, repaired and manufactured guns using Harper's Ferry parts.

BARRY, Capt.—Purchased 80 altered muskets from U. S. Government.

BASTROP, Texas.

BENNETT, J. D., Col., Pittsylvania Courthouse, Va.—Given contract to alter and make muskets.

BILBERS, C., Pittsylvania Courthouse, Va.—Given contract to alter and make muskets.

BILLINGS AND HASSELL, ————, Texas—Made rifles for the State of Texas.

BRANDON, (Miss.) ARMORY.

BRIARSFIELD ARSENAL AND ARMORY, Columbus, Miss. —Machinery moved there from Memphis, Tenn. Arms repaired. Machinery removed later to Selma, Ala.

BRISCOE, W. S. N., Tyler, Texas—Made guns.

BROADWELL, L. W. ———— —Offered breech-loading carbine to C. S.

BURKHART, ———— In charge of Harper's Ferry rifle factory for C. S.

CAMDEN, (Ark.) ORDNANCE DEPOT.—Removed to Shreveport, La.

CANFIELD & BROTHER, Baltimore—Arms dealers and military outfitters.

CASTLEMAN, E., Alexandria, Va.—Arms dealer.

CHAPMAN, C.—His name appears on Confederate rifle lock plates. Probably a master armorer.

CHARLESTON, S. C.—Confederate Arsenal.

CHURCHILL, C. B. & COMPANY, Natchez, Miss.—Arms dealers.

CLAXTON, F. X., "late Consul at Moscow."—Offered breech-loading carbine to Confederate War Dept.

CLAYTON, E.—Connected with the Asheville Armory.

CLINTON, (La.) ARMORY.

COFER, Thomas W., Portsmouth, Va.—Invented and manufactured revolvers.

COLUMBIA, S. C. (see Palmetto Armory).

COLUMBIA, (Tenn.) ARMORY.

COLUMBUS, (Ga.) ARMORY—Confederate Ordnance Depot.

COLUMBUS FIREARMS MANUFACTURING COMPANY, Columbus, Ga.—Trade name of the Haiman Brothers revolver factory.

COOK & BROTHER, New Orleans and Athens, Ga.—Made Enfield model rifles and carbines, swords and saber bayonets for the Government. Largest private arms plant in the C. S.

COURTNEY & TENNANT, Charleston, S. C.—Arms importer and military outfitters.

DANCE BROTHERS AND PARK, Columbia and Anderson, Texas.—Made Army and Navy revolvers for the State of Texas.

DANVILLE, Va. (See Read Carbines)

DAVIS & BOZEMAN, Coosa County, Ala.—Made rifles for the State of Alabama.

DICKSON, NELSON & COMPANY (Shakanoosa Arms Company), Dickson, Ala, Rome, Dawson and Adairsville, Ga.— Made rifles and carbines for the State of Alabama.

DIMICK, H. E., St. Louis, Missouri—Not a Confederate arms maker, but made sharpshooter rifles for the Union.

DITTRICH, J. F., Mobile, Ala.—Gunsmith.

DIXIE WORKS, Canton, Miss.

FAYETTEVILLE, N. C.—Machinery for making the short rifle sent there from Harper's Ferry.

FEUCHTWANGER, E., Macon, Ga.—Arms dealer.

FISHER, W. B. & C., Lynchburg, Va.—Arms dealers and gunsmiths.

FOSTER, W. E., Norfolk, Va.—Arms dealer.

GALLAGHER, Dr. M. J., Savannah, Ga.—Invented rifle.

GARRETT, J. & F., Greensboro, N. C.—Made the Tarpley breech-loading carbine.

GEORGE, Asa, Charlotte, N. C.—Invented revolving gun.

GEORGIA ARMORY, Milledgeville, Ga.—Made rifles for State of Georgia.

GIRARD & COMPANY, Paris—Made LeMat revolvers.

GLADDING, W. H., Savannah, Ga.—Invented rifle.

GLASSICK, F., Memphis, Tenn.—Gunsmith and arms dealer.

GLAZE, WILLIAM & COMPANY, Columbia, S. C. (See Palmetto Armory)

GODWIN, Thomas W., Norfolk, Va.—Invented nine-shot revolver.

GREENWOOD & GRAY, Columbus, Ga. (See J. P. Murray)— Made rifles for State of Alabama.

GRISWOLD, A. B., of Thomas, Griswold & Company, New Orleans—Military outfitters.

GRISWOLD & GRIER, also called Griswold & Gunnison, Griswoldville, near Macon, Ga.—Made brass frame Confederate "Colts."

GRISWOLDVILLE, Ga.—Site of the Griswold & Grier revolver factory.

HAIMAN, Louis, Columbus, Ga.—Head of L. Haiman & Brother and the Columbus Firearms Manufacturing Company. Made swords, rifles and revolvers.

HALL, George H., Pittsylvania Courthouse, Va.—Given contract to alter and make muskets.

HEATH, A. J., Sumner Armory, Tenn.—Made rifles.

HENRY, George, Columbus, Miss.—Inventor of breech-loading rifle.

HILL RIFLES—Made first at Arkadelphia, Ark., and later at Tyler, Texas.

321

HODGKINS, D. C. & COMPANY, Macon, Ga.—Arms dealers, also made carbines, Springfield model 1854, for the Confederacy.
HOFFMAN, Louis, Vicksburg, Miss.—Arms dealer.
HOLLY SPRINGS ARMORY, Miss. (See Jones, McElwaine & Company)—Awarded first contract by C. S. to make rifles.
HOWLETT, J. W., Greensboro, N. C.—Inventor of breech-loading gun.
HUEY, James G. L.—Associated with Sturdivant in Alabama arms contract.
HYDE & GOODRICH, New Orleans—Arms dealers and military outfitters. Partnership dissolved July 1, 1861.
JOHNSON, Rev. Felix, Florence, Ala.—Inventor of revolver.
JONES, Peter—Armorer at Georgia Armory.
JONES, McELWAINE & COMPANY, Holly Springs, Miss., also Marshall Manufacturing Company.—Awarded first C. S. contract for manufacture of 30,000 rifles.
KEEN, WALKER & COMPANY, Danville, Va.—Probably made the so-called rising breechblock carbine.
KENT, PAINE & COMPANY, Richmond—Military outfitters.
KERNAGHAN, D., New Orleans—Arms dealer.
KNOXVILLE, TENN.—Arms altered for Confederate service. Confederate Ordnance Depot.
KRAFT, P. W., Columbia, S. C.—Arms dealer. Made swords.
KREUTNER, C., ————, Alabama—Made rifles for State of Alabama.
LAMAR, G. B. ————————. — Purchased 10,000 altered muskets from U. S. Government.
LAMB & BROTHER, Jamestown, N. C. (Also H. C. Lamb & Company)—Made rifles for the State of North Carolina.
LAQUEQUIST, Carl, Macon, Ga.—Inventor of breech-loading gun.
LEDBETTER, W., ————, Tenn.—Made muskets for State of Tennessee.
LEECH & RIGDON, Memphis, Tenn., Greensboro, Ga.—Made imitation Colt navy revolvers for C. S.
LEONARD, Charles, Petersburg, Va.—Arms dealer.
LEYDEN, Maj. Austin ————————. — Inventor of breech-loading gun.
LIGON, E. T., Demopolis, Ala.—Invented breech-loading pistol.
LINCOLN, Thomas B., ————, Texas—Invented gun.

LITTLE ROCK (Ark.) ARSENAL—Machinery removed to Tyler, Texas.

LONDON ARMOURY COMPANY—Supplied C. S. with large quantity Enfield rifles and Kerr revolvers.

LYNCHBURG, Va.—Confederate Ordnance Depot.

MACON, Ga.—Confederate Arsenal.

MARSHALL, J. H., Columbus, Ga.—Gunsmith.

MAXWELL, A. L. & CO., Knoxville, Tenn.—Made muskets for State of Tennessee.

McELWAINE, W. S., Holly Springs, Miss. (See Jones, McElwaine & Co.)

McLEAN ———— Associated with Zuccarelle in Pulaski Armory.

McNEILL, Thomas—Organized company in Richmond for making of breech-loading carbine.

McRAE, Colin—Started works at Selma, Ala.

MEMPHIS (Tenn.) ARMS COMPANY—Incorporated in 1861, but never operated.

MENDENHALL, JONES & GARDNER, Jamestown, N. C.— Made rifles for State of North Carolina.

MILLS, Benjamin—Assistant armorer at Harper's Ferry and accompanied the machinery to Fayetteville.

MITCHELL & TYLER, Richmond, Va.—Military outfitters.

MOBILE, Ala.—Confederate Ordnance Depot.

MONDAY, W. S., Tenn.—Made guns for C. S.

MONTGOMERY, Ala.—Confederate Ordnance Depot.

MONTGOMERY ARSENAL, Ala.—Guns altered to percussion.

MORSE, George W., Nashville and Greenville, S. C.—Made breech-loading carbines and muskets at the State Works, Greenville.

MORSE, Thomas, Richmond, Va.—Invented breech-loading gun.

MOUNT VERNON, ALA.—Confederate Arsenal.

MURRAY, J. P., Columbus, Ga.—Gunsmith, altered and repaired guns for C. S.; later master armorer for Greenwood and Gray's rifle factory.

OLLIS & TOULMIN, Mobile, Ala.—Arms dealers.

O'NEAL, ————, Tenn.—Made rifles.

PAERACH, Adalbert, New Orleans—Inventor of breech-loading musket.

PALMETTO ARMORY, Columbia, S. C.—Made muskets, rifles and pistols for the State of South Carolina, in 1852-1853. Altered and repaired arms, 1861-65.

PARK, LYONS & COMPANY, Mobile, Ala.—Arms dealers.
PECK & BOWMAN, Atlanta, Ga.—Arms dealers and gunsmiths.
PETERSON, W. & COMPANY, Richmond, Va.—Gunsmith.
POLLEYS, Capt. George S.—Superintendent Tyler Armory.
PULLIAM, Col. Robert William—Organized Asheville Armory.
RADCLIFFE, T. W., Columbia, S. C.—Arms dealer and importer.
READ, John B.—Patented muzzle-loading firearms and projectiles.
READ, N. T.—Patented breech-loading firearms.
READ, R. H.—Connected with Holly Springs Armory.
RIGGINS, Thomas—Gunsmith; worked at Knoxville on alterations.
ROBINSON, ADAMS & COMPANY, Richmond—Arms dealers.
ROBINSON, S. C., ARMS MANUFACTORY, Richmond, Va.—Made breech-loading carbines on the Sharps model for C. S.
ROBINSON & LESTER, Richmond, Va.—Established pistol factory, character and quantity of output, if any, unknown.
RODGER & BOWEN, Augusta, Ga.—Arms dealers.
ROGERS, E. H., Augusta, Ga.—Arms dealer.
S. & K.—Mark of an English firm, unidentified, which supplied the C. S. with large quantities of war munitions.
SCHNEIDER & GLASSICK, Memphis, Tenn.—Arms dealers; made model revolver in 1861.
SELMA, Ala.—Confederate Ordnance Depot.
SHAKANOOSA ARMS COMPANY (See Dickson, Nelson & Co.)
SHAWK & McLANAHAN, Carondelet, St. Louis, Mo.—Made revolvers before the War, solicited Union contract, but was refused.
SHELTON, ———— Foreman of one of the Tallassee Armory shops.
SHEPARD, MAXWELL & HOYT, Knoxville, Tenn. (See A. L. Maxwell & Co.)
SHORT, BISCO & COMPANY, Tyler, Texas—Given contract to make 5,000 Mississippi rifles for the State of Texas.
SHORT, J. S., Tyler, Texas—Connected with the rifle plant at Tyler, Tex.
SHRIVER, G. B., ————, Alabama (?)—Inventor of the Confederate carbine on the Maynard model, commonly and erroneously known as the Confederate "Perry."
SIBERT, Lorenzo, Staunton, Va.—Inventor of the Sibert repeating rifle.

SLOAT, J. P., Richmond, Va.—Proprietor of Sloat's gun factory.

SMITH, A. J., Augusta, Ga.—Member of the firm of Rigdon, Ansley and Company, makers of the 12-stop Confederate "Colts."

SMITH, RHODES & COMPANY, Richmond—Arms dealers.

SOWERS, E. N., Danville, Va.—Repaired arms for C. S.

SPENCE, E. B., Richmond, Va.—Arms dealer.

SPILLER & BURR, Atlanta, Ga.—Made revolvers on the Whitney model with brass frame.

SPRATTY, W. S., Norfolk, Va.—Arms dealer.

STAUNTON, Va.—Arms repaired.

STREET & HUNGERFORD, Memphis, Tenn.—Repaired and made guns.

STREETER, McDANIEL & CHAMBERLAND, Memphis, Tenn.—Planned in 1861 to make revolvers.

STURDIVANT, L. G., Talladega, Ala.—Given contract to make rifles for State of Alabama.

SUMNER ARMORY, Tenn.

SUTER, C. & COMPANY, —————————. — Made rifles for State of Alabama.

SUTHERLAND, Samuel, Richmond—Gunsmith and arms dealer, maker of fine sporting rifles and pistols before the War. Altered and repaired thousands of arms for the C. S. Known locally as the "Armorer of the Confederacy."

SWIFT, W. C. N.—Purchased 480 altered muskets from U. S. Government.

TALLADEGA, Ala.—Two small gun plants there.

TALLASSEE, Ala.—Site of the Confederate carbine works.

TANNER, N. B., Bastrop, Texas—Given contract to make rifles for State of Texas.

TARPLEY, J. H., Greensboro, N. C.—Inventor of Tarpley breech-loading carbine.

TODD, George, Austin, Texas and Montgomery, Ala.—Armsmith, worked on revolvers at Tucker, Sherrod & Company's plant and made rifles at Montgomery, Ala., in 1864.

TUCKER, SHERROD & COMPANY, Lancaster, Texas—Made revolvers on the Colt dragoon model for the State of Texas.

TYLER, (Tex.) ARMORY—Made rifles.

UNION MANUFACTURING COMPANY, Richmond, Va.—Also known as Sloat's Rifle Factory. Started early in 1861.

VAN WART SON & COMPANY, London—Supplied the C. S. with large stores of munitions.

FIREARMS OF THE CONFEDERACY

VIRGINIA MANUFACTORY, Richmond, Va.—Started in 1799.

WALLIS, Daniel, Talladega, Ala.—Given contract to make 1,000 rifles for State of Alabama.

WALSH, James, Richmond—Dealer in arms and military goods.

WANT, Edward, Newberne, N. C.—Awarded contract to make 5,000 pistols for C. S., 1861. Never operated.

WEB, ———— Associated with Zuccarelle in Pulaski Armory.

WEIGLE, John, Augusta, Ga.—Made the brass frames for the Spiller & Burr revolvers.

WERNAC, W. B.—Master armorer, Georgia Armory.

WHITE, John, Jr., Citronville, Ala.—Invented breech-loading gun.

WHITESCARVER, CAMPBELL & COMPANY, Rusk, Texas— Awarded pistol contract. Made rifles for State of Texas.

WHITNEY, Eli—Made Whitney-Enfield rifle for Mississippi.

WHITSON, G. W.—Connected with the Asheville Armory.

WILMINGTON, N. C.—Confederate Ordnance Depot.

YARBROUGH, George—Of the Tyler, Texas, Armory.

ZACHARIE, J. W. & CO.—Purchased 4,000 altered muskets from U. S. Government.

ZUCCARELLE, N. B.—Made arms at Pulaski, Tenn.

FIREARMS OF THE CONFEDERACY

CONFEDERATE STATES PATENTS
ON
SMALL ARMS

A list of small arms patents granted by the Confederate States Government in 1861-'62-'63 as gleaned from the reports of the Confederate Commissioner of Patents, Mr. Rufus R. Rhodes, which reports are now in the Congressional Library at Washington. There were no small arms patents in 1864 and no record of any patents in 1865.

It is of course regrettable that there are no drawings or specifications covering these patents available as that information would no doubt clear up some of our present Confederate *mysteries.*

1861

No. 9—August 12, Thomas E. Cofer, Portsmouth, Va.; revolving pistol.

No. 24—September 24, E. T. Ligon, Demopolis, Ala.; breechloading pistol.

No. 54—December 7, John White, Jr., Citronville, Ala.; breechloading gun.

1862

No. 58—January 21, Carl Laquequist, Macon, Ga.; breechloading gun.

No. 91—May 10, J. W. Howlett, Greensboro, N. C.; breechloading firearm.

No. 108—September 27, George Henry, Columbus, Miss.; breechloading firearm.

No. 111—October 3, A. J. & T. O. Clanton, Panola, Miss.; breechloading firearm.

1863

No. 148—February 14, J. H. Tarpley, Greensboro, N. C.; breechloading firearm.

No. 151—March 10, A. Legden, Atlanta, Ga.; revolving firearm.

No. 154—March 20, N. T. Read, Danville, Va.; breech-loading firearm.

No. 163—April 18, C. W. Alexander, Moorfield, Va.; breechloading firearm.

No. 178—June 10, Asa George, Charlotte, N. C.; revolving firearm.

No. 199—September 10, Thomas Morse, Richmond, Va.; breechloading firearm.

Confederate Ordnance Depots and Officers
From the Confederate Ordnance Manual of 1862

Col. J. Gorgas, Chief of Ordnance, Richmond, Va.
Maj. S. Stansbury, Arsenal, Richmond, Va.
Capt. G. T. Getty, Ordnance Depot, Lynchburg, Va.
Lt. Col. J. A. d'lagnel, Arsenal and Armory, Fayetteville, N. C.
Maj. F. L. Childs, Arsenal, Charleston, S. C.
Lt. Col. G. W. Rains, Arsenal, Augusta, Ga.
Maj. R. W. Cuyler, Arsenal, Macon, Ga.
F. C. Humphreys, M. S. K., Ordnance Depot, Columbus, Ga.
Capt. J. L. Henderson, Ordnance Depot, Selma, Ala.
C. C. Wagner, M. S. K., Ordnance Depot, Montgomery, Ala.
M. Gayle, M. S. K., Arsenal, Mt. Vernon, Ala.
Commanding officer, Ordnance Depot, Wilmington, N. C.
Commanding officer, Ordnance Depot, Knoxville, Tenn.
Commanding officer, Ordnance Depot, Mobile, Ala.
Commanding officer, Ordnance Depot, Briarsfield Armory, Columbus, Miss.

INDEX